Contents

	Acknowledgments	**v**
INTRODUCTION	*Sexual Fear, Sexual Pain*	**1**
ONE	*The ABCs of Sex: Anatomy, Behaviors, and Cycles*	**13**
TWO	*Terra Incognita: Charting Your Own Sexual Map*	**37**
THREE	*Sexual Dysfunction in Women: Identifying the Landmarks on Your Map*	**59**
FOUR	*Filling in Your Map: Other Factors Associated with Sexual Dysfunction*	**89**
FIVE	*Changes along Your Pathway: The Impact of Life Change on Sexual Dysfunction*	**119**
SIX	*Beginning Treatment for Sexual Disorders*	**135**
SEVEN	*Sensate Focus Exercises*	**147**
EIGHT	*Overcoming Roadblocks and Resistance*	**175**
NINE	*Individualizing Your Treatment*	**201**
TEN	*Working with Partners, Physicians, and Therapists*	**231**
APPENDIX	*Readings, Resources, and Referrals*	**261**
INDEX		**273**

Acknowledgments

From the Authors

The staff at New Harbinger has been wonderfully supportive every step of the way in bringing this book to fruition. Special thanks go to Kristin Beck, who was an enthusiastic and friendly support from the very beginning, and to Angela Watrous, who was consistently helpful and kind in her feedback during the editing process.

Aurelie Jones Goodwin, Ed.D.

I would like to thank the following people for their support and encouragement in the writing of this book. First, my understanding of women's sexuality is based on thousands of hours listening to women talk about their intimate lives. To the women and men who have shared their sexual stories with me, I owe my gratitude. I also want to acknowledge my family for their loving emotional support.

I also wish to thank my coauthor Marc Agronin for his optimism and enthusiasm, constant cooperation, careful work, and compassionate insight about the human spirit. I am grateful to the friends and family who read the book at various stages and offered invaluable comments which have clarified the content and enriched the writing. Rosemary Lawson and Jennifer Campion offered their expertise both in the organization, content, and understanding of the process of therapy. Alexandra Myles read the section of lesbian sexuality and was helpful in many ongoing conversations about lesbian sexuality. Arthur Cobb, Rosalie Brown, Judy Silverstein, Judy Leavitt, and Kathleen Logan-Prince are all sex therapists, and their comments enriched the text and helped clarify clinical issues.

Marc Agronin, M.D.

I am grateful to Aurelie Jones Goodwin for her wonderful collaboration on this book. I have benefited greatly from her wisdom, experience, and friendship. My wife, Robin, encouraged and supported my efforts, and my son Jacob provided endless hours of necessary distraction. I would like to thank Ellen Agronin and Elyse Levine Less for their careful and insightful assistance in the editing process. Dr. Ron Less and Dr. Neal Foman provided valuable technical assistance. I would like to dedicate my efforts in this book to my grandfather, Dr. Simon Cherkasky (1914–1997), who inspired my career as a physician and was a constant source of wisdom and guidance in my life.

Sexual Fear, Sexual Pain

Are you experiencing difficulties with your sex life? Are these difficulties creating problems in your personal life or in your relationships? If so, ask yourself the following questions:

- Do you have a lack of sexual desire?

- Is it difficult for you to become sexually aroused during sex?

- Do you avoid sex? Do you dread sex?

- Does the idea or experience of sex fill you with fear, panic, or disgust?

- Do you find sexual intercourse painful?

- Do you have trouble with vaginal penetration?

- Are you unable to have an orgasm?

If you answered "yes" to any of these questions, this workbook may be for you. It has been written as a guide to help women overcome sexual difficulties.

There are many books available on the "art" of sex. Some books focus on sexual communication and intimacy, while others offer strategies to improve both the emotional and physical relationship with a sexual partner. It can be frightening to get the impression that having good sex requires some sort of academic degree, perhaps in advanced acrobatics and international diplomacy. When all goes well, however, sexual function does not require instruction or training; without impediments it flows in predictable ways. Sexual function in every aspect—from desire, to arousal, to orgasm—is already wired into our bodies. Sexuality is not a unique skill or art form, but a bodily function as natural as eating and sleeping. All people have equal access to it. This workbook offers you a straightforward series of readings and exercises to help restore this natural flow of sexual function.

The two main obstacles to healthy and satisfying sexual function are fear and pain. For many women, sexual relations are accompanied by vivid, unpleasant physical or emotional reactions. For other women, however, sexual experiences may cause vague, uncomfortable sensations instead of overt fear and pain. Not surprisingly, the pleasure of sex is diminished when it is accompanied by any form of fear and pain. Negative sexual experiences can bring intense frustration, especially when sexual expectations seem hopelessly unattainable. Over time, sex may be viewed with great indifference or distaste, perhaps for no conscious reason. Many women suffer silently with sexual problems, avoiding or limiting sexual relationships, or dreading gyne-cologic exams, and feeling unable to share such painful secrets with anyone. When a partner is involved, sexual problems can complicate the affected couple's ability to communicate about their sexuality, feel good about themselves, and enjoy physical affection.

Sexual dysfunction is the term used to describe a person's diminished or absent capacity for specific aspects of sexual relations, including

- interest or desire in sexual activity,
- physical and mental sexual arousal and pleasure before, during, and after sexual activity,
- pain during or after sex, and
- capacity for orgasm.

Sexual dysfunction can occur at any point or at multiple points along this sexual response pathway. The normal sexual anatomy and function will be described in chapter 1.

Sexual dysfunctions in their many forms are relatively common. A study of one hundred happily married couples found that 63 percent of the women had experi-enced difficulty with sexual arousal or orgasm at some point in their lives (Frank, Anderson, Rubenstein et al. 1978). When all forms of sexual difficulty were included, such as low interest and problems with relaxation, the rate of difficulty rose to 77 percent. And these were rates for happily married couples! These sexual difficulties may be episodic and related to obvious causes. Temporary sexual dysfunction can be due to exhaustion from work, an argument or tension with one's partner, preoc-cupation with a newborn child, a physical illness, or anything else that increases stress, anxiety, or physical pain. Sexual dysfunction is more long lasting when it occurs frequently; when there is no obvious, reversible cause; or when it is related to a stressor that cannot be changed easily. In these situations, it is usually an ongoing fear or pain reaction that has established the difficulty, and is perpetuating it.

What can be done? You can use this workbook as a guide if you and your partner suffer from sexual problems. It has been written to help you better understand your own body and sexuality, unblock the natural flow of sexual function, and feel more relaxed and comfortable with sexual relations. It is intended to guide you on a safe and comfortable journey towards recognizing and reversing fear and pain reactions, and achieving happier physical and emotional relationships with others. Finally, it has been written to help you enjoy a sexual life based on your own ideas, capabilities, and values, instead of based on sexual myths or on idealized descriptions of peak sexual experiences. Sexual dysfunction is often readily treatable, and its reso-lution brings benefits to overall sexuality, relationships, self-esteem, and personal well-being. You may feel more hopeful and relieved with this knowledge, even as you struggle with a problem that seems insurmountable.

For most women, there is a fundamental sense of relationship and relatedness to the world—to one's self, as well as to beloved family and friends, romantic and sexual partners, co-workers, bosses and mentors, acquaintances, animals, and even the natural world. Women are taught to connect to others, and to make relationships work. This orientation can cause difficulty, however, if a woman feels selfish when she attends to her own needs. If a woman is deeply concerned about pleasing others, she seldom has the time to think of pleasing herself. As a younger woman she may not know herself well, or know her own body, wants, and needs. Cultural restrictions and stereotypes sometimes make women feel out of touch with their deeper selves, and cause them to react in rigid and conflictual ways. Even when a woman knows that something is not her inner truth, she may be uncertain how to both give to her relationships and be true to herself. The goal for a woman in this predicament is to make the exploration of her inner self as important as listening to others, so she can attain the wisdom to see herself as equally worthy of attention and love.

Starting Your Journey

This book will guide you on a journey through your body, mind, and spirit. All travelers journey in their own way. You may prefer to know where you are going, and use many maps and guides. Or perhaps you prefer the challenge of uncertainty while you explore the unknown, and relish a sense of risk and adventure. You may let go of the familiar and set off towards the unknown future, able to move from one moment to the next with confidence, or move with caution when you are unsure of the terrain. At times the journey is easy, and you can see a clear path to the goal ahead. Other times the goal seems out of reach, and the road is bumpy or blocked as you leave the known behind and go through rough patches of fear, anxiety, uncertainty, and loneliness. You may decide to travel alone or choose to have company along the way. Sometimes you will follow in a well-worn pathway, and sometimes you must cut through the weedy undergrowth alone. When you go on a journey you always reach a point of no return, a place where the familiar is no more and the unknown lies ahead. Going beyond this point requires belief in yourself, courage to continue, and faith in a safe and happy future.

We have written this book, then, as a companion guide for you as you embark on a journey of growth and change. Women experience a variety of changes in their bodies and sexuality: puberty and the beginning of menstruation, adolescence and sexual awakening, the intimacy of young adulthood, pregnancy and childbirth (for some women), menopause, and the post-menopausal years. In a world that has been patriarchal for centuries, womens' sexuality has usually been defined by men. Many women have been influenced by a biased cultural version of feminine values and beliefs and may need to reexamine these values and determine from where and whom they came. But when questioning these values, some women may feel disloyal to beloved parental figures and confused about trying to maintain connections to traditions and yet be true to their own sexuality. It is important for each woman to look inward towards her own body and mind, to her deepest sense of self, and discover her own sexuality. Then she can share what she has learned with others.

Terra Incognita

In this workbook we want to emphasize that the goal of treatment goes beyond just achieving comfortable and pleasurable sexual intercourse. A woman with sexual problems may view her genitals with indifference, unease, or disgust, or she may act as if her body has no sexual purpose. Her genitals may be associated with unpleasant sensations, emotions, or experiences. As a result, her body image is obscured and distorted by boundaries that have put her out of touch with her genitals. If we compare her body to a map of a great territory, her map has a hidden, unexplored, and unknown region—a *terra incognita*. The exercises in this workbook will help her locate, illuminate, and explore this territory, to feel a sense of harmony and control in its boundaries, and to make it a truly known and understood place—a *terra cognita*.

How to Use This Workbook

The purpose of this workbook is to engage your participation in a challenging but pleasant journey. If you suffer from a sexual difficulty, the very presence of this workbook may bring many emotions and reactions with it: trepidation, anxiety, fear, anger (what took so long?!), denial, indifference, and, hopefully, a degree of relief and anticipation. Your initial reaction to the book is very important, because it says a lot about what the experience of sexual dysfunction has been like for you.

You may have ascribed your sexual problem to many factors in yourself, a particular relationship, or the setting. For instance, you may feel that you're not ready, too anxious, or unsure about sex. It may not seem to be the right person, place, or mood. You may feel angry at your partner, or fearful and apprehensive about his or her expectations. You may feel too much pain or discomfort when you attempt physical intimacy and intercourse. In other words, you may ascribe your difficulties to a distinct cause that you feel you need to change. Or you might be experiencing indifference or denial, perhaps feeling unsure whether you really need this book. If your partner gave you this workbook and told you (perhaps indirectly) that you have a problem, you may feel angry and humiliated. All of your emotional responses are important and deserve recognition.

Think about how you feel as you hold this book, and consider why you might feel this way. Think about the possible explanations for your difficulty, whether it involves minimal interest in sex, painful or unsuccessful gynecologic exams or attempts at sexual intercourse, or other inhibitors to enjoying sex. Now consider whether, in addition to these factors, there is a more basic problem, such as uncontrollable, subjective feelings of fear, anxiety, disgust, indifference, or confusion. By asking questions of yourself about these feelings, you are taking the first step in understanding your own sexuality. If any of these emotions seem to characterize your reaction, we suggest jumping into the initial exercises in this introduction to clarify if, how, and why this workbook can be helpful.

If you are certain that you have a sexual dysfunction, you may feel great relief when you finally have a name and a solution for your difficulty. You may also feel angry for not having had a guide much earlier, nervous that this workbook will make you confront your fears, or doubtful that a workbook can help you. If your emotions have been shaped by years of difficult and painful experiences, they may have a depth and intensity that seems impossible to surmount. These painful feelings are perfectly normal and can be a first step in opening yourself up to new understandings and possibilities. Give yourself time to absorb these emotions if they haven't been fully conscious before. Let them flow unhindered, and give yourself time to overcome them and chart a new course.

The presence of this book in your life might be a closely guarded secret, unknown to your partner, physician, or even therapist. That's okay at this point. There is no immediate obligation to share it with anyone. If it was given to you by a therapist or physician, it is important to discuss with him or her how it will be used. If a partner gave it to you, it is important that you assume responsibility for it without feeling that someone is looking over your shoulder and monitoring your progress. Whatever the situation, this workbook is your possession to do with as you wish. We do recommend, however, that at some point you share your experiences with a trained professional, such as a certified sex therapist or psychotherapist (see chapter 10 for descriptions of each specialty), in order to maximize your progress. Although it is possible, it is also difficult and lonely to overcome sexual dysfunction on your own. You may decide on one of three routes:

- Use this workbook as an adjunct to sex therapy or psychotherapy, under the guidance of your therapist.

- Use this workbook alone or with a partner for a certain period of time, and then assess your progress before deciding whether to seek professional assistance.

- Use parts of this workbook, such as the journal writing and relaxation exercises, on your own, but have a therapist help you with exercises specifically designed to help you overcome your specific sexual problem.

If you are reluctant to share your difficulties with anyone now, we hope that the pace and direction of this workbook will help you journey to a more comfortable point where you can do so. In chapter 10, we discuss how to include your partner in your journey. We will also recommend ways to approach your gynecologist, internist, or psychotherapist to discuss your problem. Chapter 10 may also help you decide how and when to bring the workbook to these specialists to seek their advice. Finally, at the end of each chapter and in the resources in the appendix, we will provide lists of helpful and relevant references, referral sources, support groups, catalogs, products, and Web sites. Whatever you decide, remember that you are not alone in your journey.

Each chapter in this book will provide numerous exercises to help you map out your sexuality and begin to overcome your sexual difficulty. The workbook is designed to be followed in the order of its chapters, with the exception of chapter 10 "Working with Partners, Physicians, and Therapists," which may come in handy as you begin treatment in chapter 6. The exercises within each chapter are intended to build upon information and skills learned in previous chapters, so even if you are tempted to skip ahead, we caution against it. Skipping ahead may shorten your course initially, but will inevitably require that you backtrack to acquire missed skills. You are learning a new language and mapping a new territory for yourself, and this takes time. Because every woman's sexuality is unique, and every sexual problem is different, we do not prescribe a certain timetable or set of norms. You and your body will determine how long and in what manner your journey will progress. No matter how long it takes, trust in your ability to succeed.

Mapping Out Our
Treatment Philosophy

Before you get started, we'd like to introduce ourselves and acquaint you with the guiding philosophy of this book. We are both mental health professionals who treat a wide variety of individuals and disorders. Dr. Goodwin is a certified sex therapist and educator who has worked for over two decades conducting individual, couples, and group therapy with women and men with sexual dysfunction. Dr. Agronin is a psychiatrist and psychotherapist who specializes in psychopharmacology and geriatric psychiatry and has specialized interests in sexual dysfunction and personality disorders. We are strong advocates of psychotherapy, sex therapy, and, if needed, medications to treat sexual dysfunction. Although we are confident that many women can make great progress using this workbook alone, we do not offer it as an equivalent to therapy. Sexual difficulties are distressing and complex, and are certainly not easy to face alone.

The philosophy we present in this book has several components. We believe that sexual problems must be approached in an open and honest manner, and that it is critical for every affected woman to educate, or reeducate, herself about her own sexuality. Chapter 1 will discuss genital anatomy and sexual functioning in detail. Chapters 2 through 5 will help you gain a deep understanding of your own sexuality and sexual functioning. We also believe that many sexual problems cannot be separated from their context within the couple, and we support the concept of *conjoint* (couple-based) therapy to resolve them. It may be tempting for one partner to blame the other for the sexual problem, but this approach frequently leads to a cycle of shame, anger, resentment, and more conflict. Although many exercises are geared towards the woman with the identified problem, others require participation of a partner, and all of them can be adapted for the couple. The introduction to chapter 10 discusses this in more detail.

Although we support an honest and informed perspective on sexual function, we do not attempt to endorse any particular liberal or conservative agenda, nor do we wish to endorse any particular social or political philosophy towards sex. It is important to us that women in all stages and situations, and with all manner of philosophical and religious views on sex, be able to recognize and understand sexual dysfunction and receive treatment commensurate and appropriate to their unique situation. Although the language in this book is often geared towards women in heterosexual relationships, we have tried to provide balanced use of pronouns and a variety of case examples to represent and support all types of women in all types of relationships: heterosexual, bisexual, and homosexual women who are single, dating, or married. If you are in a lesbian relationship, we have tried to address your concerns throughout the book and have provided resources that can help in this regard. The exercises in this book can be adapted for almost any situation, and we have tried to suggest ways to do so throughout the book.

This is not to say that we do not have any professional biases. We do represent the medical, psychological, and psychiatric views of sexual dysfunction as put forth by our respective professional affiliations. Thus, all diagnoses of sexual dysfunction we describe in this book are based upon the standard *Diagnostic and Statistical Manual for Mental Disorders*, 4th Edition (1995), otherwise known as DSM-IV. With respect to the technical information in this book, we have tried to draw upon a wide range sources and theorists, and have tried to find the most up-to-date statistical information. We have based many of the treatment strategies on the work of several major pioneers and theorists in the field of sex therapy, including William Masters and Virginia Johnson, Helen Singer Kaplan, Joseph LoPiccolo, and David Snarch. We must mention, however, that given the pace of change in medical and sexual research, and changing medication formularies, we cannot guarantee the absolute accuracy of all technical information. This caveat applies particularly to the sections on medical illnesses and medications. We urge you to work with your physician and therapist to confirm medical information in this workbook and to obtain the most up-to-date perspective.

Learning Skills

As you use this book, you will be learning many new concepts and practicing new skills. A few important words about how humans learn may prove useful. Think back to your childhood and try to remember what it was like to learn a physical skill for the first time, like riding a bike or skateboard. How did you approach this new experience? Did you feel excited, anticipate success, and enjoy the challenge? Or did you worry that you might not succeed, or would hurt or embarrass yourself?

What kind of instruction, encouragement, and feedback did you receive? These learning experiences can be triumphant, or painful and humiliating. All people begin a learning task with some degree of anxiety towards the unknown. You may believe that you *ought* to know already, or you may fear that the task is too hard. You may doubt the instructions you are given, or question their value to you. You may try to go too fast, or take a big leap and get discouraged if you fall backwards.

Humans learn best when they are neither "scared out of their wits" nor "bored to tears." A mild amount of anxiety helps the learning process best. Thus, when a situation such as a sexual problem causes you to feel mildly anxious, you are likely to be motivated to take in new information and make changes to alleviate this anxiety. But when the anxiety level rises beyond a certain threshold, your mind and body become so preoccupied with survival and so busy erecting safe defenses that you lose

terror or physically flee. On the other hand, once you attain a goal, and gain mastery over it, you may become bored without a new challenge. It is important to have a new goal at that juncture, and a reason to pursue it. Unfortunately, it can be all too easy for most people to let this boredom steer them away from their larger goal, especially if they lack the confidence to attain it, or feel a lot of anxiety about it.

As you work through the material in this book, try to balance your learning so that you are challenged to increase your level of skill in gradual increments, without becoming so anxious that you freeze up, "flee" the book, or lose interest altogether. Don't let boredom lead you to abandon the larger goal. If you are bored, it often means that you have accomplished something. However, boredom is sometimes a defense against high levels of anxiety that are out of conscious awareness. Your boredom may cause you to avoid your sexual problem rather than stay with the problem and fix it. It can be difficult to know the true reason for your boredom, and a therapist can be helpful here. In any event, it is important to forge ahead and achieve a comfortable balance between these extremes.

How can you find this balance? We recommend that you start by setting a large goal (e.g., *I'm going to learn how to have an orgasm*), and then set a series of small goals which lead toward your larger goal (e.g., *I'm going to get to know my body. I'm going to try touching myself to discover what arouses me, etc.*). Each goal you reach will give you a sense of pride and accomplishment, and the self-confidence you need to pursue a slightly more challenging goal. We have designed all of the exercises in this book to help you identify goals and pace yourself, as you work in a logical and comfortable flow. Mihaly Csikszentmihalyi (1990) has written about the experience of *flow*, which describes optimal learning experiences in which people feel happiness and joy. His model describes how to achieve this optimal flow in all life experiences, and we have adapted it in the diagram on the following page.

To understand this diagram, imagine a woman's experience as she learns about her sexuality. (A) In the beginning, she has little sexual experience and few skills in how to please herself or her partner. But she feels challenged to learn more. She enjoys the new sensations of arousal and isn't worried because she knows she will not be pushed to do more than she wishes; she is in the flow of her experience and feels happy. (B) After a while she wants to learn to have an orgasm, but as she experiments she becomes anxious in anticipation of intense sexual sensations; she is out of the flow. (C) As she slows down her pace and practices newly learned skills of gradually touching herself, she feels less anxious and more comfortable; she is back in the flow. (D) Suppose her pace slows down to the point where she becomes bored with doing the same thing and is not learning anything new; she is again out

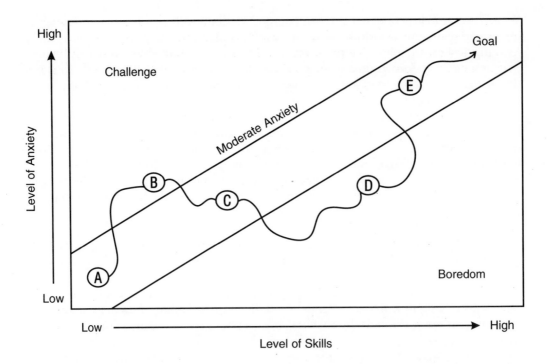

Figure 1. The Way We Learn—The Experience of Flow

of the flow. (E) Boredom is unpleasant, so she becomes motivated to learn new skills, and thus returns to the flow experience. As this flow progresses, she gradually acquires more skills, and these allow her to meet new challenges and eventually achieve her goal. Optimal learning is thus a dynamic flow towards your goals, in which you acquire more complex and highly developed skills along the way. You must balance your journey between experiencing too much anxiety or too much boredom, or run the risk of getting stuck or moving backwards.

⤳

Exercise 1—Keeping a Travel Log

Have you ever kept a diary or journal of your experiences? Journal writing helps to crystallize thoughts and emotions and provide healthy self-awareness and acceptance. It helps chronicle your path, providing you with a personal history and showing you where you've been and where you're going. It allows you to track your progress. Journal writing should be private in all respects. Purchase or make a notebook in which you can keep a journal of your experiences as you begin this process of self-exploration. You can use any loose-leaf or spiral-bound notebook, but many women prefer a hardcover-bound book in which to write. Find a place to keep it where you are assured of privacy. We will provide suggested topics along the way, but feel free to write about anything that comes to mind. You can record a major goal that you've set for yourself, as well as smaller, achieved goals along the way. You can draw, make graphs, lists, write about family history, make up fairy tales that tell your story, and record progress as well as obstacles along the way. It is important to write about the difficulties you encounter, since these will help set and adjust goals. Find a special pen or pencil to write with and designate a private time and space to do your writing. You may want to preview the initial sections in chapter 8, where we discuss how to find a private place and space for writing and relaxation. Once you are ready, there are several important issues to write about:

- What thoughts and emotions do you have about this workbook?

- What is your sexual difficulty? How has it affected your life?

- Have you tried to "fix" your problem? How?

As you think about your emotional reactions to your problem and write about them in your journal, remember that they will change as you progress through this book. Use the following scales to rate several emotions at this point and time.

Emotional Preparedness
How ready do you feel emotionally to use this workbook to tackle your problem? Rate your level of emotional preparedness from 0 to 10, with 0 = I feel energized, 5 = I feel tired, and 10 = I feel exhausted.

0	1	2	3	④	5	6	7	8	9	10
Energized										Exhausted

Anxiety
How nervous or anxious about your problem do you feel? Rate your level of anxiety from 0 to 10 with 0 = I am calm, 5 = I am anxious, and 10 = I am panicked.

0	1	2	3	4	5	⑥	7	8	9	10
Calm										Panicked

Anger
How angry do you feel about your problem? Rate your level of anger from 0 to 10 with 0 = I am content, 5 = I am angry, and 10 = full of rage.

0	1	2	3	4	5	⑥	7	8	9	10
Content										Rageful

Hope
How hopeful do you feel about overcoming your problem? Rate your level of hopefulness from 0 to 10 with 0 = I am hopeful, 5 = I am worried, and 10 = I am full of despair.

0	1	2	3	4	⑤	6	7	8	9	10
Hopeful										Despairing

Self-Esteem
How do you feel about yourself knowing that you face a sexual problem? Rate your level of self-esteem from 0 to 10 with 0 = I am proud, 5 = I am embarrassed, and 10 = I am humiliated.

0	1	2	3	4	⑤	6	7	8	9	10
Proud										Humiliated

You can return to these scales at any stage in your journey to gauge the intensity of your feelings. You may want to make several copies of the scales and rate your feelings after completing each chapter in the book. Doing this will allow you to see how your feelings change over time.

🙠

EXERCISE 2—THE ASSOCIATION WEB

An association web will take you into many unexplored realms. You will be surprised at how well it will help bring out thoughts and feelings about your sexual difficulty. A web makes use of something called *free association*. In free association, you simply start with one word or phrase and write down words and phrases that jump into your mind. Don't worry about the connections between them—they will emerge later on.

Start with a generic word or phrase about sex, such as "sex, intercourse, love-making," etc., and write it in the center of your web. Or, you may select a word or phrase which best describes your problem, such as "low sexual desire, pain during intercourse, no orgasm," etc. Then, let your mind wander freely. What words, thoughts, phrases, emotions come to your mind? Write them down around the word in the center of the web, and link them to it. What associations come into your mind next? Let them flow freely. Do not try to outline. Do not worry about neatness. When you run out of words, take few minutes to rest and look over your web. Begin to

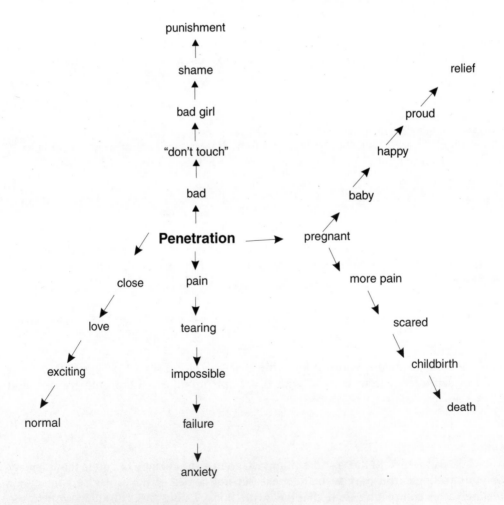

Figure 1. Sample Association Web

write your reaction in your journal. You will be surprised at how your mind will organize the ideas you've generated into a more coherent theme. To get started, you might want to review the sample association web we've provided in figure 1, drawn by a woman with painful vaginal penetration. Then try making your own association web in your journal or on a separate sheet of paper. Make as many webs as you wish. When you feel stuck in treatment, an association web is a good jumpstart. It may reveal previously unknown blocks

Feel Free to Write Us

We welcome your comments and suggestions on ways in which this workbook could be more helpful. Feel free to write either author at the following addresses:

Aurelie Jones Goodwin, Ed.D.
165 Hunnewell Avenue
Newton, MA 02158

Marc Agronin, M.D.
Department of Psychiatry
VA Medical Center, One Veterans Drive
Minneapolis, MN 55417

References

Csikszentmihalyi, M. 1990. *Flow: The Psychology of Optimal Experience.* New York: Harper Perennial.

Goldberg, N. 1986. *Writing Down the Bones: Freeing the Writer Within.* Boston: Shambhala.

Frank, E., C. Anderson, D. Rubenstein. 1978. "Frequency of Sexual Dysfunction in Normal Couples." *New England Journal of Medicine* 299:111–115.

Rainer, T. 1978. *The New Diary: How to Use a Journal for Self-Guidance and Expanded Creativity.* Los Angeles: J. P. Tarcher.

Rico, G. L. 1983. *Writing the Natural Way: Using Right-Brain Techniques to Release Your Expressive Powers.* Los Angeles: J. P. Tarcher.

CHAPTER ONE

The ABCs of Sex:
Anatomy, Behaviors, and Cycles

Sex is an intensely physical experience. In ideal conditions, you are able to focus on pleasurable sexual sensations and feelings as they stream continuously through your mind and body. When everything works, you are most alive and joyous, fully present in the moment, and aware of the variety and richness of your experience. However, sometimes you feel pressure to shift your mental focus from this stream of inner awareness to an external focus on sexual performance and goals. When this shift occurs, you can lose track of both your internal emotional state and the sexual sensations moving through your body. What causes this shift? Fear and pain are two main causes, because they shift your attention to more pressing bodily sensations. Cultural and societal values also exert pressure. Everywhere you turn the media presents models of peak sexual performance, prowess, and physical appearance. Many people aspire to a sexual experience informed more by cultural images than by their own minds and bodies. As a result, it is easy to lose touch with their own personal sexual potential.

Some women are out of touch with their sexuality for other reasons. Many parents are uncomfortable talking about sexuality, and don't know how to provide their daughters with appropriate education about their sexual selves. When parents attempt to teach about sexuality, their messages may be distorted by sexual taboos, ignorance about body image, or narrow-minded beliefs about female gender roles. Sometimes parents attempt to transmit sexual information and values without honest accounts of sexual anatomy and function. By the beginning of puberty, many girls have only a foggy concept of their genitals. The word "vagina" may be a catch-all phrase for the whole complex of genital structures, whose true locations and functions remain a mystery. This mystery may deepen and inspire discomfort, fear, and anxiety when it is accompanied by negative messages that portray genitals as unclean, embarrassing, burdensome, dangerous, or fragile.

Consider the analogy of visiting a city without the aid of a map or an informational brochure. Without information, you might avoid certain parts of the city that seem mysterious or dangerous. With only a sketchy account of the city, you would not know the location of landmarks and main streets, or how the transportation system works. What would your visit be like? It would be difficult to focus on enjoying the visit without some guideposts. Even the smallest threat or discomfort could inspire fear, aversion, or panic—out of proportion to the stimulus. Every approaching stranger could be a cause of discomfort—friend or foe? Your visit might be full of inner tension and preparation to either flee danger or fight back. For some women, their experience of sexuality is similar to such a visit. Not surprising, largely due to lack of familiarity with their bodies, they find it difficult to relax in the sexual moment and to focus on pleasurable bodily sensations.

The exercises in this workbook are designed specifically for sexual dysfunction but may also benefit components of other problems. For instance, we teach relaxation and concentration techniques for sex that can also be used to treat chronic pain, anxiety, and panic disorder. Sensate focus exercises will provide more relaxing sexual relations, and will also help improve communication between partners. The techniques presented in chapter 8 to recognize cognitive distortions regarding sex can also apply to the treatment of depression, anxiety, panic, chronic pain, and post-traumatic states. These exercises will help you start along a path towards resolving many disorders, but they are not a substitute for professional therapy.

A Is for Anatomy: Female Genital and Reproductive Organs

In the next few sections we will help you gain an initial sense of comfort and control by providing you with a basic road map of sexual anatomy, behaviors, and cycles. In addition, we will provide exercises to help you begin creating a personal mental map of your sexuality.

Development and Differentiation

Although men and women have very different sexual anatomy, both develop from the same embryologic and fetal tissue. Figure 1.1 illustrates the male and female genitals, which appear structurally different but are actually similar in many ways. If you compare them you can see that they have the same erectile tissue and nerve endings, even though the genital structure is different. Thus, the glans of the clitoris and the glans of the penis are analogous tissue. Since heterosexual couples often wonder how sensations are experienced by the opposite sex, this diagram can be especially helpful.

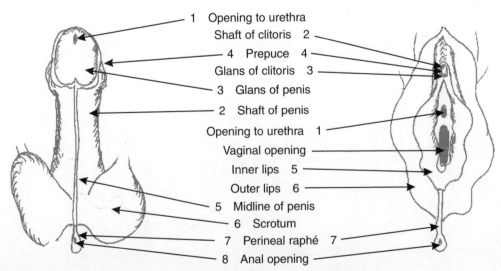

1   Opening to urethra
Shaft of clitoris   2
4   Prepuce   4
Glans of clitoris   3
3   Glans of penis
2   Shaft of penis
Opening to urethra   1
Vaginal opening
Inner lips   5
Outer lips   6
5   Midline of penis
6   Scrotum
7   Perineal raphé   7
8   Anal opening

Figure 1.1. Analogous Tissues of Male and Female Genitals

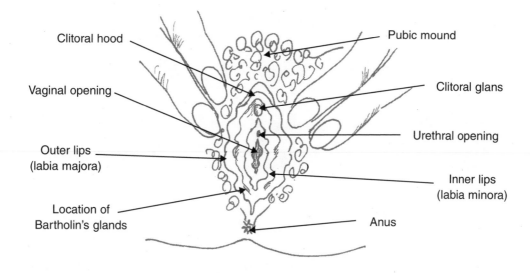

Figure 1.2. External Female Genital Anatomy

External Female Genital Anatomy

The external parts of the female genitalia are referred to as the *vulva*. If you look at figure 1.2, you will see that the vulva is composed of many different structures. At the top of the diagram is the *mons pubis*, or *pubic mound*. This cushion of soft, fatty tissue and skin is covered with hair and overlays the pubic bone. Many women find that pressing on the mons is sexually arousing. The *anus*, or opening to the rectum, lies in back or posterior to the other structures. The *labia majora*, or outer lips, are the large, soft outer lips, or folds, surrounding the vaginal opening; they are covered with pubic hair. Within the labia majora lie a smaller pair of smooth and shiny, pink or brown-colored, hairless lips called the *labia minora*, or inner lips. They are very sensitive to stimulation.

The inner lips, or labia minora, are joined together at the top where they meet above the *clitoral glans*, forming the clitoral hood. The clitoris is actually a large complex system of blood vessels, erectile tissue, and nerve endings that lie under and surround many of the structures of the inner lips. The clitoral glans, which most people call the clitoris, is only the external part of the clitoris. The glans of the clitoris, a small button of sensitive flesh, lies under the clitoral hood. It has as many nerve endings as the glans of the penis but is much smaller in size, which may account for its exquisite sensitivity to touch. The clitoral shaft stretches back and splits into two legs that lie on either side of the vagina.

Below the clitoris lies the opening to the urinary canal called the *urethral orifice*. Urine flows through this orifice. Directly below the urethral orifice is the entrance to the vagina. In most women who have not yet had intercourse there is a thin membrane called the *hymen* partially covering the vaginal opening. After intercourse, the remnants or tags of the hymen sometimes remain. Opening into the vestibule of the vagina are two small glands (called *vestibular* or *Bartholin's* glands), which secrete a thin mucus to lubricate the area. Although most lubrication comes from within the vagina, this secretion increases during sexual stimulation. The *perineal sponge* lies under the skin between the opening of the vagina and the anus and is richly supplied with nerve endings. Stimulation of this area can provide intense pleasure.

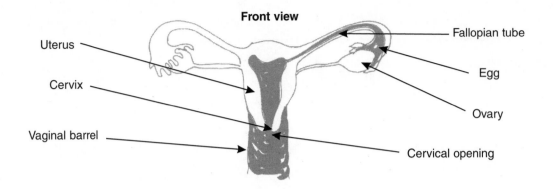

Figure 1.3a. Internal Genital Anatomy

Internal Female Genital Structures

The internal female genital structures pictured in Figure 1.3a and 1.3b are involved in both sexual activity and reproduction. There are several muscles that surround the vaginal orifice and enclose the bulb of the clitoris. When contracted, these muscles reduce the size of the vaginal opening and help to make the clitoris erect. There is also a much larger muscle, shaped like a double figure eight, that encircles the urethral orifice, the vaginal opening, and the anus. We will refer to this muscle throughout the book as the *pubococcygeus,* or *PC,* muscle. A woman may have voluntary control over contracting and releasing the PC muscle by practicing Kegel exercises (described in chapter 6). Learning to strengthen and control this muscle with rhythmic contracting and relaxing exercises may improve pushing during childbirth and help correct urinary incontinence, which sometimes occurs as a result of childbirth. Contracting and relaxing the PC muscle during sex may enhance pleasure and even induce orgasm in some women.

The vagina is a tube of soft muscular tissue about three to five inches long. In a resting state it is a potential space with the walls touching one another. During sexual arousal it lengthens and stretches to accommodate a penis, and during birth it stretches to allow the passage of a baby. Small glands in the walls of the vagina secrete a thin mucus, which increases during sexual activity. Several areas within the vagina respond to stimulation, including the cervix, the perineal and urethral sponge, and the legs of the clitoris that surround it. The vaginal walls do not have the same nerve endings as skin, and so the sensation is different.

There is a highly sensitive area, called the *Gräfenberg Spot (G-Spot)* or *urethral sponge,* running along the urethra in the upper part of the vagina. This structure surrounds and protects the urethra by filling with blood during excitement. When this area is stimulated with a finger, penis, or other object, some women report exquisite sensations leading to an explosive type of orgasm, during which there may be an expulsion of fluid from the urethra. This fluid continues to be the subject of controversy, with some scientists believing it to be urine and others describing it as a fluid similar in composition to seminal fluid (but without sperm, obviously).

Extending beyond the vagina is the *uterus,* a pear-shaped muscular organ about the size of a fist. The uterus opens into the vagina at the *cervix,* which extends into the vagina about one-half inch. The cervix allows for the passage of menstrual material and serves as the passageway for sperm on their way to the egg.

The fallopian tubes travel along both sides of the uterus and open up into fingerlike projections which surround each *ovary* and catch the egg expelled during

Side view

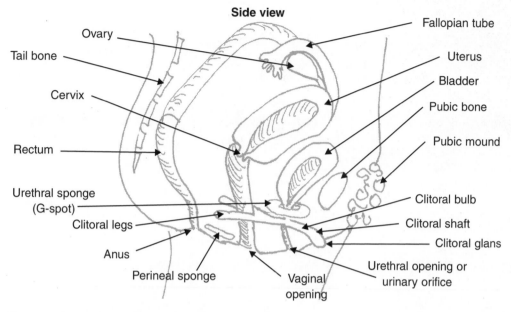

Figure 1.3b. Internal Female Genital Anatomy

ovulation. The uterus has a thin cavity surrounded by *endometrial tissue.* This tissue is richly supplied by blood vessels, which cause it to engorge prior to ovulation in anticipation of supporting a fertilized egg. When conception does not occur, the endometrial tissue sloughs off during menstruation. The uterus, fallopian tubes, and ovaries are supported in the pelvis by a series of strong, pliant ligaments.

EXERCISE 1.1—VIEWING YOUR OWN MAP

Review the diagram of external genitals pictured in figure 1.2. Then look at your own genitals by holding a small mirror between your legs while you are sitting down. Locate each of the various structures on yourself as you look at the diagram. Write about this experience in your journal. Draw a picture of your genitals using figure 1.2 as a guide. Really look carefully at yourself. Label the various parts. As you locate each part of your genitals, notice how you feel. Do you feel comfortable using the clinical names? If not, make up your own names.

EXERCISE 1.2—A SYMBOLIC PICTURE

Here is another exercise that can help clarify how you feel about your genitals. This time make a symbolic picture of your genitals using different colors, lines, spaces, and shapes to represent your thoughts and feelings about them. For example, different colors or patterns may represent certain emotions, thoughts, memories, or images. This drawing may not physically resemble your genitals at all but will still convey meaning. One woman used red to color in areas of pleasure, and blue to represent the expansive feeling during orgasm. Another woman drew jagged black lines to represent the barrier which kept her from feeling pleasure and a green pasture to represent the pleasure she couldn't quite reach.

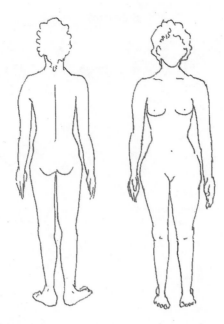

Figure 1.4. Body Drawings

Exercise 1.3—Body Image

Body Image refers to the way you feel about your body and is directly connected to your sexual experience. Look at yourself nude in a full-length mirror and draw yourself from both a front and a back view. Add a side view if you wish. You don't have to be an artist to do this. If you wish, you can enlarge the template provided in figure 1.4 as a guide, or draw your body in a notebook. Using several different colors, shade in areas of your body to indicate: (1) the parts of yourself you like, (2) the parts of yourself you don't like, (3) the parts of yourself where you like to be touched, and (4) the parts of yourself where you don't like to be touched. Then, show areas that evoke the following emotions: happiness, joy, excitement, shame, guilt, anger, grief, anxiety, pain, and fear. Use other symbols to indicate where you feel pleasure and pain.

Male Sexual Anatomy

Although we will not discuss male anatomy in the same detail as female anatomy, we feel that it is important for heterosexual women to know the names, locations, and functions of their partners' genitals. This information may demystify male sexual anatomy for some women, and teach others how to best respond to their partners' requests during lovemaking. The *penis* is usually in a flaccid, or non-erect, state, and in adult males averages three to five inches long. It is surrounded at its base by pubic hair, and by the *scrotum,* hanging below. The scrotum is a hair-covered, wrinkly sack roughly two to three inches long, with two testicles inside (with the left testicle often hanging slightly lower). The enlarged head, or *glans,* of the penis contains the *urethral opening,* or *meatus* (mee-ay-tus), through which urine and semen pass. The underside of the glans is the most sensitive and therefore most sexually stimulated part of the penis, and although there is sensation elsewhere, this part of the glans is the male equivalent of the clitoris and inner labia. In uncircumcised men, a hood of

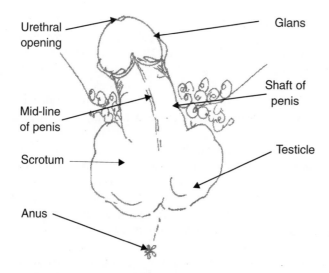

Urethral opening

Glans

Shaft of penis

Mid-line of penis

Testicle

Scrotum

Anus

Figure 1.5. Male Genital Anatomy

skin called the *foreskin* covers the head of the penis and retracts when it is pulled back during erection. There is no foreskin in circumcised men.

Inside of the penis are tubes of spongy tissue known as the *corpus cavernosa*. The urethra is surrounded by a third tube of spongy tissue known as the *corpus spongiosum*. Several nerves and blood vessels also run through the penis. During sexual arousal, these spongy tissues become engorged with blood, causing the penis to become hard and erect, averaging four to six inches long. When erect, the thickened veins cause the penis to appear darker in color, feel warm, and possibly appear to throb or pulse. A man with an *erectile dysfunction* or *impotence* may not get an erection if the spongy tissue of the penis does not fill with blood, or he may lose his erection when the blood drains out of his penis before orgasm.

The testicles' main function is to produce sperm and the sex hormone *testosterone*. The immature sperm cells originate in the testicles but do not mature into fertile and mobile cells until they travel into the *epididymus*, a coiled structure sitting atop each testicle. During *ejaculation*, which is a series of rhythmic muscle contractions that accompany orgasm, the sperm travel from each epididymus through a tube known as the *vas deferens* and out the urethra. As the sperm pass through the *prostate gland*, nutrient-rich fluid from the prostate and secretions from the connected *seminal vesicles* are added. One to two tablespoons of semen or "*cum*" are expelled during ejaculation. The bladder is closed off during ejaculation so that only semen—and not urine—exits the penis.

The Sexual Response Cycle

A woman's reproductive anatomy is exquisitely designed to accomplish the act of sexual intercourse and consequent reproduction. There are several theoretical models of sexual behaviors that have been developed by sex researchers, or sexologists, over the past thirty years. All sex therapists work from some variation of the models presented in this section. The *sexual response cycle* refers to a recurrent series of physical changes in the body during sexual activity. Accompanying these physical changes are changes in emotions, behavior, and patterns of thought as a woman deepens her involvement in a sexual encounter.

In 1966, renowned sex researchers William Masters and Virginia Johnson published their first laboratory findings based on several thousand sexual experiences of nearly seven hundred men and women. They were the first to study and describe in detail the physical changes that take place in the body during a sexual experience. Masters and Johnson (1966) proposed four stages in this cycle: *excitement, plateau, orgasm,* and *resolution.* Soon after, Helen Singer Kaplan (1974) added a fifth, psychological stage preceding the excitement stage, which she labeled the *desire stage.* Since that time, however, Zilbergeld and Ellison (1980), Levine (1988), and Snarch (1991) have elaborated on the phenomenon of desire, conceptualizing it as existing before, during, and after a sexual encounter. Other researchers have described specific changes in thought patterns as a person deepens involvement in sexual activity. Because of this new conceptualization of sexual desire, we are describing it as a phenomenon throughout the sexual response cycle and not as a separate stage.

Figure 1.6 represents the sexual response cycle. The numbers from 1 to 10 on the vertical axis represent increasing degrees of sexual excitement or arousal. This is, in part, a subjective rating, and you can base you own "level" on your personal experiences. The horizontal axis represents the time course of a sexual experience. The threshold of physical arousal above the level 1 involves the beginning of vaginal lubrication and genital swelling and overall muscle tension in preparation for sex. Sexual excitement can wax and wane between levels 2 and 9, when it reaches the plateau stage, experienced as a sense of urgency and wish for orgasm. Orgasm occurs at level 10 of the diagram. The resolution stage represents that portion of the curve falling from 10 after orgasm back to a state with no sexual arousal. This is just one model of the cycle: each woman has her own unique pattern for each sexual experience. The degree of rise and fall in sexual excitement and the time spent in each stage will vary, depending on the circumstances. It is important to note that the line representing arousal does not go up in a straight line: human arousal level rises and falls depending on how much attention is focused on the sensations being experienced. There are many reasons why attention moves away from experience. During lovemaking when you are giving pleasure to your partner, your attention is focused externally; consequently, arousal drops temporarily since you are not fully concentrating on your own pleasurable sensations. Arousal may also fluctuate if you are preoccupied with performance goals, such as whether you will reach orgasm. Instead of taking in sexual sensations, you may then be focused on self-evaluation, and end

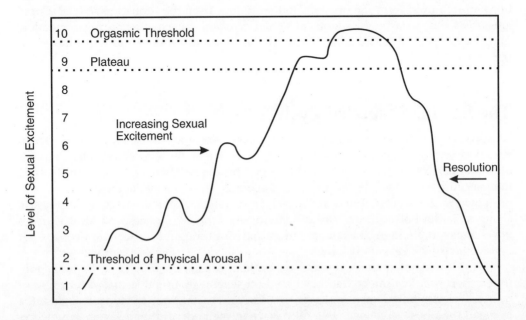

Figure 1.6. The Sexual Response Cycle

up trying to force pleasurable feelings. Or you might drift off into a reverie that is nonsexual in nature. However, when you focus on yourself again, arousal generally grows.

We will now explore the sexual response cycle, beginning with a description of sexual desire. Then we will explore the four stages of the cycle which involve physical changes, and conclude with a discussion of the psychological changes that occur.

Sexual Desire

Helen Singer Kaplan (1995) has defined sexual desire as the urge to seek out and respond to sexual activity. It is a drive, or appetite, dependent upon specific centers in the brain's *limbic system* (particularly the hypothalamus). The limbic system is a collection of deep brain structures regulating many fundamental emotional and motivational states. The limbic system guarantees self-preservation by helping the person avoid pain and seek pleasure. Sexual desire is stimulated in both sexes by testosterone. In women, testosterone is produced in both the ovaries and the adrenal glands. Women also depend upon the hormone *estrogen* to stimulate female sexual characteristics and promote healthy genital function. *Oxytocin* may stimulate affilliative behavior and mother-infant bonding, while *vasopressin* may stimulate monogamous behaviors. Put together, all of these hormones allow for a balanced and appropriate mechanism to regulate sexual activity. Over the course of a lifetime, a women's sexual desire may be affected by hormonal changes during her monthly cycle, and during and after pregnancy and menopause.

Sexual activity depends upon a sex drive. We often describe this drive as an instinct because it is preprogramed into the brain. In evolutionary terms, the survival of a species requires this instinct in order to reproduce, but the sex drive is not the most immediately important instinct: the survival instincts to protect yourself from danger and feed yourself take precedence. The sex and survival drives cannot occur simultaneously. The nervous system is wired so that when you sense danger your body must forget about sex and focus on survival, and that is where fear and pain play important roles. Fear reactions signal danger and prepare your body to either flee or to defend yourself. Pain reactions signal tissue damage and cause you to withdraw from the source of pain and seek safety and comfort. Without fear and pain, people could not respond to danger and would quickly succumb to the elements.

The sex drive depends upon a woman's ability to perceive and respond to sexual cues and stimulation. To respond to these cues, the sex drive has a dual-steering mechanism: it is both excitatory and inhibitory, depending on the circumstances and stimuli (Kaplan 1995). For example, in safe, comfortable surroundings, with proper stimulation (an attractive partner, physical touching, sensual scent, pleasing music, etc.) the sex drive is likely to be excited. If a woman perceives unsafe or dangerous surroundings, more immediate self-preservative drives take over, and her sex drive is likely to be inhibited.

Sexual desire waxes and wanes over time. Desire is highly influenced by life stressors, such as relationship difficulties, financial strain, work-related demands, and major life changes such as marriage, divorce, or death of a loved one. Many theorists believe that sex is grounded in the dynamic system of the couple, and that desire waxes and wanes depending on the thoughts and feelings the couple have for each other. Snarch (1991) conceptualized desire as the passion that accompanies arousal throughout the sexual response cycle. During a specific sexual encounter, desire may rise and fall several times, usually resulting in similar changes in the level of physical arousal. Anything that interrupts the process of physical arousal, such as medication side effects, or physical ailments, can derail the interaction between desire and arousal. In chapter 3 we will discuss this process in more detail.

Desire or Will? Beginning the Sexual Response Cycle

Women who are satisfied with their sexuality often say that for them, the sexual response cycle does not start with desire (Goodwin 1989). They are more likely to say that even if they have no desire for sex or feelings of arousal, they deliberately make a choice to be sexual. They know from many good sexual experiences that once they begin they will like it and enjoy the physical and emotional intimacy sex brings.

Loulan (1984) calls this stage *willingness,* a preliminary stage to the sexual response cycle which may replace desire for some people. Willingness is a decision to have sex for the reasons which are meaningful to you. This differs from desire, which includes feelings of yearning and inner need for sexual connection. It is a proactive stance rather than one of passive receptivity. Usually if you are willing, and sexual activity begins, you will become aroused.

Snarch (1991, 1997) suggests that low desire is often based on "not wanting to want", a decision that is often based on nonsexual reasons. The reasons are varied, but often are based on unresolved issues from childhood or the dynamics of the current relationship. For example, a woman might be fearful of abandonment from her past or might have unspoken resentment with her partner. She might be aware of either of these reasons or they might occur below the level of her awareness.

It is very important to understand that willingness to be sexual comes from inside and that you should not feel obligated to be sexual if you feel aversive or actively unwilling. Rather, it is a willingness to allow yourself to enter into a physical connection that may lead to sensuous and sexual pleasure. You can enjoy pleasure at any stage of the sexual response cycle and stop when you feel you have had enough. There is no need to continue through to orgasm unless you decide to do so.

Stage One—Excitement

During the excitement stage of the sexual response cycle, a woman's body undergoes several critical physical changes to prepare for sexual relations. Sexual arousal leads to lubrication, or the release of slippery secretions in the vagina and vulva in a process likened to sweating. These secretions lubricate the vaginal area in preparation for sexual intercourse. It is important to note that although lubrication begins with sexual arousal, being lubricated does not necessarily mean that a woman is ready for intercourse. Sexual arousal also creates an increase blood flow to the genitals and breasts in a process called *vasocongestion.* Vasocongestion in the vulva results in the swelling of the inner and outer lips and a darkening of their color. The clitoris increases in size and the hood expands and swells. Breasts and nipples enlarge as well. As sexual excitement builds, there is an increase of muscular tension throughout the body known as *myotonia.* Other physical signs of sexual excitement include increases in perspiration, heart rate, and respiration, and a skin-flushing reaction known as *sex flush,* which spreads from the abdomen upwards to the neck. Internally, the uterus and cervix are pulled up and the vaginal walls expand and lengthen to allow room for the penis.

During the excitement phase, all women experience a varying level of sexual tension. As with sexual desire, sexual excitement may decline when attention is focused on the partner, and the woman is not perceiving her own incoming sensations. Excitement rises when she returns her attention to her own experience, and concentrates on pleasurable stimulation. Most women like to be aroused gradually before they are ready for genital touching and they experience soft caresses over their entire body as relaxing and highly erotic. Gentle stimulation of the face, neck, hands, feet, inner thighs, and breasts can begin the process of sexual excitement before any genital contact occurs. Each woman is unique in the type and amount of stimulation she needs in order to become sexually aroused. The pattern of arousal may change over the course of her life, depending on her partner, the nature of her relationship, and the level of daily stresses she experience. Arousal can also be highly influenced by hormonal changes during monthly menstrual cycles, pregnancy and lactation, and menopause.

David Snarch (1991) discusses how sexual excitement—and sexual desire—are interrelated, proposing a model in which the total amount of stimulation is comprised of both external physical sensations and internal psychological perceptions. In this mind-body perspective, there is an important and continuous interaction between mental and physical changes during sexual experience. Snarch proposes two different thresholds during the sexual response cycle. The arousal threshold is reached when adequate physical and psychological stimulation leads to the physical changes experienced during the excitement stage. The orgasmic threshold is reached when the amount of physical and psychological stimulation is dense enough to trigger orgasm. In Snarch's model, the amount of physical sexual excitement does not necessarily indicate positive or negative emotions. A woman might have relatively low levels of physical excitement during a sexual experience, but enjoy the intimacy and love she feels. On the other hand, she may experience high levels of physical excitement, but not enjoy the experience.

Stage Two—Plateau

The plateau stage is experienced as an urgent flowing towards orgasmic release. Muscle tension increases, extending to the neck, face, hands, and feet. Both the inner and outer lips of the labia may appear to be swollen, blood pressure and heart rate increase, and breathing becomes faster. Sex flush is more noticeable on the upper part of the body, and the chest and breasts may show a blushing of red or brown that looks somewhat like a rash. The breasts and nipples become more engorged, as does the outer third of the vagina.

The outer vaginal lips are parted and the inner lips are swollen and darkened. Masters and Johnson found that, if appropriate stimulation continues, this color change signals approaching orgasm. However, unlike men, who experience a period of inevitability after which they cannot stop an orgasm, a woman's orgasm may stop at any stage if she does not receive enough continuous stimulation. At this stage, the clitoral glans is now extremely sensitive and withdraws under the clitoral hood where it continues to respond to indirect stimulation.

Stage Three—Orgasm

Orgasm is the climax of sexual excitement and provides intense pleasure that lasts anywhere from two to fifteen seconds. It may be experienced deep within the pelvis or pulse throughout the body or may be focused in the clitoris and surrounding genital area. Orgasm begins with a sensation of mental and physical suspension, followed by an intense sensual awareness that starts in the clitoris and radiates upward through the pelvis. At the same time, awareness of other bodily sensations is reduced. The cervix opens and enlarges to prepare the way for sperm to enter the uterus. There is often a feeling of bearing down or expelling during orgasm.

The second phase of the orgasmic experience involves a suffusion of warmth that begins in the pelvic area and spreads throughout the body. This is quickly followed by a release of sexual tension involving a series of muscular contractions at intervals of eight-tenths of a second. These contractions gradually fade, and are often followed by sensations of pelvic throbbing. The strength and number of these contractions varies depending on the intensity of the orgasm. Contractions may be felt in the uterus, around the vaginal and anal area, or in the entire PC muscle. Some women experience contractions as intense sensations, while others are less aware of this experience. Contractions of the cervix and uterus may create a sucking effect which helps bring semen though the cervix and into the uterus.

There are several kinds of orgasms, each of which results from the stimulation of different genital areas. A clitoral orgasm occurs when a woman focuses her attention on the sensations of clitoral stimulation, which must be prolonged and dense enough to reach the threshold in which orgasm is released as a reflex. If stimulation stops or changes to a less dense type of stimulation, the orgasm may stop partway through. Clitoral orgasm can occur with direct manual or oral stimulation of the clitoris, or indirect stimulation during intercourse when the in-and-out motion of the penis stimulates the clitoral legs. A uterine orgasm can result from the penetration and thrusting in and out of a penis or other object, such as a dildo. The motion of the penis, as it bumps into the cervix and jostles the uterus and other reproductive organs, may cause intense pleasurable contractions of the uterus, and is felt deep within the pelvis and throughout the body.

A G-spot orgasm occurs when the G-spot, or urethral sponge, along the upper wall of the vagina is stimulated with a penis, finger, or dildo. Unlike some types of orgasm, which can stop partway through, once a woman begins a G-spot orgasm it continues through to the end of the climax with intense internal sensations. A blended orgasm refers to the simultaneous release from two areas, such as the clitoris and uterus, or the clitoris and nipples, and is intensely pleasurable. Some women experience multiple orgasms, either immediately following their first one or shortly thereafter as stimulation continues. Some women strive for this experience, while others feel completely satisfied with one orgasm.

There continues to be controversy among researchers regarding the variety and nature of women's orgasms. Some sexologists distinguish between vaginal and clitoral orgasms, while others believe all orgasms are the result of stimulation of the clitoral system, which is integrated into the rest of the reproductive structures. Subjectively, some women experience different types of orgasm, while others notice no distinctions. Clitoral stimulation can be a reliable form of orgasm for many women when a partner is not available, or for a woman who wants to enjoy sex without vaginal penetration. As with sexual excitement, the amount and type of stimulation needed to reach orgasm varies widely. Although intercourse provides intense stimulation to the penis, it may not provide enough stimulation to release orgasm in a woman. According to a number of researchers, only 25 to 30 percent of women experience orgasm during intercourse.

Stage Four—Resolution

The resolution stage begins with a release of physical tension after orgasm, as a woman returns to an unstimulated state. Muscle tension is relieved with orgasm, and heart rate, breathing, and blood pressure return to normal. The sex flush disappears and the genitals return to their normal resting condition. The uterus descends, allowing the cervix to drop into the end of the vagina where the penis has deposited sperm. The resolution stage may last a long time in women, and it is often a luxuriating and sensuous experience, during which a gradual diminishing of excitement occurs. If adequate stimulation is resumed, further orgasm may follow. If a woman has not had an orgasm but has reached a high level of arousal, this stage may last for several hours as her body gradually returns to normal. In this situation, the swollen genitals may create an uncomfortable or cramping sensation, along with a physical and emotional sense of frustration

Psychological Changes During the Sexual Response Cycle

In order to understand the psychological changes that take place during a sexual experience, you must first understand ordinary waking consciousness. Conscious awareness is rational, sequential, and analytic in nature. You are oriented toward the external environment as you evaluate, problem solve, and make moment-to-moment decisions. Generally, awareness of ongoing physical sensations is minimal as you focus on the external world.

As you become more deeply involved in a sexual experience, you undergo a cascade of psychological changes. There is a gradual dimming of awareness of the external environment, sometimes described as a *trance*, as your attention is focused more and more deeply on the immediate experience. During this sexual trance you become more receptive to the nuances of emotion and may be in touch with earlier experiences, images, and feelings about yourself as a sexual person. Several sex researchers have described this psychological response as a withdrawal from higher mental activities into a dreamlike experience where past and present become one and connect to currently experienced physical sensations. Fried (1960) and Kaplan (1974) have commented on the ability to abandon oneself to pleasure both as a positive capacity and a learned skill.

Mosher (1980) conceptualized a model to account for the deepening of psychological awareness during the sexual response cycle. The trancelike state during a sexual encounter is accomplished in two ways: by giving up a hold on external awareness and by increasing focus on internal experience. Mosher suggested that during a sexual episode a women's striving toward pleasure occurs in an altered state of consciousness that is qualitatively different from psychological functioning during normal waking consciousness. During this altered state of awareness, there is a shift in orientation from outside reality to an inner preoccupation with sexual sensations and mental processes. Mosher proposed that high levels of sexual arousal which ultimately lead to orgasm are based on the density of the sensation experienced while the person is deeply fascinated and involved with the stream of inner experience.

Building on Mosher's model, Goodwin (1989) interviewed women who described the changes in psychological processes they experienced as they went through the physical processes of the sexual response cycle. Women described this experience in many ways: decreased awareness of their surroundings; dreamlike images; a sense of timelessness; a surrender to the moment; intense connection to a partner; changes in body image described as flowing, pulsating, tingling, or tickling sensations; warmth; loosening; lightheadedness; and waves of emotions or intense pleasure.

The following summary describes the psychological changes which occur during the sexual response cycle:

Early Stage of Sexual Arousal and Dalliance

The excitement stage of the sexual response cycle corresponds to an early and middle stage of psychological processes. Early stages of arousal include making eye contact, agreeing verbally or nonverbally to be sexual, caressing, nongenital touching, stroking, and holding. As thoughts of potential sexual activity occur, the person makes associations to earlier experiences. Attention oscillates between the growing sexual encounter and the environment. Thoughts are concerned with safety and privacy issues and feelings about the self and the partner. The person is easily distracted from the sexual experience by external or internal events. A decision is made to engage in sex. Body sensations may be felt as erotic or as pleasantly neutral. Communication is often both verbal and nonverbal.

Middle Stage of Sexual Arousal and Lovemaking

This stage of lovemaking involves increasing physical excitement with an accelerating shift in focus from stimuli in the outside environment to more immediate sexual sensations. As concentration on the partner or the self increases, distractions from the environment, as well as internal distracting thoughts, diminish. However, a woman is still vulnerable to the self-evaluation of performance. Physical touch is increasingly erotic. Wholebody pleasure is sought, with a gradual emphasis on genital sensations. Communication is increasingly less verbal.

Plateau Stage: Subjective Sexual Awareness

As a woman surrenders herself to the sexual experience, a shift of thought occurs that is not noticed at the time, but can be remembered later. The shift in thought is a psychological marker for the physical plateau stage. Only urgent stimuli will create distraction from her involuntary focus on genital pleasure, bodily sensations, and accompanying positive sexual images and associations. Evaluative, sequential thought does not occur. There is a sense of timelessness. If something in the experience causes the woman to stop and evaluate, she may drop out of this stage. If she returns her awareness to her sensations and sexual thoughts, she can then return to this stage.

Bodily perceptions change and there is a developing loss of sensory capacity for other parts of the body as sensation increases and becomes totally oriented in the genital area. Sense of touch is diminished so that pain may not be felt, and a woman may not hear sounds—even those that are close at hand. The sense of taste and smell are reduced, temperature sense is diminished, and peripheral range of vision is narrowed. A woman may perceive parts of her body to be seemingly expanded or distended, and she may have sensations of floating, flying, warmth, or buzzing, which become faster and faster as they move into orgasm. She may feel a sense of intense connection or even merger with her partner or a need to concentrate on herself. An image, often nonsexual in nature, may arise unbidden to her mind. Communication is nonverbal. A woman may sigh, moan, or use broken sentences, but she does not converse. This stage is apparently a prerequisite to orgasm.

Orgasm and Complete Subjective Sexual Awareness

Orgasm occurs with a simultaneous flowing of sensations, images, and feelings in a woman's mind. Communication is nonverbal. The body as a whole is involved as the orgasmic experience fills the mind. Women use the following words to describe the experience: dreamlike images, timelessness, surrender to the moment, intense connection to my partner, changes in my body image such as flowing, pulsating, tingling or tickling, warmth, loosening, lightheadedness, waves of emotion or intense pleasure.

Another curious phenomena appears to occur for many women. They have an image that is nonsexual in nature which enters the mind. The image which occurs before and during orgasm takes different modalities. These images often occur in the mode of sensation that is the strongest for a women, such as visual, auditory, or kinesthetic (body feelings). For instance, a sculptor whose strongest experiential mode was kinesthetic spoke of her orgasmic experience as if she were a boulder rolling more and more rapidly down a hill until she rolled into orgasm. A visually oriented woman remembered a violin-shaped space which changed in color from a light red to a darker brownish red and finally to a brilliant sky blue as orgasm approached. A singer, whose favored mode is auditory, described orgasm as a rising note which reached a peak and then diminished.

Resolution: Return to Conscious Awareness

After orgasm occurs, the woman usually drifts down in a luxuriating sense of peace and pleasure. The mind returns to the reality orientation of nonarousal.

A woman's attention to her sexual sensations, thoughts, and emotions plays a critical role in allowing the sexual response cycle to proceed pleasurably to orgasm. High levels of anxiety create a cognitive state in which a woman either becomes distracted from the sexual scene by nonerotic stimuli or focuses obsessively on her sexual behavior. The flow of sexual activity—the taking in of and attending to pleasurable stimulation—is disrupted when these situational factors are perceived as unsafe, fearsome, painful, or demanding. Sex therapists commonly try to help women focus attention on more positive sexual thoughts, expectations, and sensations during sexual arousal.

The Relationship between Sexuality, Fear, and Pain

The sexual response cycle depends upon very different signals in order to be activated: erotic sights, sexually stimulating sounds and scents, and a physical capacity for sexual pleasure. Sexual response also requires the absence of fear and pain to prepare the body for sexual relations and ultimately for reproduction. The line between the competing sex drive and survival instincts can easily become blurred, and sexual dysfunction may result.

Fear: The Fight-or-Flight Response

When you perceive a dangerous situation, your body reacts quickly to protect yourself.

How does this occur? Deep in the brain, a group of interconnected centers, collectively called the limbic system, processes incoming sensory stimuli (that is, visual, tactile, auditory, and olfactory sensations) and assess in a split second the significance of these stimuli. You could liken the limbic system to a guard who sits in front of a video monitor, observing the scene for dangerous situations. If the limbic system perceives danger, it evokes the urge to either fight off or flee from the danger. The reaction is called the *fight-or-flight response.*

The emotion of fear is associated with this nervous response and signals the body to react. The response is then mediated by activation of an automatic part of the nervous system called the *sympathetic nervous system.* Sympathetic nerve pathways prepare the body for fight or flight by increasing heart rate and breathing, raising blood pressure, shunting circulation to critical organs, tightening muscles, raising hair on end, increasing sweat, dilating pupils, and increasing vigilant scanning of the environment. Neurologic pathways for sex and feeding are inhibited. Pain sensation in the body may be dulled as the body concentrates fully on the danger. Each of these changes in the body serves a unique purpose and guarantees the best chance of survival. When there is no danger, an opposing set of automatic nerve pathways called the *parasympathetic nervous system* relaxes the body and mediates other functions such as digestion and sexual arousal.

Although our bodies react physically in similar ways to animals during the fight-or-flight response, the human psychological response to danger is more complex. A cat or bird may need to raise its fur or feathers (called piloerection) to frighten off predators and to appear too large to be eaten, but piloerection in humans (experienced as goosebumps) doesn't do much good. Similarly, a racing heartbeat and shaking muscles may allow a frightened deer to quickly flee a hunter, but it doesn't help a frightened person make a speech to a large crowd of people. Yet human bodies respond to all perceived dangers in the same way. This fear response is critical when facing actual physical danger and plays an important role with less-threatening situations as well. A small amount of fear and physical, or *sympathetic,* arousal in humans actually enhances performance, but as it increases beyond a certain point, performance begins to decrease, and this progression can lead to total inhibition.

The emotion of fear can be triggered by actual danger, situations only perceived as dangerous, or situations that have come to be associate with danger. This is called a *conditioned response.* The experience of fear, unease, or discomfort when no threatening object is in sight is *anxiety.* Anxiety can be mild, waxing and waning over minutes to hours, or it can become sudden and severe and involve an incapacitating physical response called a *panic attack.* A person experiencing a panic attack often feels as if they will die, and may engage in frantic behaviors to escape the situation. Panic attacks in response to specific triggers are called *phobias.*

Under ideal conditions, the parasympathetic nervous system prepares the body for relaxing, playful, and sexually pleasurable activity. When the body is relaxed, it is maximally responsive to sensual touch, and both the mind and body allow for the buildup of sexual excitement and eventually of sexual climax. What happens when sex becomes associated with fear, anxiety, or panic? More research has begun to focus on phobias of sexual intimacy, including fear of male or female genitals or fear of vaginal penetration. The panic reaction in these phobias can be so severe that people adapt their lives to avoid them, by giving up sexual relationships or limiting sexual contact to only certain activities.

A woman may be anxious about a sexual situation for many different reasons. She might anticipate that sex will hurt. She might be worried about her body image, angry at her partner, concerned about whether she's a good lover, or upset about something outside the sexual realm (such as job-related or financial concerns). Her anxiety may be related to unknown and wholly unconscious causes, such as underlying guilt about sex, uncertainty about her partner, or conflict over her sexual orientation. As anxiety increases in those circumstances, her body might react as if she were in real danger and activate the fight or flight response, which in turn inhibits the sexual response cycle. This inhibition may occur at any point along the pathway, from desire, to arousal, to orgasm. It may not be experienced as an obvious response to danger, especially when the anxiety is less tangible or unconscious. Instead, a woman might be aware of her sexual problem and not recognize the fear or anxiety that inspired it. This reaction, in turn, could lead to more anxiety and new emotions of frustration, disappointment, and shame.

Pain

Pain is the subjective experience of tissue damage and serves as the immediate and most telling indication of injury and disease. Pain can result from actual tissue damage, such as a cut, or from potential damage, such as the heat from a flame before it actually burns your hand. Pain may be acute, such as the sharp hurt of a twisted ankle, or chronic, such as the ache of a degenerative disc in the back. The tissue damage may be mild, but interpreted as severe, and hence the pain feels worse than what would be expected. Pain can even result from imagined tissue damage, such as when someone believes that they've been injured more seriously than they have been. The actual tissue damage may not bear any relation to the degree of pain, but the pain is still real. Too often, pain is only taken seriously when we can see its source, such as the pain from a large gaping wound or an angry sore. Patients and physicians can get into endless struggles over the discrepancy between test results and complaints of pain. It is difficult to really understand someone's pain without actually experiencing it. But pain depends on the experience of the injured and the manner in which the individual views it. Regardless of the type of pain, your take on the pain will influence its experience.

How does this happen? Pain is a complex interaction between nerve pathways, the spinal cord, and centers in the brain, particularly a deep cerebral nucleus called the *thalamus.*

What is the source of the pain? Pain is transmitted from peripheral pain receptors, called *nociceptors*, to a gatelike mechanism in a part of the spinal cord called the *dorsal horn.* There are several types of peripheral nerve endings, and each detects a different source of painful stimulation; the three possible sources are intense pressure, thermal damage, and inflammation. Certain nerve pathways transmit painful stimuli from peripheral endings to the spinal cord and then up into the brain. Other peripheral pathways serve to "close the gate" in the spinal cord and inhibit transmission of pain. Still other pathways travel downward from the brain and interact with this gate. Thus, the perception of pain is influenced by peripheral nerve pathways traveling to the brain as well as by central nerve pathways traveling from the brain—a true mind-body interaction.

How does the body respond to uncomfortable or painful stimulation? The most basic response is a reflexive withdrawal from it; your hand jerks away from fire, you jump and turn towards a loud startling noise, your eyes blink, and your hands fly in front of your face when a blinding light is suddenly shone on you. A simple reflex occurs in an arc, in which a painful stimulus is felt by peripheral nociceptors, sent to our spinal cord, and then relayed back to the appropriate muscles to withdraw from the stimulus. When actual tissue damage occurs, you might wince, cry, or scream in response. Your body responds physically by mounting an inflammatory immune response to fight off microscopic invaders. Swelling, redness, warmth, and more pain result. Pain eventually subsides as tissue repair proceeds. A severe or repeated injury can sometimes lead to chronic pain. Chronic pain may not always have the same intensity as acute pain, but its experience over time can be extremely frustrating and debilitating, leading to social and occupational disability and often depression.

When painful sensations occur regularly during sexual activity, a woman may begin to view sex as dangerous, which then inspires apprehension, anxiety and the predictable fight-or-flight response. *Dyspareunia* is the condition where genital pain is caused by sexual intercourse (discussed in detail in chapter 3). Sexual dysfunction may also result from discomfort or pain which occurs during sexual intercourse but in other parts of the body, such as joint pain, shortness of breath, or chest pain due to physical exertion. Such nongenital pain during sex can decrease pleasurable sensations and lead to inhibited sexual arousal, orgasm, and, eventually, decreased desire.

Everyone reacts to fear and pain differently; for instance, some try to bear it stoically, others need to wear it on their sleeves, and still others bury it and become angry and depressed. In the exercises at the end of this chapter, you will spend some time thinking about your own fear or pain, examining how it has had an impact on your life in general and your sex life in particular. Now that you have an understanding of both the sexual response cycle and fear and pain mechanisms, it is important to begin to find connections between the two in your own life.

Your Fear, Your Pain

The purpose of the following exercises is to get a sense of the relative role of fear and pain in your life and the degree to which it affects you. There are often connections between the ways in which a woman experiences and copes with fearful and painful experiences in her day-to-day life and in her sex life. It is often possible to transfer coping skills from one experience to another. You will first need to examine all of the fears and pains in your life—past and present, sexual and nonsexual. Then you will be asked to look for common themes and assess their overall impact on your life. Chapters 3 and 4 will focus in on your sexual fears and pains.

EXERCISE 1.4—MY FEAR

List up to ten things in your life which have caused you fear, using grid 1.1 found on page 34. Rate the intensity of each fear from 1 to 5, based on the following scale:

Intensity

1 = mild fear or apprehension

2 = mild to moderate fear with some physical arousal

3 = moderate fear with definite physical arousal

4 = severe fear or phobic reaction with high physical arousal.

5 = one of the most extreme fears ever; a traumatic experience

Describe the impact of the fear on your life. If you rated the fear as involving physical arousal, specify your reaction. Here are several examples from one woman:

Fear	Rating	Physical Arousal and Impact on Life
Spiders	1 (mild)	Made me afraid to explore our basement.
Being Separated from My Parents	3 (moderate)	Caused muscle tension, crying, sweating, and jumpiness. My friends called me a crybaby. I didn't like going to grade school.
School Tests	3 (moderate)	Caused stomachaches and muscle tension. Resulted in poorer performance than I was capable of achieving.
Car Accident	5 (traumatic)	Resulted in a broken leg and a feeling of "spaciness" for several hours. Afterward I had nightmares for several months and fear of driving at night for several years. I no longer think about it when driving, although I am still apprehensive about driving late at night.
Dating/Sex	3–4 (moderate to severe)	Anxiety, stomachaches, headaches, diarrhea for several days prior. I have little appetite and feel tongue-tied during the date. I try to avoid blind dates and only go out with men I've met in "non-date" settings. The idea of sex makes me very nervous.

The list above is just a sample of how to describe your fears. You may want to use your journal or a separate sheet of paper if the grid does not provide enough room to describe the impact of the fear on your life.

Exercise 1.5—My Pain

Now think about experiences of physical pain in your life, and list up to 10 on grid 1.2 found on page 35. Rate each pain on a scale of 1 to 5 for each category listed below. Because pain can be so difficult to describe and quantify, don't worry about assigning the "perfect" number; just try to get it in the ballpark.

Duration

1 = acute; seconds to minutes

2 = short; minutes to hours

3 = medium; hours to days

4 = long; days to weeks

5 = chronic; months to years

Intensity

1 = mild (e.g., a pinprick)

2 = mild to moderate (e.g., stinging, aching pains)

3 = moderate (e.g., cramping, pinching pains)

4 = severe (e.g., tearing, piercing, crushing pains)

5 = most severe pain I've experienced

Severity

1 = minimal injury or illness (e.g., minor bump, abrasion, injection, recurrent cold or sore, etc.)

2 = minimal to moderate injury or illness (e.g., more extensive minor injury, irritation, or infection; perhaps requiring medical intervention)

3 = moderate injury or illness (deep wound, broken bone, surgical wound, minor functional or neurological disability, anything requiring surgical repair)

4 = severe injury or illness (loss of sense, major trauma, severe neurologic or functional disability, illness requiring major surgery, cancer requiring chemotherapy or radiation)

5 = catastrophic, life-threatening injury or illness

Exercise 1.6—Fear and Pain Connections

Now that you have an inventory of the major fearful and painful experiences in your life, re-read the two lists. Are there any connections between these experiences? Do several experiences have a common cause or represent a common theme? How many of these experiences are relevant to your sexual problem? Consider writing in your journal your thoughts about these experiences. For example, one woman with dyspareunia made a connection between painful intercourse, her symptoms of endometriosis, her painful loss of virginity, and her fear of painful medical and dental procedures. When she thinks about intercourse, memories from each experience flood her mind, and make her even more apprehensive about sex.

Exercise 1.7—The Impact of Fear and Pain

Begin this exercise by reviewing your lists of fears and pains. Think about which experiences have had the most significant impact on your life and list up to ten of them on grid 1.3 on page 36. Then, use the scale below to rate each experience on a scale of 1 to 5 on how much influence it still exerts on your life.

1 = It's no longer a factor in my life. I've moved beyond it. (e.g., The broken arm was painful and scary, but that was years ago.)

2 = I think about it often, but its major impact has passed. It only affects my life in infrequent and minimal ways. (e.g., I remember my ex-boyfriend, but with less painful emotions. I won't date a man like him again.)

3 = The experience has passed, or is only an occasional part of my life, but still exerts some impact on my life. (e.g., I finished chemotherapy five years ago, and still worry about a recurrence. I have become somewhat of obsessive about my health.)

4 = The experience is current or frequent, and exerts a significant impact. (e.g., My back and neck pain is always with me. Sometimes I just can't take it. I feel very depressed.)

5 = The experience has exerted a major, defining impact on your life. (e.g., Ever since the rape, I haven't dated again. I often have nightmares and painful, terrifying recollections.)

By going through and ranking each experience by its life impact, you will gain a clearer picture of the overall role of fear and pain in your life. You may begin to understand how you cope with these experiences, and this in turn may give you insight into the roots of your sexual problem.

References

Federation of Feminist Women's Health Centers and S. Gaye. 1981. *A New View of a Woman's Body.* New York: Simon & Schuster.

Fried, E. 1960. *The Ego in Love and Sexuality.* New York: Grune & Stratton.

Goodwin, A. 1989. *Subjective Sexual Awareness: An Investigation of these Phenomena in Women's Sexual Arousal.* Dissertation. Boston University.

Haas, A., and K. Haas. 1990. *Understanding Sexuality.* St. Louis, Miss.: Times/Mirror College Publishing.

Kaplan, H. S. 1974. *The New Sex Therapy.* New York: Brunner/Mazel Publications.

Kaplan, H.S. 1995. *The Sexual Desire Disorders.* New York: Simon & Schuster.

Ladas, A.K., B. Whipple, and J. D. Perry. 1982. *The G-Spot and Other Discoveries About Human Sexuality.* New York: Holt, Rhinehart & Winston.

Levine, S. B. 1988. "Intrapsychic and Individual Aspects of Sexual Desire." In S. R. Leiblum and R.C. Rosen (Eds.), *Sexual Desire Disorders.* New York: Guilford.

Loulan, J. 1984. *Lesbian Sex.* San Francisco: Spinsters/Aunt Lute.

Masters, W.H., and V. E. Johnson. 1966. *Human Sexual Response.* Boston: Little, Brown and Company.

Mosher, D. 1980. "Three Dimensions of Depth of Involvement in Human Sexual Response." *Journal of Sex Research,* 16(1):1–42.

Snarch, D. 1991. *Constructing the Sexual Crucible: An Integration of Sexual and Marital Therapy.* New York: W. W. Norton.

Snarch, D. 1997. *Passionate Marriage: Sex, Love, and Intimacy in Emotionally Committed Relationships.* New York: W. W. Norton.

Snell, R.S. 1986. *Clinical Anatomy for Medical Students, Third Edition.* Boston: Little, Brown and Company.

Stewart, F., F. Guest, G. Stewart, and R. Hatcher. 1987. *Understanding Your Body.* New York: Bantam Books.

Zilbergeld, B., and C. Ellison. 1980. "Desire Discrepancies and Arousal Problems in Sex Therapy," in S. Leiblum and L. Pervin (Eds.), *Principles and Practice of Sex Therapy.* New York: Guilford Press.

Grid 1.1. My Fears

Fear	Rating	Physical Arousal and Impact on Life

Grid 1.2. My Pains

Pain Description	Intensity	Duration	Severity

Grid 1.3. Life Impact	
Experience of Fear or Pain	**Impact Rating**

CHAPTER TWO

Terra Incognita:
Charting Your Own Sexual Map

What causes sexual dysfunction? Why do certain fearful or painful experiences affect some women severely and other women not as much? How have your own sexual experiences led to difficulties? These are important—*critical*—questions, for which you will soon begin to discover some answers. Sexual difficulties are caused by several factors that interact with one another. Once you understand how your unique life experiences have led to sexual problems, you can make a personal plan to resolve them.

This chapter will help you create a map of your sexual experiences. Each question will address a different aspect of your sexuality, starting from a general description of your difficulty and then moving through several topics. As you work through this questionnaire, keep in mind how each of the following factors has influenced your sexual functioning: physical and sexual development, previous sexual experiences, early learning experiences, current attitudes about sexuality, relationship issues, medical and psychiatric problems, and life stressors.

It is important to be as straightforward as possible with your answers. You may want to write your answers in your journal or photocopy these pages and attach them to your journal. The spaces provided do not reflect how much space you should use—that's up to you.

Sexuality Questionnaire

Overview of Sexual Function and Dysfunction

This first series of questions will provide an overview of your current sexual function and main difficulties. These difficulties will become the focus for later chapters regarding treatment.

1. Describe your current difficulties with sexual function. _____

_____

_____

_____

_____

2. If you are in a relationship, is your partner aware of this problem? If so, what has your partner said to you? _____

_____

_____

_____

3. Is this a recent problem? If not, how long has it affected you? _____

_____

4. Describe any recent changes in your sexual function. _____

_____

_____

_____

_____

5. Was the onset of your difficulty related to a specific event, medication, health problem, or relationship? Describe briefly. _____

_____

_____

6. Are you currently sexually active? If so, describe the frequency and nature of your sexual practices (e.g., foreplay, intercourse, oral sex, masturbation, etc.). _____

_____

_____

_____

_____

7. Are you able to masturbate to orgasm? _____

8. What is your sexual orientation? Has this always been the case? If you are bisexual or homosexual, are you "out of the closet"? Do you have someone with whom you can discuss your feelings about this? _____

_____

9. Have you had a recent gynecologic examination? If so, did you describe to your physician your difficulties with sexual function? _____

_____

10. Have you sought any treatment for this difficulty? If so, what? _____

_____

_____

The answers to these questions may have raised several issues:

- Is your sexual problem clear to you, or do you have trouble describing it?
- Is it an active problem? A recent problem? A long-standing problem?
- What is the nature of your current sexual functioning—active, abstinent, intermittent, varied, or limited?
- What help, if any, have you sought for this problem?

Write about your reflections in your journal. As you forge ahead, upcoming questions may help clarify these issues.

Sexual Response Cycle

The next set of questions will elicit details from each stage of sexual functioning to illuminate both function and dysfunction. If you are not currently sexually active, some of these questions may not apply. If that is the case, try to answer based upon your most recent relationship or your personal experiences (e.g., masturbation, reading or viewing erotic materials, sexual thoughts or fantasy).

1. Rate the level of your sexual desire in the last month from 0 to 10. _____

> 0 = no desire whatsoever
>
> 5 = moderate amount of sexual desire
>
> 10 = strong desire all of the time

2. Does this number change with sexual stimulation? To what number? _____

_____

3. What specific factors negatively influence your level of desire (e.g., daily stressors, relationship issues, physical turnoffs)? _____

_____

_____

4. Are there specific factors (e.g., physical acts, music, scents) that positively influence your level of desire? If so, list them. _____

_____

_____

5. How has your level of desire changed over the course of your current relationship? If you are not in a relationship, has your level of desire changed in the last year?

_____

_____

6. How has your level of desire affected the frequency of your sexual experiences?

_____

_____

_____

7. Do you have sexual thoughts or fantasies? How often? Are you comfortable with the fact that you have such fantasies? When do you fantasize: during masturbation? during sex? other times? _____

_____

_____

_____

8. Do you experience rising levels of sexual arousal when you make love? Do you notice fluctuating levels of arousal? Describe your pattern of arousal. _____

_____

_____

_____

9. Circle those responses that you experience during sexual arousal: _____

    Sexual thought or fantasies   decreased awareness of surroundings

    heavy or rapid breathing   muscle tension   genital swelling

    feeling of fullness in your genitals   vaginal lubrication   sweating

Others: _____

_____

10. Are any of the preceding factors noticeably absent? How does that affect you? Do any of these factors decrease during sexual activity? If applicable, describe how fluctuating levels of arousal affect your body. _____

_____

_____

_____

11. Do you use anything for lubrication during sexual activity (e.g., KY jelly, Replens, Astroglide, saliva, oils, etc.)? What would happen if you didn't use a lubricant?

_____

_____

12. Does sexual arousal make you feel anxious or panicky? In what way? _____

_____

_____

13. When you are in a sexual encounter, or a potential encounter, do you have feelings of anxiety? Panic? Disgust? How strong are these feelings? If your answer is no, skip to question 16. _____

14. Do these feelings always arise or do they only occur with a specific partner or in a particular situation (e.g., specific sex act, bodily secretions, location, or time of day)? _____

15. How do these feelings affect your level of arousal? _____

16. Do you experience any pain or discomfort when your genital region is stimulated? If so, where exactly is the pain? What type(s) of stimulation elicits it? _____

17. Describe the intensity and duration of the pain. How do you react? _____

18. How does the pain affect your level of sexual arousal? _____

19. Are you able to reach orgasm currently, under the following conditions?

Self-stimulation	YES	NO
Partner stimulation	YES	NO
Intercourse	YES	NO

20. If you answered no for all three conditions, have you ever been able to have an orgasm? _____

21. Describe how your orgasm feels for all three of these conditions. (For example, see the section on orgasm in chapter 1.) _____

22. If you are having difficulties reaching orgasm, what factors inhibit it (e.g., poor concentration, discomfort, bothersome thoughts, etc.)? _____

23. Describe your current method of birth control, if applicable. Are you satisfied with it? Does it inhibit sexual experiences with your partner? _____

24. Do you practice safe sex? If so, how? Does that affect your sexual response? How? _____

25. Have you had difficulty with birth control methods in the past (e.g., allergic reactions to latex condoms or spermicides, retained ("stuck") sponges, side effects from the Pill)? How did these difficulties affect your sex life? _____

You should now have a clearer idea of when your sexual difficulties occur during the sexual response cycle, the extent of the difficulty, and obvious associated factors. The next step is to examine possible causes of sexual stress and dysfunction.

Relationship Issues

These questions will not immediately apply if you are not in a relationship. Some women find that sexual interest diminishes when they don't have a partner, but increases when they are in a relationship. If that is the case, answer based on your most recent or significant sexual relationship. Relationship issues are sometimes the single most important factors in sexual dysfunction and are always addressed in therapy. These issues play a role regardless of whether you are currently in a relationship, because sometimes the absence of a relationship is in itself revealing.

1. Describe your current, most recent, or most significant relationship in terms of duration, satisfaction with the relationship in general, and satisfaction with the sexual relations in particular. _____

2. Is your partner aware of your sexual problem? If so, how have they reacted? __

_____

_____

_____

3. Does your partner have any current or past sexual dysfunction? If so, did the problem begin during the course of your difficulties? _____

_____

_____

_____

4. What general features attracted you to your partner? What features makes him or her sexually attractive to you? _____

_____

_____

_____

5. How has your sexual relationship changed over time? _____

_____

_____

_____

6. What sexual activities do you enjoy together? Do you engage in foreplay? Do you engage in a variety of sexual and sensual activities (e.g., oral sex, various positions, massage, kissing, snuggling, etc.)? _____

_____

_____

7. Describe your general communication style with your partner: Can you confide in each other? Do you discuss your emotions? _____

_____

_____

_____

8. Do you talk about sex? Have you talked about your difficulties? _____

_____

_____

9. Who is responsible for contraception? Can you talk about it with your partner?

_____

10. When you fight, what is it usually about? _____

_____

_____

11. Have you had serious relationship problems? Describe briefly. If so, have you sought professional counseling? With whom? What was the outcome? _____

_____

_____

_____

_____

12. Who usually initiates sexual relations? Do you feel comfortable initiating? Are you able to say "no"? _____

_____

13. Have you had similar sexual problems in previous relationships? Have things changed with your current partner? If so, how? _____

_____

_____

_____

_____

14. Have you or your partner had a sexual affair outside of your relationship? If so, did your sexual functioning change due to that affair? How did it affect your relationship with your partner? _____

_____

_____

_____

_____

15. Are there aspects of your overall relationship you think have helped, hindered, or perhaps even caused your sexual problem? _____

_____

_____

_____

_____

As you review your answers, think about the strengths and weaknesses that have characterized your relationship. Hopefully, you are beginning to understand why it is so helpful to have your partner involved in sex therapy. The goal is not to place blame on you or your partner, but to recognize all possible contributing factors to your sexual problem and then work together to overcome them. Write your thoughts in your journal.

Medical and Psychiatric Factors

Any medical problem that limits physical ability or interferes with the sexual response cycle can cause sexual dysfunction. Psychiatric problems are also frequently associated with sexual dysfunction, especially depressive and anxiety disorders. Substance abuse is a common cause of sexual problems. There are also many medications that impair the sexual response cycle.

The connection between physical and psychiatric problems and sexual dysfunction is sometimes direct, such as when a sexually transmitted disease causes pain that interferes with sex. Other times the connection is indirect, such as when work-related stress increases anxiety, which in turn leads to decreased energy and motivation for sex. Still other times the connection is mysterious. The questions in this section will help you explore the links between physical and mental health and sexual function.

1. Do you have any congenital (from birth) problems that have affected your physical functioning? If so, how have they affected your sexual function? _____

_____

_____

_____

_____

2. Do you have any major medical problems? If so, how has each one affected your sexual function? _____

_____

_____

_____

_____

3. Have any medications affected your sexual function? _____

_____

_____

4. Do you use alcohol or street drugs? Have you ever been in treatment for substance abuse? Have these substances affected your sexual desire and function? If you are now sober, how did sobriety affect your sex life? _____

_____

_____

_____

_____

_____

5. Have you been treated for any psychiatric disorders (e.g., depression, anxiety, phobias, eating disorders, reactions to trauma, psychosis, etc.)? Describe briefly. _____

_____

_____

_____

_____

_____

_____

_____

6. If applicable, have these disorders affected your sexual function? _____

_____

_____

_____

7. How often do you see your gynecologist? Have you had any specific gynecologic problems? Describe briefly. _____

_____

_____

_____

8. How many times have you been pregnant? How many children do you have? (If you have never been pregnant, go to question 14.) _____

_____

9. How did pregnancy affect your sex life? _____

_____

10. If you have given birth, did you have any postpartum (after birth) medical, psychiatric, or sexual problems? _____

_____

_____

11. How did having children affect your sexual relationship? _____

_____

12. Have you had an abortion? If so, did it affect your sexual functioning or sexual relationship with your partner? _____

_____

13. Have you given up a child for adoption? How did this affect your sexuality?

_____

_____

14. Have you had any problems with infertility? If so, how has your sex life been affected? If applicable, how did infertility treatment affect your sexual function? Did it inhibit desire? Or create more tension with your partner? _____

_____

_____

_____

_____

History of Sexual Function

So far, you have reviewed your current difficulty and placed it within the context of your relationship and overall health. Next, you will attempt to discover how your sexual dysfunction developed. It is sometimes possible to discover the roots of sexual problems in childhood or adolescent experiences. Early emotional, physical, or sexual abuse can set the stage for later trouble with sexuality. Insufficient sex education can complicate your understanding of sexual experiences. Families with overly strict or punitive attitudes towards sex can create an association between sex and shame. These early experiences have important influences on adult sexuality.

1. How did you first learn about sex? From books? friends? siblings? parents? What did you learn from each source? _____

_____

_____

_____

_____

_____

_____

2. What were your parent's attitudes towards sex? Did they discuss it openly?

_____

_____

_____

_____

3. Did you grow up with negative values or attitudes about sex? Where did these come from—your parents? influential friends or family? yourself? _____

_____

_____

_____

_____

4. Describe the attitude towards sex you perceived from the religious or philosophical beliefs you were taught as a child and adolescent. _____

_____

_____

_____

_____

5. Did your parents display physical affection toward each other? Were your parents affectionate with you? How did other family members display affection? _____

_____

_____

_____

6. Were your parents at ease with sexuality? Could you ask them questions about sex? Did they provide age-appropriate sex education? _____

_____

_____

_____

7. Did your parents make clear boundaries about privacy—both theirs as well as yours? Could/would family members close doors? have privacy in the bathroom? ask before entering a bedroom? _____

_____

_____

_____

_____

8. What attitudes regarding nudity existed in your family? _____

_____

_____

9. What sexual values did your parents have? Was the parental attitude prosexual or antisexual? Do you think they enjoyed their sex lives? _____

_____

_____

_____

10. Were specific gender roles and behaviors expected of family members? If so, list some examples. Was there any flexibility? _____

_____

_____

_____

11. Did your siblings affect your sexual beliefs and attitudes? How? _____

12. What attitudes did your family express about the following aspects of sexuality: masturbation, premarital sex, homosexuality, contraception, pregnancy (planned and unplanned), and abortion? _____

13. How did you relate personally to your mother and father? Were you close or distant? Did you want to be like your same-sex parent? opposite-sex parent?

14. What messages did family members give you about your body? Your genitals? How did the men in your family talk about women's bodies? How did the women talk about men's bodies? _____

15. Did you learn about male-female anatomy by playing games like "doctor" or "house" with children your age? (This is often the way children learn about sexual anatomy.) Were you ever discovered by adults while playing these explorative games? How did they react? _____

16. Did you touch your genitals to give yourself pleasure? (This is a normal stage of sexual development.) How old were you? What happened? Did anyone catch you or scold you? _____

17. At what age did you first try masturbation? What feelings resulted? Did you learn to have an orgasm this way? _____

_____

_____

_____

18. Did you ever have an upsetting or frightening sexual experience as a child? Could you talk about it? If yes, with whom? Were they supportive of you? _____

_____

_____

_____

_____

19. Did you talk to your peers about sex? What were your discussions like? Did you tell jokes? Discuss seriously? How did you feel about these discussions? Embarrassed? Relieved? Pressured? Supported? _____

_____

_____

_____

_____

20. Did you have a best friend you could confide in? What did you confide? What did that feel like? _____

_____

_____

21. When did your menstrual periods begin? What was the experience like for you?

_____

_____

22. How did you learn about menstruation? Did you know in advance, or were you surprised when you got your first period? Did your mother provide you with feminine hygiene supplies? If not, who did? What was the attitude of this person about how you should take care of yourself at this time in the month? Were you pleased to become a woman or dismayed? What did family members say to you? _____

_____

_____

_____

_____

_____

_____

23. Did you discuss menstruation with your friends? What terms did you use? What attitudes did you internalize about your bodily processes? _____

_____

_____

_____

_____

24. What was your adolescent experience regarding social and sexual contact with boys? If you are lesbian, your experiences may have been quite different, and you may choose to describe your experiences with boys, girls, or both. _____

_____

_____

_____

_____

25. Describe your first romantic experience (e.g., first kiss, physical touch, date). How do you remember it? Fondly? With embarrassment? _____

_____

_____

_____

_____

26. Learning to touch includes all the steps of holding hands, kissing, necking, and petting. What kinds of touching did you do? How did it develop over time into genital touching? Could you talk to your partner about what you were doing? How long did you engage only in sexual touching before you had intercourse? Did you learn to have an orgasm during this sexual touching? _____

_____

_____

_____

_____

27. Describe your first sexual encounter that included genital contact. How did you feel? What did you enjoy about it? Did you experience any problems, guilt, fear, anxiety, discomfort, or pain? _____

_____

_____

_____

_____

28. Intercourse is a major step in sexual development. Since many skills are involved in enjoyable intercourse, first intercourse experiences are often disappointing, embarrassing, or painful. How old were you the first time? What was this experience like? Were you aroused? Did you have an orgasm? Did you talk about or use contraception? Did you get "caught" by adults? Could you confide in anybody? your partner? your friends? others? _____

_____

_____

_____

_____

_____

_____

29. Did you set sexual boundaries and maintain them? How? If you were put in a position where you had to say "no," what happened? _____

_____

_____

_____

30. Some problems with sex during adolescence include confusion of sexual values, restraint against bodily urges, different cultural expectations among peers and parents, and difficulty knowing what you want or how to ask for it. What struggles did you have? With whom? _____

_____

_____

_____

31. How did you learn about sexually transmitted diseases? Did you know how to protect yourself? Did you contract a sexually transmitted disease and, if so, how did you deal with it? How did it make you feel about yourself? How did others react?

_____

_____

32. Have you had any ongoing problems with irregular or exceptionally painful menstrual periods? Do you have premenstrual symptoms (PMS; i.e., cramping, bloating, irritability)? Describe briefly. _____

_____

_____

33. If you are primarily heterosexual, did you have any homosexual experiences? If you are primarily homosexual, did you have any heterosexual experiences? If so, what was it like? _____

_____

_____
_____
_____

34. Did you have any pregnancy "scares" (missed period, but no pregnancy)? or accidental pregnancy? How did you react? What did you do? Did the experience leave any lasting effects on your sexual function? _____

_____
_____
_____
_____

35. Did you have any traumatic sexual encounters with a consenting partner? Describe briefly. _____

_____
_____

36. Were you ever physically attacked? raped? sexually humiliated? traumatized? How has that affected your sexual function? _____

_____
_____
_____
_____
_____

Attitudes and Self-Image

Your psychological attitudes towards sexuality have a significant influence on how you anticipate sex, how you experience and remember sex, and your understanding of your sexuality. The ability to enjoy sex is highly influenced by your beliefs, values, attitudes, and memories, which are shaped by significant cultural and social influences. Myths and misunderstandings about sex often play a role in sexual dysfunctions. Your views on your body and physical appearance are intertwined with your sexual identity. Your attitudes towards sex have an enormous influence on your ability to seek sex, enjoy it, and work through sexual problems. Again, if you are currently not in a sexual relationship, you may want to use your most recent or significant partner when answering.

1. How do you feel about your body? Do you find it attractive? overweight? underweight? well-proportioned? _____

_____
_____
_____
_____

2. How did your parents influence your body image? _____

_____

_____

_____

_____

3. Do you have any physical scars? deformities? If so, how have they affected your self-image? _____

_____

_____

_____

4. How do you feel about yourself in general? Do you like yourself? Are you hard on yourself? _____

_____

_____

_____

_____

5. Do you feel comfortable with your nude body? Do you feel comfortable being nude around your partner? Why or why not? _____

_____

_____

_____

_____

6. How do you feel about your partner's body? Do you feel comfortable when your partner is nude around you? _____

_____

_____

7. How do you feel about sex? What words come to mind (e.g., pleasurable, sensuous, comfortable, painful, fearful, dirty, etc.)? _____

_____

_____

_____

_____

8. Are there certain sexual acts (e.g., oral sex, various sexual positions, anal sex) that you find objectionable? disgusting? Do you engage in these acts regardless of your feelings? _____

_____

_____

_____

9. How often do you desire or prefer sex? How does this compare with your partner?

10. What are your attitudes about pornography and erotic materials (e.g., pictures, books, videos)? Do you view them? Does your partner? If not, do either of you want to? _____

Potential Stressors

This next set of questions is designed to elicit any transient or ongoing stressors that may be affecting your sexuality. Any stressful event in the present can trigger a sexual problem. These may include trouble with your partner, pressures at work, illness of friends or family, relocation, etc. Such triggering events often serve as the "last straw" in a cascade of other factors. Stress can perpetuate existing sexual problems. The sexual dysfunction itself can then become an even greater source of stress. It is important to inventory all of these stressors and understand how they relate to one another.

1. Check any of the following stressors that have either occurred in the last year or occurred prior to that but are still a significant source of stress.

___ Loss of friend	___ Loss of partner
___ Loss of family member	___ Loss of job
___ Financial strain	___ Legal problems
___ Birth of child	___ Family fight
___ Purchase of house	___ Separation or divorce
___ New job	___ Victim of crime
___ Natural disaster	___ Serious injury
___ Marriage	___ Major illness
___ Relocation	___ Major illness in family member
___ Serious injury of family member	

For each item you have checked, consider whether it has had any effect on your sexual desire or sexual performance:

2. If you have kids at home, does their presence inhibit sexual activity? _____

3. Do work commitments interfere with your sex life? _____

_____

_____

4. When you don't want sex what is your typical reason? _____

_____

_____

5. Do you worry that you or your partner might be unfaithful? _____

_____

_____

6. Are you having second thoughts about your current relationship? _____

_____

_____

7. Are there any other stressors influencing your sex life? _____

_____

_____

Putting It All Together

Take some time now to review the answers to the previous questions. Think about each section and then answer the following:

1. Have you identified specific sexual problems? What are they? _____

_____

_____

_____

2. Based on your answers, what factors in your life seem to be associated with your sexual problem? List them as follows:

Potential causes of the problem: _____

_____

_____

_____

_____

Factors that created a vulnerability to the problem: _____

_____

_____

_____

_____

Factors that perpetuate or exacerbate the problem: _____

_____

_____

_____

_____

3. Finally, what strengths have emerged? Try to list up to ten sexual strengths; that is, people or circumstances that have been positive, supportive, and potentially curative for your problem (e.g., a strong relationship, a supportive partner, a supportive therapist or physician, physical health). _____

1. _____

2. _____

3. _____

4. _____

5. _____

6. _____

7. _____

8. _____

9. _____

10. _____

◇

EXERCISE 2.1—MAKING YOUR SEXUAL MAP

Now that you have explored so many areas of your sexuality, you are ready to map out what you've discovered. We have provided a "map" (figure 2.1) to list the discoveries you've made relative to your sexual functioning. These include a general description of your problem, and lists of the most relevant fears, pains, medical and psychiatric problems, relationship issues, attitudes, stresses, early learning experiences, and strengths that have influenced your sexuality. Select up to three of the most influential factors to put on your map. These factors should have appeared in your answers to question 2 under "Putting It All Together." This map will be your guide for the rest of the book. It will evolve as you add new items, drop ones that seem less relevant, and discover new links between certain life experiences and your current sexual difficulty. Make several copies of the map template to write on. Date each version so that you can chart your evolving understanding of your sexual map.

References

Kaplan, H. S. 1974. *The New Sex Therapy.* New York: Brunner/Mazel.

Kaplan, H. S. 1983. *The Evaluation of Sexual Disorders: Psychological and Medical Aspects.* New York: Brunner/Mazel.

Risen, C. 1995. "A Guide to Taking a Sexual History." *The Psychiatric Clinics of North America,* March, 18(1):39–53.

Wincze, J. and M. Carey. 1991. *Sexual Dysfunction; A Guide for Assessment and Treatment.* New York: The Guilford Press.

My Sexual Map
Terra Cognita

Sexual Difficulties

1.

2.

3.

Major Fears/Pains

1.

2.

3.

Medical Problems

1.

2.

3.

Psychiatric Issues

1.

2.

3.

Sexual Strengths

1.

2.

3.

Relationship Issues

1.

2.

3.

Attitudes Toward Sex

1.

2.

3.

Early Experiences

1.

2.

3.

Sexual Dysfunction in Women: Identifying the Landmarks on Your Map

If you go to a therapist and explain your problem, the therapist uses a model called a *diagnostic decision tree* to understand and diagnose the problem and then design a course of action. This model is like a mental road map, with numerous forks in the road where the therapist must identify problems and choose which path to take, depending on where your symptoms occur in the sexual response cycle. To illustrate this model, in this chapter we will describe the recognized sexual disorders that appear in the current diagnostic manual used by sex therapists. After reading this information, you may discover that you suffer from one or more disorders or a variant of one. The exercises in this chapter will assist you in developing a working definition of your disorder. Your symptoms may be *primary*, meaning that you have always had them, or *secondary*, meaning that you have acquired them after a period of successful sexual functioning. These symptoms may be episodic in nature or may occur on a chronic basis.

Reading this chapter, you may find yourself feeling discouraged, anxious, angry, or depressed as you become more aware of the details of your problem or causes that are unpleasant to consider. Don't jump to any conclusions: every affected woman has a unique, multifaceted reason for her difficulties. Just because a certain percentage of women with a given sexual disorder have certain underlying characteristics doesn't mean you do as well. Rely on your journal to chronicle your own thoughts and feelings, and refer back to your sexual map created in chapter 2 for guidance (the actual map is printed in figure 2.2). Try to determine which factors have played a role in your life. At the end of the chapter, an interactive diagnostic flowchart will help guide you to an appropriate diagnosis.

The Common Elements of Sexual Dysfunction

There are several common elements running through the types of sexual dysfunction seen in women. All of them involve some interruption at a specific point in the sexual response cycle. This interruption usually results from many factors rather than from a single cause. Although these factors can be either physical or psychological, it is not possible to reduce the problem to being "all in the mind" or "all in the body." Successful treatment requires that both be considered, since all of the factors affecting sexual dysfunction interact with one another.

Several components contribute to sexual dysfunction. Inner psychological conflict between a woman's sexual desires and her inhibitions can play an important role in sexual dysfunction. Psychoanalytic or psychodynamic models suggest that a person is often not aware of these conflicts because they are unconscious, but the effects are still felt. Successful treatment depends upon uncovering and working through these conflicts. Masters and Johnson (1970) felt that most sexual dysfunction in women was psychological in origin, but now research on sexuality has shown that there are several different causal models. Conjoint sex therapy, which involves both partners, is based on the premise that sexual problems are directly related to the dynamics of the relationship. A history of sexual trauma or other serious problems in early life also creates sexual difficulties. Physical problems such as illness, injury, and medicinal side effects serve as an additional source of sexual dysfunction. These problems are discussed in more detail in chapter 4.

Another important dimension contributing to sexual problems includes the many social and cultural factors that influence a woman's sexual education, values, attitudes, and behaviors. Women are sometimes less apt to recognize sexual dysfunction as problematic because our society often perpetuates negative attitudes towards female sexuality. Because male sexual dysfunction can prevent sexual intercourse from occurring, it is more widely recognized as a dilemma. Sexual dysfunction in a heterosexual woman inhibits her enjoyment of sex but does not necessarily prevent intercourse from occurring. Cultural myths in this society suggest two opposing views of women, both of which are powerfully present in most women's consciousness. The media presents women as figures of sexual fantasy and portrays women as young, thin, scantily clad, and writhing with sexual desire. At the same time, children are trained to believe that women should be either wholesome and innocent virgins untouched by sexuality or nonsexual mothers. Consequently, women have few or no models of sexual women with whom they can actually identify. Although these factors serve to protect and enhance the sanctity of monogamous sex, they can sometimes inhibit sexual arousal and produce unwarranted shame or guilt, leading to further inhibition. This is not to say that a liberal view of sex is necessarily free of shame, guilt, or sexual conflict, because sexual dysfunction can be found in all contexts. The problem is complicated when attitudes or values—regardless of whether they are liberal or conservative—inhibit a woman from recognizing sexual dysfunction and seeking help.

Most sex therapists use a model that integrates the psychological, interpersonal, physical, and sociocultural factors just described. They also incorporate a behavioral model that identifies specific fearful or painful stimuli that interrupt one or more phases of the sexual response cycle. When a woman perceives these stimuli as dangerous, her concentration on sexual sensations is disrupted and the flight-or-flight response occurs. For example, when Betty felt a painful twinge at penetration, she became so nervous and tense that she pushed her partner away. The sense of relief that occurs when the fear or pain is removed can be highly reinforcing, even though it disrupts the sexual response cycle. A reinforced behavior becomes conditioned when it occurs predictably and repetitively without the original stimulus. Even though Betty felt no pain the next time, she was so fearful of pain she was reluctant to be sexual. Consider the following case:

Case 3.1—Meg

Meg grew up in a home where sex was never discussed, and she didn't learn much about it until her first college romance. Even into her twenties she knew little about sexual function and felt uncomfortable talking about it. She enjoyed sexual relationships with several boyfriends in college and could reach orgasm with clitoral stimulation. However, intercourse was always uncomfortable, and at times it was so painful that she had to stop. She never discussed this with her gynecologist or any of her boyfriends, and she never made the connection between the painful intercourse and her later diagnosis of endometriosis.

Meg then met Paul at a work function and became quite infatuated. Despite her eagerness to be with Paul, she was ambivalent about having a serious relationship with him since they worked in the same company and she didn't want to start rumors. She also felt uncomfortable because she was his boss, and she didn't want their sexual relationship to affect their professional one. Nonetheless, a relationship developed. During their first lovemaking, she was excited and easily aroused. However, her endometriosis had recently flared up and intercourse was painful. She began to hurry Paul through intercourse by pretending to have an orgasm, because she was so fearful of pain. She continued to feel ambivalent about their relationship and found, to her dismay, that she could not reach orgasm through any kind of sexual stimulation. Although this had never been a problem in the past, after several bad experiences, she was completely unable to have an orgasm with Paul. Even when her pelvic pain resolved, and Paul had transferred to a new division, she still was unable to reach orgasm with him. This problem continued with her next partner, James. Since Meg was unable to talk about her sexual problem it remained an uncomfortable secret.

A behavioral perspective of Meg's situation would suggest that during her initial lovemaking with Paul, she experienced pain due to endometriosis and anxiety due to her ambivalence about having a serious relationship with him. Pain interfered with her ability to enjoy sexual arousal. Unconsciously, letting go to orgasm was symbolic of letting go of her control over the relationship. Her pain and fear reactions during sex interfered with increasing levels of sexual arousal during the excitement stage. Her concentration shifted from her own body's pleasurable sensations to the more immediate and threatening pelvic pain and inner anxiety. Because she didn't understand how or why she was losing her sexual concentration, Meg was not able to pass through the excitement stage and achieve orgasm. However, not being highly aroused decreased her anxiety about the relationship, since she no longer worried about symbolically losing control to Paul. It also shortened the duration of their lovemaking, bringing her pelvic pain to a quick end. This decrease in anxiety and pain reinforced her orgasmic failure, and after several repeat performances, it served to condition her response. As a result, even when the pelvic pain and mental anxiety were resolved, she still was not orgasmic.

This case is fairly typical of sexual problems since the causes are often difficult to recognize. However, Meg's case illustrates that sexual dysfunction often serves a purpose by preventing even more distressing fear or pain. All sexual dysfunction serves a purpose even though that purpose may be puzzling or unknown. This underlying problem creates a major roadblock along the road to sexual fulfillment. We will focus on these roadblocks and how to get around them in later chapters. First, though, it is important to understand the nature of your sexual problem and to identify potential causes by taking a closer look at specific types of sexual dysfunction.

Hypoactive Sexual Desire

Sexual desire exists in the mind as wanting and wishing for sexual pleasure. Unlike the physical stages of the sexual response cycle, desire is experienced as a receptivity toward sex, a feeling of vague restlessness in the body, being "horny," or as a passionate interest in the ongoing experience of making love. Hypoactive Sexual Desire (HSD) involves an absence or loss of sexual interest, desire, and fantasy, and can lead to personal distress and/or relationship difficulties. High levels of anxiety and unexpressed anger are major psychological factors in low or absent desire.

When HSD is primary, or lifelong, it can be difficult to treat because usually these women have never had an interest in any form of sexual expression, and the reasons not to be sexual far outweigh the reasons to change. Secondary, or acquired, HSD follows after a previous period of active sexual desire and has a variety of causes, including relationship problems, chronic stress, religious conflict, sexual trauma, medical and psychiatric disorders, medications, and substance abuse. HSD may involve a lack of interest in sexual fantasy, a partner, and any other form of sexual activity. Hypoactive desire may also be specific to a particular partner or sexual activity. There is no clearly established average amount of sexual activity, although many surveys have proposed certain norms. It is more important to note whether a woman's low desire represents a change for her and whether it creates personal distress or relationship problems.

Studies have found that HSD is more common in women than men by a greater than 2:1 ratio, and is seen in anywhere from 30 percent to over 60 percent of women in sex therapy clinics (Lief 1988, LoPiccolo and Friedman 1988). HSD is frequently associated with other sexual dysfunctions; one study found a 40 percent rate of sexual arousal or orgasm disorders among women with HSD. Depression is commonly a precipitating factor for HSD. Schreiner-Engel and Schiavi (1986) found that 70 percent of women with HSD had a lifetime incidence of a mood disorder (e.g., depression or mania), compared to a 27 percent rate of mood disorders among a group of women without HSD. It should be noted that a decrease in sexual desire is a cardinal symptom of depression.

Kaplan (1995) describes HSD as an imbalance in the regulatory mechanism of sexual motivation. In normal desire, a woman fantasizes about sexual activity and imagines of erotic thoughts and feelings that trigger arousal. Desire fluctuates depending upon the content of her thoughts and their frequency. In Kaplan's model, HSD results when sexual desire is blocked by an unconscious selection of negative thoughts, feelings, and sensations.

HSD is also affected by hormones. Fluctuating hormonal activity over the monthly cycle has a direct relationship to feelings of desire. During and after menopause, the decrease in estrogen leads to the thinning of vaginal mucous membranes and decreased lubrication. These changes can indirectly lead to decreased sexual desire, since intercourse may be painful and potentially traumatic to dry and fragile vaginal tissue. Estrogen supplementation has been helpful for many women in counteracting these effects. The hormone testosterone also plays an important role in producing sexual desire in both men and women. Women with low levels of sexual desire may have little or no testosterone in their system. Testosterone supplementation is sometimes used as a treatment to increase sexual desire but must be carefully monitored to avoid the risk of masculinizing side effects.

Before deciding that your problem is HSD, it is important to view the level of sexual interest within the context of your relationship. If a couple has sex once a month, but is satisfied with that frequency, it does not represent a problem. But if one or both partners want sex more often, this problem should be addressed. Issues usually arise when there is a marked discrepancy between each partner's level of sexual desire. That situation can sometimes highlight a problem in one partner or reflect unrealistic expectations that are amenable to compromise. In some couples, one partner will tolerate low desire in the other as long as she or he agrees to sex. Since couples often have different sexual needs and notions of how frequently they want sex, it is helpful to talk about it. This subject, however, is emotionally charged and requires tact, patience, and understanding from both partners. Low desire may also result from other dynamics of the couple's physical and emotional relationship. If a woman's earlier attraction to her partner was based exclusively on nonsexual factors, a change in these factors over time may lessen her sexual desire. Poor love-making techniques or the presence of erectile dysfunction or premature ejaculation in the male partner may lead to hypoactive desire in one or both partners.

Case 3.2—Cindy and Tony

Cindy and Tony had been married for only two years, but they were very unhappy. Although Cindy had enjoyed sex and orgasm in previous relationships and with Tony before they got married, she now had no desire for sex. She put it off as long as she could and gave in only when Tony got mad at her. His anger was upsetting for Cindy, since she hated conflict. She had been brought up as a peacemaker, and as long as Tony didn't complain, she imagined that their marriage was fine. She had originally been attracted to Tony's emotional style because it seemed to balance her quieter approach to things. Now she disliked his insistence that she enjoy sex more. Cindy resented Tony's advice on how she could be a more sensuous woman.

Tony was unable to understand how Cindy could live without a sexual outlet. Sometimes he deliberately waited, secretly counting the days to see if she would show any sexual interest, but she never did. He loved her and wanted to make love to her, but regardless of whether he got really angry or kept his anger to himself, she seemed disinterested. Tony eventually decided that if they didn't go to therapy, their marriage would end.

As therapy proceeded, several reasons for their sexual problems emerged. Tony was active about initiating sex, while Cindy passively opposed his efforts. Tony was furious at Cindy for this, but beneath his anger he felt hurt when she rejected his sexual advances. No matter what Tony did, Cindy felt no sexual interest. She was angry at his criticism of her, but she had never told him how she felt. Since it was hard for her to defend herself against his verbal insistence, she used a passive opposition. As a result, on those occasions when she gave in and had sex to please him, she felt no pleasure and was not orgasmic. Over time, any desire she once had disappeared since she felt no sexual pleasure.

The first task the couple worked on was to rebalance the power in their relationship. The therapist requested that Tony stop pursuing Cindy. Once Cindy no longer had to push Tony away, she was able to feel sexual desire rising inside herself. Tony learned to be less critical, and Cindy learned to be more direct about her feelings. They worked out a plan to enjoy intimate time together, going at Cindy's pace. Cindy realized that she had not taken any responsibility for her own sexuality. She had expected Tony to know what she liked without having to tell him, and had blamed him when he didn't know how to please her. Tony felt confused and helpless because he did not know how to please Cindy. The sexual exercises recommended by their therapist helped them both discover how to give each other sexual pleasure. Gradually, Cindy and Tony began to enjoy a new sexual relationship together.

Sexual Phobias and Aversion

Unlike desire problems, where a women feels a pervasive lack of interest in sex, but may enjoy sex once she begins, sexual phobia is associated with feelings of severe anxiety or panic, and sexual activity is actively avoided. It is not clear whether sexual aversion represents a distinct form of sexual phobia or an entirely different entity. Aversion is usually associated with a sense of disgust, rather than panic, but both states end up in the same pattern of avoidance. A woman who is sexually aversive may feel numbed and "not present" during sex, or if she does experience arousal and orgasm she may not remember that she enjoyed the experience. Phobic and aversive reactions are not just related to performance anxiety, but represent fundamental, severe reactions to the possibility of having sex.

Panic attacks in sexual phobias are more than just a sense of anxiety or inner discomfort, but are an overwhelming sense of immediate threat or terror, accompanied by hyperventilation, palpitations, dizziness, choking sensations, chest tightness, numbing or tingling sensations, faintness, and other fight-or-flight symptoms. Not surprisingly, a woman avoids this reaction by staying away from situations that evoke it. The degree of phobic avoidance or aversion, however, varies depending on the stimulus. For some women, erotic thoughts, images, and conversation can lead to severe anxiety. For others, all physical contact or sexual foreplay can inspire panic attacks. For still other women, only certain types of sexual contact, such as oral sex or intercourse, evoke panic attacks or aversive responses. Thus, a woman with a sexual phobia or aversion may enjoy some aspects of romance or sex but have strong reactions to other aspects. Or, she may be able to tolerate sexual contact, but regard it with the same enthusiasm or pleasure as having a dental procedure. Over time, however, phobia or aversion may lead to total avoidance of sexual activity or physical affection. An affected woman may develop extensive strategies to avoid the possibility of sexual contact.

How common are these disorders? At one sex clinic, approximately 20 percent of women suffered from sexual phobias or aversion, while the other 80 percent had HSD. Research has indicated that a high percentage of women with sexual phobias have other phobias as well or suffer from a panic disorder. Kaplan reported that 25 percent of her patients who phobically avoided sex had definitive diagnoses of panic disorder while over 60 percent had some symptoms of it.

What happens to individuals with sexual phobias or aversion? The severity of their initial experiences of anxiety, disgust, or panic often leads to avoidance of sex and sometimes of romantic relationships. Some women remain single and adapt to a life without a committed romantic relationship or marriage. They may sublimate such needs or desires into platonic and familial relationships, work, or other life projects. For other women, the inability to have these relationships can lead to loneliness and depression, especially if they believe that marriage and family are the measures of success. Most affected women are loving and giving and have children and relatively stable marriages despite their feelings of sexual discomfort. Their partners often tolerate the woman's avoidance of sex, perhaps because of their own conflicts over sex and relationships. Over time, however, some partners are unable to tolerate a marriage or relationship devoid of sex or physical affection. (It is important to clarify that a celibate lifestyle (abstaining from sex and marriage) is often not an indication of a sexual disorder, but a chosen path by an individual as part of religious vows or personal philosophy.)

The causes of sexual phobias and aversion are similar to those for panic symptoms in general. Kaplan suggests that these individuals probably have an inborn vulnerability to anxiety and panic, often manifested early in life by marked separation anxiety from their parents. They may also suffer from rejection sensitivity and an intolerance of criticism. Their threshold for anxiety and panic is low and may be triggered spontaneously. This vulnerability to high anxiety is shaped by parents' re-actions to it. Parents who reject a daughter's anxiety and are not empathic for her fears may end up viewing her behaviors as annoying, embarrassing, or disappointing. As a result, this child may grow up feeling ashamed of her fears and undeserving of help. Her attitudes make it difficult for her later in life to engage in therapy or accept help from her partners. Overprotective parents, on the other hand, may give too much attention to their daughter's fears, going out of their way to prevent frus-tration and pain. As a result, the child may not have limits set on her behaviors or be given the opportunity to try to soothe herself. She may end up avoiding oppor-tunities later in life to solve her own problems. The most helpful parents accept their daughter's difficulties, acknowledge her emotions, and help her to find ways to accept her anxiety and deal with it.

The use of relaxation techniques and antianxiety and antidepressant medications has revolutionized the treatment of phobias and panic disorder. Cognitive-behavioral therapy can help desensitize a woman's extreme fears, while judicious use of medi-cations can eliminate the threat of panic attacks. The class of medications known as *benzodiazepines* are short-acting tranquilizers that can be taken on a regular or an as-needed basis for anxiety and panic. There are several types of benzodiazepines, including Ativan (lorazepam), Valium (diazepam), Xanax (alprazolam), and Klonopin (clonazepam). The downside of these medications is that they can cause excess se-dation, are potentially habit-forming (especially in individuals with a history of sub-stance abuse), and can be dangerous when mixed with alcohol. A more fundamental approach to the treatment of panic is the use of antidepressant medications. There are a variety of effective medications that work differently than the short-acting tran-quilizers. Antidepressant medications must be taken on a daily basis and require several weeks before they have an effect. They work extremely well at preventing panic attacks, but may have problematic side effects. In fact, many of them actually cause sexual dysfunction. Medications are often necessary to treat sexual phobias and aversion, either by actually eliminating the phobia or by lowering anxiety enough so that a woman can work through her sexual fears in therapy.

❦ *Case 3.3—Lou Ellen and Richard*

Lou Ellen had been a fearful person for most of her life. Her father was a charismatic preacher, and she had been brought up with strict religious beliefs that women should never show themselves to men in any way that might be considered sexual. As a result, Lou Ellen was reserved around men. She also suffered from many forms of anxiety, including her fears of flying, being in tunnels or crowded places, and having sex. She had faced many anxious situations by gritting her teeth and bearing her panic, but in general she tended to avoid places and situations that caused such feelings. Lou Ellen was a twenty-five-year-old virgin when she married Richard. Although she loved Richard, she was so frightened of intercourse on their first night together that she broke down and sobbed that she couldn't have sex with him. Richard was confused but also soothing and understanding, and he didn't force the issue.

As time went on, things didn't get much better. Occasionally Lou Ellen and Richard would have a sexual encounter, but something was clearly wrong. Even the thought of sex or anything that might lead to sex caused Lou Ellen to cringe with disgust. What confused Richard was that on the few occasions when they did have sex, Lou Ellen seemed to enjoy herself. However, afterward she would deny that she liked sex and would be filled with guilt, shame, and revulsion. She would then refuse to let Richard touch her. This state of affairs lasted for about two years, until both Lou Ellen and Richard felt miserable. Lou Ellen loved

Richard, but felt hopeless that she would be able to include sex as part of their married life. Richard described the situation to his physician, who gave him the name of a sex therapist. Lou Ellen agreed to go for a consultation but was skeptical.

The therapist realized that Lou Ellen's aversion to sex was strongly connected to her lifelong anxiety, and recommended the use of an antidepressant and antipanic medication. When the medication took effect, Lou Ellen was able to tolerate sexual exercises without feeling anxious or panicked. Through therapy, Richard realized that one reason he had chosen Lou Ellen as his wife was because he unconsciously felt comfortable with the emotional and physical distance she kept between them. Lou Ellen realized that she had internalized her father's rigid antisexual values but had attributed them to divine proscription. She reevaluated her religious belief system and gradually felt freer to experiment with sensuous touching. The couple used a gradual method to desensitize Lou Ellen's anxieties about sexual contact. They moved from nonsexual touch, to genital touch, and eventually to intercourse. Each step required reassurance, education about normal sexuality, and permission to go slowly. The very slow pace allowed Richard to become accustomed to deepening emotional intimacy, while Lou Ellen learned to tolerate and enjoy her sexuality.

Sexual Arousal Disorder

As described in chapter 1, sexual arousal has both psychological and physical components. It differs from sexual desire, which is entirely psychological. The basic psychological process is a dimming of consciousness of the external environment, with a mental focus on pleasurable stimuli flowing into the mind. Sexual arousal depends upon an open, unhindered mind-set during this stimulation, so that a woman becomes increasingly focused on pleasure and loses herself in the experience. Further dimming of conscious awareness leads to the point where orgasm occurs. The physical process of arousal prepares the body for sexual intercourse and ultimately successful conception. Lubrication begins in the external genital area, particularly in the vestibule, and in the vaginal canal. Genital tissues swell as blood rushes to them in a process called *vasocongestion*. This process enables genital and pelvic muscles to maintain adequate tension, and properly aligns the cervix to receive sperm.

In some women this normal process of arousal occurs only partially or never takes place. Sexual Arousal Disorder involves a recurrent inability to achieve or maintain a state of sexual arousal during sexual activity and is sometimes called *generalized sexual dysfunction*, since it is such a fundamental difficulty. The term *frigidity* is no longer considered to be an accurate or particularly kind label—but you may have heard it before. Women with Sexual Arousal Disorder experience little pleasure from sexual stimulation. Stimulation may be experienced as ticklish, annoying, or boring. Sex is often viewed as a chore, an obligation, or as something to endure. If a woman does not go through increasing levels of arousal, she doesn't achieve orgasm. Lack of arousal is evident in a lack of lubrication, making intercourse painful, and reinforcing her lack of arousal and desire to be sexual. Over time, many women with inadequate sexual arousal feel anger and resentment towards their partners, or they may create excuses to avoid sex. It is not known exactly how common Sexual Arousal Disorder is, but in one study of couples who consider themselves happily married, 33 percent of the women reported some difficulty in maintaining adequate sexual excitement for a variety of reasons (Frank, Anderson, Robenstein et al. 1978). This figure may overestimate the number of women with a true disorder, but probably reflects the fact that a significant number of women experience some degree of arousal difficulty at one point or another.

What causes a lack or loss of sexual arousal? It is important to understand that the capacity for sexual arousal is programmed into the body, so if it isn't happening, something must be in its way. Inhibited sexual desire can sometimes handicap sexual arousal, but many women with low desire are still able to become sexually aroused and orgasmic if they let themselves enter into a sexual encounter. A more likely cause of inhibited arousal may be a strong psychological defense mechanism that blocks sexual sensations from entering into conscious awareness. Lack of arousal acts as a signal to ward off sexual activity by blocking sexual sensations. Typically, this is accomplished by tensing muscles in the entire body. When this occurs, a woman may not be consciously aware of fear or anxiety during sex; instead she notices only a lack of sexual excitement. Often, she fears that becoming aroused will lead to unknown harm or danger.

Lack of the appropriate kind of stimulation is another major cause of arousal disorder. Many woman don't really know what sexual stimulation they want, or if they know, they aren't able to ask for it. They may fear that if they appear interested in sexual arousal, they will be seen as too demanding of their partner. Sometimes a woman tries to position her body so that she will receive the stimulation she wants, rather than by directly letting her partner know. However, since partners are not mind readers, such signals are often not understood.

⇙ Case 3.4—Janet and Todd

After ten years of marriage, Janet and Todd felt that sex was boring. Early in their relationship sex had been wonderful, and they had planned a future together that had now come true. They had three children, and Todd's busy law practice afforded them enough money to buy their dream house. Janet had turned her interest in gardening into a successful landscape-design company. In fact, their lives were so busy that they only had time for sex late at night. They would fall into bed at midnight after a hectic weekend filled with activities. Janet didn't feel aroused when Todd touched her, and she had given up hope that things would change. Her mind was continually distracted with thoughts of new business deals, of plans for the children, and of a host of nonsexual thoughts. Besides, she knew exactly what to expect. After three minutes of foreplay they would have intercourse in the missionary position. Since Janet was not aroused, intercourse felt scratchy and uncomfortable, and she often encouraged Todd to finish quickly. After Todd had his orgasm they would both fall asleep.

A change occurred when they made arrangements for a weekend away from the family and went to the country inn where they had often stayed before their marriage. After a typical sexual encounter, they began to talk about how they had lost the passion they had enjoyed so much. They agreed to consult a sex therapist. The therapist suggested that they had allowed sex to become routine, and that both were using their passionate energy in other parts of their lives, giving little attention to their intimate life. As they did the sensate focus exercises (described in chapter 7), the couple began to expand their sexual repertoire and open up communication. Janet realized that she didn't allow Todd to touch her in ways that would arouse her. Todd realized that his arousal level was low and he feared losing his erection. Both had somehow agreed to hurry through intercourse.

The couple soon looked forward to the sensate focus exercises and the chance afterwards to talk about their experience together. Therapy helped them discuss their reactions to a variety of touch activities, and soon they were talking easily about their sexual responses. They agreed that their sex life was important and set aside private "date" time, free of interruption. As they invested their energy in their sexual relationship they began to experiment with new positions and different types of touch. Both Todd and Janet found that when they were "giving a performance" they were not in touch with their experience. Janet learned to show Todd how to touch her by guiding his hand with her own. Each new exercise felt more arousing than the last. The therapist encouraged the couple to use their time together to learn about touching and temporarily suspend a focus on orgasm. They found they were enjoying leisurely, sensuous lovemaking without thinking of the goal of orgasm. As therapy ended, they were enjoying their sexual experiences with pleasure.

Sexual Pain Disorders

The two sexual pain disorders, *dyspareunia* and *vaginismus*, are common and extremely frustrating conditions. Even in loving, stable relationships with strong sexual desire, adequate arousal, and orgasmic capacity, these disorders rob a woman of what should be pleasurable and sensual sexual relations. Vaginismus refers to an involuntary spasm at the opening of the vagina that makes penetration difficult or impossible. Dyspareunia refers to genital pain, usually during intercourse. It is important to understand genital and pelvic anatomy because sexual pain disorders can affect any part of a woman's genitals and reproductive structures. Locating the area and extent of pain or discomfort is key to diagnosis. A thorough gynecologic exam can confirm a diagnosis of sexual pain, but may not be able to easily discern a cause.

Vaginismus

In vaginismus, the outer muscular opening of the vagina involuntarily contracts in a spasm when vaginal penetration is attempted, making gynecologic exams and sexual intercourse painful and almost always impossible. This may be a guarding reaction similar to how a woman blinks her eye to protect it from being hurt. Sexual relationships often go unconsummated for years because of the stress and pain of unsuccessful attempts at sexual intercourse. Some individuals avoid sexual relations or romantic relationships in general. The majority of women with vaginismus are unable to tolerate vaginal penetration during gynecologic exams, and as a result may avoid recommended follow-up visits. Sexual phobias and aversion may develop from vaginismus. The impact on relationships can be devastating, and sometimes male partners begin to experience difficulty with sexual desire and erectile function.

The term *primary vaginismus* is used when a woman has never been able to have a gynecologic exam or engage in vaginal penetration. *Secondary vaginismus* may develop due to numerous physical and psychological factors in a woman who has previously been able to have sexual intercourse. Whatever the route, many women are reluctant to bring this problem to the attention of professional help. They often feel alone and different from other women, when in fact vaginismus is not uncommon. Although its true prevalence is not known, it is estimated that nearly two out of every one thousand women in the general population and twenty percent to forty percent of women seeking sex therapy suffer from vaginismus. Many more women may suffer from intermittent pain or muscular spasm during intercourse due to the same factors that lead to chronic vaginismus. The good news about vaginismus is that treatment is relatively straightforward, and the success rates are close to 100 percent in women and couples who stick with treatment.

A woman with vaginismus often suffers from a sense of failure because she is not able to express her love through sexual intercourse. Rather than having control over her body, it seems as if her body has arbitrary control over her. The involuntary vaginal reflex usually occurs at the moment of attempted penetration, but may also occur in response to mental images of penetration or anticipated penetration, such as during foreplay. This contraction involves several muscles that surround the vaginal opening and effectively close it off, especially the *pubococcygeus* or PC muscle. The PC muscle contraction sometimes feels painful, like a muscle cramp, especially when pressure is exerted against it. Consequently, the discomfort often escalates during heated attempts at penetration or with repeated attempts to insert a speculum during an exam. A reflexive tightening of other muscles in the pelvis, thighs, abdomen, and legs may also occur, as the affected woman tries to close her legs and withdraw from the painful stimulus. Some women reflexively scream out or begin crying as they try to withdraw from penetration. Most women who suffer from vaginismus are very frightened of being hurt and deeply ashamed of their inability to have intercourse or penetration of any kind.

Vaginismus becomes chronic when the muscular spasm becomes a conditioned response to attempted penetration. In other words, it occurs repetitively upon stimulation, even without the initial precipitating cause. The pain, confusion, frustration, and humiliation that can accompany vaginismus eventually leads to avoidance of sex or physical affection, creating a vicious cycle of fear and pain. This cycle is illustrated in figure 3.1.

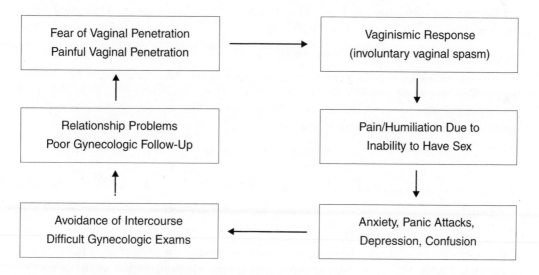

Figure 3.1. The Cycle of Vaginismus

What causes vaginismus? Sex researchers do not know why some women develop vaginismus, but they do have a good idea of what factors are commonly associated with it. The immediate cause of vaginismus is the involuntary contraction of the PC muscle. The initial occurrence may be an acute response to vaginal or pelvic pain during intercourse or an exam, or a reaction to an upsetting or traumatic experience that induces fear and aversion. Any physical condition that causes vaginal pain, including all of the causes of dyspareunia, are possible factors. Physically or sexually abusive experiences can induce fear of vaginal penetration, or phobias about sex, which in turn can result in vaginismus. Other potential antecedents of vaginismus include frightening medical procedures experienced during childhood; painful first intercourse; irritation from condoms, spermicides, or lack of lubrication; sexual relations without strong desire; and fear of pregnancy.

Since these experiences of pain and fear are fairly common, why don't all women who experience them have vaginismus? Sex researchers have studied women with vaginismus in order to identify psychological factors that may create a predisposition to the disorder. Based on their case studies, Masters and Johnson (1970) suggested that important factors include religious orthodoxy, inadequate or shaming sexual education, sexual inhibition, sexual abuse, rape, and anger towards partners because of infidelity. Kaplan (1974) believes that ignorance and misinformation about sex can exaggerate fear and pain during early sexual encounters. It has been suggested that fears of intimacy, pregnancy, and aggression, or the belief that one's vagina is too small, can sometimes predispose a woman to vaginismus (Leiblum, Pervin, Campbell 1989; Silverstein 1989). Women with vaginismus often possess learned, negative attitudes towards sex. We have listed many factors associated with vaginismus in table 3.1.

Psychoanalytic views of vaginismus focus on the important role of psychological conflict, in which a woman would indirectly express anger, hatred, or envy towards men by closing off her vagina. Kaplan has called this theory into question, however, by describing how elated her patients have felt once their vaginismus is resolved. Other theories of vaginismus have looked at developmental factors. In one study of twenty-two women with vaginismus, Judith Silverstein (1989) found that nearly all of the women grew up as obedient girls who had difficulty expressing anger and had a constant need for approval. This study and one by Kennedy, Doherty, Barnes

Table 3.1. Factors Associated with Vaginismus

Physical Pain with Intercourse	Pelvic pain; Dyspareunia; Imperforate hymen; Painful loss of virginity.
Sexual Anxiety or Panic	Sexual phobia or aversion disorder; Fear of intimacy; Fear of pain or injury during sex; Fear of pregnancy; Fear that vagina is too small.
Sexual or Physical Abuse	Sexual trauma, rape, or molestation.
Negative Sexual Attitudes	Intercourse viewed as a violation or invasion; Religious proscription against sex; Misinformation or ignorance about sex; Negative or shaming sex education; Anger, envy, or hatred of partner or of men
Associated Personality Features	Obedient, "good" girl in family; Difficulty expressing anger; High need for approval; Fearful of aggression.
Associated Family Features	Grew up with domineering, critical, or overly seductive father; Witnessed physical violation in family; Grew up with parental conflict and abuse; Kind, gentle, passive husband (opposite of father); Husband with erectile dysfunction (impotence); History of husband's infidelity.
Other	Low sexual desire; Prior or unrecognized lesbian orientation (for women with male partners); History of painful childhood medical procedures.

(1995) have suggested that many of these women grew up with critical, domineering, and/or seductive fathers, and married kind, gentle, and passive men—the opposite of their fathers. Vaginismus may thus serve to protect these women psychologically, and unconsciously, from their symbolic "fathers," represented by a sexual partner, while indirectly expressing anger.

❧ Case 3.5—Lorraine and Kevin

When Lorraine and Kevin went for their first sex-therapy appointment, they were both upset and nervous but determined to understand what was wrong with their sex life. No matter what they did, Kevin was not able to penetrate Lorraine, and they had not yet consummated their two-year-long marriage. Lorraine enjoyed being intimate with Kevin, and both of them had orgasms through oral sex or mutual masturbation, but every time they tried to have intercourse she would be reduced to tears of frustration. They wanted children and were embarrassed when family members and friends asked if they were starting their family. No one knew that they had never actually had intercourse, and they felt ashamed, embarrassed, and angry that their lives had stopped moving forward.

Lorraine told the therapist that she had recently seen her gynecologist, who found her to be healthy with no physical reason to prevent penetration. As the couple talked about their childhood experiences, Lorraine remembered that when she was three years old she had been hospitalized for a bladder infection. She had been terrified when the staff held her down for the doctor to examine her. Lorraine became fearful as a six-year-old when she overheard her mother talking to a friend about labor pains. She also had a friend who told her that sex was horribly painful and that women bled when they had sex the first time. When she added up these experiences, Lorraine began to see why she was afraid of vaginal penetration. Both Kevin and Lorraine felt discouraged after she described these early life experiences, and they wondered if she would ever overcome them. The therapist said that vaginismus could be easily resolved if the couple followed a program of graduated assignments.

The therapist first encouraged both Lorraine and Kevin to learn about their sexual anatomy by taking turns looking at their genitals and naming the structures they saw. Next she taught Lorraine how to do Kegel exercises to tighten and loosen the muscle at the opening of the vagina. Lorraine soon realized that she had conscious control of this muscle, which she used every time she urinated. The therapist taught a series of relaxation and deep breathing exercises and asked that the couple practice these on a regular basis. She explained that unconscious anxiety caused the muscle to spasm, but that relaxation would lessen this anxiety. Next, she presented Lorraine with a set of vaginal dilators in graduated sizes. She instructed Lorraine to use progressive-relaxation exercises with deep breathing, followed by Kegel exercises and the insertion of the tiny dilator into her relaxed vagina. Over time, Lorraine gained control over the use of dilators.

The next step was to include Kevin in these activities. Through sensuous exercises, Kevin gradually learned to insert the dilators with Lorraine guiding his hand. Meanwhile, the couple practiced gentle touching exercises designed to teach them how to arouse each other. Soon, Lorraine was ready to try intercourse. The therapist instructed the couple to first arouse each other; then, with Kevin lying on his back, Lorraine could lower herself onto his erect penis. Much to their surprise, she was able to do this as soon as she slowed her breathing and relaxed.

Dyspareunia

The term dyspareunia refers to recurrent and distressing genital pain associated with sexual relations. It is classified into *primary dyspareunia* when it has always occurred during sexual relations and *secondary dyspareunia* when it has occurred after a period of pain-free sexual activity. Although dyspareunia is usually described as occurring during intercourse, it can occur during any point in the sexual response cycle when genital stimulation occurs. Dyspareunia is often a cause of vaginismus; it can also result from vaginismus. In a recent study of 155 women referred to a sexual dysfunction clinic, 14 percent complained of dyspareunia. A review of other studies estimated that from 8 percent to 23 percent of women in the general population suffer from dyspareunia (Spector and Carey 1990). Women with this condition are seen often in gynecological offices, but are rarely referred to sex therapy. However, many women never even contact a physician. Technically, the diagnosis of dyspareunia is reserved for those women in whom there is pain but no specific medical or organic cause. In our experience, however, genital pain from any cause that eludes quick diagnosis or is not easily treatable can lead to significant emotional distress and sexual problems, including vaginismus, hypoactive sexual desire, and avoidance of sexual encounters.

When a woman experiences genital pain, it is critical to first rule out specific, treatable physical causes. Gynecologists were traditionally taught that pain at or near the opening of the vagina was related to psychiatric issues, whereas pain during the deep thrusting of intercourse was usually due to a physical cause. These explanations are no longer considered useful. When assessing genital pain, physicians basically try to identify

1. The history of the pain (location, duration, associated factors, intensity),

2. The presence of visible and *palpable,* or able to be felt, abnormalities,

3. The impact on sexual function.

A physical examination may not be enough to make a diagnosis; sometimes tissue samples are needed for microscopic analysis. Dyspareunia can be classified by its location, with pain occurring in the vulva and vestibule (*superficial dyspareunia*), in the vaginal canal, or deep in the pelvis. The physician determines the cause of pain partly by its location.

Vulvar Disorders and Dyspareunia

Dyspareunia due to vulvar disorders is common and has many variants and causes. As a result, the diagnosis can sometimes be difficult and the course of treatment frustrating due to repeated attempts to find and treat the actual cause of the problem. Vulvar disorders are especially problematic because they can produce unremitting vulvar pain. Vulvar pain may be experienced as burning, itching, or stinging. Skin may feel or appear dry, swollen, or inflamed. Pain is sometimes felt in the clitoral or anal region and occasionally felt in the abdomen. Vulvar pain is associated with painful sexual stimulation and intercourse and sometimes vaginismus. Some women experience discomfort only when the region is stimulated, while other women experience pain all of the time. In postmenopausal women the loss of estrogen can lead to marked thinning and dryness of the vulvar and vaginal tissue, causing pain when stimulated.

Vulvitis refers to inflammation of the skin of the vulva and may have both infectious and noninfectious causes. Sexually transmitted diseases are sometimes the culprit. *Vulvodynia* refers to a condition of vulvar pain that is *idiopathic*, or lacking a clear cause. *Vulvar vestibulitis* (also called *focal vulvitis* or *vestibular adenitis*) refers specifically to a condition characterized by inflammation, irritation, and painful burning sensations of the tissue surrounding the vaginal opening or *vestibule*, ranging from the base of the labia to the urethral opening. Physical examination in this area will reveal red and swollen tissue that is often quite tender. Vulvar Vestibulitis is seen commonly by gynecologists. Although the cause of vulvar vestibulitis is not clear, it has sometimes been associated with a history of multiple yeast infections or with infection from the Human Papilloma Virus (HPV). More recently, a Denver research group led by Dr. Clive Solomons (1991) has proposed a theory that vestibulitis, and other forms of chronic vulvar pain, may be due to abnormal systemic and urinary levels of calcium oxalate. Women with vulvar vestibulitis often face repeated, frustrating visits to the gynecologist due to persistent symptoms. Many women have good symptomatic relief from daily application of topical estrogen cream, along with a regimen of biofeedback to deal with chronic pain. Topical anesthetic jelly applied to the vulva prior to intercourse helps reduce pain. The addition of a diet low in calcium oxalate and supplemented by calcium citrate has helped upwards of 60 percent to 70 percent of affected women.

Another source of vulvar inflammation are the *vestibular glands,* or Bartholin's glands, which can develop infections and cysts. *Urethritis* produces discomfort and pain when the urinary opening or urethra becomes inflamed. Pain, irritation, and inflammation of the vulva can also result from trauma due to inadequate lubrication or irritative agents such as dyes or detergents in clothes, spermicidal foams, infected urine or cyst secretions, and douching. Inadequate lubrication is probably the most common cause of secondary superficial dyspareunia. Stimulation of dry vulvar tissue by rubbing or by penile thrusting in the dry vestibule can cause a great deal of pain. All of these conditions can worsen or lead to secondary infections when a woman further injures vulvar tissue by scratching the vulva in an attempt to relieve intense itching.

Lichen sclerosis, also known as *vulvar dystrophy* and *atrophic dystrophy,* refers to abnormal thickening followed by eventual thinning of the outer layer of skin of the vulva. Examination reveals patches of *hypopigmented skin,* or loss of normal color, with white plaques, sometimes labeled *leukoplakia.* As the condition progresses, the labia may thin, flatten, and lose their elasticity. The thinning of vulvar skin can greatly distort the appearance of the external genitals and lead to scarring and constriction of the vaginal opening. A number of benign and a few malignant lesions can lead to vulvar dystrophy. Biopsy is important to rule out cancerous lesions.

Note: If you suffer from chronic vulvar pain, please read about the Vulvar Pain Foundation in the appendix.

Vaginal and Pelvic Disorders and Dyspareunia

Vaginal pain is less common because the nerve endings in the vagina differ from those in the skin and are less sensitive. Pain is usually experienced at the opening of the vagina or deeper in the pelvis. As with superficial dyspareunia, however, lack of vaginal lubrication can cause discomfort and irritation. Vaginal infections from yeast and bacteria can cause vaginal itching and pain. Vaginal tightness due to *strictures,* or the narrowing of the vaginal canal, or muscle spasm, as seen in vaginismus, can create pain and cramping. Any urethral problems, such as a diverticulum, which is a small pouch, or a congenitally shortened distance from the lower joining of the labia, can create pain in the vaginal region.

Superficial and deep dyspareunia are extremely common following childbirth, gynecologic surgery, and radiation treatment. The sites of vulvar or vaginal tears or surgical episiotomies from delivery can be markedly tender and painful during intercourse for several weeks or months. A certain type of suture used to close surgical episiotomies has been associated with cases of dyspareunia that last for several years after childbirth. Pelvic surgery can lead to *adhesions,* in which adjacent tissues scar together (i.e., become attached) abnormally. Pelvic structures are thus less pliable and can produce pain when stretched during intercourse. Radiation treatment for gynecologic cancer can also cause pelvic adhesions and can sometimes cause *radiation vaginitis*, characterized by inflammation, dryness, vaginal ulcers, poor healing, and eventual scarring. Pain from radiation may increase over time and last from months to years.

Deep dyspareunia is often described as a pain resulting from penile and pelvic thrusting during intercourse. Any pelvic infections, in particular *pelvic inflammatory disease* (PID) can cause pain during intercourse. The presence of inflammation, scarring, or adhesions in the uterus or pelvis due to endometriosis is a significant cause of deep dyspareunia. Pelvic tumors or masses such as ovarian cysts or uterine fibroids are also causes. Finally, uterine position can be a cause of deep dyspareunia. In the majority of women, the uterus is bent forward over the vagina and flexed slightly downward. Other women have a normal variation of this, in which the uterus is facing and flexed backwards over the vagina. For those women, deep thrusting during intercourse may have more contact with the uterus, which sometimes causes pain. Table 3.2 summarizes the many causes of dyspareunia.

A thorough gynecologic examination is necessary to determine the cause of deep dyspareunia. The problem with dyspareunia is that repeated sexual pain can set up a cycle of apprehension, avoidance, and further sexual dysfunction, all out of proportion to the initial cause. It is critical for physicians to take a woman's complaints seriously and to consider all possible causes. Women with dyspareunia must educate themselves about female genital anatomy, function, and disease, and must become advocates for their health care and well-being. Dyspareunia is never simply psychological and should be treated medically before any psychological components are considered. Careful follow-up, judicious treatments, biofeedback, relaxation tech-

Table 3.2. Major Causes of Dyspareunia

Superficial Vulvar Pain	Vulvitis, vulvovaginitis; Vulvodynia; Vulvar vestibulitis; Lichen sclerosis or vulvar dystrophy; Bartholin Gland infection; Genital herpes; History of vulvectomy; Urethritis; Inadequate lubrication during sex; Irritation from spermicides, latex, or chemical agents.
Vestibular or Vaginal Pain	Imperforate (intact) hymen; Sexually transmitted diseases; Episiotomy pain; Pain following childbirth; Radiation vaginitis; Vaginal strictures, scarring; History of vaginal surgery; Vaginal atrophy (post-menopausal); Inadequate lubrication during sex; Irritation from spermicides, latex, or chemical agents; Sexual trauma (i.e., rape or molestation); Vaginismus.
Deep Pelvic Pain	Congential malformations of genitals; Pelvic Inflammatory Disease; History of gynecologic, pelvic, or abdominal surgery: Hysterectomy (removal of uterus), Salpingo-oopherectomy (removal of fallopian tubes and ovaries), Cystectomy (removal of bladder), Colonic resection; Endometriosis; Pelvic adhesions; Genital or pelvic tumors; Urinary Tract Infection; Ovarian cysts; Uterine retroversion or retroflexion; Interstitial cystitis; Uterine fibroids.

niques for pain, and a lot of support can help break the cycle of pain, fear, and sexual dysfunction.

∞ Case 3.6—Helen and Cal

Helen and Cal had been married for thirty-seven years and had enjoyed a satisfying sex life for most of that time. Then Helen was diagnosed with endometrial cancer and underwent surgery, chemotherapy, and radiation treatment. These medical interventions were successful and she was declared to be free of cancer. However, as the couple began to rebuild their lives and recover from the threat that Helen might die, they found that intercourse was very painful for her. Since she had an excellent relationship with her doctor, she asked for a consultation for her dyspareunia.

Helen's doctor acknowledged that radiation and chemotherapy often cause dyspareunia and referred her to a sex therapist to discover how she could cope with the changes in her sexuality. The therapist talked about the changes in her vaginal tissue as a result of the treatments that might be causing pain. Adding to the problem was the fact that Helen had to stop taking estrogen replacement therapy for other medical reasons, so she did not have the hormonal support necessary to keep vaginal tissue supple. After surgery, the loss of elasticity and shortening of her vagina coupled with loss of lubrication all added to the vaginal pain she felt during penile thrusting. Since she had to live with these changes, the couple worked on measures to make intercourse manageable.

Through trial and error Helen and Cal found several solutions to the problem. First, Helen began using a moisturizing lubricant which she inserted in her vagina several times a week. When they planned to have sex she used an additional liberal supply of lubricant in and around her vagina. Helen did a relaxation exercise before they began lovemaking and waited until she was highly aroused before letting Cal know that she was ready for penetration. Once he entered her, they would stop until she adjusted to the sense of his penis and then moved gradually until they got a sense of what she could enjoy. They were able to talk about what to do sexually, both during and after a sexual encounter. Intercourse often worked best when she knelt on top of him and was thus able to control the depth and speed of thrusting. They also found that a side-to-side position was good. While intercourse continued to be a problem for Helen, and she and Cal missed the easy intercourse which was no longer possible, they were still able to engage in other forms of sexual pleasuring.

∞ Case 3.7—Betty and Quinn

Betty and Quinn were very discouraged about sex. Betty found intercourse to be painful and began to avoid intimacy with her husband. Quinn felt baffled by Betty's experience, but he didn't want to hurt her. The whole topic of sex was embarrassing to him. Both Betty and Quinn grew up in strict religious homes where premarital sex was considered sinful and punishments were harsh. They met at a seminary where they were both studying religion. Betty told Quinn she wanted a family with traditional values, and he agreed that this was also his dream. Neither had any sexual experience, and they decided to wait until after marriage to have sex. Although they had once kissed each other on the lips, they both agreed afterward that it was too exciting and tempting, and they wanted to enter marriage as virgins.

Before the wedding, Betty went to a gynecologist to obtain birth control pills, since she didn't want a child right away. Her doctor told her that while her body was healthy, she might need to adjust to intercourse since her vagina was relatively tight. But she reassured Betty that her genital anatomy was well within a normal size range. During their three years of their marriage, Betty and Quinn had intercourse less than ten times, because Betty experienced severe pain each time and felt sore and miserable for several days afterward. Since he lacked experience, Quinn felt awkward and unsure how to approach Betty sexually, so he seldom initiated sex. After years of frustration and pain, they eventually talked with their minister, who referred them to a marriage counselor who was also trained in sex therapy.

The therapist asked Betty to see her gynecologist to rule out a physical reason for her pain. Betty's doctor found her reproductive system to be completely normal, but told her that the side effects of her birth control pills might cause a lack of lubrication and consequent pain. She also suggested that the couple was attempting intercourse when Betty was not aroused or lubricated. She recommended that Betty use a water-based lubricant during sex. At their next appointment, the therapist questioned the couple about how they touched each other. They admitted that they were afraid to touch each other's genitals and usually went straight to intercourse. The therapist then suggested they take a vacation from intercourse while they explored their sexuality.

Betty saw the therapist alone for a few sessions and was surprised to find that all sexual activities frightened and upset her. She listed twenty items of sexual activity from easiest (holding hands in the movies) to hardest (having intercourse under the covers with the lights out). Next, Betty learned deep muscle relaxation, and imagined each successive scene while she was deeply relaxed. She made fast progress once she understood the process, and couple therapy was resumed. The couple learned about touch and communication as they used sensate focus exercises to illuminate areas of fear and embarrassment.

Their progress was steady until they had a setback when they became aroused and began intercourse too soon, resulting in the return of Betty's vaginal pain. Talking about the experience helped them realize that their expectations for "perfect sex" were unrealistic. Soon Betty was enjoying the touching exercises so much that she asked Quinn if she could guide his penis into her. He was delighted, and Betty realized that she had enough control over the sexual situation to feel safe and free of pain. Lovemaking with sexual intercourse became a regular event in their lives.

Orgasmic Disorder

Orgasmic disorder involves a recurrent and persistent delay in or failure to achieve orgasm after a normal excitement phase. Also called *anorgasmia*, it is the most common sexual dysfunction in women, and accounts for nearly 50 percent of women's primary sexual dysfunction. Many affected women have normal sexual desire and arousal but are not able to progress beyond the plateau stage. Like other sexual disorders, orgasmic disorder may be primary or secondary, and may occur only in certain situations or with all sexual stimulation and all partners. Lonnie Barbach (1973) coined the term "pre-orgasmic" to describe primary orgasmic disorder in which a woman has not yet had an orgasm. Part of the difficulty in defining this disorder is first knowing what is considered a normal orgasmic stage. Women vary greatly in the time it takes for them to reach orgasm and the type of stimulation they require. Some women require direct clitoral stimulation, while others prefer indirect clitoral contact. Although achieving orgasm during intercourse is often cited as the ultimate goal, this is not necessarily the norm for women. In fact, studies show that only 25 to 30 percent of women can consistently reach orgasm during intercourse.

Helen Singer Kaplan (1974) based her thinking about the causes of orgasmic disorder on what she calls the *reflex* concept of orgasm. Sexual sensory input is centered in the clitoris, from where neurologic pathways flow to the lower spinal cord. The spinal center is also influenced by neural pathways from the brain, which can both facilitate as well as inhibit input from the clitoris. Sensorimotor output travels from the spinal cord to the muscles surrounding the vagina, which contract rhythmically during orgasm. The reflex arc thus goes from clitoris to spinal cord and back to vaginal muscles, with much influence from higher brain input. This arc explains how orgasm is facilitated by both clitoral stimulation as well as by brain activity, presumably experienced as a narrowing of attention to pleasurable and erotic thoughts, images, and sensations. Orgasm can be inhibited by a disruption in either pathway—clitoral or cerebral.

On a broader level, there are many conditions associated with orgasmic disorder. Lack of sexual desire or arousal often sets the stage for making orgasm difficult or impossible. Dyspareunia can have the same effect, although women with vaginismus are often orgasmic. Relationship conflicts and internal psychological conflict such as fear of pregnancy or rejection can cause transient orgasmic dysfunction. Many women who are not orgasmic feel uncomfortable with the loss of control during orgasm, perhaps associating it with sexually improper or unacceptable aggressive impulses. Severe guilt or religious proscription can also inhibit orgasm.

Many women with orgasmic disorder are often able to enjoy sexual relations or orgasm during masturbation. Other women with more global inhibition may lose interest in sex altogether. Sometimes a woman adapts to her situation by faking orgasm so as not to disappoint her partner, leading to an inevitable loss of interest in sex. As a consequence, her partner usually remains unaware of the problem and doesn't learn how to please her. If a woman feels she has to perform adequately by producing an orgasm, she is likely to focus on and evaluate her level of arousal during lovemaking. This "spectatoring" or watching herself leads to a drop in arousal as she removes her attention from sexual stimulation. As we will detail in chapter 9, the treatment of orgasmic disorder involves progressive masturbation exercises, the use of vibrators, and specific lovemaking techniques to maximize erotic stimulation.

✎ Case 3.8—Marcia and Ron

Marcia and Ron were very much in love and wanted to marry. Although Marcia enjoyed the closeness of making love, she was not able to have an orgasm. Neither wanted to start their marriage with a sexual problem, and they agreed to see a sex therapist. At their first appointment, the therapist asked Marcia a series of questions to see if they could discover what was causing this block in her sexual response to stimulation. As Marcia explained her past sexual history it became clear that there were several problems that were interfering.

She had grown up in a strict religious household where sexuality was considered sinful unless it was for procreation. Because of these strictures against sexual expression, the family believed that to protect their innocence the girls should not be taught about sexuality. For example, Marcia was not told about menstruation and was very frightened when she got her first period because she thought she had been injured. In high school she had many friends and excelled in academics and sports, but she didn't date.

When Marcia went to college she fell in love with Ron, but she didn't know enough about sex or contraception to protect herself and she got pregnant. She decided to have an abortion and Ron was supportive during this period, but she was filled with guilt and shame and was not able to tell her family or friends. After the abortion she found that she didn't get aroused when they made love, although she still liked the closeness and love she felt for Ron.

As they talked to the therapist, Marcia began to realize that she knew very little about her body and how it worked and that the shame about sex and the guilt she felt from the abortion also acted as a barrier to letting go. The therapist recommended that Marcia join a sexuality group for women. The group met for ten weeks and Marcia learned about the physical and emotional components of her sexuality. She examined her family's religious attitudes and beliefs about sex and explored her own value system. At the same time, she began practicing masturbation assignments to discover how her body worked. Gradually over the ten week period she learned how to bring herself to orgasm. At that point she and Ron returned to their couples therapist and learned how to talk about sexuality and express their wants and needs. Even with the rush of wedding plans they continued their sexual assignments and were delighted when their lovemaking led to orgasm for Marcia on a consistent basis.

Other Notes on Sexual Disorders in Women

We have just described the main sexual disorders in women. We have not discussed *paraphilias* (e.g., repetitive and distressing sexual fantasies or urges, such as sexual sadism, masochism, exhibitionism, pedophilia, voyeurism, and others) and gender identity disorders because few women experience these conditions. If, however, you believe that you suffer from one of these disorders, we recommend that you discuss it with a certified sex therapist.

EXERCISE 3.1—THE DIAGNOSTIC FLOWCHART

This exercise is designed to help you identify whether you have a sexual dysfunction. It is important that you complete the questionnaire in chapter 2 in order to begin this exercise. We are modeling this exercise on a diagnostic tree, starting with the trunk and moving outward to the limbs and then leaves. The "roots" of the tree will be discussed at the end of the exercise. This tree may help clarify your problem with sexuality. However, any potential diagnoses that emerges from it should be confirmed by a formal diagnostic exam from a certified sex therapist or mental health professional with training in sexual dysfunction.

Your responses should be based on either your current relationship or on your most recent relationship. Don't worry about distinguishing between generalized and situational problems, or between primary and secondary problems—just check them off and we will help you qualify them at the end.

Trunk

Based on your map from chapter 2, list the major sexual difficulties you have experienced.

1. _____

2. _____

3. _____

4. _____

5. _____

These difficulties form the basis of your sexual dysfunction. Depending on what you wrote, the diagnosis may already be obvious. Still, it is important to complete the exercise to get a full diagnostic picture. Keep these problems in mind as you proceed through the diagnostic tree.

Limb One—Desire (I)

1. How often do you desire sexual activity? Rate your desire using the scale provided.

Never	Less Frequently than Monthly		Monthly		Weekly		Daily		
0	1	2	3	4	5	6	7	8	9	10

2. How would you rate your level of sexual desire?

None	Minimal		Mild/Episodic		Moderate		Frequent		
0	1	2	3	4	5	6	7	8	9	10

3. If you answered less than six on either items 1 or 2, go to item 4. Otherwise, skip to the next limb.

4. Your answers may fall in the range of hypoactive desire. On the following check-list, rate your level of interest, enthusiasm, or participation in the following over the last twelve months:

   0 = never

   1 = once or twice, with little interest

   2 = several times, with minimal interest

   3 = infrequently, but with some interest

   4 = occasionally, with mild interest

   5 = sometimes, with mild to moderate interest

How often do you:

Have sexual fantasies?	0	1	2	3	4	5
Daydream about sex or romance?	0	1	2	3	4	5
Masturbate?	0	1	2	3	4	5
Read erotic materials?	0	1	2	3	4	5
View erotic pictures, photos, or videos?	0	1	2	3	4	5

5. If your responses were all less than four, go to item 6, otherwise skip to item 7.

6. Do you find your lack of sexual desire distressing? To what extent?

Not at all	Minimally		Somewhat		Very		Severely		
0	1	2	3	4	5	6	7	8	9	10

7. How has your level of sexual desire affected your relationship? Check all that apply:

   _____ I don't have any romantic relationships as a result.

   _____ I have a romantic but nonsexual relationship.

   _____ I agree to sex but don't seek it out.

   _____ Sex with my partner is not pleasurable.

   _____ My partner and I argue a lot because of my low desire.

   _____ One or more relationships have ended because of my low desire.

8. If you rated your level of distress as greater than three, or checked off at least two items in 7, go to item 9. Otherwise, skip to item 10.

9. Your responses indicate a high likelihood that you have *hypoactive sexual desire disorder.* Put a check mark in the margin next to this item. Now go to Limb 2.

10. Your responses indicate relatively low sexual desire, but perhaps not to the point of representing *hypoactive sexual desire disorder.* Put a check mark in the margin next to this item. Now go to Limb 2.

Limb Two—Desire (II)

11. Does sexual activity or the possibility of sexual activity make you feel anxious? If so, go to item 12. If not, skip to item 15.

12. Check off the degree(s) to which you feel anxious during sexual activity:

    _____ A. Mildly anxious, but sex is tolerable.

    _____ B. Moderate to severe anxiety, but no panic during sex.

    _____ C. Panic during sexual activity.

    _____ D. Panic attacks that prevent sex from occurring.

    _____ E. Sexual or erotic images or conversation cause panic.

    _____ F. Panic prevents romantic and sexual relationships.

13. If you checked off any of items C through F, go to item 14. If you checked off A or B only, skip to item 15.

14. Your responses indicate the likelihood that you are suffering from a *sexual phobia.* Put a check mark in the margin next to this item. Now go to item 15.

15. Check off the items that apply:

    _____ A. Sexual thoughts, images, or discussions make me nervous or uncomfortable.

    _____ B. I tolerate sex with my partner for the sake of the relationship.

    _____ C. Sexual thoughts, images, or discussions are disgusting.

    _____ D. I tolerate physical contact but avoid all sexual contact.

    _____ E. I avoid both physical and sexual contact with my partner.

    _____ F. I have had few or no sexual relationships and have no interest in it.

16. If you checked off any of items C through F, go to item 17. If you checked off A or B only, skip to item 18. If you didn't check off any item, skip to Limb 3.

17. Your responses indicate a high likelihood that you have a *sexual aversion disorder.* Put a check mark in the margin next to this item. Now go to Limb 3.

18. Your responses indicate that you have a degree of sexual anxiety and/or aversion, but not to the degree of a phobia or aversion disorder. Now go to Limb 3.

Limb Three—Arousal

19. Does the following happen to you during any sexual activity (alone or with a partner):

    _____ A sense of sexual arousal?

    _____ Genital lubrication?

    _____ A sensation of genital swelling?

    _____ Pleasurable sensations with clitoral stimulation?

20. If you checked off every item, skip to Limb 4. If not, go to item 21.

21. Do you experience any of the following:

    _____ Little or no pleasure or excitement during sex?

    _____ Numbness or lack of sensation during sex?

    _____ Difficulty maintaining sexual arousal during sex?

22. If you checked any of above, go to item 23. Otherwise, skip to item 26.

23. How does your lack of sexual arousal affect you? Check all that apply.

    _____ A. It doesn't bother me or my partner.

    _____ B. I still have sex and enjoy it emotionally, but without any physical pleasure.

    _____ C. I find sexual activity upsetting.

    _____ D. It has led to relationship problems.

    _____ E. I don't have any form of sex as a result.

24. If you checked A or B, skip to item 26. Otherwise, go to item 25.

25. Your responses indicate a high likelihood that you have a *sexual arousal disorder.* Put a check mark in the margin next to this item. Now go to Limb 4.

26. Your responses indicate some degree of inhibited arousal, but it hasn't caused either significant problems or prevented you from having romantic and/or sexual relationships. Now go to Limb 4.

Limb Four—Sexual Pain

27. Do you experience pain or discomfort during sexual intercourse? If yes, go to item 28. If no, skip to item 32.

28. Describe your pain during intercourse:

    _____ A. Only intermittent, mild pain that doesn't prevent intercourse.

    _____ B. Pain has only occurred once or twice and hasn't restricted sex much.

    _____ C. The pain was significant but due to a specific cause that was resolved.

    _____ D. The pain has recurred and is due to a specific cause.

    _____ E. Frequent, significant pain that has restricted or prevented sexual intercourse or genital stimulation.

_____ F. Significant pain without any known cause.

_____ G. Significant pain, and a physician has suggested possible causes, but without any treatment success to date.

29. If you checked any of items A through D only, skip to item 31. If you checked any of items E through G, go to item 30.

30. Your responses suggest that you are suffering from *dyspareunia.* Check the primary location(s) of your pain below:

_____ Superficial: pain located in vulva or vestibule.

_____ Vaginal: pain located in vagina during penile insertion or thrusting

_____ Deep: pain felt in pelvis or abdomen during penile thrusting

Put a check mark in the margin next to this item. Now go to item 32.

31. Your responses indicate that you have experienced intermittent sexual pain with a clear and treatable cause, or that you have experienced mild *dyspareunia.* Put a check mark in the margin next to this item. Now go to item 32.

32. Have you experienced any of the following:

_____ Partner is unable to insert finger, dildo, penis, or other object into your vagina?

_____ Physician unable to insert speculum during gynecologic exam?

_____ A sensation of muscle tightness that severely restricts insertion of a tampon, finger, penis, or any other object into your vagina?

33. If you answered yes to any of the above, go to item 34. If you answered no to them all, skip to Limb 5.

34. Your responses suggest a diagnosis of *vaginismus.* Put a check mark in the margin next to this item. Now go to Limb 5.

Limb Five—Orgasm

35. Are you able to have orgasms consistently by any method (e.g., masturbation, vibrator, clitoral stimulation from partner, intercourse)? If yes, skip to the Diagnostic Summary. If no, go to item 36.

36. How do you feel about your orgasmic capacity:

_____ A. I achieve orgasm consistently, but it takes *longer* than either I or my partner thinks is normal.

_____ B. I achieve orgasm consistently, but it *requires more stimulation* than either I or my partner thinks is normal.

_____ C. I achieve orgasm infrequently, and when I do it requires excessive time and stimulation.

_____ D. I am unable to achieve orgasm by any means.

37. If you checked off items A and/or B only, skip to item 41. If you checked off items C or D, go to item 38.

38. How does your orgasmic delay or inhibition affect you?

_____ It distresses me quite a bit.

_____ It has caused relationship problems.

39. If you checked off either option, go to item 40. If you didn't check either option, skip to item 41

40. Your responses suggest a diagnosis of an *orgasmic disorder.* Put a check mark in the margin next to this item. Now skip to the Diagnostic Summary.

41. Your responses suggest one of the following:

1. Your expectations and those of your partner for your orgasmic capacity may be discrepant or unrealistic. If you are able to have orgasms and enjoy them despite your concerns, it is less likely that you have a true orgasmic disorder.

or

2. You have inhibited orgasm but it doesn't bother you or your partner or have a significant impact on your sexual activity. This situation does not therefore qualify as a true orgasmic disorder.

or

3. You have an orgasmic disorder but are either denying the significance of the problem, hiding it from your partner by faking orgasm, or not mentioning it to your partner, and he or she hasn't asked.

or

4. You have a degree of inhibited orgasm at some times but are still able to experience and enjoy orgasm. The main problem may be inadequate lovemaking techniques or relationship problems.

Diagnostic Summary

42. Did you arrive at one or more working diagnoses (the items next to which you put a check mark in the margin)? If you did, go to item 43. If you did not, skip to item 44. (**Note:** We use the term "working diagnosis" to indicate that although we assume this diagnosis to be correct, and will have you work on solutions in this book, it is still important to confirm it through a formal diagnostic interview with a certified sex therapist.)

43. List the working diagnosis(es) below.

A. _____

B. _____

C. _____

Now skip to item 45.

44. If you did not reach any definitive working diagnoses, did you arrive at any problem areas that emerged from the diagnostic tree? If not, skip to item 46. Otherwise, list the problems below.

A. _____

B. _____

C. _____

The Leaves of the Tree—Qualifying Your Working Diagnosis(es) or Problems

45. Think about the time course and settings for your sexual dysfunction, and check the following qualifying characteristics for each one:

Diagnosis/Problem A _____

_____ Lifelong: I've always had this problem.

_____ Acquired: I didn't always have this problem; it developed after a period of normal sexual function.

_____ Generalized: I have this problem in all situations with all partners.

_____ Situational: I only have this problem with my current partner, in specific sexual situations, or with specific sexual acts.

Diagnosis/Problem B _____

_____ Lifelong: I've always had this problem.

_____ Acquired: I didn't always have this problem; it developed after a period of normal sexual function.

_____ Generalized: I have this problem in all situations with all partners.

_____ Situational: I only have this problem with my current partner, in specific sexual situations, or with specific sexual acts.

Diagnosis/Problem C _____

_____ Lifelong: I've always had this problem.

_____ Acquired: I didn't always have this problem; it developed after a period of normal sexual function.

_____ Generalized: I have this problem in all situations with all partners.

_____ Situational: I only have this problem with my current partner, in specific sexual situations, or with specific sexual acts.

46. If you did not identify any working diagnosis or problem from the Diagnostic Tree, you might want to review it again. If you still do not identify anything, go back to the problems listed in the trunk of the tree and use those to think about where in the sexual response cycle you are having difficulty. Otherwise, consider why you feel that you need to use this workbook. Have you identified relationship problems as sexual ones? Is your partner more concerned about these problems than you? Think about whether you are facing problems too difficult to admit to yourself. If you are at an impasse here, but are indeed experiencing some sort of sexual problem, it is critical to discuss this with a therapist experienced in the treatment of sexual and relationship problems.

The Roots of the Tree

Now that you have identified specific sexual disorders or problems, reread those sections in this chapter that describe them. Then review your map from chapter 2. Try to make a list of those factors in your sexual education and development, family life, personal history, attitudes and beliefs, physical and mental health, and relationships that might be causal factors. Try to list at least five possible causes.

1. _____
2. _____
3. _____
4. _____
5. _____
6. _____
7. _____
8. _____
9. _____
10. _____

✍

EXERCISE 3.2—SEXUAL STRENGTHS

Having just delved into a possible diagnosis for your sexual dysfunction, you might be experiencing a lot of emotion. You may be relieved to finally have a name for your problem and an understanding of it. You may also feel shocked, afraid, depressed, anxious, angry, or even hopeless. Perhaps you are confused as to why this problem has emerged. It is important to document these reactions in your journal. It is also important to remember that sexual dysfunction is treatable. In this exercise, focus on sexual *function* and look at specific areas of sexual strength you have upon which to build successful sexual experiences.

The following is a list of sexual abilities and strengths. Check all of those that you have. Feel free to list more at the end.

Desire

_____ I have a lot of sexual desire in certain situations.

_____ I have frequent, vivid sexual fantasies.

_____ I enjoy erotic discussions, books, pictures, or videos.

_____ I enjoy masturbation.

_____ I enjoy physical affection with my partner.

_____ I love my partner.

_____ I feel relaxed during sex.

_____ I can feel relaxed with my partner.

_____ I feel good being sexual by myself.

Arousal

_____ I become sexually aroused easily.

_____ Sexual stimulation is pleasurable for me.

_____ I enjoy being physically intimate with my partner.

_____ My genitals provide pleasurable sensations.

Orgasm

_____ I am able to achieve orgasm in different settings.

_____ I enjoy orgasm immensely.

_____ Clitoral stimulation provides reliable orgasms.

_____ I can bring myself to an orgasm using a vibrator.

_____ My partner can bring me to orgasm.

Sexual Comfort

_____ Sexual stimulation and intercourse do not cause pain.

_____ I enjoy vaginal penetration.

_____ I am able to ease pain through relaxation.

What other sexual strengths do you have?

_____

_____

_____

_____

Having completed this diagnostic flowchart and sexual strengths questionnaire, it is now time to explore potential causes and associated factors to your sexual dysfunction. The next two chapters will discuss a range of physical and emotional issues and problems that may lie beneath or close by your sexual problem. Now that you have a sense for your specific sexual difficulties and strengths, you can begin to put the pieces of your map together and attain a clear picture of your journey before beginning treatment in later chapters.

References

Abramov, L., I. Wolman, and M. P. David. 1994. "Vaginismus: An Important Factor in the Evaluation and Management of Vulvar Vestibulitis Syndrome." _Gynecology and Obstetrics Investigations_, 38:194–197.

American Psychiatric Association (APA) 1995. _Diagnostic and Statistical Manual for Mental Disorders, 4th Edition_ (DSM-IV). Washington: APA Press.

Barbach, L. 1975. _For Yourself: The Fulfillment of Female Sexuality_. Garden City, New York: Doubleday and Co., Inc.

Barbach, L. 1980. _Women Discover Orgasm: A Therapist's Guide to a New Treatment Approach_. New York: The Free Press.

Doe, Jane. "The Secret Pain that Kept Us Apart." _Redbook_, (October 1996):77–82.

Frank, E., C. Anderson, and D. Rubenstein. 1978. "Frequency of Sexual Dysfunction in Normal Couples." _New England Journal of Medicine_ 299:111–715.

Gottlieb, A. "The Pain that Wouldn't Go Away." _Ladies Home Journal_, (December 1993): ___.

Kaplan, H. S. 1974. _The New Sex Therapy_. New York: Brunner/Mazel, Inc.

Kaplan, H. S. 1987. _Sexual Aversion, Sexual Phobias, and Panic Disorder_. New York: Brunner/Mazel, Inc.

Kaplan, H. S. 1995. _The Sexual Desire Disorders_. New York: Brunner/Mazel, Inc.

Kennedy, P., N. Doherty, and J. Barnes. 1995. "Primary Vaginismus: A Psychometric Study of Both Partners." *Sexual and Marital Therapy* 10(1):9–22.

Knopf, J. and M. Seiler. 1990. *Inhibited Sexual Desire.* New York: William Morrow and Company.

Lieblum, S. R., L. A. Pervin, and E. H. Campbell. 1989. "The Treatment of Vaginismus: Success and Failure." In *Principles and Practice of Sex Therapy, Update for the 1990s,* edited by S. R. Leiblum and R. C. Rosen. New York: Guilford Press.

Lief, H. I. 1988. "Sexual Desire Disorders." In *Principles and Practice of Sex Therapy: Update for the 1990's,* edited by S. R. Leiblum and R. C. Rosen. New York: Guilford Press.

LoPiccolo, J. and J. M. Friedman. 1988. "Broad Spectrum Treatment of Low Sexual Desire: Integration of Cognitive, Behavioral, and Systemic Therapy." In *Principles and Practice of Sex Therapy: Update for the 1990's,* edited by S. R. Leiblum and R. C. Rosen. New York: Guilford Press, 107–144.

Masters, W. H. and V. E. Johnson. 1970. *Human Sexual Inadequacy.* Boston: Little, Brown and Company.

Meana, M. and Y. M. Binik. 1994. "Painful Coitus: A Review of Female Dyspareunia." *Journal of Nervous and Mental Disease,* 182(5):264–272.

Ogden, J. and E. Ward. 1995. "Help-seeking Behavior in Sufferers of Vaginismus." *Sexual and Marital Therapy,* 10(1):23–30.

Rosen, R. C. and S. R. Leiblum. 1995. "Hypoactive Sexual Desire." *Psychiatric Clinics of North America,* March, 18(1):107–121.

Sarazin, S. K. and S. F. Seymour. 1991. "Causes and Treatment Options for Women with Dyspareunia." *Nurse Practitioner,* October, 16 (10):30–41.

Schreiner-Engel, P. and R. C. Schiavi. 1986. "Lifetime Psychopathology in Individuals with Low Sexual Desire." *Journal of Nervous and Mental Disease,* 174:646–651.

Silverstein, J. L. 1989. "Origins of Psychogenic Vaginismus." *Psychotherapy and Psychosomatics,* 52:197–204.

Solomons, C. C., M. H. Melmed, and S. M. Heitler. "Calcium Citrate for Vulvar Vestibulitis." *Journal of Reproductive Medicine,* 36(12):879–882.

Spector, I. P. and M. P. Carey. 1990. "Incidence and Prevalence of the Sexual Dysfunctions: A Critical Review of the Empirical Literature." *Archive of Sexual Behavior,* 19:389–408.

Steege, J. F. and F. W. Ling. 1993. "Dyspareunia: A Special Type of Chronic Pelvic Pain." *Obstetrics and Gynecology Clinics of North America,* December, 20(4):779–793.

The Vulvar Pain Foundation. 1994. "A Conversation with Clive C. Solomons, Ph.D." *The Vulvar Pain Newsletter,* no. 4, (Spring):1–5.

Walker, E. A. and M. A. Stenchever. 1993. "Sexual Victimization and Chronic Pelvic Pain." *Obstetrics and Gynecology Clinics of North America* 20, no. 4 (December):795–807.

Ward, E. and J. Ogden. 1994. "Experiencing Vaginismus—Sufferer's Beliefs About Causes and Effects." *Sexual and Marital Therapy,* 9(1):33–45.

CHAPTER FOUR

Filling In Your Map:
Other Factors Associated with Sexual Dysfunction

Many women have trouble separating their sexual dysfunction from other major medical or psychiatric disorders or traumas. These other disorders may actually be the main cause of their sexual problem and create a major roadblock towards getting better. In that case, successful treatment of the sexual disorder must involve simultaneous treatment of the other disorders. This does not mean that the other disorder must be completely cured, since it may be a chronic illness, but it cannot be ignored or left to progress without therapeutic attention or the sexual problem can recur indefinitely. In this chapter we will focus on sexual dysfunction due to sexual abuse or trauma, physical illness or disability, chronic medical disease, psychiatric illness, medications, and sexually transmitted diseases. We will also discuss the importance of guidelines for safe sexual practices.

Sexual Trauma and Abuse

Sexual, emotional, and physical abuse of children always carries a legacy of sexual problems into adulthood. Sexual abuse may take on many forms, ranging from inappropriate comments and threats to forced physical exhibitionism, fondling, forced oral sex, and rape. The abuse is perceived by the victim as frightening, painful, and confusing, and most often is perpetrated by a close relative or friend. Children who are victims of sexual abuse do not always understand what is happening and are emotionally overwhelmed and powerless to resist. Whatever their understanding, these experiences evoke strong, confusing emotions, and adjustment problems can appear immediately or later in adulthood. Some children will repress memories of abuse, only to have memories or problems reemerge in puberty or adolescence during consensual sexual experiences. Deep feelings of powerlessness, fear, anxiety, panic, and shame are common. Usually post-traumatic episodes are triggered by a recent sexual experience and may consist of intrusive memories, flashbacks, physical or emotional numbing, and dissociation. For example, whenever Ann would try to be intimate with Paul, she would feel spaced out, as if she were outside her body. She felt numb and could barely sense Paul's caresses.

Westerlund (1992), Maltz (1992), and Herman (1992) indicate that many women with a history of sexual abuse in childhood experience sexual dysfunctions in adulthood. Complications include problems with desire, arousal, and orgasm, as well as negative feelings about themselves, their partners, and sexuality in general. Complicating this problem is the fact that survivors of abuse are unlikely to seek help from a sex therapist (Westerlund 1992). If a woman is in therapy because of a history of either physical or sexual abuse, she may have many nonsexual issues that crowd into the foreground and need attention. Often this early work must be completed before she can focus on reclaiming her sexuality, yet the problems of compromised sexuality in relationships confront her on a regular basis.

First, we will address the problems of women who have experienced sexual, physical, and emotional abuse. In general, abuse leads to four areas in which adult sexuality is compromised:

1. Physical problems including discomfort or pain

2. Emotional problems including depression, anxiety, and fear

3. Cognitive problems including mistaken beliefs, cognitive distortions, and negative attitudes about sex

4. Relationship problems including difficulty with trust and control

In order to survive the overwhelming experience of sexual and physical abuse, a child learns certain coping skills that include numbing their body, dissociating from their bodily experiences, and maintaining a vigilant hyperarousal in which the nervous system prepares the body for fight or flight. Adult survivors of abuse experience an oscillation between the passive numbing phase and the active stage of fearful arousal. Chronic anxiety, fear, and pain are common aftereffects of abuse.

Abuse victims often experience disturbances in all phases of the sexual response cycle. These disturbances may flair up episodically or become chronic. The following sexual disturbances can occur as the result of physical or sexual abuse:

- Lack or loss of desire

- Arousal difficulties leading to lack of lubrication and consequent pain during intercourse or other sexual behaviors

- Problems with orgasm (often experienced as an inability to "let go")

- Vaginismus

- Negative and distorted perceptions of the body

- Fantasies that are unacceptable to the woman (e.g., feeling aroused when remembering the abuse)

- Triggers during current sexual experiences that cause flashbacks of the early abuse

- Repeated promiscuous sexual experiences because of inability to say "no," giving up power to the partner, or feeling compelled to repeat the behavior in order to gain a sense of control over anxiety

There are several ways in which survivors of childhood or adolescent abuse cope with their sexuality as adults. Research by Westerlund (1983) suggests that upwards of one-third of abused women go through a stage in adolescence and early adulthood of compulsive or promiscuous sexual behaviors. Often this period of acting out is followed by inhibited sexual response within a subsequent monogamous relationship. Some women alternate between these two types of sexual behaviors. Many survivors feel highly sexual with new partners and believe they will continue to relate to their life partner in this way. But sexuality is split off from emotional intimacy and love, so as they become closer and more intimate, the partner begins to feel more like family and therefore is perceived to be like the dangerous perpetrator or a part of the incest taboo. Consequently, these women view sex as an aversive experience and withdraw from it. This is confusing to both partners as they cycle through a pattern of little or no sex, distance, anger, fear, fights, and hopeful reconciliations.

The woman may wonder why her partner can't love her for herself and leave sex out of the relationship. Yet few partners are willing to live without a sexual relationship. Many women with incest histories hold themselves responsible for all their sexual experiences including what happened when they were children. They tend to blame themselves for what happens sexually with both perpetrators and partners, and they feel high levels of guilt and shame. It is not surprising that many eventually feel a sense of hopelessness and despair because they cannot integrate sexuality into their life.

Relationships after Sexual Trauma

Relationships are often deeply affected by past abuse. Many survivors feel unsafe when they are in the presence of others. Sexual difficulties can follow as a woman avoids sex because of her expectations of pain, shame, isolation, fear, and anger. Although the major negative charge is toward the childhood abuser, many abused women find themselves with negative sexual feelings about their partners. A typical comment of a survivor is: "I saw him change before my eyes into my father." Since her basic trust has been violated, a sexually abused woman has difficulty allowing herself to relax and let down her guard in the presence of another. She has no sense of her own personal boundaries and is often not clear that her body belongs to herself. She may believe that she has no right to refuse if her partner asks for sex, and may think that she must please her partner and ignore her own needs. She may pretend to be aroused but learn to dread the next sexual encounter—creating anger at her partner and frustration and anger at herself. This can recreate early abusive situations in which she was treated as if she existed only for the pleasure of the abuser.

Many incest survivors experience conflict about the meaning of sex. Sex becomes a duty rather than an expression of love, pleasure, or comfort. As intimacy increases, so does the survivor's fear of being dependent, vulnerable, and unable to protect herself. Commitment begins to feel like being trapped in an unsafe situation. The abused woman may begin to view her partner through the same lens with which she views family members or others who have hurt her. She may handle all of these conflicts by separating sex from emotional intimacy. Many abuse survivors describe feeling highly sexual when they have been with new, casual, or inappropriate partners, but find themselves losing their sexual feelings with a loved partner.

PTSD and Sexual Dysfunction

Many survivors of sexual and physical abuse find it difficult to feel safe from harm. They often avoid and dislike sex because they find it to be both physically and emotionally painful. For some of these women, many of the sexual difficulties described in therapy are closely linked to common manifestations of post-traumatic stress disorder (PTSD). PTSD symptoms reflect extreme psychological and physical reactions through which the mind copes acutely with trauma, and include

1. A state of hypervigilance and physical hyperarousal that includes fear, anxiety and possibly terror

2. A numbing and constriction of both psychological and physical awareness, sometimes referred to as dissociation, possibly leading to amnesia for aspects of the trauma

3. A reexperiencing of the trauma afterward through repetitive memories, nightmares, and flashbacks

4. Sensitivity to sensory stimuli (noises, smells, sights, etc.) that trigger memories

How are these reactions to trauma linked to sexual dysfunction? Hyperarousal and high anxiety levels signal the body to prepare for danger, in part by shutting down the sexual response cycle. Physical touch may be experienced as unpleasant, ticklish, and/or painful, or may trigger memories of abuse. Thus, the affected woman does not feel aroused, does not lubricate, and guards herself against genital stimulation and penetration. Numbing or dissociation also occurs with high levels of anxiety. As the woman directs her attention towards the perceived threat, she directs it away from her bodily sensations, thus blocking the experience of pleasure and making arousal or maintenance of arousal impossible. If she is dissociated from the experience she may not feel anxious, but only notice a sense of boredom and numbing.

Cognitive Aftereffects of Sexual Trauma

Many cognitive distortions result from a history of abuse. Self-esteem is always damaged. An abused woman may sexualize events that are not experienced that way by others. Negative messages about the self include a host of ideas such as the following:

- *My partner is only nice to me so they can have sex.*

- *I'm bad.*

- *I don't deserve pleasure.*

- *Sexual pleasure is for others.*

- *Sex and love are the same as pain, fear, anger, and hate.*

- *I'm only good for sex.*

- *If I'm sexual, I'm bad.*

- *Sex will lead to bad things happening.*

Efforts to be in control and avoid vulnerability often lead to troubles with a partner. An abuse survivor may not know how to allow affectionate touch, fearing that it will become sexual. So, she prevents or avoids all touching; as a result, she may feel a sense of safety but may also experience a disconnection from her partner. Or, in order to feel safe, she may shut down arousal to a manageable level. She may set limits on being touched in any way that would lead to sexual arousal. Her mental script becomes full of avoidant thoughts:

- *I gave in last week, maybe I can avoid it tonight.*

- *My partner will notice if I don't agree soon.*

- *If I feel sick I should be able to avoid sex.*

- *I'm so busy that there isn't time for sex.*

- *I've worked too hard and I'm tired.*

- *If my partner could just live without sex our lives would be fine.*

Avoidance of sex provides temporary relief, only to be followed by feelings of guilt, failure, and shame.

Confusion of the meaning of touch is common. Pleasure is mixed up with pain— a soft touch may seem to hurt. The past and present flow together, so that a survivor is not sure who is touching her—her loving partner or an abuser from the past. The meaning of love and hate may seem confused, since she may have loved, as well as hated, her abuser. Trust and distrust are difficult to sort out since she should have been able to trust adults as a child, but they were not always trustworthy. She may feel unsure whether she can trust her partner's touch when she is sexually vulnerable. Flashbacks are sometimes triggered during sexual experiences, when stimulation of some parts of her body trigger memories of abusive touching and lead to vivid reexperiencing of the original abuse. Any sensory experience can be a vivid reminder of past traumatic experiences [e.g., a certain odor, a particular quality of light (such as candlelight) music, a voice, or a taste].

The sexual response cycle produces a change in thought patterns as a woman becomes more highly aroused, leading to an altered state of awareness somewhat like a trance. This normal process is similar to the abnormal but protective change in thinking that occurs when a child is abused—she protects herself by dissociating from the experience into an altered state of awareness—which is also like a trance. Thus, when an abuse survivor engages in sexual experiences, she may revive memories by returning to this altered trance state. Memories of abuse are so unpleasant that the woman may not want to continue making love. She may try to continue despite her misgivings and pain, or she may have to stop.

Under ordinary circumstances, during the highest levels of sexual arousal just prior to orgasm, a woman will focus more and more intently on her genital sensations. This leads to a dimming awareness of her surroundings. However, if a woman is afraid and guarded she will be unwilling to let go of cognitive control long enough to surrender to the experience of orgasm. She may fear attack, pain, or even annihilation, and guard herself against these unbearable experiences at the expense of her sexuality.

The emotional damage for survivors of abuse occurs before, during, and after a sexual encounter. They often expect to dislike the experience, which they may associate with negative emotions including fear, shame, guilt (for refusing the partner), and resentment (at feeling pressured to consent to sex). During the sexual experience women who've been abused are often caught between two negative experiences. If they enjoy themselves, they may feel confusion, disgust, revulsion, self-hatred, or anger toward their partners. If they don't enjoy themselves, they may feel sad, guilty, angry at themselves or their partners, ashamed, or dissatisfied. After sex, a woman may feel relief that it is over, but this relief may be followed by a new wave of guilt and shame. Many of these emotions are the same ones felt during abusive experiences. In chapter 9, we will present a treatment module for women facing these difficulties.

Physical Illness and Disability

The impact of physical illness and disability on sexual function warrants its own book—perhaps several volumes. Practically every chronic and debilitating illness and injury has the potential to cause sexual dysfunction, often in unique ways. In this section, we will provide an overview and focus on several disorders. If you suspect that a physical illness is causing your sexual problems, it is imperative to review this with your physician. Without optimal treatment of your condition, neither the exercises in this book nor a sex therapist can adequately help you make progress. Unfortunately, many physicians do not inquire about sexual functioning during routine exams. Like the rest of us, physicians may entertain stereotypes that individuals who are ill or disabled have no interest in sex. If you suffer from a major physical problem and are reading this book, then you certainly know better. Sexual functioning remains an active and important issue for most people with an illness or disability. Adequate functioning requires an understanding of the specific effects of the illness on sexual functioning, as well as empathic counseling on how to continue sexual practices or modify them to meet special needs. If your physician hasn't addressed this issue during an appointment, bring it up. They can often reassure you, provide guidance, and refer you to other health professionals who specialize in sexual function. Also, we have provided a list of helpful booklets in the appendix.

What aspects of physical illness or disability create sexual problems? Perhaps the most common culprit is pain. As both your mind and body are programmed to prioritize survival over sex, your body will shut down sexual desire and arousal in the face of pain, in order to tend to more important, restorative activity. In chapter 1 we discussed how acute pain can interrupt the sexual response cycle. Chronic pain or discomfort is often characteristic of physical illness and can have an impact on sexual response in similar ways. When this pain is preoccupying, debilitating, unpredictable, or fought on a daily basis, it can lead to loss of sexual desire and arousal. The ghost of recurrent pain can induce states of anxiety and apprehension prior to sex. For example, a woman with severe cardiac disease may avoid sex because she fears a recurrence of angina pain during sexual exertion.

A second major factor that creates sexual dysfunction is the direct effect a physical disorder has on neurologic, vascular, and endocrine function. The sexual response cycle is dependent on a healthy brain and peripheral nervous system, intact genital nerve pathways and blood vessels, and adequate supplies of sex hormones. When any of these functions are compromised, sexual arousal can suffer. In turn, sex becomes more difficult and painful, and desire lessens.

A third complicating factor of physical illness or disability is the negative effect on body image and overall self-image. The discomfort and pain of chronic illness can cause a woman to feel less attractive to her partner and less able to please and be pleased. Relationships are complicated when one partner becomes dependent on the other for major caretaking responsibilities. It is not uncommon for the partner whose role is caretaker to suffer a loss of sexual desire when the loved partner is ill and in pain. Both partners may lack confidence that they know how to deal with the physical limitations that restrict the repertoire of sexual activity. The continuing stress of illness, pain, and worry about the future can shut down sexual desire for both partners. Even during periods of relative tranquility and recovery, women with chronic illness may have persistent problems if they are unable to break long-standing patterns or conditioned behaviors that contribute to their sexual dysfunction.

It is important to emphasize that physical disability does not automatically prevent an active and satisfying sexual life. The main stumbling block is not necessarily a lack of adequate sexual capacity; instead, it may be a lack of guidance and counseling provided by health care professionals who assume that disabled patients are either asexual or have minimal sexual desire or interest. This guidance is critical because many disabled women have normal levels of sexual desire but do need to make changes in their patterns of sexual behaviors to accommodate their physical limitations.

Individuals with congenital defects or disability in early childhood often face the additional burden of lifelong stigmatization, which may have led to social isolation, lack of opportunities for intimate relationships, and lack of sexual education. A disability that begins in adolescence is complicated by simultaneous struggles to establish an identity and seek initial intimate relationships. Adult-onset disability may involve a period of mourning for lost physical and sexual attributes, which in turn can harm self-image and self-confidence. Despite these challenges, sexual experiences can be satisfying and fulfilling. We have included a special treatment module in chapter 9 for women with physical disabilities.

Cancer

Cancer and cancer treatment can severely affect sexual function, especially cancers that affect genital structures or other parts of the body associated with sexuality. According to Parker, Tong, Bolden, and Wingo (1997) breast cancer is the most common cancer in women in the United States. It is estimated that it will be diagnosed in over 180,000 women in the United States in 1997, representing 30 percent of all new cases of cancer. Lung cancer will account for an estimated 13 percent of all new cases of cancer in women in 1997 and is the leading cause of death by cancer, killing an estimated 67,000 women this year. It is the only type of cancer in women with a sharply increased death rate since 1960, most likely due to the increase in female smokers. Colon cancer is the third most common cancer, representing 11 percent of all new cases. Gynecological cancers, including those of the vulva, vagina, cervix, uterus (endometrium), and ovaries will affect an estimated 82,000 women in 1997. Of these, the most common are endometrial and ovarian cancer. The rate of cancer in women is highest after the age of sixty, affecting nearly one in four women. As these statistics show, a large number of women will face cancer at one point or another in their lives.

If you have cancer, it is important for you to know what sexual changes to expect both from the illness and from the various treatments. You can feel a sense of control if you know what will happen and are able to make some decisions on how to cope with the situation. You may need to face changes in your appearance after surgery or other procedures and decide about options for reconstructive surgery. Partners can provide important emotional support when they become involved in continuing a physical relationship, even if it is not sexual. Touching, bathing, cuddling, kissing, and, eventually, sexual activity show love and concern. In fact, partner acceptance of a woman's body after treatment helps her accept her altered appearance. Physicians and allied health care professionals (social workers, physical and occupational therapists, etc.) involved in cancer treatment and rehabilitation must take active roles in educating a woman with cancer and her partner by providing appropriate resources and counseling. If you are not receiving this assistance, ask for it! The American Cancer Society (ACS) offers free support groups in all major cities for cancer patients to talk with others coping with the same problems. People in these groups express enormous relief that, at last, someone else understands. The ACS also publishes outstanding brochures on sexual function and cancer; these are listed with other helpful resources in the appendix. We have also provided a detailed treatment module for women with cancer in chapter 9.

Several dimensions of cancer affect sexual function. The initial diagnosis of cancer is the first main hurdle and can lead to significant stress as a woman becomes involved in a battle for survival, regardless of how favorable the prognosis may be. Glasgow and colleagues (1993) have described a number of important potential reactions to this diagnosis; some women may feel anxious and guilty, fearing that their illness is punishment for real or imagined past sins, such as masturbation, promiscuity, affairs, abortions, or incest. Gynecological cancers may be more likely to inspire such fears. As a result, a woman may feel that her survival depends upon her giving up or curtailing sexual activity. Initial diagnosis may be especially difficult for single young women, who are in the midst of learning about their sexuality and trying to form intimate relationships. Women in their childbearing years may fear that cancer treatment will interfere with having a baby, and this anxiety can be transferred into their sex life. Thus, even before treatment begins, many women face serious anxieties about their survival as well as their sexual and reproductive potential.

The impact of cancer on sexual dysfunction will ultimately depend on the type of cancer and its severity, the extent and duration of treatment, residual physical effects, and the availability of social and family supports. Certain cancers, when diagnosed early, involve curative and short-term surgery, radiation, and/or chemotherapy and leave minimal physical damage. Other types of cancers, and all late-stage cancers, may require more extensive and repetitive surgical procedures and long-term or intense radiation and chemotherapy with greater potential for damaging side effects. In addition, a woman must cope with the possibility of cancer recurrence—a fear that is reinforced if metastases were present initially or when a woman is asked to return for routine surveillance for several years after treatment.

In general, as a cancer progresses it causes systemic symptoms such as decreased appetite, weight loss, anemia, fatigue, and muscle weakness. The loss of sexual desire is a common result, probably related in part to actual physical impairment from the cancer. Loss of desire may play a role as a psychological defense, allowing the affected woman to focus on more immediate issues and to avoid sex with her partner if she feels less attractive or less able to perform. Loss of desire can also be a symptom of depression, which is a common occurrence in cancer patients.

Cancer treatment involving surgery, radiation, and/or chemotherapy can have profound effects on sexual function. Sexual dysfunction has been seen in 30 to 90 percent of women with gynecological cancer (Andersen 1985; 1987), usually occurring in the first few months after diagnosis and treatment and resolving in about half of these women by six to twelve months after completion of treatment. This dysfunction may be related to either psychological factors or to the primary effects of the cancer. For instance, dyspareunia and postintercourse bleeding may be symptoms of vulvar, cervical, and uterine cancer. Deep dyspareunia may occur from endometrial/uterine and ovarian cancer, although it is not a reliable diagnostic sign.

Surgery, Radiation, and Chemotherapy

The most profound effects of gynecological cancer on sexual function come from surgery, radiation, and chemotherapy. For example, body image can be affected by surgical removal or disfigurement of body parts, especially the loss of breasts due to mastectomy, large scars in prominent locations, loss of limbs, or loss of genital structures. As a result, some women feel less attractive and less sexually desirable. Sexual arousal can be diminished by surgical removal of sexually sensitive breast tissue or genital structures. The effects of chemotherapeutic agents can be temporarily devastating to physical appearance (e.g., hair loss, weight loss) and function (e.g., fatigue, weakness, nausea, general malaise, potential for infection, gastrointestinal disturbances) and can inhibit sexual desire and arousal.

Breast cancer raises sexual concerns for many women. Even though the breast is only indirectly involved in sexual response, it has an important role in many cultures as a symbol of sensuality and sexual attraction. A woman may feel less attractive, less feminine, self-conscious, or even mutilated after having a *lumpectomy*, breast tissue removal, or a *mastectomy*, full breast removal, due to cancer. This alteration in her body image can lead to decreased sexual desire and activity. Sexual dysfunction has been seen in 20 to 40 percent of women treated for breast cancer (Lamb 1995).

Treatment for localized vulvar cancer involves removal of superficial tissue. Consequently, genital sensitivity may be lessened, and many women report a decreased frequency of sex. More extensive vulvar cancers may require surgical removal of the vulva, clitoris, and part of the vagina, which will decrease genital sensitivity and prohibit deep thrusting during intercourse due to a shortened vagina. Many women describe a dramatic drop in sexual activity after such surgery, despite the fact that they probably retain the physical capacity for sexual arousal and orgasm.

Schover, Fife, and Gershenson (1989) report that cervical cancer has been associated with all forms of sexual dysfunction, both before and after treatment. More than 60 percent of affected women experienced sexual pain and bleeding prior to diagnosis. In their review of women with early-stage cervical cancer, rates of hypoactive desire and decreased frequency of sex ranged from less than 10 percent to 60 percent. Inhibited arousal affected 20 to 30 percent of the women depending on the time frame after treatment. Orgasmic disorder occurred in 25 percent to 50 percent of the women, and dyspareunia affected upwards of 90 percent of the women. In one study, however, all of these sexual problems peaked in incidence by four months after treatment and dropped to much lower levels by one year after treatment.

Women with cervical or endometrial/uterine cancer who were treated surgically with *hysterectomy*, the removal of the cervix and uterus, with or without *salpingo-oopherectomy*, the removal of the fallopian tubes and ovaries, tended to have much less dysfunction than women treated with radiation (either external beam or intra-cavitary placement). Women receiving radiation often experience significant sexual dysfunction (Schover 1988). Unfortunately, sexual dysfunction due to radiation is delayed in many women and actually was worse at one year posttreatment due to the residual effects of radiation, which tend to be cumulative. Radiation can cause a number of problematic effects:

- Decreased genital lubrication and sensitivity
- Thinning of vaginal tissue with resultant irritation and bleeding
- Vaginal sores or ulcers
- Scarring that causes shortening of vaginal length and a narrowing of the vaginal cavity
- Scarring of pelvic structures
- Ovarian failure, or *premature menopause*

Scarring refers to the buildup of fibrous tissue, in a process called *fibrosis*, which can distort, shrink, and decrease the pliability of genital structures, and make them more prone to injury and cause poor healing. The common result may be pain whenever these structures are stretched or have pressure applied, such as during intercourse. Ovarian failure without appropriate hormone replacement can then worsen all of the effects of radiation. Not surprisingly, women can experience the whole range of sexual dysfunction after radiation therapy, including low desire, arousal difficulty, orgasmic inhibition, dyspareunia, and vaginismus. Most women had sex less frequently after radiation treatment, and a small but not insignificant number of women gave up sexual activity entirely (Schover, Fife, Gershenson 1989; Anderson 1987, 1989).

A significant number of women with colorectal cancer need to have a surgical *ostomy*, or artificial opening created in the skin in order to allow for emptying of fecal material from the intestines. Wearing an ostomy bag may also have a negative impact on body image, especially during sexual activity when it may be exposed. Hypoactive desire has been reported in 28 percent of women, and dyspareunia in 20 percent after surgery for colorectal cancers (Andersen 1985). Women who have had surgery for bladder cancer, which often involves total removal of the bladder, may have the same concerns about their urostomy bag. These women often experience dyspareunia, which sometimes progresses to vaginismus. In pelvic surgery, in which the bladder, colon, or other tissue is removed, the source of dyspareunia may be the lack of adequate cushioning for the vagina during the thrusting movements of intercourse. To lessen this pain, there are several recommended sexual positions that are more comfortable. These are illustrated in chapter 8.

✒ Case 4.1—Rachel and Steven

Six months after her surgery for endometrial cancer, Rachel went to see a sex therapist on the advice of her oncologist. She and Steven had been married for forty years and were comfortable with their marriage and with each other, but they were having persistent difficulties with their sexual relations. They both had a bad scare during Rachel's illness, but the hysterectomy and radiation treatment had eradicated all evidence of cancer. Now that the crisis was over, they wanted to return to their normal life and resume the comfortable and richly varied sex life they had always enjoyed.

The therapist discussed possible residual sexual side effects of the cancer treatments and asked Rachel if she felt physically and psychologically ready to evaluate her sexual responses. Rachel did feel ready to reintroduce herself to sexual arousal and accepted her therapist's suggestion to start with some masturbation exercises. Steven was supportive and offered to do whatever would help. Rachel agreed to let the therapist know if any genital pain occurred. On her next visit, Rachel reported that she had been able to get sexually aroused, but that her genitals did not lubricate well, and it was painful to insert anything into her vagina. She was afraid of hurting herself.

Rachel's sex therapist gave her a water-based lubricant and a set of four dilators of graduated sizes. She was able to relax her body and insert the smallest dilator into her vagina, using plenty of lubrication. She practiced daily, increasing to the largest dilator over a period of several weeks. At that point she was no longer in pain and was less fearful that she would injure her vagina. While Rachel practiced with the dilators, the therapist helped the couple set up a comfortable and sensuous program for resuming their sexual life. They learned to plan ahead and take advantage of when Rachel felt rested. They learned to use relaxation exercises so that Rachel felt at ease. They bought luxurious new sheets and pillows for the bed and surrounded themselves with cushions to support their bodies. Rachel and Steven were instructed to start with simple nongenital touching and gradually move to genital stimulation when Rachel felt ready.

After two months of weekly therapy, Rachel was ready to try intercourse. For several difficult and unsuccessful sessions she and Steven tried out a variety of different positions. They found that it was most comfortable when Rachel sat astride Steven while he lay on his back; this way he could stimulate her clitoris while she moved up and down at a pace that felt good to her. They also enjoyed lying side by side. As her therapist suggested, Rachel helped Steven stimulate her by guiding his hand towards erogenous zones or away from tender spots. He was appreciative to know she enjoyed his touch, and his own fears of hurting her diminished. However, even after they were able to resume lovemaking, they both agreed that their sexual life was changed and they missed the old days when sex was carefree.

Diabetes Mellitus

Diabetes mellitus (DM) is a chronic sugar or glucose metabolism disorder caused by the absence of or bodily resistance to insulin. Insulin is produced by cells in the pancreas and is required by liver, muscle, and fat cells in order to take up and utilize glucose from the bloodstream. *Type I*, or *insulin-dependent diabetes mellitus* (IDDM), usually begins in childhood or adolescence and is due to prior destruction of insulin-producing cells in what is believed to be an autoimmune process. IDDM, also called juvenile diabetes, requires strict dietary control of glucose along with daily injections of insulin. In *type II*, or *noninsulin-dependent diabetes mellitus* (NIDDM), the cells in the body become resistant to insulin. This disorder often occurs in overweight individuals with a family history of diabetes. NIDDM, also called adult-onset diabetes, can be treated with sugar-restricted diets, weight loss, and oral medications. Even with adequate control of blood sugar, the chronic excess glucose in the body causes damage to small blood vessels and the tissues and organs they support.

Women with DM have higher rates of sexual dysfunction than nondiabetic women. In one study, 35 percent of diabetic women reported anorgasmia compared to 6 percent of women in a control group. The diabetic women reported a gradual onset of orgasmic problems (Kolodny 1971). Another study found rates of sexual dysfunction in diabetic women to be closer to 20 percent (Ellenberg 1977). Diabetic women often have an increased rate of vaginal infections, which may affect sexual functioning. In general, diabetes does not affect sexual desire and arousal and does not directly cause dyspareunia in women (although secondary infections can be a cause). DM-related sexual dysfunction has been more of an issue for men due to erectile dysfunction caused by nerve and blood vessel damage.

Endometriosis

Endometriosis is probably the most common cause of pelvic pain. It occurs when clusters of endometrial cells (from the *endometrium*, or lining of the uterus), ranging in size from tiny specks to coin-sized clumps, are present in abnormal sites in the pelvis outside of the uterus. It is not known precisely how these cells get outside of the uterus; one theory suggests that they come from cells sloughed off during menstruation that travel backwards through the fallopian tubes and out into the pelvic cavity. Another theory is that these cells originate from primitive cells already outside of the uterus but are transformed into endometrial cells. No matter what the cause, these cells can appear on both the inner and the outer lining of the uterus, fallopian tubes, vagina, ovaries, bladder, rectum, and pelvic ligaments.

Pain may result from direct pressure on these cell clumps and is heightened during menstruation, when normal hormonal flux causes the endometrial cells to release excess *prostaglandin*, a hormone that causes uterine muscles to contract; in turn, these contractions help expel menstrual material. Excess amounts of prostagladin released from clusters of endometrial cells throughout the pelvis lead to painful uterine and rectal cramping, sometimes causing heavy periods and diarrhea. Under these conditions sex is very uncomfortable and is often avoided.

Endometriosis also leads to the formation of inelastic scar tissue within the pelvis that can cause pain when pelvic tissues are stretched during intercourse. The degree of pain caused by endometriosis is believed to be more related to the location of cells than the size or amount. In a study of over two hundred women with endometriosis, lesions in the vagina were associated with more frequent symptoms and more severe deep dyspareunia (Vercellini, Cortesi, Trestidi et al. 1996). Diagnosis and surgical treatment for endometriosis is often by *laparoscopy*, in which thin metal rods with attached fiber-optic cameras and surgical instruments are inserted into the pelvis through small abdominal incisions. These devices help to locate, and if necessary remove, abnormal tissue. Endometriosis is also treated with different forms of the pill and other hormonal agents to eliminate the effects of the normal menstrual cycle.

Interstitial Cystitis

Interstitial cystitis (IC) is a relatively uncommon disorder, characterized by pain in the region of the bladder and frequent urges to urinate. It affects an estimated 450,000 individuals, 90 percent of whom are women (Webster and Brennan 1994; Gillenwater and Wein 1988). Symptoms of IC vary among affected women, but in the more serious cases the urge to urinate, often in small amounts, can occur several times an hour. The experience of pain ranges from a dull or heavy ache in the bladder or back to sharp pains and even shocklike sensations. Some women experience pain within the region of the urethra and may have accompanying urethral inflammation. The cause of IC is unknown, although some researchers believe it is related to reduced bladder capacity. Urine cultures are often negative, and antibiotics have not proven beneficial. Over half of women with IC also suffer from dyspareunia, usually occurring with penile insertion or deep penetration. A smaller percentage of women have pain during foreplay or orgasm, or during the resolution stage (Webster 1996). IC can also interfere with sex due to urinary urgency during lovemaking. Fatigue and lack of sleep due to IC symptoms can sap libido, and nearly 60 percent of women with IC report decreased sexual desire (Webster 1996). There are various treatment options for IC, but many women have chronic symptoms.

Multiple Sclerosis

Multiple Sclerosis (MS) is a progressive neurologic disease in which accumulating lesions in the central nervous system lead to motor, sensory, and cognitive impairment. The onset of MS is usually between the ages of twenty and fifty, and women are affected in a 2:1 ratio over men. Symptoms fluctuate over decades, with episodic exacerbations ranging from mild numbness or tingling sensations in a limb to debilitating and transient loss of sight or the ability to walk. Symptoms usually improve over weeks or months—with or without treatment; but over time they leave increasing disability. There is much research being done on MS, and recent breakthroughs have led to treatments that both decrease the frequency and blunt the symptoms of MS attacks. The exact cause of MS is not known, but it is believed to be an autoimmune disease in which an individual's own immune cells begin attacking the insulating sheath around nerves. It is hoped that the pace of research will provide more effective treatments in the near future.

Women with MS have significant physical disability over time, and up to 50 percent of sufferers report sexual dysfunction (Mattson 1995; McCabe, McDonald, Deeks et al. 1996). Many of these women have sex less frequently, and 30 percent lose their desire for sex. Inhibited sexual arousal and orgasm affect 20 percent of women with MS, while anywhere from 1 to 7 percent of women suffer from dyspareunia or vaginismus. Sexual dysfunction is most prevalent during periods of symptom exacerbation but can improve significantly during subsequent remission.

Myocardial Infarction (Heart Attack)

Despite the high incidence of cardiovascular disease in this country, few studies have looked at its effects on sexual function in women. Many women suffer heart attacks each year, and 65 to 75 percent of these women report sexual dysfunction in the weeks following (Tardiff 1989). Not surprisingly, much of this dysfunction involves hypoactive desire since the women are dealing with a life-threatening situation. Most of these women resume a normal sex life once they have recovered. However, a persistent fear of angina pain or a recurrent heart attack during sexual exertion is common, even though the risk of actual heart attacks or death during sexual activity is very low among women.

Sexual exertion involves a 40 to 100 percent increase in heart rate (averaging 114 to 180 beats per minute) and blood pressure with the maximum stress on the heart occurring during orgasm. These parameters quickly return to normal during the resolution phase. Although the exertion of sex is often compared to walking up two flights of stairs, this is not an optimal comparison, and only a stress test can provide a more definitive answer as to whether sexual activity is safe. In general, physicians usually recommend avoiding sex (and any exercise for that matter) for two months after suffering an MI. Less strenuous but equally sensuous physical contact should be substituted. Large meals and the use of alcohol should be avoided prior to sex since they can put more stress on the heart during exertion. Anal sex should also be avoided since it can cause parasympathetic nervous stimulation that can decrease cardiac performance. If you have suffered from a recent heart attack, or have cardiovascular disease, it is important to ask your doctor if you should consider any possible limitations or modification in sexual activity.

Pulmonary Disease

Chronic pulmonary diseases are extremely common and affect upwards of one out of every three individuals. The two major pulmonary diseases we will discuss are *asthma* and *chronic obstructive pulmonary disease* (COPD), commonly known as *emphysema*.

Asthma occurs across the life span but is particularly prevalent in children and young adults. It is characterized by sudden, often violent, attacks of wheezing, coughing, and breathlessness, and responds to both short-acting and long-term medications, usually administered as inhalers. In general, asthma does not cause any direct sexual impairment. Women who experience an asthma attack during sexual activity might fear similar attacks in the future, and this anticipatory anxiety can precipitate wheezing. The use of inhaled bronchodilator medications prior to sex can prevent or lessen this occurrence. If asthma attacks are recurrent, a better strategy would be the long-term use of inhaled steroids and attention to relieving coexisting symptoms of anxiety. A less common reaction in some women involves allergic asthmatic symptoms in response to environmental allergens during lovemaking or due to sensitivity to a male partner's semen. In these cases, a visit to the allergist is recommended.

Emphysema is a lung disease characterized by loss of supportive pulmonary tissue and symptoms of chronic shortness of breath, oxygen deprivation, and fatigue. Chronic steroid treatment and portable oxygen are the eventual mainstays of treatment. Smoking is the leading cause of emphysema, and as a result it is often associated with cardiovascular and other tobacco-related diseases. Emphysema is commonly seen in later life and has traditionally affected more men, although the percentage of women has increased in the last decade. While this disease does not have a direct effect on physical sexual function, its symptoms and treatment have numerous indirect effects. Women with emphysema may be less interested in sex due to symptoms of fatigue and shortness of breath and feel less attractive due to chronic coughing and odorous breath from recurrent bronchial infections. They may also feel less attractive and sexually capable due to steroid-related side affects including weight gain from fluid retention, fragile and easily bruised skin, acne, muscle weakness, and/or abnormal hair growth. Chronic use of theophylline and bronchodilators can cause nausea, irritability, and headaches, which can interfere with sexual desire and function. Anxiety from oxygen deficiency, fear of increased shortness of breath, and depression are all related issues that can decrease sexual interest. The use of antianxiety drugs can sometimes decrease overall anxiety. Oxygen and inhalers used before and during sex may alleviate breathlessness. Certain positions can decrease exertion during sex; these are illustrated in chapter 9.

General Medications and Sexual Dysfunction

Medications can have the following sexual side effects in women:

- Loss of sexual drive

- Decreased lubrication

- Inhibited arousal and/or orgasm

- Painful clitoral engorgement

These effects do not always occur immediately after starting a medication, but can occur days, weeks, and even months afterward. As a result, it can be difficult to know whether the sexual problem is due to other causes, such as the underlying disease being treated or another medication. Surprisingly, physicians often fail to talk about sexual side effects and patients may not think to ask or may feel embarrassed to mention it. Because almost all medications are potential culprits, the best rule of thumb is always to rule out the possibility of medication-induced sexual side effects.

Although we have listed medications in table 4.1 that are frequently associated with sexual dysfunction, the list is by no means complete. Chapter 9 has a section about how to deal with sexual side effects from medications. It is important to remember that only some women on a drug known to cause problems will actually experience these side effects. When they do occur, the type and severity of problems will differ for each woman. Only medications with a direct effect on sexual dysfunction, not those that cause side effects that in turn lead to sexual problems are listed. For example, many medications cause sedation that in turn can decrease sexual interest, but this loss of interest is not a primary side effect of the medication.

Psychiatric Illness and Psychotropic Medications

Symptoms of sexual dysfunction are commonly seen with most psychiatric disorders. These symptoms may range from transient dysfunction present only during episodes of illness, to full-blown sexual disorders independent of the primary psychiatric disorder. Because sexual dysfunction can also result from most psychotropic medications, it is important to determine when exactly the symptoms began. Treatment of the sexual dysfunction will depend upon its relationship to the psychiatric disorder and on the ability of the patient to tolerate sex therapy during or between episodes of illness.

Depression, Mania, and Bipolar Disorder

Decreased sexual desire is a cardinal symptom of depression. Other depressive symptoms include depressed or irritable moods, loss of pleasure or interest in previously enjoyed activities, loss of energy, decreased concentration and memory, suicidal thoughts, guilty feelings, and changes in appetite, weight, and sleep. Along with low desire, depression is also associated with inhibited arousal and orgasm. Sexual dysfunction that is caused by depression will not improve until the depression is resolved; sex therapy must be deferred until after that time. Psychological conflicts or stressful relationships can cause a reactive depression. This type of depression is often less severe and usually disappears when the sexual problem is resolved. The flip-side of depression—mania—can cause hypersexual behavior, but sexual dysfunction cannot cause mania.

Most antidepressant and antimanic medications can cause sexual dysfunction in women including problems with desire, arousal, and orgasm. See table 4.1 for a complete list of medications. The most commonly prescribed antidepressants are the *selective serotonin reuptake inhibitors,* or SSRIs. These include fluoxetine (brand name is Prozac), sertraline (Zoloft), paroxetine (Paxil), and fluvoxamine (Luvox). The SSRIs can be used for depression, dysthymia, panic and anxiety disorders, eating disorders, somatization disorders, obsessive-compulsive disorder, and premenstrual syndrome. Anywhere from 10 to 40 percent of women on SSRIs may experience some degree of decreased desire, inhibited arousal, poor lubrication, and/or delayed or inhibited orgasm (Segraves 1992; Gitlin 1994; Margolese and Assalian 1996). There have also been reports of painful clitoral engorgement from SSRIs. The tricyclic and tetracyclic antidepressants (TCAs) are used to treat the same disorders as SSRIs, and are also used frequently for migraine headaches, attention deficit hyperactivity disorder (ADHD), and chronic pain syndromes. Several of the most popular TCAs include amitriptyline (Elavil), imipramine (Tofranil), sinequan (Doxepin), nortriptyline (Pamelor), desipramine (Norpramin), and clomipramine (Anafranil). The TCAs and SSRIs tend to cause similar rates and types of sexual dysfunction in women. A newer antidepressant called venlafaxine (Effexor) causes less sexual dysfunction in women than men and probably less dysfunction in women when compared to other antidepressants. Three antidepressant medications associated with fewer sexual side effects include bupropion (Well- butrin), nefazodone (Serzone), and trazodone (Desyrel). It is not clear how a relatively new medication called mirtazapine (Remeron) affects sexual dysfunction. There are several potential dosing strategies and antidotes to minimize or eliminate sexual dysfunction caused by antidepressants; these are discussed in chapter 9.

Medications used to treat bipolar disorder, recurrent depression, agitation, and aggressive/impulsive behaviors include lithium (sold under the names lithium carbonate, lithium citrate, Lithobid, Lithonate, and Eskalith), valproic acid (also called divalproex sodium and Depakote), and carbamazepine (Tegretol). These medications, referred to as mood stabilizers, have not been associated with high levels of sexual dysfunction when used alone but are often used in combination with benzodiazepines and antipsychotic medications that do cause dysfunction. Studies have shown mild to moderate degrees of sexual dysfunction in 5 to 15 percent of women taking lithium alone (Ghadirian, Anable, Bélanger 1992).

Anxiety

Sexual fear and anxiety are major causes of sexual dysfunction and act as primary sources of resistance to treatment. In turn, sexual dysfunction can lead to high

Table 4.1. Medications Associated with Sexual Dysfunction in Women

Medication	Loss of Desire	Impaired Arousal	Anorgasmia
Acetazolamide (Diamox)	✔		
Alprazolam (Xanax)	✔		✔
Amiloride (Midamor)	✔		
Amiodarone (Cordarone)	✔		
Amitriptyline (Elavil)	✔	✔	✔
Amoxapine (Asendin)	✔	✔	✔
Amphetamines			✔
Barbiturates	✔		
Birth Control Pills	✔		
Chlorpromazine (Thorazine)	✔	✔	✔
Cimetidine (Tagamet)	✔		
Clofibrate (Atromid-S)	✔		
Clomipromine (Anafranil)	✔		✔
Clonidine (Catapres)			✔
Danazol (Danocrine)	✔		
Desipramine (Norpramin)	✔	✔	✔
Diazepam (Valium)	✔		✔
Digoxin	✔		
Doxepin (Sinequan)	✔	✔	✔
Fluoxetine (Prozac)	✔	✔	✔
Fluphenazine (Prolixin)	✔	✔	✔
Fluvoxamine (Luvox)	✔	✔	✔
Haloperidol (Hadol)	✔	✔	✔
Imipramine (Tofranil)	✔	✔	✔
Isocarboxazid (Marplan)	✔	✔	✔
Lithium	✔		
Lorazepam (Ativan)	✔		
Methadone (Dolophine)	✔		✔
Methazolamide (Neptazane)	✔		
Methyldopa (Aldomet)	✔		✔
Metoclopramide (Reglan)	✔		
Metoprolol (Lopressor)	✔		
Mexiletine (Mexitil)	✔		
Molindone (Moban)	✔	✔	✔

Table 4.1—*Continued*

Medication	Loss of Desire	Impaired Arousal	Anorgasmia
Norethindrone (Norlutate)	✔		
Nortriptyline (Pamelor)	✔	✔	✔
Paroxetine (Paxil)	✔	✔	✔
Perphenazine (Trilafon)	✔	✔	✔
Phenelzine (Nardil)	✔	✔	✔
Phenytoin (Dilantin)	✔		
Pimozide (Orap)	✔	✔	✔
Primidone (Mysoline)	✔		
Propranolol (Inderal)	✔		
Ranitidine (Zantac)	✔		
Reserpine (Diupres)	✔		
Sertraline (Zoloft)	✔	✔	✔
Spironolactone (Aldactone)	✔		
Thioridazine (Mellaril)	✔	✔	✔
Thiothixene (Navane)	✔	✔	✔
Trifluoperazine (Stelazine)	✔	✔	✔

Note: This list is based upon reports that (1) may have only involved men or very few women, (2) may have involved few cases, and (3) may not have properly described sexual side effects. As a result, this list is not complete, and the effects of any medication cited above should be reviewed with your prescribing physician. (Abramowicz 1987)

levels of anxiety during sex, although this anxiety usually abates outside of sexual activity and may not indicate a primary anxiety disorder. For example, Janet had a deep fear of being hurt by vaginal penetration which led to vaginismus. As a result, anticipation of sex was so unpleasant that her anxiety rose even higher. General anxiety and panic disorders often coincide with sexual disorders, in particular sexual phobias and aversion.

Antidepressant medications are commonly used to treat these generalized anxiety disorders. These medications may take several weeks to take effect and then work by preventing recurrent symptoms. Short-acting tranquilizers, on the other hand, are used for acute symptoms of anxiety and panic, and last only for several hours until they need to be taken again. The main class of these antianxiety, or *anxiolytic*, medications are the benzodiazepines and include diazepam (Valium), lorazepam (Ativan), alprazolam (Xanax), clonazepam (Klonopin), oxazepam (Serax), and chlordiazepoxide (Librium). Several other benzodiazepines are used primarily as sleeping pills: flurazepam (Dalmane), temazepam (Restoril), and triazolam (Halcion). Benzodiazepines have been associated with decreased sexual desire and anorgasmia in women, in particular when combined with lithium. In one study, nearly 50 percent of women on that combination experienced sexual difficulties, mostly reporting decreased desire (Ghadirian, Anable, Bélanger et al. 1992). Another medication, Buspar (buspirone), is commonly used to treat anxiety and has not been associated with significant sexual side effects.

Psychotic Disorders

Schizophrenia and other psychotic disorders often involve sexual problems. Individuals with predominant symptoms of social withdrawal or discomfort in the presence of others, apathy, and/or a blunted emotional tone or affect often have little interest in relationships and sexual activity. Those with more extreme symptoms, such as delusions, hallucinations, and bizarre thought patterns, will have difficulty relating to others and interacting in sexually comfortable or appropriate ways. During periods of symptom remission, however, sexual relationships can be perfectly normal. But the impairment in interpersonal relating that is common with psychotic disorders can have a markedly negative impact on sexual function and sexual relations. In addition, sexual dysfunction might serve a purpose for the individual—for example, protection from stressful relationships—or have idiosyncratic meanings that might threaten the individual's stability if altered. For this reason, sex therapy must be approached with caution and with the assistance of the individual's treatment team. It must be deferred during periods of active psychosis.

Medications used to treat psychosis (as well as states of severe mania, agitation, and delirium) are called *antipsychotic*, or *neuroleptic*, medications. Some of the more frequently used antipsychotic medications included haloperidol (Haldol), fluphenazine (Prolixin), perphenazine (Trilafon), risperidone (Risperdal), clozapine (Clozaril), olanzapine (Zyprexa), thioridazine (Mellaril), and chlorpromazine (Thorazine). All of these medications can cause sexual dysfunction, usually in proportion to the dose being used. As with the antidepressant and anxiolytic medications, the antipsychotics can decrease libido, interfere with sexual arousal, and/or inhibit or block orgasm.

Substance Abuse

Substance abuse can lead to severe sexual dysfunction, and sex therapy must be deferred until the person has achieved a period of sobriety. Although some individuals may use alcohol in order to relax during sex, or ingest marijuana, cocaine, amphetamines, or amyl nitrate in hopes of enhancing sexual pleasure, these practices inevitably disrupt relationships and precipitate sexual dysfunction. Such usage may also reveal underlying sexual problems; for instance, the women who must have a drink before sex may have an underlying sexual aversion or phobia. Addiction to most drugs will eventually interfere with sexual desire and desensitize sexual arousal, in turn increasing the chance of orgasmic impairment.

Sexual problems also arise during recovery from substance abuse. There is often a drop in sexual desire following sobriety. For some women, sexual activity is associated with being intoxicated or high. Consequently, sober sex may bring up negative memories or associations between sex and substance use, often linked to a history of abusive experiences or promiscuous behaviors that occurred while under the influence. Sexual activity may also bring temptations to use the substances again, especially if a woman used substances to enhance sex or decrease sexual anxiety, or if she was used to meeting sex partners in bars or with other substance abusers. Coping with sober relationships and trying to establish intimacy with partners can be difficult and frightening. Many women with a history of substance abuse also have problems with self-esteem, guilt, anxiety, and depression, and these problems can further complicate sexual relationships and functioning.

Personality Disorders

Personality disorders (PDs) are characterized by chronic and pervasive impairment in several areas: interpersonal relationships, emotional expression, impulse control, and interpretation of experiences. An individual with a PD demonstrates a history of maladaptive behaviors and ways of viewing the world that start in late adolescence or early adulthood and usually lead to frequent conflicts with other people. The main PDs and their characteristic features include

- Schizoid (aloofness and indifference towards social relations)

- Schizotypal (odd beliefs and behaviors)

- Paranoid (tendency towards suspiciousness and hostile reactions to perceived insults)

- Avoidant (oversensitivity to social scrutiny; social avoidance due to feared rejection)

- Dependent (excessive dependency on others for daily functioning and guidance)

- Passive-aggressive (passive resistance to demands, scorn for authority)

- Obsessive-compulsive (rigid, detailed, stubborn, and counterproductive adherence to schedules, procedures, ideas, and thriftiness)

- Depressive (excessive tendency towards gloomy, pessimistic, and critical outlooks on life)

- Histrionic (seductive and provocative, but shallow behaviors and emotional expressions)

- Narcissistic (excessive grandiosity, sense of entitlement, and disregard for feelings of others)

- Borderline (unstable interpersonal relations, poor self-identity, and impulsive, self-injurious, or reckless behaviors)

- Antisocial (disregard for social rules and civil conduct, lack of empathy for others, criminal behaviors)

Behaviors characteristic of PDs are usually more pronounced during periods of stress or in the context of other psychiatric disorders such as depression or substance abuse. Personality disorders do not have direct effects on physical sexual functioning but can be associated with poor sexual relationships, inappropriate sexual expectations or attitudes, and strong resistance towards therapy. They pose severe problems when one partner is affected and refuses to engage in therapy or is suspicious of the therapist. Sexual dysfunction may serve a defensive role in some individuals with a PD, preventing them from engaging in certain relationships or dealing with intimacy. It may also cause severe psychological or interpersonal stress, leading the individual to become withdrawn, suspicious, or rageful towards the partner. These reactions will depend on the PD in question but are often exaggerated and counterproductive responses. Depression and anxiety are common in PDs and can complicate sexual function by disrupting the sexual response cycle.

Sexually Transmitted Diseases

Sexually transmitted diseases (STDs) are relatively common infectious ailments that result from sexual contact with an infected person. STDs are only transmitted by person-to-person contact and require close sexual contact: contrary to popular fears, you cannot become infected from public objects such as toilet seats. It is possible to have more than one STD at the same time, and because there are no vaccines for most STDs and no immunity, it is also possible to become reinfected. Understanding the facts about STDs and practicing safe sex can greatly reduce the chances of getting an STD, or can help you get prompt treatment if you contract one.

The United States has one of the highest rates of STDs in the Western world. Twelve million citizens a year are diagnosed with STDs, and three million of these are adolescents. Two-thirds of those infected with STDs contract the illness before age twenty-five. According to public health officials, the main barrier to preventing STDs is people's refusal to acknowledge and address sexual issues. Unfortunately, many people who know they have symptoms of an STD continue to have sexual relations without going for treatment or telling their partners.

Why discuss STDs in this chapter? There are several reasons. First, many women who contract an STD experience emotional turmoil, and this frequently precipitates sexual dysfunction. There is often an initial sense of shock and disbelief, which may give way to feelings of anguish, fear, self-blame, helplessness, and anger. Some women may consequently feel disgusted by their bodies and revolted by sex, and others may have hesitations and misgivings about future sexual behavior. Some women can't imagine that they will ever be able to enjoy sex again. Although there is nothing inherently "bad" or "dirty" about a person who contracts an STD, many individuals feel guilty. All of these emotional reactions to STDs can lead to low desire, as well as to sexual anxiety and aversion. In addition, the symptoms of STDs may include a rash, itching, irritation, discharge, or odor, all of which can severely limit sexual relations. Fear of infecting one's partner acts as a major factor in loss of sexual interest. Dyspareunia may be secondary to an undetected STD. Also fears of infection or re-infection, whether conscious or not, may lead to sexual aversion, phobia, vaginismus, and/or difficulty with arousal and orgasm.

Transmission of STDs

Unfortunately, many sexually active individuals think they are immune to STDs or assume that their partners are not infected. To give you an example of how STDs can be spread, consider how many people you could be linked with. Think about your past partners and assume that each person had at least two sexual partners in their lifetime. Now assume those partners also had at least two partners, and so on. If even one of the previous partners had an STD, it could have been passed on, thus exposing you to the sexual practices of many people you have never met. Anyone who is sexually active can be at risk for STDs, regardless of their social standing or serial monogamous behavior.

Possible Signs of a Sexually Transmitted Disease

The following signs and symptoms may indicate the presence of an STD:

- Burning or itching around your vagina or vulva.
- An unusual discharge or smell from your vagina.
- Bleeding from your vagina between periods.
- Sores, blisters, or bumps on or around your vulvar or anal regions.

- Pain in your abdomen.

- Pain in your pelvic area—between your navel and pubic bone.

- Pain deep inside your vagina when you have intercourse.

- Pain or a burning sensation when you urinate.

- Frequent or urgent need to urinate.

- Swelling in your neck, armpits, or groin area.

- Flu symptoms, such as aches and pains in joints, fever, and/or chills.

- Night sweats, recurring fever.

- No symptoms (but you suspect the possibility of an STD).

Bacterial, Parasitic, and Fungal STDs

Chlamydia trachomatis is the most common bacterial cause of STDs. It affects 3–10 million adults in the United States (Stewart, Guest, Stewart et al. 1985). It is transmitted by genital secretions.

Common symptoms include abnormal vaginal discharge (yellowish) or bleeding, urinary discomfort and frequency, painful intercourse, and pelvic pain. Many women have no symptoms, so they never suspect infection and consequently go untreated. Some women may discover they have chlamydia because their male partner has symptoms such as burning during urination, or discharge from his penis.

If it is not treated, chlamydia can affect the uterus and fallopian tubes and cause a more extensive infection known as pelvic inflammatory disorder (PID). Upwards of 50 percent of PID cases are the result of chlamydia. Chlamydia is associated with newborn infection and a higher rate of miscarriage. Inflammation and scarring that results from infection can increase the chances of ectopic pregnancy (non-uterine implantation) and fertility problems. Given these potential problems, women with multiple partners may want to consider regular testing for chlamydia.

Tetracycline, erythromycin, and related antibiotics are the treatment of choice. It is imperative that both sexual partners be treated.

Gonorrhea A common and serious sexual infection caused by the *Neisseria gonorrhea bacterium.*

Its symptoms and its route of transmission are identical to those for chlamydia, making the two STDs difficult to distinguish clinically. Women are often free of symptoms of gonorrhea and may not notice subtle symptoms including urinary burning or discharge. Thus, they may be unknowing carriers of the disease. It is not uncommon for women to discover they are infected when their male partner shows symptoms such as a burning sensation during urination and a discharge from the penis.

Like chlamydia, untreated gonorrhea is responsible for upwards of 50 percent of PID, with the same risks of pregnancy and fertility problems.

Gonorrhea can be cured with penicillin, tetracycline, and related antibiotics.

Trichomoniasis (trick-oh-moh-nigh-ah-sis), or Trichomonis Vaginitis, a very common STD caused by a one-cell protozoa called a *trichomonad.*

Usual symptoms include severe itching and a greenish-white or gray discharge with a bad odor. Intercourse is often quite uncomfortable, and many women feel sexually undesirable.

Some affected women and most men are asymptomatic, and can thus unknowingly pass trichomoniasis to partners. Although trichomoniasis is transmitted via sexual intimacy, the trichomonad can survive in wet towels or clothing and sometimes be passed along when someone else comes into genital contact with those items. Trichomoniasis does not cause any serious long-term problems.

It is treated with a medication called metronidazole (Flagyl). Both partners must be treated or the infection will pass back and forth between them.

Syphilis is caused by the *Treponema pallidum bacteria* and was once a major epidemic. Prior to the development of penicillin, syphilis frequently caused severe illness, insanity, and death, often decades after an initial unsymptomatic infectious stage. It is now considered the least common of the STDs. Syphilis is very contagious during sexual intimacy, and symptoms may appear several weeks after initial exposure.

The first sign is an infectious sore called a chancre, which appears where the disease entered the body. The chancre is usually painless during the first stage of the disease. This stage, called *primary syphilis*, is the time to seek treatment. If a woman does not get treatment, the second stage, known as *secondary syphilis*, occurs as the infection enters her bloodstream. Symptoms include rash, fever, large genital warts, and joint pains. Commonly, there is a rash on the soles of the feet and the palms of the hands. If untreated, a woman enters the third stage of the disease, known as *tertiary syphilis*, and may be free of symptoms and not contagious.

In about one third of infected individuals the disease continues slowly and invades several organs of the body over the course of ten to thirty years. Tertiary syphilis can cause heart disease, dementia, blindness, and, eventually, death. Syphilis is easily detected by several blood tests, one of which is known as the VDRL.

Penicillin has remained the best treatment for all stages of syphilis.

Bacterial vaginosis, also known as Gardnerella vaginalis, and **Candidiasis,** or yeast infection are common genital infections that can be transmitted by sexual contact but are not necessarily known as STDs. Bacterial vaginosis involves overgrowth of normal vaginal bacteria.

Bacterial vaginosis causes itching, dyspareunia, urinary discomfort, and a copious white or gray vaginal discharge with an objectionable odor. Candidiasis causes vaginal discomfort, itching, burning, and a thick whitish discharge. Bacterial vaginosis is usually treated with metronidazole, ampicillin, or amoxacillin. Candidiasis is usually treated with antifungal creams and suppositories. For both of these infections, your partner does not necessarily have to be treated, but treatment should be considered if you have recurrent infections.

Pubic lice, or "crabs," are small parasites that infect pubic hair and cause intense itching. *Scabies* are tiny mites that burrow into genital skin and cause small bumps and itching. Both pubic lice and scabies are both treated with a solution containing the pesticide lindane.

Viral STDs

Human Immunodeficiency Virus (HIV) is a viral STD that produces Acquired Immune Deficiency Syndrome (AIDS). According to the Centers for Disease Control and Prevention, there are about 1 million Americans infected with HIV. AIDS is the third leading cause of death for women aged 25–44 in the United States. Women accounted for 20 percent of all new AIDS cases in 1996. HIV is particularly devastating because it infects and kills human immune cells—the same cells that are supposed to be fighting off an infection. It is transmitted through intimate exchange of infected blood, semen, vaginal fluid, and anal secretions. HIV has commonly been transmitted by sexual contact (both homosexual and heterosexual), sharing of needles, and blood product transfusions. Transmission of HIV from urine or saliva has not been demonstrated. HIV is not transmitted by sharing household items or touching an infected person, and cannot be contracted from public items such as toilets, telephones, water fountains, doorknobs, or swimming pools. Women with herpes are at increased risk of HIV infection.

An individual with HIV infection but without clinical symptoms of AIDS can still infect other individuals.

There is a delay of two to ten years between inoculation with HIV and the development of symptoms, at which point it is formally described as AIDS. A person is also said to have AIDS when the number of CD4 lymphocytes drops below 200 cells/μL. Antibodies to HIV show up in the body within 6 months, so testing shortly after exposure may not show signs of infection. Initial symptoms may include chills and fevers, night sweats, fatigue, unexplained weight loss of more than ten pounds, swollen glands that last for more than two months, and persistent diarrhea. Although the virus itself can cause devastating neurologic and kidney damage, the main problems occur as the virus kills off immune cells, thus allowing opportunistic infections and cancers to run rampant. Common infections include pneumocystis pneumonia, fungal meningitis, tuberculosis, and fungal gastroenteritis. Common opportunistic cancers include Kaposi's sarcoma, manifested by purplish skin lesions, and lymphomas. Many individuals develop depression and other psychiatric illnesses, including a form of dementia known as AIDS encephalopathy.

Although medicine is making giant steps in understanding and treating this illness, there is no known cure. HIV infection is treated with a cocktail of antiviral drugs including a new class known as protease inhibitors, which inhibit the replication of new virus, but do not eradicate it entirely. AZT is the most well-known antiviral medication, but used alone it does not always have an appreciable effect on life span, which may range from 6 to 24 months or longer following the onset of AIDS. Since the advent of protease inhibitors, however, many previously ill individuals have returned to previous levels of health, and might live indefinitely if the virus can be kept at bay. One recent study of a new 3-drug therapy showed that it reduced the rate of deaths and AIDS-related illnesses in individuals with AIDS by 50 percent compared to a 2-drug regimen (Baker 1997). However, not everyone can tolerate these regimens, and the long-term prognosis is unknown. Aside from antiviral therapy, regular check-ups, exercise, good nutrition, and aggressive treatment of opportunistic infections have greatly improved the prognosis for individuals with AIDS.

Genital herpes is caused by the Herpes simplex type 2 virus and is the most common viral STD. This relatively mild but incurable disease is spreading rapidly through the population and currently affects anywhere from 10 to 20 million Americans. Herpes is spread by genital contact from an infected person with a lesion. A person with herpes is most contagious when there are sores, but the virus can be expressed or *shed* at any time.

Initial symptoms for herpes are tingling or painful lesions that appear on the genitals, and may be accompanied by fever, body aches, swollen lymph nodes, and exhaustion. The herpes blisters may be pin-sized or larger, and are extremely contagious. If the lesions are near the vaginal opening, there may be burning or stinging during urination. After a few days the lesions scab over and eventually come off. It is usually safe to begin sexual relations again if you use a condom. Episodes vary with women, some lasting a week, others a month, or even years. Some women experience severely painful symptoms, others very few symptoms. Most women discover that herpes lesions become less problematic over time, heal more rapidly, and occur less often. Although it is uncomfortable and annoying, herpes it is not life threatening.

If you have herpes, it is very important not to reinfect yourself by touching the infected spot and then some other part of your body. The most dangerous concern is that you could infect the cornea of the eye. Women with herpes are at greater risk for cervical cancer and should have regular pap smears. Women who are pregnant can infect their child during delivery through the infected birth canal. These women will have a caesarean delivery if herpes lesions are apparent at the time of birth. Most women with herpes have no problem with the safe delivery of a healthy child.

There is no cure for herpes, but some antiviral drugs can reduce the frequency and severity of the attack. Acyclovir (Zovirax), for instance, can be taken daily and may help mitigate symptoms. Recently, a herpes vaccine has been found to be quite effective in preventing the spread of genital herpes from an infected person to his or her partner. Stress can induce symptoms, and a routine of stress reduction techniques may help women avoid an attack. Support groups for people with herpes can provide needed reassurance, as well as a meeting place for people who are afraid to date because they have herpes.

Condylomata acuminata, or genital warts, are caused by the *human papilloma virus (HPV)*, and affect over 3 million Americans each year. Genital warts appear as painless growths on the vulva, around the anus, or inside the vagina. They are spread through oral sex as well as anal and vaginal intercourse. The warts are flat, brownish-pink, small in size, and often appear in clusters. They are contagious until removed because the virus can shed at any time. Cervical infection by HPV is often a cause of abnormal Pap smears. It is important to recognize and treat this condition because certain strains of HPV have been clearly linked to cancer of the cervix. Treatment involves removal of the warts through laser surgery, freezing, electrocautery, or the use of certain chemicals. Treatment may require multiple visits to your physician, but is usually only mildly uncomfortable.

Hepatitis is a liver disease with several strains; the major strains include hepatitis A, hepatitis B, and non-A, non-B hepatitis. Hepatitis A is often spread by ingesting contaminated oral or fecal secretions from an infected individual. This may occur by eating uncooked shellfish from sewage-contaminated water, or food prepared by an infected person who uses the bathroom and has not washed her or his hands. Hepatitis A can also be sexually transmitted. Hepatitis B is found in saliva, blood, semen, vaginal fluids, and sweat. A person can be infected if she comes into contact with infected body fluids through any body opening. It is often transmitted through needle sharing, as well as through oral sex and vaginal and anal intercourse. Non-A, non-B hepatitis is similar to Hepatitis B, and may represent a different form of the virus.

Symptoms of all forms of hepatitis include nausea, loss of appetite, abdominal pain, fever, muscle aches and pains, fatigue, jaundice (yellow color in eyes and skin), and liver enlargement.

The illness has few remedies, and recovery usually occurs within 1 to 4 months. Rest, freedom from stress, avoidance of alcohol, and good nutrition may help a person recover more quickly. A small percentage of people with Hepatitis B or non-A, non-B develop chronic hepatitis and cirrhosis of the liver. There is no cure for Hepatitis B, but immune globulin given shortly after exposure can prevent it. There is also a vaccine for Hepatitis B, but is usually reserved for individuals at high risk for contracting Hepatitis B, such as health care workers, highly promiscuous individuals, partners of infected individuals, travelers to infected areas, and institutionalized individuals.

Molluscum contagiosum is caused by a pox virus and transmitted through skin contact. It causes small, painless, skin-colored bumps throughout the genital areas, and usually resolves on its own after months to years.

Molluscum is cosmetically unappealing, and can be removed in similar ways that warts are removed.

Testing for STDs

If you suspect that you have an STD it is critical to visit a physician, particularly a gynecologist, to have a pelvic exam and be tested. Hepatitis and HIV infection do not require a pelvic exam, but do require blood testing and a general physical exam. For any STD, once you suspect infection or learn you have one, your partner must be tested as well to prevent reinfection to you as well as to prevent spread to future partners. You should abstain from sex until your physician indicates that you have been cured, or if cure is not an option, until you have adopted safe sex practices and have a partner willing to assume the risk of exposure. When you are given medication, be sure to take the whole course, and then return for follow-up.

If you don't want to see your regular physician, most cities have special STD clinics. Call your local family planning clinic for information. We have listed several STD hotlines in the appendix. Some clinics allow for anonymous testing if you are concerned about confidentiality. All cities have clinics and agencies where you can receive anonymous testing for HIV, and there is now an over-the-counter product called Confide that you can purchase to mail in your own blood sample and receive results over the phone. If you go to a clinic for HIV testing, you are often given a number to use rather than your name. Most clinics offer counseling before and after the test. This is very important; testing positive for HIV can be traumatic. With any STD it helps to talk with a counselor about your feelings and what you can do to cope with symptoms and avoid future problems.

Safe and Unsafe Sexual Practices

You can protect yourself from STDs to differing degrees. The only total protection occurs if you abstain altogether from sexual contact. If you have a monogamous relationship and you both agree not to have sex with other partners (and can trust each other), you are certainly safer if both of you start off the relationship without infection. At the outset of any relationship, then, it is important to discuss the possibility of STDs in previous sex partners and ask whether your partner has ever shared needles with anyone. Unless you are 100 percent certain that neither you nor your partner have an STD, safe sexual practices should be followed.

Talking about safe sex is often much harder than engaging in sex. Many women worry that they will turn their partner off, or that he or she will leave if they bring up this sensitive topic. Remember, however, that you have a right to be free of an STD. Do not let your partner talk you out of your concerns for planning safe sex. Beginning a discussion about safe sex is always hard. Some women like to role-play how to have a frank sexual conversation. Find a friend or a counselor with whom to practice. Make a time and place to talk with your partner when you are both dressed and not planning to make love soon. It helps to "telegraph ahead" by starting the conversation with, "This is hard to talk about but . . ." or "I feel embarrassed discussing safe sex but . . ." Talk about past sexual partners and intravenous drug use, if relevant. Some people may not realize that their behavior was risky. Some people do not like to admit that they don't know how to use condoms or how to make them a part of sex.

If your partner is reluctant to discuss safe sex, is scornful towards the topic, or is not willing to practice safe sex, you are at an increased risk. It is your right to refuse to engage in any risky behaviors until you come to agreement regarding safe sex. Risking your health, your future sexual relationships and sexual partners, your fertility and the safety of future pregnancies, and your life is not worth a relationship with an uncooperative partner.

In order to protect yourself, you need to know safe sex guidelines. Here are some lists of sexual activities categorized by their relative risk for contracting an STD:

Safe

- Masturbation
- Touches, massages, and body caresses
- Tickling, wrestling
- Talking, dancing, fantasizing, flirting, nongenital touching
- Closed-mouthed kissing

Some Risk

- Vaginal intercourse with a properly used condom and spermicide
- Anal intercourse with a condom and spermicide
- Oral sex with a condom or dental dam
- Open-mouthed kissing
- Watersports (sexual contact with urine)

Unsafe (High Risk)

- Unprotected vaginal intercourse
- Unprotected anal intercourse
- Sex play involving direct contact with blood
- Oral sex without a condom or dental dam
- Oral-anal contact
- Anal-manual contact (insertion of fingers or hands into the anus)
- Partner masturbation involving contact with cut or broken skin
- Sex while under the influence of drugs or alcohol
- Sharing sex toys

Mistaken Beliefs About Safe Sex	Reality
• Sometimes using safe sex protects you.	• You must *always* use safe sex.
• Withdrawal method will prevent STDs.	• Preejaculate can carry STDs.
• Washing or douching afterwards protects you from STDs.	• STDs can enter the body immediately on contact.

- Using birth control methods other than condoms such as the pill, a diaphragm, cervical cap or a variety of spermicidal jellies, creams or foams can protect you from STDs.

- Without a condom or dental dam as a barrier method you are not safe.

- Sex toys can't hurt you.

- Body fluids on sex toys can spread STDs.

- Prospective partners will tell you if they have an STD.

- Sometimes a person may not be aware they have an STD. Sometimes they don't believe they will pass it on to you. Sometimes they don't care.

Even if you use another form of birth control, safe sex requires the use of a latex condom every time, the avoidance of exchanging any bodily fluids, and possibly the use of a spermicidal agent known to kill most STDs, such as nonoxynol-9. Remember, to be safe you have to practice safe sex every time you have sex. Here are some tips on using condoms, spermicides, and other barrier contraceptives:

- Keep a supply of condoms near your bed and in your bag or purse: nobody wants to interrupt sex to make a run to the drugstore.

- Have a variety of different sizes, colors, and brands on hand (but always latex). Your partner may be more willing to use one if he has either a preferred brand or a variety to try.

- Talk about condom use. Make sure that you both understand how to use it. No man is too big or too small to get a condom to fit.

- Use only new latex condoms. Lambskins or natural condoms are not safe. Read the directions on the package. Save the box to check the date on the package. Don't use novelty condoms; they may not provide a true barrier. Do not store condoms out of the wrapper, or in a hot location.

- Remember that STDs can be transmitted via vaginal fluids or pre-ejaculate, which is the fluid on the tip of the penis before ejaculation. Put the condom on early in foreplay.

- Some men lose their erection while putting on the condom. If this happens, explore ways to stimulate him to get it back.

- Some condoms have a reservoir tip to collect semen. If you use one that does not, squeeze the air out of the tip of the condom. Then, carefully unroll the condom all the way onto the base of the erect penis, leaving a space at the top. This leaves room for the ejaculate, or cum.

- Use a water-based lubricant that contains nonoxynol-9, if possible. Oil- or petroleum-based lubricants or lotions can weaken the condom and lead to tearing. Lubrication inside the condom may increase sensation for the man but also runs the risk of having it slip off.

- After ejaculation, have you partner slowly withdraw his penis before the erection diminishes. Remove the condom carefully and tie a knot in the top before disposing of it.

- Use unlubricated condoms or a dental dam for oral sex.

- A dental dam is a square of latex that you place over the vaginal opening or anus while you have oral sex. You can make a dental dam by cutting the end off a condom, and then cutting up one side of the tube to create a flat surface. Never turn over a dental dam once you have used it. Throw it away instead.

- Spermicides containing nonoxynol-9 come in foams, creams, suppositories, and films. You can find them in a drugstore, usually next to the condoms.

- For sex play use disposable latex gloves.

- Diaphragms and cervical caps should always be used with a spermicidal jelly or foam to maximize their contraceptive protection. However, without the additional use of condoms, they are not effective against STDs.

- Always wash sex toys with soapy water after use and before you share them with another person.

Eroticizing Safe Sex

Making safe sex practices a part of the erotic experience of sex is the best way to insure their use. We will suggest several ideas, but recommend that you and your partner use your collective creativity and humor to come up with your own erotic safe sex.

- Using humor is important. Even though safe sex is a serious matter, laughter may help lighten the mood. For example, you may want to come up with funny expressions, such as "let's put on your party hat," when referring to using a condom.

- Slow down lovemaking to include safe sex preparation. Help put the condom or dental dam on your partner, stroking them as you do it. Once safe sex becomes part of your routine, the very sight, feel, and smell of a condom or dental dam may be a turn-on.

- Have a fun "grab bag" full of your safe sex items (condoms, dental dams, gloves, spermicides, etc.) near the bed, and make a game or ritual out of making a choice. As we mentioned above, a variety of choices can make the experience more enjoyable and spontaneous.

- Before leaving for vacation, go on a shopping spree and have some fun choosing a supply of condoms and other sex toys. Vibrators and dildos come in all shapes and sizes, and massage oils or lotions can add sexual variety.

Eroticizing safe sex not only makes it an integral part of foreplay, but often ends up extending foreplay and enhancing sensual aspects of sex. Practicing and enjoying safe sex with your partner improves your communication and helps build a sense of trust. It can also prevent disease and may very well save your life.

References

Ambramowicz, Mark, ed. 1987. "Drugs That Cause Sexual Dysfunction," *The Medical Letter.* 29, No. 744 (July 17):65–68.

Andersen, B. L. 1985. "Sexual Functioning and Morbidity Among Cancer Survivors: Present Status and Future Research Directions." *Cancer,* 55:1835–1842.

Andersen, B. L. 1987. "Sexual Functioning Complications in Women with Gynecologic Cancer." *Cancer,* 60(8):2123–2128.

Andersen, B. L., B. Andersen, and C. deProsse. 1989. "Controlled Prospective Longitudinal Study of Women with Cancer: I Sexual Functioning Outcomes." *Journal of Consulting and Clinical Psychiatry,* 57(6):683–691.

Baker, R. 1997. "Three-Drug Therapy Reduces Deaths and New AIDS-Related Illnesses by 50 Percent." *Bulletin of Experimental Treatments for AIDS* (BETA), March:3–4.

Barbach, L. 1976. *For Yourself: The Fulfillment of Female Sexuality.* New York: Anchor Books.

Barbach, L. 1982. *For Each Other: Sharing Sexual Intimacy.* New York: Anchor Press.

Ellenberg, M. 1977. "Sexual Aspects of the Female Diabetic." *Mt. Sinai Journal of Medicine,* 44:495–500.

Garner, W. E. and H. A. Allen. 1989. "Sexual Rehabilitation and Heart Disease." *Journal of Rehab,* January-March:69–73.

Ghadirian, A., L. Annable, and M. Bélanger. 1992. "Lithium, Benzodiazepines, and Sexual Function in Bipolar Patients." *American Journal of Psychiatry,* 149(6):801–805.

Gillenwater, J. and A. Wein. 1988. "Summary of the National Institute of Arthritis, Diabetes, Digestive, and Kidney Diseases Workshop on Interstitial Cystitis, National Institutes of Health, Bethesda, Maryland, August 28–29, 1987." *Journal of Urology,* 140:203–206.

Gitlin, M. 1994. "Psychotropic Medications and Their Effects on Sexual Function: Diagnosis, Biology, and Treatment Approaches." *Journal of Clinical Psychiatry,* 55(9):406–413.

Glasgow, M., V. Halfin, and A. F. Althausen. 1987. "Sexual Response and Cancer." *CA—A Cancer Journal for Clinicians,* 37(6):322–333.

Hana, L. 1997. "Recent News About Women and HIV." *Bulletin of Experimental Treatments for AIDS* (BETA), March:18–20.

Heiman, L ., J. LoPiccolo, and L. LoPiccolo. 1976. *Becoming Orgasmic: A Sexual and Personal Growth Program for Women.* New York: Prentice Hall.

Herman, J. L. 1992. *Trauma and Recovery, The Aftermath of Violence—From Domestic Abuse to Political Terror.* New York: Basic Books.

Hollander, H. and M. H. Katz. 1990. HIV Infection. In *Sexually Transmitted Diseases, 2nd Edition,* edited by K. K. Holmes, P. Mårdh, P. F. Sparling, and P. J. Wiesner, New York: McGraw-Hill.

Hutchinson, M. G. 1985. *Transforming Body Image: Learning to Love the Body You Have.* Freedom, Calif.: The Crossing Press.

Kitzinger, S. 1983. *Women's Experience of Sex: The Facts and Feelings of Female Sexuality at Every Stage of Life.* New York: Penguin Books.

Kolodny, R. C. 1971. "Sexual Dysfunction in Diabetic Females." *Diabetes,* 20:557–559.

Kunzman, K. 1990. *The Healing Way: Adult Recovery From Childhood Sexual Abuse.* San Francisco: Harper & Row.

Lamb, M. A. 1995. "Effects of Cancer on the Sexuality and Fertility of Women." *Seminars in Oncological Nursing,* 11(2):120–127.

Loulan, J. 1984. *Lesbian Sex.* San Francisco: Spinsters/Aunt Lute.

Love, P. 1991. *The Emotional Incest Syndrome: What to Do When a Parent's Love Rules Your Life.* New York: Bantam Books.

Maltz, W. 1992. *The Sexual Healing Journey: A Guide for Survivors of Sexual Abuse.* New York: W. W. Norton.

Margolese, H. C. and P. Assalian. 1996. "Sexual Side Effects of Antidepressants: A Review." *Journal of Sex and Marital Therapy,* 22(3):209–217.

Mattson, D., M. Petrie, D. K. Srivastava, and M. McDermott. 1995. "Multiple Sclerosis: Sexual Dysfunction and Its Response to Medications." *Arch Neurol*, 52 (September):862–868.

McCabe, M. P., E. McDonald, A. A. Deeks, et al. 1996. "The Impact of Multiple Sclerosis on Sexuality and Relationships." *Journal of Sex Research*, 33(3):241–248.

McCann, M. E. 1989. "Sexual Healing After Heart Attack." *American Journal of Nursing*, September:1133–1138.

Meiselman, K. 1978. *Incest: A Psychological Study of Causes and Effects with Treatment Recommendations*. San Francisco: Jossey-Bass.

Napier, N. J. 1993. *Getting Through the Day: Strategies for Adults Hurt as Children*. New York: W. W. Norton.

Nosek, M. A., D. H. Rintala, M. E. Young, C. A. Howland, C. G. Foley, D. Rossi, and G. Chan Pong. 1996. "Sexual Functioning Among Women with Physical Disabilities." *Archives of Physical Medicine Rehabilitation*, 77, February:107–115.

Parker, S. L., T. Tong, S. Bolden, and P. A. Wingo. 1997. "Cancer Statistics, 1997." *A Cancer Journal for Clinicians*, 47:5–27.

Schlesinger, L. 1996. "Chronic Pain, Intimacy, and Sexuality: A Qualitative Study of Women Who Live with Pain." *Journal of Sex Research*, 33(3):249–256.

Schover, L. R., M. Fife, and D. M. Gershenson. 1989. "Sexual Dysfunction and Treatment for Early-Stage Cervical Cancer." *Cancer*, 63(1):204–212.

Schover, L. R. and S. B. Jensen. 1988. *Sexuality and Chronic Illness*. New York: Guilford Press.

Schover, L. R. 1988. *Sexuality and Cancer: For the Woman Who Has Cancer and Her Partner*. Cleveland, Ohio: American Cancer Society, Inc.

Segraves, R. T. 1992. "Overview of Sexual Dysfunction Complicating the Treatment of Depression." *Journal of Clinical Psychiatry*, monograph 10(2):4–10.

Stewart, F., F. Guest, G. Stewart, and R. Hatcher. 1987. *Understanding Your Body: Every Woman's Guide to Gynecology and Health*. New York: Bantam Books.

Tardiff, G. S. 1989. "Sexual Activity After a Myocardial Infarction." *Archives of Physical Medicine Rehabilitation*, 70 (October):763–766.

Thompson, W. L. 1986. "Sexual Problems in Chronic Respiratory Disease." *Postgraduate Medicine*, 79(7):41–52.

Unsain, I. C., M. H. Goodwin, and E. A. Schuster. 1982. "Diabetes and Sexual Functioning." *Nursing Clinics of North America*, 17(3):387–393.

Vercellini, P., I. Cortesi, L. Trestidi, F. Parazzini, O. DeGiorgi, and P. G. Crosigano. 1996. "Endometriosis and Pelvic Pain: Relation to Disease Stage and Localization." *Fertility and Sterility*, 65(2):299–304.

Walbroehl, G. S. 1992. "Sexual Concerns of the Patient with Pulmonary Disease." *Postgraduate Medicine*, 91(5):455–460.

Webster, D. C. 1996. "Sex, Lies, and Stereotypes: Women and Interstitial Cystitis." *Journal of Sex Research*, 33(3):197–203.

Webster, D. and T. Brennan. 1994. "Use and Effectiveness of Physical Self-Care Strategies for IC." *Nurse Practitioner*, 19(10):55–61.

Weinberg, J. R. 1977. *Sex and Recovery*. Minneapolis, Minn.: Recovery Press.

Westerlund, E. 1983. "Couseling Women with Histories of Incest." *Women and Therapy*, 2:17–31.

Westerlund, E. 1992. *Women's Sexuality After Childhood Incest*. New York: W. W. Norton.

Whitfield, C. L. 1989. *Healing the Child Within: Discovery and Recovery for Adult Children of Dysfunctional Families*. Deerfield Beach, Fla.: Health Communications, Inc.

Whitfield, C. L. 1993. *Boundaries and Relationships: Knowing, Protecting, and Enjoying the Self*. Deerfield Beach, Fla.: Health Communications, Inc.

CHAPTER FIVE

Changes along Your Pathway: The Impact of Life Change on Sexual Dysfunction

Your sexuality changes over the course of your life—the sexual person you were at eighteen years old will be quite different from the one you'll be at sixty-five. Your personal expectations, needs, and limitations shape your view of sex and determine which experiences you will actively seek or avoid. In this chapter we will focus on several major life changes that have an impact on sexual function. First, we will examine how physical and psychological changes during pregnancy affect a woman's experience of sexuality and her interactions with her partner. Next, we will look at the role of fertility problems in a couple's sexual relationship. Finally, we will discuss the impact of menopause and aging on sexual function and relationships.

Sex During and After Pregnancy

It is common for a couple to go through profound physical and sexual changes during and after pregnancy without understanding the changes in their sexual relationship. Although they love each other as much as ever, they may feel uncomfortable sharing with each other or anyone else their distressing or uncomfortable thoughts about these sexual changes. Obstetricians and gynecologists will give advice on the medical aspects of sexuality and pregnancy but often do not talk in depth to their patients about their psychological experiences of sexuality. Their partners are left even more in the dark.

Pregnancy is a mysterious time, when a woman's psychological focus turns ever inward. She has to come to terms with her image of her changing body and may need reassurance from her partner that she is still attractive and sexually interesting. Your partner may also need reassurance of your love and sexual interest, and that your focus is not only on the baby. Lovemaking can be a reassuring way to give and receive attention, affection, and passion. Pregnancy offers a special opportunity for couples to deepen their understanding of each other's emotional and physical needs and to enrich their relationship while they await a new addition to their family.

Common Concerns

Every woman responds differently to sexual experiences during pregnancy. According to Bing (1977), the most common pattern among women seems to be an increase in sexual interest during the first and second trimester and then a gradual decline in the third trimester. Some women who are pleased to be pregnant want to celebrate their femininity and fertility. Others relax and enjoy sexuality without worry about contraception. Women who feel high levels of sexual arousal may enjoy masturbation more than usual. The couple may feel a sexy pride and joy in the pregnancy. On the other hand, some couples feel anxious and require time to adjust to the idea of parenthood, during which time sex becomes low priority. Sexual interest may decline during the first trimester if a woman experiences a lot of nausea, vomiting, or exhaustion due to hormone surges. Tender and enlarged breasts may make even the most gentle touch seem like too much. Sexual desire may also fall if the woman feels ambivalent about being pregnant or is having relationship problems with her partner. These days there are many alternatives for women and some single women are having a child alone. Some lesbian couples are choosing for one or both members of the couple to have a biological child. The sexual dynamics will differ if a pregnant woman has a male or female partner who is committed to the relationship, or if she is alone or with a partner who is not the biological father.

The major physical concern during pregnancy is the safety and comfort of the mother and baby, and all couples must find comfortable positions and decide whether arousal or orgasm is safe for the mother. Penetration, whether by a penis, finger, dildo, or other object may be cause for concern for physical reasons.

The First Trimester

It is common for couples to worry that having intercourse will cause pain or injury to the woman or to the fetus or will bring on premature labor or miscarriage. These concerns are often amplified in a woman who has had a previous miscarriage. A man may worry so much that he has difficulty maintaining an erection, or begins to avoid sex altogether. Both the woman and her partner may panic if she has any bleeding after intercourse. This is commonly due to deep thrusting during intercourse, when an object bumps up against the cervix. This problem is usually nothing to worry about but can be avoided by choosing positions that do not provide deep penetration. However, if a woman has spotting after intercourse, it is important to consult with an obstetrician. Many doctors will recommend abstaining from intercourse and orgasm if significant bleeding occurs during the first trimester.

During a first pregnancy each partner may worry that the other has reservations about being sexual, especially if there has been a change in the type or frequency of sexual activity. If a couple doesn't talk about this, both people can feel hurt and rejected. Talking things over can help you avoid misunderstanding and resentment, and increase emotional intimacy. When partners feel loved and included, they will usually be more than willing to find alternative sexual expressions that are mutually satisfying. Intimacy can be experienced through massages, caresses, holding, cuddling, and talking in bed together. If your doctor suggests abstaining from sex, find out if you should abstain from intercourse only, or from all types of sexual activity. Remember that for the vast majority of couples, sex during pregnancy is perfectly safe and remains an important part of their relationship.

Many couples wonder whether oral sex is safe during pregnancy. There is no reason to avoid oral sex at this time, although couples sometimes abstain for several reasons. Some partners object to the smell and taste of vaginal secretions which are different during pregnancy. Women commonly have an extra amount of discharge during pregnancy due to the increased blood supply to the genitals. Occasionally a pregnant woman may get a vaginal infection such as yeast or trichomoniasis, and if so, her vagina may also smell or taste different than usual. These infections are no more serious during pregnancy than at other times and can be easily treated. Vaginal infections are not harmful to the fetus since the cervix seals the uterus from the vaginal canal. A word of caution if you engage in oral sex; at no time should a woman ever have air blown into her vagina, regardless of whether she is pregnant or not, since air could theoretically pass into the bloodstream through the uterus and create a life-threatening embolism.

The Second Trimester

Many women feel wonderful during the second trimester as the fatigue and nausea of the first trimester diminish. At this stage the woman's belly is usually not so big and most sexual positions are still comfortable. Physical changes in the breasts and pelvic area may actually increase sexual interest and arousal for many women. There is an increase in blood flow as estrogen levels rise and the pelvic area feels slightly swollen and sensitized. Some women feel sexually aroused much of the time and are easily orgasmic. Although couples worry about hurting the fetus during intercourse, orgasm apparently has no harmful effects. It is clear that the fetus is well protected as it is surrounded by a literal "bag" of water within the tough uterine muscle and protected by the sealed cushion of the cervix below.

As pregnancy advances, most women look for more comfortable positions for making love in order to avoid pressure on the breasts and abdomen. Also, pressure on the diaphragm can aggravate common symptoms of indigestion and heartburn. A sitting position using cushions and a lot of pillows can lessen the pressure and allow for more comfort. Lying together in a spoon position can provide connection, stimulation of breasts and clitoris, and a sense of comforting enfolding. The partner of a pregnant woman needs to be gentle during lovemaking and must explore new ways to adapt to the changes in their lover's body. Using the guiding exercises in chapter 7 may help a woman show her partner what feels good as her pregnancy continues.

Couples who want to continue with intercourse as a part of lovemaking may find some positions more comfortable for the pregnant woman. In a spoon position the woman lies with her back to her partner as they both lie on their sides. This position allows for breast and clitoral stimulation during intercourse and leaves her belly free from pressure. In a scissors position, the partner lies on his side and the pregnant woman lies on her back and raises both legs over her partner's pelvis while he enters from under her legs. This position allows the lovers to look at each other during intercourse while the pregnant woman's abdomen is free from pressure. In the kneeling position, a woman kneels so that the baby is suspended in her abdomen and her partner can enter from behind, providing clitoral stimulation if the woman wishes. The drawings in figure 5.1 show these three positions.

Some men lose sexual desire as their partner becomes more obviously pregnant; the men are unable to connect the image of a mother with a sexual partner. Men might be influenced by cultural images of the "good asexual mother," of incest taboos, and of the pure Madonna, all of which may suggest that sexual relations should not be associated with bearing children. Even though he knows that his partner is not *his* mother, he may still lose sexual interest as he sees her as a forbidden sexual object in her role as the mother of his children.

The Third Trimester

The third trimester often brings a decline in sexual interest and activity. A woman generally feels uncomfortable and tired and has a big belly that makes it more awkward for her to move. Finding a comfortable sexual position becomes more problematic. The rate of orgasm seems to drop as the delivery date draws nearer. Thus, the woman who reaches orgasm three out of four times during sex before pregnancy may only experience orgasm every one out of four occasions. Although this continues to be a time for intimacy and physical closeness, many couples find that they gradually enter a period of abstinence from intercourse.

For many years there was a general belief among obstetricians that intercourse in the last trimester could cause premature deliveries or maternal infections. Goodlin (1971) studied a small group of women and suggested that orgasm could cause the uterus to contract, leading to a slight increase in premature deliveries. Naeye (1979) reported on a large sample of women that there was a higher rate of infection for women who had intercourse more than once a week after the thirty-seventh week of pregnancy. He also noted that fetal mortality was slightly higher. Mills (1981), however, conducted a large-scale study and found that there was little danger to the baby, either before or after birth. Sex during the last trimester of pregnancy is probably safe for most women, provided that they have no history of miscarriage or of premature ripening of the cervix. If you are concerned whether it is safe for you, ask your obstetrician.

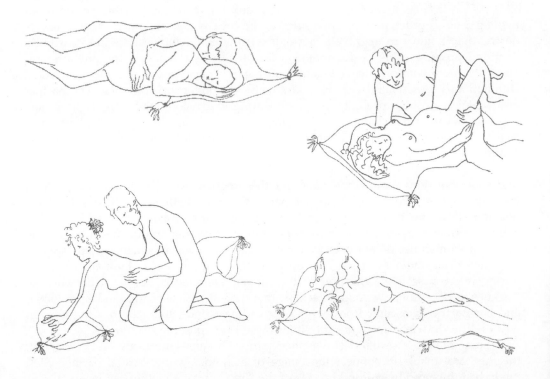

Figure 5.1. Sexual Positions that Minimize Exertion: Modified for Pregnancy

After Delivery

After the baby's birth, a couple may feel very excited and joyous. In the first few days after delivery, however, they will also be exhausted and emotions may run high as the couple faces many new challenges. Some partners who have attended the birth have to readjust their thinking about sex and reproduction. It may take a while before they can think of their partner's body as a sexual turn-on after watching labor and delivery. Especially with a first child, the couple usually focuses on immediate aspects of newborn care and their own intimate relationship becomes secondary. As they get to know their new infant, they may pay less attention to each other. Both may feel this loss of attention and some couples worry that the baby will always come first in their partner's affection.

A woman's vagina and perineum is often sore after childbirth, especially if there was tearing during delivery or if an episiotomy was performed. An episiotomy is an incision which is sometimes made during delivery to enlarge the vaginal opening to allow for the baby to be born. It is done sometimes to avoid tearing of perineal tissues but is not always necessary. As a result, intercourse can be distinctly painful and should be postponed until the discomfort passes. If a woman is nursing, her breasts may be too sensitive for sexual stimulation. Breast and nipple stimulation during nursing can repress ovarian function, which in turn can cause vaginal dryness and painful intercourse. If a woman is not nursing, there is still a period of breast sensitivity as the milk supply is repressed. Both emotional adjustment and hormone fluctuations after childbirth contribute to changes in mood that can decrease sexual desire. Postpartum blues are common but short-lived, though they occasionally progress to more serious states of depression. All of these physical and emotional adjustments to childbirth may have an impact on sexual function for four to six weeks. This time can prove frustrating and disappointing for women who expected to return to sex with their usual pleasure.

The following suggestions can be helpful in maintaining fulfilling sex during and after pregnancy:

- Unless your physician tells you otherwise, it is perfectly safe to have sexual intercourse and orgasm during pregnancy.

- Pregnancy is a special and exciting time to share feelings and sensations with your partner. They want to be included as much as possible. Communicate with them about your experience of pregnancy. Share thoughts and feelings about intimacy—before, during, and after sex.

- Neither you nor your baby is fragile. Don't worry about anyone getting hurt when you engage in normal sexual practices.

- You cannot get pregnant again (i.e., have twins) once you conceive. Enjoy not using contraception during this time, provided that you know for sure that neither of you has an STD.

- Later in your pregnancy you may need to be creative about finding comfortable positions for making love. Keep several pillows handy to use as props during intercourse.

- Take a romantic vacation together before your baby is born (and while you are still comfortable traveling.) Once your infant arrives it will be harder to find time to be alone together.

- You can resume sexual activity within a few weeks after delivery, as long as you are comfortable and your doctor agrees. Don't assume that breast-feeding will prevent a new pregnancy. Use birth control until such time as you are ready for another baby.

- Most obstetricians and midwives recommend Kegel exercises for the new mother to regain pelvic muscle tone.

Infertility

Infertility is defined as a couple's inability to get pregnant after one year of normal, unprotected sexual intercourse and affects roughly one in six couples in the United States (Stetson 1996). Rates of infertility have increased in the past few decades, partly because more women want to conceive in their late thirties and forties, and also because more women have contracted sexually transmitted diseases that impair reproductive function. In over 90 percent of cases of infertility, a physical cause is identified usually involving one partner and occasionally both partners. Failure to ovulate is one of the most common reasons for infertility.

Infertility is a major developmental crisis in the life of a couple. The psychological and physical pain which accompany treatment for infertility strongly affect a couple's sexuality. As a couple slowly becomes aware of the problem, they often feel an initial sense of disbelief followed by frustration and deep disappointment. Infertility can be especially difficult for a woman who bases a large part of her identity on the idea of becoming a mother.

As a woman realizes she may not be able to bear a child, she may undergo a cascade of painful emotions: grief that she cannot produce a biological child, anger at the circumstances that have brought this about, and shame at what others may think of her. She must cope with negative feelings she has about her body, which may not go through pregnancy, delivery, and the birth of a child.

A woman's struggle with the realization of infertility is made more painful by the uncertainty that accompanies infertility treatment. Each month is greeted with hope for a pregnancy, followed by disappointment, anger, helplessness, and sadness once menstruation starts, indicating failure of conception. The couple must struggle to maintain a loving relationship while they are preoccupied with medical procedures. Treatment for infertility can involve time-consuming and uncomfortable procedures, rigid schedules, time-limits for sexual activity, and distressing side effects from fertility medications. In addition, a couple must commit substantial financial resources to infertility treatments, which may require cutting back on vacations or other luxuries. For both partners the whole process can be exhausting and enormously stressful and can take a toll on mental health.

A woman facing infertility may experience many unpleasant, negative thoughts. She may fear that people will blame her or belittle her for not producing a child and feel humiliated in front of unaware or insensitive family and friends who ask when she will have children. She may have absorbed negative cultural myths that women who don't have children are selfish, deviant, or damaged. A study by Link and Darling (1986) found that 40 percent of women coping with infertility revealed evidence of depression on a questionnaire. Couples frequently become angry at each other, and one partner may hold unspoken resentment if the other partner was identified as the source of the infertility. A woman may be very angry at her partner if they gave her an STD which caused her infertility. Or, she may feel enormous resentment if she waited too long to get pregnant because her partner was ambivalent about having a baby, and then has trouble conceiving because of her age. A woman may also be angry if her partner is infertile, even though she knows on a rational level that they, too, want a baby. A woman may be wracked with guilt and anger at herself if her age or the effects of previous STDs are a factor. She may feel that she is being punished for past promiscuous behaviors or sexual indiscretions, even though these experiences bear no relation to the reasons for the infertility. She may experience terrible guilt or regret if she had an abortion years before she felt ready to have a child. Going to a clinic and seeing pregnant women can be an unbearable ordeal.

Infertility can have decidedly negative effects on sexual function, and studies have reported the presence of sexual problems in 65 percent of women facing infertility. So much attention is focused on getting pregnant that a woman may feel little sexual desire, or she may feel numb to genital sensations and consequently have fewer orgasms. A woman may become demanding of her partner to produce an erection on time and hurry through the act of sex, or she may refuse to have sex except during her fertile period. What sex there is may be unfulfilling and mechanical, especially when it must conform to a treatment schedule. Some men have trouble with erections, especially during critical times of the month when they must have sex on demand. It is common for men to feel hurt by partners who only seem interested in their sperm and are less interested in them as a person. An infertile man may feel like a failure if he can't produce a child and ultimately become depressed, which will affect the emotional and sexual connection with his partner.

What can a couple do to address the psychological and sexual effects of infertility? The sensate focus exercises in chapter 7 can help a couple maintain a relaxed and loving sex life despite the pressures and stresses of infertility procedures. It is very important for both partners to go to a therapist together to express their feelings about infertility and to discuss its impact on their relationship. Counseling can be enormously helpful for a couple during infertility treatments and has even been demonstrated to improve the chances of conception (Sarrel and DeCharney 1985). There are also excellent support groups available in all major cities where couples can connect with other couples facing the same problems (see the appendix).

Case 5.1—Ken and Lisa

Ken and Lisa had been married for two years; they spent the second year trying to get pregnant. After eight months without success, Lisa went to see her gynecologist, who ran several diagnostic tests and then referred the couple to a fertility specialist. They went through eighteen months of expensive and time-consuming fertility testing and treatment, including numerous intrusive procedures involving contact with a whole range of physicians, nurses, and technicians. Ken and Lisa had high praise for the medical aspects of their treatment, but felt that nobody was acknowledging or addressing the enormous emotional strain they were experiencing. Sex had lost its appeal, especially after months of mechanical, scheduled intercourse. Lisa questioned her femininity, and felt an aching sadness each month when she began menstruating at the lost opportunity for a baby. Ken felt inadequate to make her happy and angry at the circumstances for which neither was to blame.

Lisa became so nervous and upset during monthly attempts at conception that she began having difficulty feeling aroused and lubricated and was never able to reach orgasm. Ken had occasional bouts of erectile problems. The added stress of sexual dysfunction was too much for them to handle, and they began seeing a sex therapist. Ken and Lisa were enormously relieved by the opportunity to vent their feelings of anger, frustration, and sadness. They discussed strategies to reduce stress and make sex more relaxing. The therapist taught them relaxation techniques and suggested exercises to focus on affectionate touching instead of intercourse and conception. They talked about how to stay emotionally connected and supportive of one another. When Lisa finally became pregnant, she and Ken agreed that they would have given up and even separated without the chance to work through their feelings about infertility.

Sexuality and Aging

A century ago, the expected life span of an adult woman in the United States was forty years; now, women are expected to live into their eighties. While the absolute life span may not go much past one hundred years, the span of active and healthy living should continue to increase (Dychtwald and Flower 1989). Thus, what it means to be an eighty-year-old woman in the 1990s will be vastly different in the 2020s. However, North American culture is oriented toward youthfulness and exhibits a strong denial of aging and death. Stereotyping based on age—or *ageism*—permeates the very texture of this culture, as people are bombarded with the glorification of youthful images in the media and the commercial world. Aging is sometimes depicted as laughable, pitiable, or cute and sweet. These stereotypes extend to the idea of sexuality in later life, which is often thought of in joking ways as impaired, unsafe, and limited, if not wholly nonexistent. Many young people have a hard time thinking about their parents and grandparents having sex, and this squeamishness is learned early and carried into adult perspectives. But as the baby boomers age and the birth rate drops, the United States is beginning to face what Dychtwald and Flower (1989) have termed a "massive age wave." As this occurs, there will be major shifts in how aging and sexuality are viewed. People who study aging often define the beginning of the second half of life the post-menopausal years (from approximately age fifty to age seventy). The term "late life" is usually used to describe the years after age seventy.

Several factors influence sexual function in late life, and their impact often depends on how a woman is able to cope with each one. For instance, some women may continue to engage in previous sexual habits, while others feel a need to impose limitations. Menopause involves many physical changes that can impair sexual function. Some women take these changes in stride and seek treatment, while other women experience them with fear and despair. Some women are fearful of changes in physical appearance, such as age-associated weight gain or loss, sagging breasts or bellies, and skin wrinkles. Concerns about attractiveness and body image can lead to constructive attempts to change it, acceptance of these inevitable changes, or resignation and distress. A particularly devastating age-related factor is the experience of acute and chronic illness. Unique to late life is the common presence of multiple simultaneous illnesses and complicated medication regimens. Another important influence on late-life sexuality is the loss of spouses and partners. This can mean the end of sexual relations for women not willing or interested in seeking new partners.

Overall, two conclusions can be drawn from looking at the relative impact of age on sexuality. First, many women may accept ageist stereotypes about sex in later life and engage in less frequent or more limited sexual activity because they view it as inappropriate, despite the fact that they may retain sexual interest. These attitudinal barriers may be more damaging to sexuality than actual physiologic changes (Starr and Weiner 1981). Second, research has shown that a lack of information about change in sexual function in later life can lead to excess fear and pain (Boyer and Boyer 1982). These conclusions will likely change, however, because they are a product of a particular generation. Most women who grew up in the earlier part of the century were taught to be chaste, mindful of their reputation, and passive during sex. Some of these attitudes have been carried through into late life, while others reemerge after divorce or widowhood, when the possibility of meeting new sexual partners arises. As the generation of women that grew up with feminism and the sexual revolution enter the second half of life, they will face different issues and have different attitudes. One such issue will be how to protect themselves from STDs, including AIDS.

It is conceivable that this society is facing the beginning of a new sexual revolution. Successful generations of older adults are in better physical health and are better educated about sexuality, consequently their sexual function has a greater chance of remaining intact. For many women, hormone replacement therapy after menopause has made a dramatic difference in maintaining general physical health and well-being, along with healthy sexual desire and function. Starr and Weiner (1981) Brecher (1984), Butler and Lewis (1986), and Goodwin (1987) have all shown that the percentage of older adults involved in sexual relationships continues to remain quite high. For many couples, sexual intimacy often grows once the children have left home. Research shows that people in their sixties through nineties continue sexual activity and interest as they did in their forties. According to Marsiglio and Donnelly (1991), 65 percent of married couples in the sixty- to sixty-five-year-old age range and 44 percent of couples older than sixty-five years reported being sexual at least once a month. The main predictors of sexual frequency are a person's sense of self-worth and confidence and the health status of their partner.

Exercise 5.1—Aging and Self-Image

If you are facing age-related changes in your body that have altered your self-image, the following exercises can help you recognize any of your own negative or ageist attitudes and replace them with more positive ones. Ageist language used to describe older women is harmful to all women, whatever their age, because it stereotypes and generalizes by appearance. Review the following words used to describe older women and circle those that you have used yourself:

Words with Negative Connotations

biddy	crone	hag	witch
old bag	old bat	old maid	old hen
granny	old girl	old crank	stuffy
oldster	dotard	prune	prude
spinster	old fuss-budget	henhussy	shows her age
in the decline of life	dealing with the infirmity of age	feeble	waning
fading	sinking	decrepit	doddering
tottering	one foot in the grave	beldam	battle-ax
frump	old heifer	old fossil	past her prime
little old lady	ancient	senile	out to pasture

Now, from the set of positive words, circle those words you would like to use about yourself as you age.

Words with Positive Connotations

elder	senior	mature	middle-aged
grown old	venerable	matriarch	dowager
older woman	ripe	mellow	wise woman

Exercise 5.2—Finding Positive Models

If you want to avoid negative images, it helps to think about the characteristics of older women whom you have admired in your life. Many people describe an attitude of embracing life, which, for want of a better term, they call "young at heart." The image implies a woman who embodies many attributes: confident, assertive, nurturing, stylish, active, involved, healthy, socially skilled, witty, intelligent, elegant, warm, empathic, friendly, and loving. But, even here, the images are not sensual or sexual.

To focus on positive images and attitudes, try the following exercise:

1. In your journal, write down the names of five older women you admire. Choose from the older women in your own family or from the world at large.

2. Next to each name, write down at least five attributes of each woman that make her important to you. For example: *honest, able to cope with illness, self-reliant, creative.*

3. Choose at least five of the characteristics you would like to have and make a list of them on a separate page.

4. Now imagine these women as sexual individuals in a way that fits your knowledge of them. Write down these characteristics. For example: *enjoyed regular sex, enjoyed secret rendezvous, liked to dress sexy, never lost sight of sensual activities.*

Write down the sexual characteristics you could imagine would fit yourself.

Exercise 5.3—Affirming Aging and Sexuality

Do the following exercise in your journal:

Identify all the negative sexual words and images regarding your aging and sexuality. List them on the left side of a sheet of paper.

On the right side of the page, change each one into a positive affirmation of your sexual self.

Here are several examples:

I am fat.	*I have a rounded and curvy woman's body.*
I am old and difficult.	*As I get older I have learned to speak my mind.*
I can't be sexual because I'm alone.	*I am a sensual, sexual, and lovable woman.*

Menopause

The major physical change for aging women is the onset of *menopause*, sometimes called the *change of life* or *climacteric.* Lonnie Barbach (1993) has suggested calling this process *the pause* to indicate that it is a transition from childbearing years to the next stage of life. Menopause occurs over a period of two to ten years and ends for most women by age fifty-one. During this time the ovaries produce smaller amounts of the female sex hormone estrogen, eventually culminating in the ceasing of ovulation and menstruation. Menopause is characterized by the following cardinal physical symptoms that occur in up to 85 percent of women at one time or another:

- Hot flashes (most common symptom), night sweats
- Headaches, pain in the neck and shoulders
- Excessive fatigue
- Vaginal dryness due to decreased lubrication
- Thinning or atrophy of vaginal tissue
- Shortening and narrowing of the vagina
- Thinning of bladder and urethral tissue, with higher risk for infections

How do these and other aspects of menopause affect sexual function? In general, most menopausal and postmenopausal women continue to enjoy sex as they have in the past. After menopause some may even feel free to enjoy sex without the need for contraception or fear of unwanted pregnancy. However, loss of estrogen has several negative effects on sexuality. A woman may find that her breasts are extremely tender and she may need a more gentle touch than before. She may also notice that her skin is more sensitive, itchy, or irritated, especially on the mons and outer lips of the vulva; she may need a different type of sexual touch as a result. In addition, 40 percent to 60 percent of women need more time for sexual stimulation before they become lubricated (Goodwin 1987). As the body provides less lubrication, a woman may experience painful penetration and intercourse. A woman who was accustomed to becoming very wet during sexual arousal may misinterpret her lack of lubrication as loss of interest, despite the fact that her subjective feelings of arousal are high.

Loss of estrogen changes the tissues in the genitals; the vagina shortens and becomes less elastic, and the vaginal walls become thinner and more fragile. As the cushion of fatty tissue thins, the genital area has less protection and can be easily irritated during sexual stimulation. There is less flow of blood to the genital area, which therefore does not swell to the same degree as before. Consequently, the experience of orgasm may be less intense or may be accompanied by a cramping sensation during or afterwards. Hormonal shifts also cause the vagina to be less acidic, which increases the likelihood of vaginal infections and consequent itching and pain during sexual stimulation.

Research shows that 50 percent of women experience a change in libido as testosterone levels drop during menopause (Sherwin 1985). Loss of testosterone causes other changes that affect sexuality. Pubic and underarm hair become sparse. The body produces less of the oil that moisturizes the skin and gives shine to the hair. Testosterone receptors located in the nipples, vulva, and clitoris are less sensitized to sexual stimulation (Rako 1996).

Estrogen replacement therapy is an effective way to restore hormonal balance and reverse many of the changes of menopause. It is usually prescribed together with progesterone to replicate a woman's previous level of hormones. Estrogen can be taken in a pill form or in a patch, worn on the skin, that provides a slow release of hormone. Estrogen cream can also be applied directly to vulvar and vaginal tissue if irritation is a problem. All of these treatments will enable a woman's genitals to produce more lubrication during sexual activity. Some doctors are now prescribing testosterone for postmenopausal women to stimulate desire. Susan Rako (1996) believes that supplementary testosterone can restore a woman's energy and sexual interest without harm, provided the doses are not too high. Although some women are pleased with the results, this treatment remains controversial because high doses can result in side effects such as weight change, facial and chest hair, lowering of the voice, or even permanent damage to the liver. Keeping the dosage low can sometimes avoid these side effects.

The use of any hormone replacement therapy is a personal decision to be made with the help of a physician (often a gynecologist). Some women opt against it or are not candidates for it because of health concerns. Some women may not need hormone replacement. Others prefer herbal and homeopathic treatments for menopause, but such treatments have not undergone rigorous study. Some of the choices include acupuncture, vitamin E capsules, and remedies including chasteberry and sepia (Weed 1992; Barbach 1993).

EXERCISE 5.4—A SEXUALITY AND AGING QUESTIONNAIRE

Read each of the following statements and circle the appropriate number from one to three.

    1 = I don't agree

    2 = I sometimes agree

    3 = I always agree.

1. I like my body as it is.	1 2 3
2. Even though I used to look younger, my body still pleases me.	1 2 3
3. I am a mature, sexually attractive woman.	1 2 3
4. My partner finds me physically attractive.	1 2 3
5. Sex can be playful.	1 2 3
6. I enjoy feeling powerful during sex.	1 2 3
7. Being sexual makes me feel attractive.	1 2 3
8. Being sexual helps me connect with my partner.	1 2 3
9. When I am sexual I feel my femininity in contrast to my male partner's masculinity.	1 2 3
10. Sexual activity makes me aware of being a woman.	1 2 3
11. Sex can be relaxing.	1 2 3
12. I can express my feelings for my partner through sexuality.	1 2 3
13. I feel my partner's love for me during sex.	1 2 3
14. I enjoy being touched even without getting aroused.	1 2 3
15. Sex can be soothing if I'm upset.	1 2 3
16. I feel taken care of when I have sex.	1 2 3
17. I continue to be interested in sex as I age.	1 2 3
18. I get sexually aroused and would like to be sexual.	1 2 3
19. I sometimes have sexual dreams.	1 2 3
20. I sometimes enjoy masturbation.	1 2 3
21. I fantasize about being sexual.	1 2 3
22. Even though it takes longer to achieve, I still enjoy orgasm as I age.	1 2 3
23. I can't have an orgasm, but I still like to be sexual with my partner.	1 2 3

24. I have found ways to make sex feel more comfortable. 1 2 3
25. Cuddling and sensual experiences feel good without intercourse. 1 2 3
26. I know my body better than I did and now I know what I like sexually. 1 2 3
27. Sex is still an important part of my life. 1 2 3
28. I would want to be sexual if I had a partner. 1 2 3
29. Lovemaking feels good even if neither of us has an orgasm. 1 2 3
30. I can enjoy solitary sexual pleasure. 1 2 3
31. Sexual expression is for both of us to enjoy. 1 2 3
32. Even though I won't have children now, I want to be sexual. 1 2 3
33. I enjoy giving and getting pleasure. 1 2 3
34. Sex is a deep way to express our love for each other. 1 2 3
35. Sex means more to me than procreation. 1 2 3
36. If I lost my partner I could eventually enjoy sex with someone new. 1 2 3

Now add up your score. If you scored below 40, you might benefit from trying to come up with some new ideas about how to increase your enjoyment of sexuality. This book has many suggestions for sexual enhancement and pleasure. If you scored between 40 and 70, you are like many women and have an average enjoyment of your sexuality. If you scored above 70, you are already enjoying your sexuality in a large variety of ways.

Exercise 5.5—Sexuality Time Line

Sometimes you may forget to stop and consider attitudes that are affecting your decisions. This exercise may help confront ageist beliefs about continuing to have sex with a partner as you age. For each event listed below, write in the chronological age you believe is correct. If you are not sure, make a guess. For instance, if your father died when your mother was seventy-five, and she didn't date other men, you could assume she stopped having sex. If possible, ask family members for more information. Or, if your grandmother married at age eighteen she probably began having sex at that age.

Your current age: _____

Your mother's age (or age she died): _____

Your grandmother's age (or age she died): _____

The age you believe you might die: _____

The age at which a woman should begin her sexual life: _____

The age you began your sexual life: _____

The age your mother began her sexual life: _____

The age your grandmother began her sexual life: _____

The age a woman should stop sexual activity: _____

The age your mother stopped having sex: _____

The age your grandmother stopped having sex: _____

The age you will stop having sex: _____

Look at the ages you have written and think about how your family attitudes have affected what you think about sex in the second half of life. If you think a woman should stop sexual activity at menopause and you expect to live to be eighty-five years old, does that mean you expect to live for thirty-five or so years with no sexual outlet? If your mother stopped having sex after the birth of her last child, will you do the same? Make at least six connections similar to the above examples. Think about the implications of these age factors and write about them in your journal.

How to Enhance Sexual Function in the Second Half of Life

Here are a number of suggestions on how to maintain and enhance sexual function in later life:

- Cultivate a positive attitude towards sex. Remember that even though sexuality changes over the years, most people continue to be sexual throughout their lives.

- Keep your body as healthy and fit as possible. Talk to your doctor about sex as a regular part of your medical checkup.

- If pain or illness is a major part of your life, try to put it aside during sexual activity. Take pain medications prior to lovemaking to insure you have maximum pain control. Keep medication bottles and other signs of illness out of view. Choose a time of day when you both feel good. Testosterone levels are highest in the morning when you are rested, and this might be a good time to make love. Being warm helps. Take a shower or bathe together to loosen stiff muscles. For some women, the release of natural painkillers, or endorphins, in the body during sexual activity can help them forget about their pain.

- Always arrange a comfortable and pleasing environment for intimate (not always sexual) time together. Start off with an activity you both enjoy: listening to music, talking quietly about your day, doing relaxation exercises, cuddling, meditating . . . whatever brings you closer together.

- Keep talking about your sexuality with your partner. Sexual interests, sensitivities, and inclinations change over time. Telling each other about your current sexual thoughts and feelings can be a pleasure in itself.

- Look back at your sexual attitudes, beliefs, and feelings over the years. You may be holding on to old ideas that interfere with current pleasures.

- Invent new approaches. Be creative about sex and enjoy the leisure to explore each other.

- Be aware of menopausal effects on sexual function and adapt to them. A woman may find that her breasts are extremely tender, similar to the tenderness she previously experienced prior to menstruation. She may want a more gentle touch during lovemaking, or she may not want to have her breasts touched. A woman may notice that her skin is more sensitive; sometimes skin might feel itchy and irritated, especially on the mons and outer lips. She may experience touch as unpleasant or want touch to be more firm or more gentle than usual. Vaginal dryness may require liberal use of water-based lubricants for stimulation and intercourse.

- Allow yourself to enjoy touching all over the body in a sensual way, rather than limiting yourself to genital pleasure. Holding, hugging, spoon breathing, massaging, gentle caressing, and snuggling can all provide the sense of love and connection you and your partner need.

Sex during the second half of life is different from the urgent drive toward sexual exploration and genital satisfaction common in younger years. During the second half of life, most women have learned more about themselves. They know about the give-and-take of relationships and have achieved the ability to share tenderness and understanding with a partner. A sexual life can provide them with affirmation that their bodies are active and lively. They can give and receive comfort, soothing, and the pleasure of touch. As older women search for a deeper sense of intimacy, they can reaffirm life and express joy through their sexuality.

References

Pregnancy and Infertility

Bing, E. and L. Coleman. 1977. *Making Love During Pregnancy*. New York: Noonday Press.

Clubb, E. and J. Knight. 1996. *Fertility*. Devon, England: David and Charles Books.

Goodlin, R. 1971. "Orgasm During Pregnancy: Possible Deleterious Effects." *Obstetrics and Gynecology*, 38:916.

Falicov, C. 1973. "Sexual Adjustment During First Pregnancy and Postpartum." *American Journal of Obstetrics and Gynecology*, December, 117:991–1000.

Franklin, R. R. and D. K. Brockman. 1990. *In Pursuit of Fertility*. New York: Henry Holt Inc.

Herbst, A. 1970. "Coitus and the Fetus." *New England Journal of Medicine*, 301:1235.

Kitzinger, S. 1985. *Woman's Experience of Sex: The Facts and Feelings of Female Sexuality at Every Stage of Life*. New York: Penguin Books.

Link, P. W. and C. A. Darling. 1986. "Couples Undergoing Treatment for Infertility: Dimensions of Life Satisfaction." *Journal of Sex and Marriage Therapy*, 12:46–59.

Mills, J. L., S. Harlap, E. E. Harley. 1981. "Should Coitus Late in Pregnancy be Discouraged?" *Lancet*. July:136–138.

Naeye, R. 1979. "Coitus and Associated Amniotic-Fluid Infections." *New England Journal of Medicine*, 301:1198.

Naeye, R. 1981. "Coitus and Antepartum Hemorrhage." *British Journal of Obstetrics and Gynecology*, 88:765.

Rany, K. J. and S. White. 1987. "Sexuality in the Puerperium: A Review." *Archives of Sexual Behavior*, 2:165–186.

Schover, L. R. and S. B. Jensen. 1988. *Sexuality and Chronic Illness*. New York: Guilford Press.

Sarrel, P. M. and A. H. DeCherney. 1985. "Psychotherapeutic Intervention for Treatment of Couples with Secondary Infertility." *Fertility and Sterility*, 43:897–900.

Stetson, R. 1996. Presentation at conference in Dedham, MA, on *Clinical Issues in the Treatment of Infertility and Adoption*. Topic: "The Impact of Infertility on Husbands and Wives."

Stewart, F., F. Guest, G. Stewart, and R. Hatcher. 1987. *Understanding Your Body: Every Woman's Guide to Gynecology and Health.* New York: Bantam.

Zoldbrod, A. P. 1993. *Men, Women and Infertility: Intervention and Treatment Strategies.* New York: Lexington Books.

Aging

Barbach, L. 1993. *The Pause: Positive Approaches to Menopause.* New York: Sutton.

Boyer, G. and J. Boyer. 1982. *Sexuality and Aging.* Nursing Clinics of North America, 17(3):421–427.

Brecher, E. M. 1984. *Love, Sex, and Aging.* Mt. Vernon, New York: Consumers Union.

Butler, R. N. and M. I. Lewis. 1986. *Love and Sex After Forty: A Guide for Men and Women for Their Mid and Later Years.* New York: Harper & Row Publishers.

Cutler, W. B., C. R. Garcia, and D. A. Edwards. 1983. *Menopause: A Guide for Women and the Men Who Love Them.* New York: W. W. Norton.

Dychtwald, K. and J. Flower. 1989. *Agewave: The Challenges and Opportunities of an Aging America.* Los Angeles: Jeremy P. Tarcher, Inc.

Goodwin, A. J. 1987. "Sexuality in the Second Half of Life." P. B. Doress and D. L. Siegal, (Eds.), *Ourselves Growing Older: Women Aging with Knowledge and Power.* New York: Simon & Schuster, Touchstone.

Kellett, J. M. 1994. "Sexual Disorders." J. R. M. Copland, M. T. Abou-Saleh, and D. G. Blazer, (Eds.), *Principles and Practice of Geriatric Psychiatry.* New York: John Wiley & Sons Ltd.

Marsiglio, W. and D. Donnelly. 1991. "Sexual Relations in Later Life: A National Study of Married Persons." *Journal of Gerontology* (Social Sciences), Vol. 46(6):338–344.

Rako, S. 1996. *The Hormone of Desire: The Truth About Sexuality, Menopause, and Testosterone.* New York: Harmony Books.

Sarrel, L. J. and P. M. Sarrel. 1984. *Sexual Turning Points—The Seven Stages of Adult Sexuality.* New York: McMillan.

Starr, B. and M. Weiner. 1981. *The Starr-Weiner Report on Sex and Sexuality in the Mature Years.* New York: Stein & Day.

Sherwin, B. B., M. M. Gelfand, and W. Brender. 1985. "Androgen Enhances Sexual Motivation in Females: A Prospective Crossover Study of Sex Steroid Administration in the Surgical Menopause." *Psychosomatic Medicine,* 47(4):339–351.

Stoppard, M. 1994. *Menopause.* London: Dorling Kindersley.

Weed, S. S. 1992. *The Menopausal Years.* New York: Ash Tree Publishing.

CHAPTER SIX

Beginning Treatment for
Sexual Disorders

*We may have the luxury of being at the top of the food chain, but our
adrenaline still rushes when we encounter real or imaginary predators ... we
still ache fiercely with love, lust, loyalty, and passion. And we still perceive the
world, in all its gushing beauty and terror, right in our pulses.*

—Diane Ackerman,
Natural History of the Senses

An essential element of sexual pleasure is to be aware of the stream of positive
thoughts and feelings which accompany your bodily sensations from moment to moment. It is essential to be in touch with your body in a relaxed and deeply comfortable
way because it is through your body that you experience everything in your life. All
of your experiences, whether emotional, physical, or mental, are perceived through
your senses, and your body responds accordingly.

People are most alive and joyous when they are fully present in the moment
and aware of their bodily sensations experiencing the variety and richness of their
environment. Yet not all of these sensory experiences provide pleasure. There are
many painful sensory perceptions, such as noxious odors, annoying sounds, or physical pains. When people face unpleasant stimulation, the natural reaction is to instinc-
tively avoid the negative experience, either by actually removing themselves or by
shutting off their awareness. When a woman perceives a sexual situation as dangerous
her body responds with a change in behavior—the fight-or-flight response. In sexual
dysfunction this may become an automatic response regardless of whether or not
there is real danger. One woman might respond by avoiding sex. Another woman
might respond by shutting down most of the sensory awareness of her body. By
doing so, her body image, or body map, would become unclear and obscured.

This chapter will explain a series of exercises you can do at home to learn about
your body and your sexuality. They are designed to teach you to relax and focus on
the experience of energy flowing through your body. As you achieve a state of relaxed
attention, you will be more open to learning about your body.

The Relaxation Response

Your nervous system is programmed for survival and enables you to carry out a number of life-sustaining functions such as eating, sleeping, and participating in sexual activity without having to think about what you're doing. As long as the situation seems safe, the nervous system manages minor changes as necessary and it is possible to feel a sense of relaxed awareness. Consider how enjoyable a meal, nap, or sex can be when you are feeling relaxed.

When a woman experiences pain or the threat of pain, or becomes afraid or anxious, her body reacts with the fight-or-flight response by preparing for physical defense or escape. When she perceives a sexual stimulus as safe, and she is willing and interested in sexual pleasure, her body relaxes enough to become sexually aroused. Sexual impulses activate physical processes that allow her body to be relaxed and responsive to touch, leading to the buildup of sexual excitement and eventually orgasm.

The challenge in fully enjoying sexuality is to provide a setting so that the body can relax and be receptive to sexual stimulation and pleasure. Understanding and using readily available relaxation techniques can be extremely helpful. Herbert Benson's (1975, 1984) conception of the relaxation response has been useful in understanding the essential elements needed to achieve a sense of relaxation. After studying many of the world's religious meditations and mystical practices, Benson distilled the necessary elements for a sense of deep relaxation into the following practices:

- Practicing in a quiet environment, free of external distraction

- Consciously relaxing the body's muscles

- Focusing for ten to twenty minutes on a mental device such as a word, prayer, mantra, sound, or object

- Assuming a passive attitude toward intrusive thoughts

Benson also recommended combining these practices with a deeply held personal philosophical or religious belief system. If you practice meditation, yoga, spiritual prayer, or any similar activity, you can use it to achieve the necessary relaxation for this chapter.

A Place of Your Own

The first step towards achieving relaxation skills is to create a space for yourself. Because many women are accustomed to thinking of the needs of others before thinking of themselves, this idea may feel unusual, awkward, or selfish. However, if you allow yourself the same compassion you give to others, you can provide yourself with this private space. As with all of the relaxation exercises, resistance to doing the sexual tasks may mask itself in a wide array of thoughts, ideas, and feelings about why you can't change. Be sure to note these in your journal since they represent your feelings at this stage. Your current task is to learn how to relax.

Most people want their sexual activity to be private. In order to fully relax and concentrate, it is important to make sure that no one will come into the room. If you intend to practice relaxation in your bedroom, you may want to get a lock for your door. Sometimes women worry that they should be available to others at a moment's notice and feel anxious at the idea of taking time for themselves. However, if family members or roommates need you, they can easily wait for you to get up and open the door. If you feel resistant to this idea, ask yourself how much of your discomfort comes from the inner belief that you should not be doing anything sexual. The relaxation exercises are not meant to be secretive, just private. You are not hiding anything; you are giving yourself some important and well-deserved solitude.

Awareness of noises from outside the room, or concerns about making sounds that other people will hear, may break your concentration. A variety of solutions are available. Some women turn on a radio, a fan, an air conditioner, or other appliance, which creates white noise and blocks the frequencies of sounds that make them aware of others. Actual white noise machines can be purchased from catalogs or specialty stores. Interruptions such as the telephone or the doorbell need to be addressed before they interfere. Allow yourself this privacy where the world does not intrude: ignore the doorbell, unplug the telephone or turn off the ringer, and set up an answering machine in another room. If you have children, a partner, or roommates, make arrangements with them ahead of time to guarantee a time and place for yourself.

Another type of privacy you will need is the sense that no one is monitoring you. You may want to temporarily move family photographs out of view if you have trouble with this symbolic presence of family in the bedroom. The space you create for yourself should be attractive and pleasant to the senses. You may want to have extra pillows, plants, flowers, burning candles or incense, and/or soft blankets. Choose pleasurable, comfortable things that help you feel safe, cozy, and relaxed. Some women like to practice relaxation while lying in a patch of sunlight, in a tub full of warm water, or in soft light or candlelight.

✒ Case 6.1—Denise

Denise decided that she was ready to be orgasmic. She needed time alone to learn about her sexual responses through masturbation. She lived in a small two-bedroom apartment with a roommate and two cats. There was little room for privacy: the bedrooms and bathroom were small, the floors creaked, and large windows faced another apartment building. However, in her room Denise did have a bay window with a built-in bench. She cleaned off the long bench and put a soft futon on it. She covered the window with a translucent shade that let in some filtered sunlight but did not allow anyone to see in. She covered the area with large soft pillows and placed some oriental screens around it to block sound and increase privacy. She had a small floral-patterned box nearby with her favorite poetry books, journal, and scented floral sachets. To complete her private space, she placed small stereo speakers in the area to play soothing music.

A Time for Yourself

Finding time for yourself can be a real problem in this busy world. If you are going to make the changes you want, however, you will need to plan time for your exercises. Look at your daily schedule and see how you can fit in the time you need. You may need to rearrange tasks or rethink how to prioritize your time. You may wish to talk to the people with whom you live to explain that you need some time alone and work out a mutually agreeable plan. At the end of this chapter you will make out an overall plan for your exercises; this will give you a pretty good idea of exactly how much time you'll need.

Some people find it helpful to make a time chart as a way of dividing up the day. You can make one for weekdays and a second for weekends. Draw a chart on a sheet of paper or on the computer, with increments for your waking hours. Schedule the day by including all of your major activities: working, eating (including food preparation and cleanup), traveling, exercising, personal grooming, doing chores, spending time with friends and family, watching TV, and running errands. Also have a miscellaneous space for activities you can't fit in elsewhere. After you have split up the chart into segments, decide how you will fit in time for yourself. Find a regular time for your relaxation exercises. Many women choose the early morning before beginning the day's activities, the late afternoon after work, or right before bed. The purpose of this chart is not to commit yourself absolutely to a regimented schedule, but to get a general idea of when and for how long you can allot yourself some special time.

Breathing Exercises

Most of the time you are not aware of your breathing, but breathing regulates both your mind and body. When you are anxious, fearful, or tense, the sympathetic nervous system is engaged and you breathe in quick, shallow breaths. In that state, you are aroused for fight or flight. But when you are relaxed, the parasympathetic nervous system is engaged and you breathe in deep, full breaths into your abdomen. This is the relaxed state needed for making love. Many meditation practices utilize deep breathing exercises as a method of relaxation and focused attention. When you deliberately change from shallow to deep breathing, you can engage the sense of calm attention needed for the exercises in this book. Deep abdominal breathing will help decrease muscle tension and create a sense of quiet concentration. The body relaxes and the mind becomes clear and peaceful. Conscious breathing helps you focus inward on your immediate experience and causes distracting thoughts to disappear.

These exercises are designed to help you relax and focus on the experience of staying in the moment. You will need to allow twenty to thirty minutes to relax your muscles, clear your mind, and focus your attention on your body. You may be surprised by how relaxed and open you feel. Before beginning, secure your private place (e.g., a bed or sofa or the floor), and arrange enough pillows to support your body so that you are not straining any muscles. Sometimes it is helpful to put a small pillow or rolled-up towel under your head, knees, or ankles. Practice each technique several times after you review how its done.

EXERCISE 6.1—ABDOMINAL BREATHING

Abdominal breathing is an essential component in learning to relax and it differs from diaphragmatic breathing in several ways. The diaphragm is a dome-shaped muscle separating the chest cavity (above) and abdomen (below). In diaphragmatic breathing, the diaphragm contracts downward and creates a vacuum in the chest cavity, into which your lungs expand to bring in needed oxygen. You can assume conscious control over it, but you don't need to—it works all by itself. When you are nervous, tense, or in a rush, your diaphragm moves more rapidly but takes in shallower breaths. You can observe this in yourself or someone else under tension—the upper chest rises and falls prominently with each breath. When someone is severely anxious or is having a panic attack, this pattern of breathing can lead to shortness of breath or hyperventilation, a feeling of faintness, dizziness, and even more anxiety. How do you correct it? The best way to counter this reaction is with abdominal breathing. Abdominal breathing is an active, conscious activity. It expands your lung capacity, and enhances oxygen–carbon dioxide exchange and tissue oxygenation.

Begin by lying in a comfortable position on your back with your arms at your sides and your legs slightly apart. Close your eyes and gradually slow your breathing with each breath. Breathe in through your nose slowly and fully, hold the breath briefly, and then breathe out through your mouth with a sigh. Put one hand on your abdomen and notice the movement as you breathe. Your hand will feel the rise of your abdomen as your lungs fill with air. As you breathe out, your hand will feel your abdomen fall. Imagine you are filling your stomach up with air. Breathe in a normal fashion but allow a pause after you inhale and before you exhale. Wait briefly after you exhale before you begin the next breath. Inhale and exhale at a rate that feels comfortable to you. Practice doing a set of ten deep abdominal breaths and gradually add more time to this exercise until you spend five to ten minutes. Your body will gradually relax. It may take a little practice, but you will soon have a reliable relaxation technique at your disposal.

EXERCISE 6.2—SYNCHRONOUS BREATHING

Synchronous breathing occurs when you match your breathing to your heart rate. First, find your pulse on your wrist, chest, or the carotid artery of your neck (just below the outer edge of your lower jaw) and rest two fingers there as you inhale slowly one time at your own comfortable rate. The number of pulses you count is called your breathing number. It may change slightly from time to time, but generally you will find an average number. Now establish a rhythm of synchronous breathing by inhaling to the count of your number, holding the breath for one-half of your number, and exhaling for the count of your number. Then wait for one-half of your number before inhaling again. For instance, Talia counted six pulses on a comfortable exhale, so she exhaled for six pulses, held her breath for three pulses, inhaled for six pulses and held for three pulses. Continue to breathe in this way for three minutes or until you feel your heart and breath are in harmony. Try not to rush your breathing if your heart rate quickens. Practice this for five minutes.

EXERCISE 6.3—PELVIC BREATHING

The muscles and organs in the pelvis are intimately involved in sexual activity. Breathing exercises that utilize pelvic rocking help to release muscle tension and stimulate orgasm. The purpose of this exercise is to enlist the energy in the pelvis to wake up your sexual system and give you a sense of control over your body.

Lie on your back on your bed or the floor and place a pillow under your head, knees, and/or ankles in order to make yourself as comfortable as possible. Close your eyes and gradually slow your breathing to a comfortable rhythm. As you inhale, arch your back slightly, press your buttocks to the floor, and fill your abdomen with air. As you exhale, let your pelvis slowly tilt up, and imagine that the front of your pelvis and your clitoris is being drawn up to the ceiling as if by a powerful magnet. Check to be sure that when you inhale you tuck your buttocks back under the arch of your back, and when you exhale you tilt your pelvis forward and up. Now gently begin to rock back and forth, matching your breathing to your pelvic movements. Experiment with moving a little faster while you speed up your breathing. Add a sighing sound if you wish. Slow down after a minute or two and then stop. You may feel the sensation of your genitals tingling, giving you a sense of vitality and exhilaration.

EXERCISE 6.4—GENITAL FOCUSED BREATHING

If you not aware of your genital sensations, this exercise will help you to connect breathing and relaxing with genital pleasure. Over many centuries, practitioners of Eastern meditations developed similar exercises to enhance awareness of sexual pleasure and to provide a relaxed attention to the genitals. The technique is simple. Breathe in through your nose and out through your mouth. As you breathe out, imagine yourself breathing out through a wide tube in your vagina. Allow yourself to notice the genital sensations you are experiencing. If you pay close attention, you will notice a myriad of changing sensations of which you are normally unaware. Do ten breaths in this way.

EXERCISE 6.5—SPOON BREATHING (WITH PARTNER)

Spoon breathing is an exercise designed to help you and a partner feel physically intimate and relaxed. It allows you to take turns being a leader and follower. In this way you can sense each other's differing body rhythms and have the opportunity to breath in unison.

Lie close together on your sides like spoons nestled together, facing the same direction. Breathe at your own pace and begin to relax. When you have achieved at least ten deep, relaxing breaths, let the person in back adjust his or her breathing to the rhythm of the person in front. Try to breath in synchrony with your partner for five to ten minutes. Then turn over and switch roles. Don't talk during the exercise; after you have both had a turn as a leader and a follower, take the opportunity to talk about how you each felt. See figure 6.1 for an example of this exercise.

EXERCISE 6.6—FOCUSING ATTENTION

During sexual activity, many women have trouble focusing on themselves and their sexual sensations. Distracting thoughts or stimuli flood into their awareness. You can increase your ability to focus attention through the use of self-hypnosis, during which all of your concentration is reduced to a small field of perception. You could compare this to looking at a picture though a rolled-up tube—you only see a small circle of color or shape. In this exercise, you will practice focusing your attention on your bodily sensations.

Allow five minutes for this exercise. Assume a relaxed posture and close your eyes. Slow your breathing to your own comfortable rate. In your mind, scan your body, starting at the top of your head. Gradually move your attention downward, noticing and focusing on the different sensations in each part of your body. Quietly name each part that you focus on: top of head, forehead, eyes, nose, cheeks, lips, chin, back of head, ears, etc., until you finish at your toes. You may notice many sensations; the warmth of sun on your head, the texture of your clothes, the way your body is positioned as you lie still. When you finish, rest and think about the things you noticed.

Then, focus your visual attention on an object, such as a burning candle or a picture of flowers. Notice everything about it in a state of relaxed attention. Absorb all of the visual details of the object: shape, color, texture, and shading. Slow your breathing to a comfortable pace as you do this and sink into a relaxed reverie as

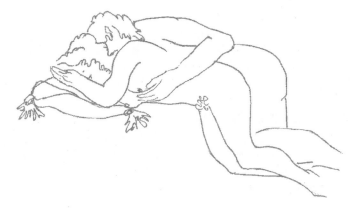

Figure 6.1. Spoon Breathing

you observe the object with total attention. When you are finished, rest and think about what you noticed. If you find this exercise particularly interesting and relaxing, you might want to read further on meditation and self-hypnosis. We have listed several references at the end of this chapter and in the appendix.

Progressive Muscle Relaxation

Progressive muscle relaxation was developed to help people deal with a variety of physical complaints that result from chronic stress. Because anxiety is often associated with uncomfortable muscle tension throughout the body, it is possible to reduce anxiety by voluntarily tightening and then relaxing your muscles. Progressive relaxation helps you gain a sense of control over your muscles by comparing them in both tense and relaxed states. This sense of muscle control reinforces your ability to relax them. Many people report that progressive relaxation leads to an overall decrease in stress and anxiety and a lasting increase in both a sense of well-being and self-esteem. You can purchase audiotapes of progressive relaxation or you can make your own tape by reading the script from this book or one you've written into a tape recorder. You may prefer instead to listen to soft, soothing music or environmental sounds while you practice this exercise. We have listed several resources for relaxation tapes in the appendix.

Exercise 6.7—Progressive Muscle Relaxation

Follow these steps as you practice the progressive relaxation exercise:

1. Settle yourself in your private space and lie on your back in a comfortable position.

2. Breathe in slowly and deeply.

3. Slowly tense a group of muscles (arm, leg, stomach, forehead, etc.).

4. Hold the contraction for a count of ten seconds.

5. Breathe out slowly.

6. Quickly release the muscles all at once.

7. Rest for a count of ten seconds.

Focus your attention on each group of muscles you are using and allow the rest of your body to relax. As you tighten and relax each muscle group, notice how you feel after the muscles are released and relaxation takes place. The following script will illustrate this in more detail.

Progressive Relaxation Script

(Optional script for tape recording. Read slowly.) *Gradually bring your attention to your body as you close your eyes. Allow yourself to sink into the bed, releasing any strain to your muscles. Breathe in through your nose and out through your mouth as you allow your breathing to deepen for several long and relaxed breaths.*

Starting at your head, breathe in and tighten the muscles of your scalp, your forehead, your eyes and ears ... hold tightly ... counting to ten ... and breathe out and now ... relax. Relax those muscles and notice them. Breathing in, tighten the muscles in your cheeks, and jaw, tighten your tongue, and the muscles in the back of your head ... tight ... and now breathe out and relax. Let those muscles go. Tighten your neck muscles, in the back and in the front, pull your head back and raise your jaw ... tight ... tight ... tight ... and relax. Now you can feel your head and neck muscles are very relaxed.

Focus on your shoulder muscles and raise your shoulders as high as you can ... hold tight ... hold ... hold and release the tension. Drop your shoulders and let the tension go. Pull your shoulders forward to stretch your upper back ... pull ... pull ... hold. And relax. Push your shoulders back and bring your shoulder blades in ... pull ... pull and tighten. Now release and breathe. Breathe in a long relaxing breath and let the tension go. Notice that your shoulders feel loose and relaxed.

Now focus on the muscles in your upper arms now and straighten out your arms, pull the muscles of your upper arms as tight as you can, hold ... hold ... hold and tighten your arms, letting the tension go as you breathe out. Tighten the muscles in your lower arms, holding them tight. Now clench your fists and hold them as tight as you can ... tighten ... tighten .. . tighten. And let them go. Let the tension go. Lie still and feel your arms, limp and relaxed.

Notice the tension in your chest muscles now. As you breathe in, hold that tension, hold ... hold ... hold ... and let the tension go as you exhale. Again, tighten the muscles at your chest and hold them tight, tight, tight. And relax. Relax and enjoy the sensation of open, expanded muscles in your chest.

Bring your attention to your stomach muscles and pull in your muscles as you breathe in, hold the tension for ten seconds, and let the tension go. Again, focus on your abdomen and tighten your abdominal muscles ... pull ... pull ... pull ... and release. Arch your back and hold ... keep the muscles tight, tighter. And let go, let the tension flow away.

Now tighten your buttocks ... feel the tension ... feel it ... feel it. And let it go. As you let go, notice how your muscles are relaxed and easy.

Now pull in the muscles of your pelvic floor, tighten the PC muscles, tighten the lower abdomen and hold ... hold ... hold ... hold ... and let go. Breathe as you appreciate your body feeling more and more relaxed and free of tension.

Now concentrate on the muscles of your thighs ... tighten ... tighten ... feel those muscles pull as you tighten. And release. Again, tighten your thighs ... pull ... pull, and let go. Let the tension go. Focus on your knees and calf muscles and pull them tight ... tight ... tighter ... and release. Tighten the muscles in your feet. Pull them tight, breathe into your feet ... pull your arches ... pull your ankles ... pull up on your toes ... tight ... tight ... and let go.

Now tighten all the muscles in your entire body simultaneously as you breathe in, hold yourself tight ... tight ... tight ... and let your body go limp, relaxed and free of tension. Notice if you feel any residual tension and if so, tighten yourself all over one more time ...

tighten . . . and relax. You feel limp and easy. Your body is completely relaxed. Lie still and feel the sense of warm relaxation flow through your body. Enjoy the sense of relaxation as you rest easy and still.

Kegel Exercises

Kegel exercises were developed by Dr. Arnold Kegel as a way for his patients to increase muscle tone and gain control over the PC muscle. The PC muscle is shaped like a double figure eight and encircles the opening to the vagina, urethra, and anus. Women who practice exercising this muscle increase their awareness and sense of control over their genital area and also increase sexual pleasure both for themselves and their partner. Kegel exercises are frequently prescribed in preparation for childbirth and as a means of correcting or preventing urinary incontinence. They are also used to help a woman with vaginismus gain a sense of control over her condition.

EXERCISE 6.8—IDENTIFY YOUR PC MUSCLE

Sit on the toilet and spread your legs apart. See if you can stop and start the flow of urine without moving your legs. The PC muscle helps to control the flow of urine; thus, if you are able to stop and start the flow, you are in control of your PC muscle. Sometimes women need to try this more than once to prove to themselves that they are in control of the muscle. If you need several times to reassure yourself, keep trying.

EXERCISE 6.9—KEGEL EXERCISES

Like all exercises, it can take a while to build strength and confidence in your ability. You can do these exercises anywhere during the day. Sometimes it helps to make it a habit and pair it with other routine activities such as brushing your teeth, showering, or starting your car. Do a set of ten contractions and relaxations three times a day. In the beginning you may feel some soreness in your abdominal muscles while you are learning to isolate your PC muscle. Or, you may notice that you have difficulty contracting the PC muscle during the slow Kegels, or that you can't do fast Kegels very quickly or easily. Once you isolate the PC muscle, you should have no trouble.

Slow Kegels

Tighten the PC muscle for a count of three, and then relax it completely. Contract again for the count of three and relax. Do a set of ten slow contractions and relaxations, three times a day.

Fast Kegels

Squeeze and relax the PC muscle as rapidly as you can, five times in a row. Do three sets of fast Kegels a day.

Pull In/Push Out

Lie on your back and pull up your entire pelvic floor, the muscles, tendons, and tissues which support the genitals, as though you were trying to suck water up into your vagina. Then push out and bear down as if you were trying to push the imaginary water out. This exercise uses stomach and abdominal muscles as well as the PC muscle. It can give you confidence in your ability to control your genital and pelvic muscles. Do a set of three each day.

Putting It All Together

Now that you have a basic understanding of your body's relaxation response and have studied several relaxation techniques, it's time to put it all together. First, try to address any possible resistance. Are you telling yourself any of the following?

- *I can't relax.*
- *This won't work.*
- *My mind won't focus.*
- *It just makes me tired.*
- *I don't have time.*
- *Is there a faster way?*

- *I'm too tense.*
- *I feel silly doing this.*
- *My body can't do this.*
- *How will this cure my problem?*
- *This is stupid.*

If you are new to relaxation techniques, it is perfectly normal (and expected) to have many of these thoughts. Don't worry—they won't prevent your progress. Keep in mind several things:

- The relaxation response is built into your body. Once you master the exercises described above, you will be able to reach a state of expansive relaxation.
- These exercises won't in themselves cure your sexual problem but will allow you to achieve a state of relaxation that will help alleviate subjective anxiety, enhance genital sensation, and gain control over your vaginal muscles.
- You do have control over your own time and space—you just have to make these exercises a priority.
- Feel too tense? Can't focus your mind? Perfect! All the more relaxed you'll feel when the natural relaxation response kicks in from the exercises.
- Feeling tired often means that the exercises are working. Don't fight it—just try to complete each exercise.

If you are feeling extreme anxiety or panic during an exercise, stop and wait until this feeling subsides. There is no reason why your body won't be able to relax at some point during the day. If you are taking medications to treat anxiety or panic, these exercises will only enhance their effect. If you are so tense that you can't even imagine beginning these exercises, you should consider consulting with a psychotherapist.

Here is a suggested routine for the exercises listed in this chapter:

9:00 P.M.   Inform the household that you will be busy for thirty to forty minutes. Turn off the phone or ask someone else to answer it. Retire to your place, and get comfortable. Put on soothing music, light candles, etc.

9:05 P.M.   Choose a breathing technique (e.g., abdominal breathing) and begin. Continue for five to ten minutes, perhaps using a second technique (e.g., genital focus breathing) for part of the time.

9:15 P.M.   Start progressive muscle relaxation with a taped script or music, and continue with relaxed breathing. Continue for ten minutes.

9:25 P.M.   When relaxed, practice Kegel exercises for five minutes. Vary the type you try.

9:30 P.M.   Relaxation exercise is complete. Consider writing in your journal for fifteen to thirty minutes. Or, repeat the exercises.

As you can see, you don't need more than thirty minutes for the exercises. We recommend that you try to do them three times a week. If you want to spend more time doing them, great! As long as you are able to feel relaxed for a sustained period of time during the exercises, you are probably spending adequate time. If you are interrupted during them, don't let that be a source of stress—just take a break to address the interruption and then resume. Once you gain confidence in yourself and get good at the exercises, you can do them anywhere you go and in almost any situation. Remember that Kegel exercises don't have to be limited to these sessions; They can be worked on throughout the day, at any time and in any situation.

References

Ackerman, D. 1990. *A Natural History of the Senses*. New York: Vintage Books.

Anand, M. 1989. *The Art of Sexual Ecstasy: The Path of Sacred Sexuality for Western Lovers*. New York: Jeremy P. Tarcher/Perigee.

Benson, H. 1975. *The Relaxation Response*. New York: Avon.

Benson, H. 1984. *Beyond the Relaxation Response*. New York: Berkley Books.

Bourne, E. J. 1995. *The Anxiety and Phobia Workbook, 2nd Edition*. Oakland, Calif.: New Harbinger Publications, Inc.

Heiman, J., J. LoPiccolo, and L. LoPiccolo. 1988. *Becoming Orgasmic: A Sexual and Personal Growth Program for Women*. New York: Prentice Hall Press.

Rossi, E. L. and D. B. Cheek. 1988. *Mind-Body Therapy: Methods of Ideodynamic Healing in Hypnosis*. New York: W. W. Norton.

Stewart, F., F. Guest, G. Stewart, and R. Hatcher. 1987. *Understanding Your Body: Every Woman's Guide to Gynecology and Health*. New York: Bantam.

Welwood, J., Ed. 1992. *Ordinary Magic: Everyday Life as a Spiritual Path*. Boston, Mass.: Shambhala.

Zinn, J. K. 1994. *Wherever You Go, There You Are*. New York: Hyperion.

CHAPTER SEVEN

Sensate Focus Exercises

In this chapter, we will build upon the relaxation techniques learned in the previous chapter so that you can involve your partner in several important exercises. *Sensate focus* means to focus your attention on the sensations you experience during sensual or sexual activity. Sensate focus exercises are designed to gradually teach a series of erotic, stimulating, and pleasurable experiences in touch during sexual activity. They were first developed in the 1960s by Masters and Johnson as part of a treatment program for couples experiencing sexual problems. Since then, many clinicians have elaborated on the original exercises. With sensate focus, the couple practices a series of exercises in the privacy of their home consisting of physical touching and caressing with gradually increasing levels of sexual arousal. These exercises are deceptively simple and straightforward, but they often evoke strong emotional responses from one or both partners. The couple discusses their reactions to the exercises with their therapist in order to tease apart the different components of sexuality, as well as to identify sexual strengths and difficulties. As the couple continues to do sensate focus exercises, the sexual problem is further illuminated, including its origins relative to each partner, the couple's behaviors that maintain it, and the resources required to fix it.

One purpose of sensate focus is to decrease, or eliminate, the anxiety that results from having to perform sexually. A therapist will sometimes recommend a ban on sexual intercourse and orgasm for a short while to remove the pressure to perform. In this way, sensual pleasure becomes the focus of sexual activity and fear of failure is removed.

Why is this ban so important? With goal-directed sex, everything you do is part of the plan to reach the end of the sexual experience with simultaneous orgasm during intercourse. This unrealistic expectation creates pressure and anxiety for both partners. Without performance goals, partners can focus on the emotional and sensual experience.

It is often helpful to use the relaxation techniques described in chapter 6 before attempting the sensate focus exercises. Deep muscle relaxation and deep breathing will help you achieve a state of relaxed but energized openness to these sensual experiences.

Sometimes relaxation techniques are also helpful if you become anxious during an exercise. If this should happen, you can stop and take several relaxing breaths during which you focus on the part of your body where you notice tension, pain, or unpleasant sensations. Imagine sending your breath to the place where you hold the unpleasant sensations; often this will relax you enough to continue with the sensate focus.

Sensate focus does not have to involve a total ban on sexual activity, but should initially be kept separate from regular lovemaking. You will find that the relaxation and serene pleasure of sensate focus can eventually be integrated with regular sexual activity as anxiety and fear of failure are removed.

A second purpose of sensate focus is for partners to learn how to touch each other in pleasurable, erotic ways. The most common complaint that women have about making love is that their partners do not spend enough time with foreplay. In one study, over seven hundred women ranked lack of adequate foreplay as a major factor in their difficulty reaching orgasm (Bechtel et al. 1993). As couples progress with sensate focus, they also learn how to both give and receive sensual pleasure. This mutuality is important for couples who normally approach sex with rigid roles that prescribe which partner does what to whom. It also helps restore balance to any power struggles during sex, making it easier for both partners to share sensual touches on equal footing.

Despite the initial appeal of sensate focus exercises to most couples, at some point one or both partners may resist carrying them out or cooperating with each other. Discussion of this resistance often reveals previously unrecognized emotions about sex, one's self, and one's partner. A sex therapist takes note of sensory numbing, fleeting thoughts and feelings, distracting images, body sensations, and negative feelings and attitudes that occur during sensate focus. If there is a clear pattern to the way in which one partner reports their reactions or resists sensate focus, a characteristic defense mechanism may be revealed. For example, one partner may always blame the other for lack of progress, when in reality they are defending themselves against performance anxiety or self-blame by projecting it onto the partner. As the sensate focus exercises continue, the origins, precipitating factors, and perpetuating factors of the sexual dysfunction become more clear. The expertise of the sex therapist lies in their ability to understand the issues that arise during sensate focus, facilitate discussion about these issues, and then modulate the exercises to match the couple's need to integrate new learning.

There are some people who are able to use these steps toward the goal of sexual pleasure without the help of a therapist. If you think that you fall into this category, this chapter will explain the exercises to you in detail. However, many people need the help of an objective person to understand the roadblocks standing in the way of progress. A sex therapist will help to maximize the benefit of these exercises—by selecting an approach, adding or subtracting elements, and adjusting the pace and structure of learning to fit each individual person. This process is illustrated in the following case:

Case 7.1—Diana and Henry

Diana and Henry went to sex therapy because Diana was not able to have an orgasm. As the couple talked with their therapist, it became evident that Diana did not know very much about her body or what she liked or didn't like in sex. She came into the session saying that she "liked everything," but didn't understand why she wasn't able to have an orgasm. During lovemaking, Diana usually became nervous, and so she hurried Henry toward his orgasm to end their sexual experience. The couple began the sensate focus exercises, starting with nonsexual touching. Diana enjoyed this step. But when the next exercise included genital touching, Diana discovered to her surprise that she blocked herself from feeling anything. When she thought about this she realized she had been taught that "sex is for men," and so she had focused on being a good lover for Henry. She pushed Henry away when his touch was arousing, because she believed that if women allowed themselves to be carried away sexually, they would end up abandoned by men. Over the course of several weeks, with the encouragement of her therapist, Diana learned to stay with her feelings and sensations, slow down, and let Henry give her pleasure. She realized that she had a right to know her own body, and during sensate focus she began to actively explore what she really liked or didn't like.

As the assignments increased the intensity of sexual feeling, Henry began to realize that he had felt good being the "sex expert" and was now worried that he knew very little about how to touch Diana as she began to understand more about her sexuality. He realized that he was drawn to Diana as a partner because she knew so little about sex, which meant that his own lack of knowledge would not be as evident. At this stage Henry began to explore his own sexuality, rather than thinking of Diana as the one with the problem. The couple learned to talk more openly about their sexuality, and began to show each other how they liked to be touched. Lovemaking became a pleasure rather than a task. The major lesson for both Diana and Henry came as they learned to stay in the stream of their experience during the time they spent together. It was hard to let go of worries and concerns, guilt and shame, and negative self-evaluation. It took several months to give up their distracting nonsexual thoughts during lovemaking as they learned to live in the sexual moment together. After several months of therapy, Diana became more in tune with her body and began to share with Henry what kinds of stimulation were most pleasing to her. They learned that Diana could have an orgasm in many ways, but not with intercourse. After several difficult sessions they both were able to accept that her sexuality was satisfying to her and that since she was orgasmic that was what really mattered. Henry also came to terms with his own fear of inadequacy and realized that it was not his responsibility to "perform" for Diana, but rather their mutual responsibility to openly communicate with each other about their desires. Together, they were able to transform their lovemaking into a leisurely and explorative process that allowed both of them to give and receive pleasure.

The case of Diana and Henry illustrates another key purpose to sensate focus: mutual involvement with your partner. Although the resolution of sexual fear and pain involves a lot of individual work, the key to success is involving your partner in a helpful, relaxing, and productive way. Many couples, however, come into therapy with long-standing conflicts, both sexual and nonsexual. Sensate focus provides a neutral arena that includes relaxed, goal-free interactions, and then provides a forum to discuss any difficulties.

Charting Your Progress

Hopefully, you have made a good start on a personal journal. We would now like to suggest the addition of a separate notebook or journal for you and your partner to keep track of progress. Or you can use the very simple and structured sensate focus checklist that follows. As you work through the sensate focus exercises with your partner, check off each one. Make notes about each exercise. The goal of your checklist or notebook is to help organize your journey together, keep track of where you going, and have a tangible record of accomplishments and challenges to serve as reminders along the way.

Sensate Focus Checklist

As you progress through the sensate focus exercises, check off each one in the following list and write about your reactions to it.

Status   *Exercise (place a ✓ under status if completed)*

_____   **7.1—Who Initiates Sex? Who Follows?**

Comments: _____

_____

_____

_____

_____   What is your plan for sensate focus? Do you have a tentative schedule?

_____

_____

_____

_____   **7.2—Sensate Focus I**

Comments: _____

_____

_____

_____

_____   **7.3—Your Responses to Sensate Focus I**

Comments: _____

_____

_____

_____

_____   **7.4—Facing Resistance**

Comments: _____

_____

_____

_____

_____   **7.5—Journal Writing**

_____   **7.6—Looking at Each Other's Genitals**

Comments: _____

_____

_____

Sensate Focus Checklist

_____ **7.7—Genital Touching and Exploration**

Comments: _____

_____

_____

_____

_____ **7.8—The Sexological Examination**

Comments: _____

_____

_____

_____

_____ **7.9—Genital Touching to Arouse**

Comments: _____

_____

_____

_____

_____ **7.10—Guiding**

Comments: _____

_____

_____

_____

_____ **7.11—Genital Stimulation to Orgasm**

Comments: _____

_____

_____

_____

_____ **7.12—The Quiet Vagina**

Comments: _____

_____

_____

_____

_____ **7.13—Non-Demand Thrusting**

Comments: _____

_____

_____

_____

The Sensate Focus Exercises

Sensate focus exercises involve both partners taking turns as *giver* and *receiver* as they gradually increase variety and intensity from nonsexual physical pleasure, to whole-body sensual pleasure, and then to genital pleasure and orgasm. Tasks of the giver and receiver differ in the following ways:

- The receiver's task is to stay in the present and experience the flow of sensations without expectations.

- The receiver is not obliged to respond except to let the giver know if something feels uncomfortable or painful.

- The giver's task is to pay attention to their own experience without trying to guess what the partner is feeling.

There is no goal, no performance demand, no rush, no demand for reassurance, and no requirements to do or not do any particular touch (aside from the basic instructions). There is no obligation that the partner should "return the favor," but rather a sense of living within the immediate experience.

Before you begin sensate focus exercises, you will have to talk about who initiates activity in general, who follows, who opposes, and/or who refuses to engage. All couples have a process, often out of their conscious awareness, by which they relate to each other both sexually and nonsexually. For instance, if one person always initiates social plans and the other always says no, that may occur sexually as well. There are many ways to learn about how your process works; first try the following exercise.

❧

EXERCISE 7.1—WHO INITIATES SEX? WHO FOLLOWS?

1. Who usually initiates sex—you or your partner? What percentage of the time do each of you initiate sexual activity? _____

_____

_____

2. Has your role changed over the course of the relationship? If so, how? _____

_____

_____

3. What factors affect your role and your partner's role both as initiator and as follower? _____

_____

_____

4. Role-play with your partner: Each of you take turns going through the motions of initiating sexual activity. What do you do? Do you ask for sex? Do you start with actions, such as a caress or a kiss? Is there no clear pattern?_____

_____

_____

5. Switch roles and try to imitate, in a respectful way, how you think your partner initiates sex. This gives both of you a chance to see what the experience is like for the other. What did you learn? _____

_____

_____

6. Demonstrate how you both would like the other to initiate sex. Then show each other how you would like to be turned down. This can avoid a sequence of hurt feelings and emotional withdrawal. _____

_____

_____

7. Practice how you would ask for affectionate touch only, with no sex to follow. How does this feel? _____

_____

_____

8. Take turns describing what you experience when you are the follower and when you are the initiator. _____

_____

_____

9. Write down how you feel about the following situations. Refer to the list of possible emotional reactions or use your own descriptions: _____

> *Sample emotions:* happy, elated, excited, apprehensive, nervous, fearful, upset, numb, sad, angry, confused, furious, horny, turned off, put off.

Initiating sex

You: _____

Your Partner: _____

Being asked for sex

You: _____

Your Partner: _____

Agreeing to sex

You: _____

Your Partner: _____

Refusing sex

You: _____

Your Partner: _____

Being turned down

You: _____

Your Partner: _____

It is very important to be clear when you are asking for physical affection only, as opposed to when you would welcome a sexual encounter. Often people mix up these two activities and cut themselves off from the pleasures of hugging, holding, kissing, and caressing because they worry it will lead to sex. Some couples have nonverbal signals, while others have a private language to make it clear. But for couples having trouble with sex, it is especially important to let your partner know what you do and don't want. In sex therapy, the therapist helps a couple work out the details of initiating and responding. Decisions are made about how often to do the exercises, who will start, and how to say "yes" or "no" to a partner's request. If a person has a low sex drive, this may be due partly to not noticing external cues that might increase desire. A partner with low desire may need to be willing to begin a sensate focus assignment even when they do not feel interested in sex. As these sensual exercises progress, interest usually grows.

Many couples often feel pressure to move quickly through these exercises, hoping for an instant cure to their problem. We caution against this attitude. In the beginning it is best to err on the side of being conservative, in order to enhance relaxation and de-emphasize sexual goals. Taking small steps is always more successful than attempting huge leaps and possibly failing. You will probably try to go too fast sometimes and then feel disappointed. If this happens, break down the exercise into smaller components. For example, if touching the whole body is too much, start with a neck or hand massage.

If you are starting off without guidance from a therapist, you should negotiate a contract with your partner, with respect to how you will initiate the sensate focus exercises, how often, when and where, and under what circumstances. It is critical to determine this before beginning and to allow some flexibility. Plans can temporarily go awry, but the important thing is that you do it at some point or another. Realistically, you should be able to find time at least once a week, preferably for an hour. If possible, three times a week is optimal. Weekends usually offer more flexible time schedules. Do not worry about spontaneity for these exercises: you may even find it is best to "schedule" an exercise like you would schedule any appointment. Consider the difficulties faced by John and Rachel, and how they overcame them.

Case 7.2—John and Rachel

John and Rachel both worked during the day and liked to exercise at the gym after work. They didn't get home until about 7 P.M., and after eating a quick dinner, usually felt too exhausted to do much more than relax in front of the TV. They began sex therapy because Rachel had admitted to John that she had lost interest in having sex. Her sexual desire had ebbed to the point that she usually refused John's requests for sex, only agreeing once or twice a month. When they began therapy, they quickly found that they didn't have any time or energy for sensate focus exercises. The sex therapist discussed their resistance to the exercises and pointed out that, in reality, they had plenty of time, but instead made other choices: working late, working out at the gym, and watching favorite TV shows. Also, their resistance reflected Rachel's resentment towards John for what she viewed as demands on her time for sex. Both John and Rachel had long-standing habits of throwing themselves into work instead of dealing with relationship issues. John usually displaced his anger with Rachel onto his co-workers, while Rachel turned her anger and frustration onto herself, always complaining about her "fat" body and going from one diet to the next.

At first the couple believed they could make the changes easily, but at their next appointment they had to admit that they had not allowed any time for the exercises until the night before therapy. As they talked about their pattern of putting off awkward assignments, they agreed to leave work early and skip working out one day a week to meet at home and spend an hour doing a sensate focus exercise. Rachel spent another hour at home alone one day a week working on some body image exercises. They also agreed to ask each other whether they were willing to do a sensate focus exercise one other night a week after dinner. Sometimes they did the exercises with the TV on, since they both always felt relaxed watching their favorite sitcom. This idea worked initially, but as they began to enjoy the exercise more and more they turned off the TV. Rachel had free reign to say "no" to any exercise, and this freedom eased the resentment she felt towards John. Their agreement allowed them to find two to three hours a week for exercises that resulted in minimal conflict and good discussions, which facilitated their progress. As the weeks of therapy progressed they began to see that if either of them got "too busy and forgot" they needed to pay attention to their resistance and why it was there. As they understood what caused them to procrastinate it became easier to talk it over and move on.

🐾 Case 7.3—Todd and Marsha

Todd and Marsha had been married for three years and had a baby boy named Zack who was eight months old. Marsha stayed home with Zack all day, and Todd usually got home around 6 P.M., when Marsha would prepare dinner. One night they had a particularly unpleasant fight about sex, one of many over the past few months when Todd initiated sex and Marsha said no. They both saw that Marsha had lost her desire to have sex and avoided Todd by going to bed before he did. They agreed they needed some professional help and got a referral for a sex therapist. At their first appointment, Todd spoke about how lonely he felt and how much he missed the warm sexuality they had enjoyed before the baby was born. Marsha talked about how she felt both exhausted and "touched out" by the skin contact she had all day long caring for a baby, and how "worn out" she felt from getting up to nurse the baby at night. Neither had realized what the other was experiencing.

Finding time for sensate focus exercises was a major problem, especially because Marsha was so tired. At first Todd defended his need for rest when he got home from a hard day at work, but as they talked he realized that if he wanted a change in their sexuality he would have to pitch in and make some changes too.

Two days a week Marsha would have a baby-sitter for part of the day so that she could spend some time away from Zack and feel more refreshed at the end of the day. Todd would make dinner while she tended to Zack and then he would put Zack to bed after dinner. They would then spend an hour on sensate focus. In addition, they would leave Zack with his grandparents twice a month on Saturday evenings, while they had a "date" for dinner and sensate focus. Having a set schedule prevented arguments, increased time they spent alone together, and allowed them to make good progress with their exercises. They also had the delight of enjoying each other's company and enjoying the warm sensuality they had lost. As they continued with therapy they faced the other underlying issues that had surfaced when Zack was born; but with their sexuality back on an even keel they were able to work through their issues.

Sensate Focus I—Nonsexual Touching Exercises

The first level of sensate focus is an experience of nonsexual touching and an emotional and physical experience of mutual trust. Sensate focus I is designed to provide a relaxing time for you and your partner with no pressure to perform. This exercise does not include sexual touching or intercourse. As with any intimate experience, you need time to make the transition into close connection. Before you begin, select a comfortable, warm, quiet, and private place in your home. Consider taking the phone off the hook and lowering the lights. Set a relaxing mood, perhaps with soft music, candles, a warm breeze from a window—anything that you both find comforting. Most people like to shower or bathe beforehand, either separately or together. For some couples, feeling fresh and clean will enhance the moment. Warm water relaxes the body and eases tension. It is common to feel uneasy when you do this exercise. If either of you begin to feel apprehension, take a few minutes to do one of the relaxation exercises described in chapter 6.

If you decide to shower or bathe together, take your time, and be playful, close, tender, and affectionate, finding your own special way to relate to each other. You may want to start the first exercise being fully clothed or perhaps wearing what you wear to sleep. If you usually sleep together nude, you can start that way. When you have settled into your comfortable space and have eliminated distractions, you are ready to begin.

Exercise 7.2—Sensate Focus I

Once you begin, use this experience as a nonverbal way to feel connected. Keep talk to a minimum. Decide who will be the first giver. Lie together for a few moments to slow down and try to settle into the experience. This exercise does not lead to sexual touching or intercourse. You may experience a sense of uneasiness as you begin to open yourself up to intimate or tender feelings. This is a normal feeling for anyone as they learn new things, especially as they allow themselves to surrender to an intimate exchange. Paying attention to your breathing can help you focus on the exercise at hand. Begin selecting a giver and a receiver.

Instructions for the Giver

The giver should begin by rubbing their hands together to warm them and generate energy. Caress your partner gently, starting with the head and touching the entire body to the feet. This touching is meant to be sensuous, not sexual. In other words, it is meant to stimulate in a comfortable and pleasurable, but not directly sexual, way. Take your time as you touch and caress your partner. Try a variety of touches: use both the palms and the backs of your hands, gently scratch with your nails, caress with your hair or lips, or use your whole body to touch your partner. Margo Anand (1989) describes fingertip stroking as a way of passing energy between the giver and the receiver. You can start with long, deep strokes at first, gradually lightening the touch. Use your fingertip like a feather, touching lightly over your partner's body, barely stroking the skin with light touches. Pay attention to the rhythms of your touch. Give full attention to the face and neck, touching behind the ears, on the eyelids, on the lips, and on the neck. Touch the palms of their hands, bottoms of their feet, backs of their knees, backs of their elbows—every delicate place you can find. Avoid the genitals and specific body regions that are potentially sexually arousing (such as breasts, inner buttocks, and inner thighs) even if you feel ready for such stimulation. The point of this first exercise is to eliminate any sense that sexual excitement is the goal.

To end this exercise, use a massage technique to integrate the whole experience. Starting at the top of the head and using your fingers loosely relaxed, stroke down over all the surfaces of your partner's body. Think of your hands as gentle, soft brooms, sweeping delightful energy evenly over your partner's body. End with their hands and feet. This first sensate focus exercise is not a test of your massage abilities,

Figure 7.2. Sensate Focus I: Non-Sexual Touching

nor is it an endurance contest. Maintain awareness of your own experience. Focus on your own feelings rather than on whether your partner is enjoying the touching. The receiver will give you feedback if necessary.

If you find yourself getting distracted or bored, shift to a different stroke. Think about what feelings you would have if you removed the boredom. Pay attention to the energy you feel coming from your partner and notice their muscle tension and strength, skin texture, hair, and the soft contours of their body.

Sometimes touching causes worry to surface in either the giver or receiver. If you feel tense, notice where you hold the tension in your body, and then breathe in through your nose while you imagine your breath is carrying healing energy and relaxation to those areas. Focus on relaxing the tension and notice how you feel more alive to touch as you relax. Use your breathing to stay in touch with your partner and yourself. If you slow down and concentrate on your own experience, chances are your partner will like it. It is often the case that when a receiver complains, it is because the giver has not been actually focusing on the touching, but thinking, worrying, or daydreaming about something else.

Instructions for the Receiver

The receiver should lie on their stomach and focus on the feelings of the moment. Let the distractions of the day go. Sometimes breathing easily and focusing attention on the exact place you are being touched helps keep your relaxed focus. Don't worry that the giver is getting tired or bored. Stay with your physical sensations. Tell your partner to change only if what is happening is unpleasant or hurts. Many women are accustomed to gritting their teeth or cringing if they don't like a particular sexual touch, waiting for it to be over. If you do this you may feel resentful and end up focusing on angry feelings instead of your experience. In this exercise, you have an opportunity to learn new responses. Giving your partner feedback in a way that is not hurtful is an important skill in achieving good sexual relations. Instead of making only a negative comment, try to also suggest something you would like. If you are feeling ticklish, show your partner how to touch you more slowly and firmly, with a deeper pressure.

Using soft tones and gentle language helps let your partner know that it's the touch you're uncomfortable with, not them. For example, suppose the giver touches you in an uncomfortable way. An aversive response would be "Stop that!" or "That hurts!" or "Come on!" This can anger or upset the giver—even when you don't mean it that way. It is hard to relax and enjoy something when you feel angry or rejected. A gentler response would be something like, "Honey, I like it best when you are very gentle on that spot," or "My shoulder is a little sensitive there—try rubbing softly." You must provide the giver with gentle feedback and this can require some practice.

❧ Case 7.4—Jenny and Steven

Jenny complained that Steven's touch felt like a "window wiper," and her skin began to hurt when he didn't move his hand from her abdomen. Steven realized that he was anxious because Jenny never gave any indication of how he was doing, so he felt too nervous to experiment. They agreed that she would moan and sigh enough so he could tell he was on the right track. This was hard for Jenny at first who had always been embarrassed to make any noises during sex. She started off by making noises very quietly, until she felt comfortable to be more audible. Steven felt more relaxed and confident with his touching since he knew what Jenny liked. It was a new and exciting thrill for him to know that he was pleasing her. Before long, both felt at ease and agreed that touching had become a wonderfully satisfying experience.

Remember, the giver will succeed most by focusing on their own experience of touching. Here is a suggested model for the exercise in which Jenny and Steven are receiving and giving touch:

Jenny lies on her stomach. Steven massages for ten minutes.
Steven lies on his stomach. Jenny massages for ten minutes.
Jenny lies on her back. Steven massages for ten minutes.
Steven lies on his back. Jenny massages for ten minutes.

They engage in pillow talk for ten minutes (see the following section on pillow talk and exercises 7.2 and 7.3).

Alternative: Steven massages both sides of Jenny for a total of twenty minutes, and then they switch.

If you wish, change places and do the exercise a second time. The suggested times are only that—feel free to agree on your own timetable. We do recommend spending at least forty-five minutes on the exercise.

Pillow Talk

After completing each of the sensate focus exercises, it is important to talk about the experience for ten to fifteen minutes to provide each other with feedback. This talking can increase intimacy, improve communication, and build confidence. If either of you have difficulty with the exercise, you may need to discuss this with a therapist. Again, this exercise can reveal many of the reasons why you are having sexual fear or pain. Resistance and roadblocks should be greeted as opportunities and challenges to learn more about yourself and your partner and to work towards a resolution.

Here is a chance for you to be honest about what you feel. Try to speak in the first person, so that your partner will not feel hurt or insulted. Here are several examples:

Instead of saying . . .	Try saying . . .
That tickles!	*I feel ticklish.*
Ouch! That hurts!	*It hurts when you touch my neck that way.*

Quit making me feel nervous.	*I feel nervous about doing this.*
You're bothering me and making me angry.	*I feel angry and I want to stop and talk.*

This type of communication accomplishes several things. First, it removes the accusation directed at your partner, and doesn't put them on the defensive. It makes you responsible for your own feelings, helping you to identify and own them. Then your partner may feel less rejected and more willing to listen and respond to your needs and requests. It is important to give both positive and negative feedback, usually starting with the positive. Often it seems difficult to tell your partner something negative, so to ensure that you are sharing true feelings, plan to mention at least two pleasant and two unpleasant types of touch. This will lead to increased intimacy if both of you can trust each other's honest responses. This is an improvement on "Everything you do feels great." For instance, Laura told Sophie that she felt protected when Sophie cradled her head when they kissed. But she felt that Sophie was not paying attention to her when she gave back rubs and her touch felt mechanical. Sophie did feel protective and was pleased that Laura noticed. Although she disagreed at first that she was not paying attention, later she realized that she really was distracted when she touched Laura's back because she was eager to move on to making love.

Responses to Sensate Focus Exercise I

Some people have a positive experience with these exercises and feel closer to their partner. They may even feel stirrings of sexual excitement that they haven't felt for a long time. If you do feel excitement, it is best not to act on it yet. Try to just enjoy the feelings and trust they will return.

Some people are surprised to discover that they have a negative response. If either you or your partner feels anxious, you may find that you begin to avoid the exercise, either by having a fight, being too busy, or feeling too tired. You may also feel bored, foolish, angry, or ashamed. You might begin to discover that you dislike your body or have a poor body image. You may blame your partner for being insensitive or awkward. You may also feel obligated to turn a sensuous experience into a sexual one, and this focus on sexual goals may cause anxiety, anger, or resentment. If you do have a negative reaction, use some of the relaxation skills you learned in chapter 6. Take several deep, relaxing breaths and breathe into the part of your body where you feel most uncomfortable. Ask your partner to stop for a moment as you breathe. If your eyes were closed, open them and look around to orient yourself to time and place. Stay focused on your feelings and the images that arise, and ask yourself how they contribute to your sexual problem. If you can continue with the exercise, do so. But if you have a strong negative reaction you may need to stop. Never continue with a sexual experience if you are afraid or in pain. Try to discuss the experience with your partner later.

EXERCISE 7.3—YOUR RESPONSES TO SENSATE FOCUS I

For both partners: In the grids below or on a separate sheet of paper, record your reactions to the sensate focus exercise in your roles as both giver and receiver. What feelings came to mind? What did you like about it? What difficulties arose? Then, write down what you imagine your partner was thinking during the exercises as giver or receiver. Now show each other what you wrote. This last instruction will help you learn how accurately you are perceiving your partner's reactions.

The following is a sample response from a couple.

Your name   <u>Leslie</u>

Role	How did you feel?	What worked well?	Problems
Giver	*I felt tense and then I gradually relaxed*	*I liked using different strokes on his back*	*Couldn't tell if Mike enjoyed it*
Receiver	*I felt embarrassed*	*Liked scalp massage*	*Felt ticklish*
Partner as giver	*He felt bored*	*He seemed to enjoy touching me*	*He thinks I'm fat*
Partner as receiver	*I don't know*	*He liked back massage*	*I don't know*

Partner's name   <u>Mike</u>

Role	How did you feel?	What worked well?	Problems
Giver	*Tense mostly*	*I liked her softness*	*I didn't know what to do when she felt tickled*
Receiver	*Felt great*	*I liked the whole massage*	*None*
Partner as giver	*Happy*	*She was really creative*	*No problems*
Partner as receiver	*She never wants to receive*	*She relaxed with the scalp massage*	*She was so ticklish it was hard to touch her*

Your name _____

Role	How did you feel?	What worked well?	Problems
Giver			
Receiver			
Partner as giver			
Partner as receiver			

Partner's name _____

Role	How did you feel?	What worked well?	Problems
Giver			
Receiver			
Partner as giver			
Partner as receiver			

After completing these grids, exchange them with your partner and discuss your reactions. Are you surprised? Are there areas of agreement? disagreement? Talking about the exercise, either alone or in therapy, will help clarify what each of you are experiencing. Try to do this without blaming the other. You may find ways to modulate the exercise, perhaps by adding or subtracting parts or dividing it into smaller segments, to meet your individual needs. Review the following case vignettes for some suggestions:

✐ Case Vignettes

Jim and Clara realized that seeing each other nude was a big jump and decided that they both wanted to spend more time opening up to each other visually before moving on to a tactile experience. They kept their clothes on and minimized touching for the first several exercises, instead speaking softly to each other about what they were looking at, what they called "visually massaging" each other. Then they decided to start doing the sensate focus with minimal light to get used to seeing each other nude. After using candle light and enjoying it, Jim wanted to move more quickly than Clara, who still felt awkward about being seen. But once they talked, he agreed to be patient with her because he could see she was really trying.

Andrea and Carl had both experienced sexual abuse as children and wanted to go slowly. They began by touching only the upper back with one finger and worked very slowly to more full-body touching.

After Miriam and Marty exchanged information about what they were really feeling as opposed to what they had each imagined, they realized that Marty really didn't know how tender Miriam's breasts were during her period. After that he softened his touch and, with some gentle reminders, he learned how to touch her in the way she liked.

Judy realized that keeping a shirt on helped her feel safer. She bought herself a soft cotton shirt that was sensuous but allowed her to remain covered.

Susan and Tamara realized they were not ready for body touching. They started seeking physical pleasure together by lying in the sun. Over time they began to hold hands and give backrubs, and then were ready to begin the sensate focus exercises with energy and commitment.

✐

EXERCISE 7.4—FACING RESISTANCE

Identify up to five areas of difficulty or resistance that arose during exercise 7.2. You may recognize resistance in negative thoughts or feelings about yourself or your partner or notice uncomfortable bodily sensations. For each item, suggest a way to correct it. For example, Leslie felt that two problems she experienced were her ticklishness and Mike's lack of communication. Since she enjoyed deep massage so much, and it was less ticklish for her, she asked Mike to focus on that technique. Also, Mike agreed to hum when he was enjoying the sensate focus and to make a quizzical "hmm" when he wasn't sure. This prompted Leslie to smile and giggle when he enjoyed something and to ask for suggestions when he didn't like something.

Resistance   **Solutions**

1. _____   _____

_____   _____

2. _____   _____

_____   _____

3. _____   _____

_____   _____

4. _____   _____

_____   _____

5. _____   _____

_____   _____

Plan to do exercises 7.2 through 7.4 at least twice a week for two to three weeks, or until you both feel relaxed and comfortable during the entire exercise. Don't move on until you have settled into a mutually comfortable pattern of nonsexual touching and communication. There is no time limit. Some couples may feel ready in two weeks—others in two months. You are ready to move on when you begin to feel relaxed enough to focus on your own sensations and enjoy the exercise. If this is not happening, you need to stick with the first exercise and reassess which area needs more work.

EXERCISE 7.5—JOURNAL WRITING

Take some time during this beginning phase of sensate focus to write about the experience. What does it feel like to begin the exercises? Have any major problems arisen? How are you and your partner interacting? Is it working out? If not, what can you do to change things? What resistance have you experienced or created? Sometimes these initial interactions with your partner can be tense and frustrating, because your sexual problems may have prompted a lot of strong emotions and conflicts that now are coming to the surface. Remember that this is to be expected: sensate focus acts as a diagnostic exercise as well as a way to learn about sensual touching. Focus on how you can remain hopeful and constructive. Try to reframe problems as challenges and opportunities towards recovery.

Sensate Focus II—Genital Touching to Explore and Arouse

We recommend that you begin sensate focus II like the earlier exercises, by gradually transitioning into a safe haven and leaving other concerns and distractions behind as you focus on the relaxed awareness of sensual touching. You may want to start with a bath or shower for two reasons. Generally, people feel more comfortable if they are clean before they engage in sexual contact. Also, the time you are bathing acts as a transition, allowing you to slow down and get in touch with each other emotionally and physically. Warm water relaxes muscles and eases body tension. Washing your hands and face and brushing your teeth can help you feel clean and refreshed. Some couples make this into a small ritual, using scented soaps or body lotions and wearing special nightclothes or lingerie. The goal is to prepare yourselves for a special, private time. Once you are ready to begin the exercise, lie together and connect at an emotional level before moving into touching. Men and women may differ about the timing of genital touch. Some men say they like genital touch immediately. Most women report that they want other types of caresses first and feel hurried if they don't receive touching all over before their partners begin focusing on their genital areas.

🐚 Case 7.5—Sandra and Jerry

Sandra believed that Jerry was selfish and interested only in intercourse and orgasm. He always wanted her to touch his penis, and he tended to grab her crotch in a playful way when they showered together. Jerry believed that Sandra was being prudish, and that if he "showed her" about physical touch she would like it. Once they began the sensate focus exercises, they each learned that their partner really did care, but didn't know how to please them. They went through several difficult therapy sessions talking about how resentful and hurt they felt before they were ready to try genital touching. Each had to remember that they had different perspectives and that neither was wrong.

EXERCISE 7.6—LOOKING AT EACH OTHER'S GENITALS

This exercise involves a visual examination of each other's genitals. Use a hand mirror so that you both can see the other's genital structures. Use the diagrams for female and male genital anatomy in chapter 2 to locate different structures. As you take turns looking at each other, decide what names or labels you want to use; this will facilitate your communication. Some people are comfortable with clinical names, while others prefer to use names they have read or heard, or use private nicknames. There are dozens of words for male genitals, but fewer to describe the different parts of women's genitals. Be creative. Kim named her vagina her "jewel case," and Mary Ann referred to her genitals as her "pretties." These names should have positive connotations—avoid derogatory labels that reinforce unpleasant thoughts or feelings. If your names inspire laughter, such humor may help both of you relax and will lighten the experience. This exercise can improve your communication and reinforce your understanding of genital anatomy. It may also reveal new difficulties: fear of exposure, shame, embarrassment, squeamishness, etc. Take time to discuss problems that arise and ways to resolve them before moving on. Once you both feel comfortable with this exercise, you can move on to exercise 7.7.

🐚 Case 7.6—Tim and JoAnn

Tim and JoAnn started the exercise on looking at their genitals, but ran into immediate problems. JoAnn began crying and refused to look at Tim's penis. They got dressed and sat down to talk, and JoAnn revealed that when she was thirteen an older friend of her brother's had exposed himself and tried to force her to fondle him. Ever since then, she had feared looking at male genitals. This now explained her extreme modesty with Tim in the bedroom: she didn't want to expose her nude body since she feared Tim would do the same. She had always insisted on sexual activity in the dark or under covers, so she wouldn't have to see him nude. To address JoAnn's anxiety, they decided to change the exercise. First, JoAnn spent several sessions alone practicing deep breathing and progressive muscle relaxation while she looked at diagrams and then photographs of men's genitals. When she felt relaxed with this, Tim joined her in looking at the diagrams. They ran into trouble when Tim got angry because "it was taking too long." A difficult conversation followed as Tim worked to realize that JoAnn did love him and was trying to change. They repeated sensate focus exercise 1 without clothes, although Tim wore loose-fitting boxer shorts. To her surprise, JoAnn was interested in looking at Tim's genitals and asked him to remove his shorts. Once she felt comfortable with this, they repeated the genital exercise without the previous difficulty. Tim still got impatient and worried that JoAnn didn't love him, but over time they were ready to move on.

EXERCISE 7.7—GENITAL TOUCHING AND EXPLORATION

In this exercise, you and your partner will begin a tactile exploration of your bodies. Start with the whole body and gradually focus on the genitals. Basically, you will be repeating exercise 7.2, but you will now include the genital regions. This touching is meant to explore and not to arouse. If you feel aroused, just let it be; arousal will diminish if you don't actively pursue it. Allow yourself to enjoy the sensations of touch without a goal. If you find yourself feeling anxious, ashamed, or other negative emotions, try breathing into the area being touched (see the section on genital-focused breathing in chapter 6). See if you can stay with the sensations and make the negative feeling diminish. After the exercise is completed, share your experiences. Follow the same schedule you used for sensate focus I, and repeat the same pillow talk exercises.

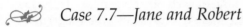 *Case 7.7—Jane and Robert*

Jane had many phobic and aversive feelings about both her own genitals and those of her partner Robert, especially during sexual activity. But she decided that she loved him and was ready to tackle difficult sexual tasks to help their relationship progress. With the help of her sex therapist, Jane located a psychiatrist and began taking antidepressant medication which helped reduce her extreme panic reactions enough to work through the behavioral tasks. Robert was eager to join her in therapy and his openness to talking about his own worries and concerns helped her express her deeply held aversion to genitals. Sensate focus exercises which involved gentle caressing of the genitals helped Jane associate them with a sense of relaxation, curiosity, and pleasure. After some intense work over a period of two years, they decided to marry and have a child. Going through childbirth also helped Jane come to terms with her body, and her aversions gradually diminished.

EXERCISE 7.8—THE SEXOLOGICAL EXAMINATION

In this exercise, you will take turns with slow and gentle exploration of each other's genital regions and discover the wide variety of touch available to you. The purpose of this exercise is to teach each other what you like or don't like. This exercise was developed to give people a simple way of expressing their experiences without talking, since it is hard to concentrate on your bodily sensations when you talk. You can indicate what you like with sighs or moans, but it's best not to use this time to chat or converse. As the giver touches a spot, the receiver will give immediate feedback as to the level of pleasure of this touch using the scale shown below. At first, the receiver may need to adjust their mind to the task by comparing several touches before being able to assign a number. But, in time it becomes easier.

Sexological Exam Scale

+3   The most pleasurable touch you can imagine

+2   Touch that feels very good

+1   Touch that is mildly pleasurable

 0   Neither pleasurable nor unpleasant—neutral

Figure 7.3. Sensate Focus II: Touching to Explore and Arouse

-1   Touch that is slightly unpleasant

-2   Touch that is quite unpleasant

-3   Touch that is very unpleasant and causes physical or psychological pain

The giver begins by touching an area an inch or so from the genitals with their fingertip. When the receiver is female, start at the pubic mound or vulva and gently stroke or pull the outer-most pubic hair. The receiver will then express a number based on the Sexological Exam Scale. The giver should then move to another part of the vulva, such as the outer lips on the right and the receiver again gives the touch a rating. Touch both sides of the vulva separately. Many people are surprised to discover that one side is more sensitive than the other. Continue in small increments of touch, progressing from the outer to the inner labia, to the region around the clitoral hood, and then to spots encompassing the entire genital area. Avoid touching the clitoris or inserting a finger into the vaginal vestibule at this point. Avoid the sensitive urethral and anal regions for now (many individuals find these areas too sensitive for sexual contact at any point). If the receiver is male, begin in the pubic hair and progress along the shaft of the penis, again avoiding the sensitive opening to the urethra. Lightly stroke the scrotum below. Remember that the underside of the tip of the penis is the most sensitive and sexually arousing location.

As the receiver feels more aroused, go over the same areas again, trying less or more pressure and faster or slower touch. The receiver will help the giver map out areas and types of touch that feel good. If there are negative numbers, move outward and use a gentler touch. As long as you have completed earlier sensate focus exercises, you will usually be able to find many areas that are erotic and exciting when touched. To enhance the experience, add a water-soluble lubricant such as Astroglide or KY jelly. This will change the experience and usually make it more erotic. If the receiver feels too sensitive, consider touching through a sheer panty or light cloth.

When you have each completed the initial exploration, consider a more in-depth exploration for the female receiver. Insert a finger into the opening of the vagina, delicately stroking in and out once. Think of the opening as the face of a clock. The receiver will notice different sensations as a finger touches twelve, three, six, nine, and again twelve o'clock. Add another level of experience by touching two places at once, such as the six o'clock position at the opening of the vagina and the twelve o'clock position at the hood of the clitoris. Or make a circling motion around a nipple as you touch a certain spot. After you have finished the exercise, change places. When you are done, rest in each other's arms and breathe slowly and comfortably together.

As long as you both feel comfortable (a lot of plus 1s through plus 3s), feel free to experiment. You will slowly create an internal image of comfortable, pleasurable, and arousing spots to guide you in future exercises. Remember that everyone has both comfortable and sensitive areas when stimulated. Everyone has times when they want to be touched and other times when they don't. Be aware of your physical experience and let your partner know what you want. You are both learning when, where, and in what manner you like to be touched. It is important to repeat the pillow talk exercises after every sensate focus. This will allow you to refocus your touching and find solutions to resistance and difficulties.

Sensate focus with genital exploration might prove to be a major hurdle for some women with sexual pain disorders. Vulvar pain might make it difficult if not impossible at times to complete the exercise. Dyspareunia and vaginismus might make vaginal insertion too difficult. If this is the case, we suggest the following:

1. Spend more time on earlier sensate focus exercises; focus on light genital stroking and visualization.

2. Share your feelings with your partner as you do the genital exploration to explain where the area is sensitive. This will help lower anxiety for both people. For instance, if you have a firm agreement not to try penetration, the receiver who is fearful of penetration might relax and be able to enjoy stimulation very much.

3. Be flexible in terms of the amount of time you explore. Better to go slowly than not at all.

4. Speak to your doctor or gynecologist about appropriate medication for vulvar disorders.

5. Discuss with your gynecologist the use of a topical anesthetic ointment (e.g., KY Jelly with lidocaine) for severely painful vulvar regions.

If you are unable to complete the exercise because of dyspareunia or vaginismus, turn to the special treatment module in chapter 9 that describes dilator exercises.

Sometimes couples abort their efforts when they start an exercise and run into a major problem. For example, if you experienced pain during genital touching, you might have jumped out of bed and asked to cancel the exercise. These incidents can easily create anger, discouragement, or even hopelessness in both partners and can lead to arguments.

How should you deal with such an occurrence? First, try to understand what is happening: the pain or fear has just overwhelmed one partner, activated the sympathetic nervous system, and led to the fight-or-flight reaction. In other words, the sexual dysfunction has just been recreated within the exercise. This *will* happen at points along the way—so expect it and don't be discouraged. Reframe your perspective; instead of seeing it as a problem, look at it as a challenge; instead of letting it stall your progress, think of ways to move beyond it. To do this, take a break from the exercise and spend ten to fifteen minutes on a relaxation exercise. This will deactivate sympathetic nervous arousal and restore a state of calm. Then try to repeat part of an earlier sensate focus exercise that worked well, such as nonsexual touching. When you and your partner are feeling calmer and more confident, discuss the problem and try to find a solution. Perhaps gentler touching is needed or slower movements towards the genitals. There are always ways to salvage exercises.

Exercise 7.9—Genital Touching to Arouse

Once you have learned to feel comfortable with exploring each other, you may want to move into the next phase of touching—sexually arousing your partner. Although you will be feeling erotic tension during this exercise, it is not meant to have a goal of high arousal. You will have a chance to explore several methods. Since this book is written about women's sexuality, we will focus on ways to touch a woman. (For suggestions of what to do for male arousal, see the resources section in appendix A.)

Suggestions for Touching a Woman

(This exercise is addressed to your partner.) Begin by general touching and caressing (as in sensate focus 1) so that you feel an emotional connection. Then, use your hands or lips to gently play with your partner, varying the types of touch and pressure, experimenting to see what is more arousing. Use the knowledge gained from the previous exercises to guide you. Many women find it most pleasurable to be aroused slowly. Play with her breasts and nipples, kissing and gently pinching or rolling the nipples between your fingers. Gradually move down the belly to the pubic area, but move slowly and do not touch the clitoris at first. Try different strokes, touches, and pressures around the vulva and clitoris. Make teasing movements around the clitoral hood to discover which area is most sensitive. As arousal increases, add lubrication and stimulate the same areas again, noting the difference in sensation. Hold the inner labial lips open and gently stroke the clitoral area and the area around the vaginal opening with your finger or tongue. Try different rhythms. Some women enjoy gentle touching around the anus. Keep in mind that the focus is on pleasurable and mildly arousing touch—not orgasm. Put aside preconceptions about what should be arousing—your partner will let you know what she finds pleasurable. Continue to focus on your own experience as well. If you get too lost in pleasing your partner, it can be hard to then shift focus to yourself.

Your Part in This Exercise

Add pelvic and genital focus breathing (exercises 6.3 and 6.4) to these exercises to enhance genital energy and pleasure. You can tell your partner what you like during or after these exercises, or you can show them with your own hand. Remember that you do need to express your preferences, because no partner is a mind reader. When you let your partner know what you like, you bring energy to the sexual experience. Many women have noticed that the touching that feels best one moment shifts to another spot the next moment. This is natural, but requires that you stay aware of this shifting arousal. Since a partner cannot know about the shift, you must show your partner what feels good as the feelings change. By this point, your improved communication and use of pillow talk exercises can keep you both in tune with each other. Take turns being the giver and receiver.

Exercise 7.10—Guiding

This exercise provides you and your partner with a physical way to communicate your likes and dislikes during sensate focus. The best way to accomplish this is through guiding the partner. To do this exercise, sit with the partner leaning against the head of the bed and encircling the woman who leans back into the partner's arms (figure 7.4). There are three stages to guiding. First, the partner rests their

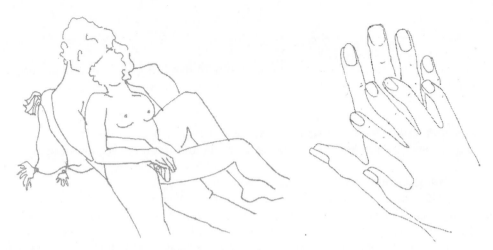

Figure 7.4. Sensate Focus II: Guiding

hand on the woman's own hand as she touches herself in the way that she prefers. Next, the partner touches the woman in a similar way, but with her hand gently guiding to show what feels best. Finally, the partner touches the woman as she has demonstrated, without her guidance. The woman receives this touching and only corrects when she wants something different. After this exercise, change places. You can also do this while the receiver lies on their back and the giver kneels or sits next to or between their legs (figure 7.5).

This exercise is especially helpful because neither partner feels criticized as both learn about touching and being touched. When you are finished, lie together and enjoy the pleasant sensations. Remember that this is a learning experience. If you feel aroused, wait for a while and let your new sensations sink in.

❧ Case 7.8—Celia and Gwen

After trying the guiding exercise, Celia and Gwen were thrilled to find a way to communicate their sexual wishes to each other. Before this each had tried to move her body into position and hope for the touch she wanted. Or they had touched each other with the hope

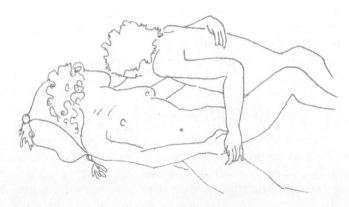

Figure 7.5. Sensate Focus II: Alternate Guiding Position

that the same touch would be reciprocated. Now they found it easy to show each other what to do. They made use of the guiding exercise several times before they were ready to move to the next sensate focus exercise.

Sensate Focus III—Increasing Genital Pleasure

Sensate focus III is designed to help you learn even more about what arouses you. Orgasm will occur if you get the stimulation you need and allow it to build to climax. While you might have an orgasm as a result of the exercise, that is not the purpose of doing the exercise. There is really no rush. If you have never had an orgasm before you may find yourself stuck at this point. If so, try the exercises provided in module 4 in chapter 9. If you have been orgasmic and feel ready to incorporate it into your lovemaking, move on to exercise 7.11.

Now is the time to let yourself feel high levels of sexual arousal that precede orgasm. Since intercourse is not a reliable way to achieve the stimulation women need to climax, do not try to use intercourse at this stage to achieve orgasm. Instead, stimulate yourself, or let your partner stimulate you while you become familiar with the sensations of the plateau stage. Orgasm will follow, but is elusive if you try to achieve it in a conscious way. If you let the sensations build, orgasm is a reflex that is a natural release of sexual tension.

✿

EXERCISE 7.11—GENITAL STIMULATION TO ORGASM

Begin this exercise in a similar manner as with sensate focus I. Then move into genital stimulation as described in sensate focus II. Go slowly, keeping in mind that the purpose of sensate focus is to relax while you and your partner share pleasure— not just to reach orgasm (even though that may be the result of the intense arousal you may feel). After you have experimented with a variety of touching, focus on those techniques that increase stimulation. If you feel ready to climax, allow yourself to surrender to orgasm. You can do this over a period of time or in one session. Remember to keep your focus on the pleasurable momentary sexual sensations, thoughts, and feelings, and not simply on the goal of orgasm.

Orgasm occurs when there is an adequate density of physical stimulation along with deep psychological involvement. It is the natural release of sexual tension, a reflex which will occur on its own. If orgasm does not occur, there are several things to try that may help trigger it. Some women need to feel tension in their buttocks and thigh muscles. Tense these muscles and relax them several times. Or push your feet hard against the foot of the bed or a wall to create muscle tension. Some women find if they stretch their neck muscles or hang their head off the edge of the bed they release orgasm. For some women, holding their breath, and letting it go all at once creates the orgasmic release. Others need to breathe deeply into their pelvis. Many women find that by squeezing the PC muscle as in Kegel exercises they can trigger orgasm. Try fast and slow Kegels to see which works best for you. At high levels of arousal, some women feel that they want something inside their vagina. This can lead to penetration with a finger or dildo, but not to intercourse during this exercise.

Using Vibrators

Many women have discovered that vibrators provide a surefire method of reaching orgasm, either alone or with a partner. In many cities in the United States you can buy vibrators at department stores, drug stores, and discount stores. In other cities they are unavailable. In the appendix we list resources on how to order vibrators through the mail. If you decide to try a vibrator, buy an electric type that provides intense stimulation. The subtle sensation provided by battery-operated, penis-shaped vibrators does not always produce enough stimulation. There is also a mistaken assumption that penetration is necessary for orgasm. You can't hurt yourself with a vibrator and you can't become "addicted." Some women use a vibrator to reassure themselves that they can orgasm. Once they know their bodies "work," they are more comfortable to move on to other types of stimulation. Feel free to incorporate a vibrator into exercise 7.11 if you and your partner feel comfortable. You do not want your partner to feel like they've been replaced, so it is important to continue with pillow talk exercises to work out any problems. To introduce a vibrator into loveplay, try using it first on the shoulder muscles or the feet. As you become more comfortable with the sensations, you can gradually try touching the genitals.

Possible Reactions to Sensate Focuses II and III

Many women feel a sense of freedom when they realize that they aren't obligated to a partner to include intercourse in their lovemaking. For a woman who is used to giving and has trouble receiving, the idea of taking turns can help because she is given a turn to be "selfish" and focus on her own pleasure. Some women have negative reactions to receiving genital pleasure. A woman may feel self-conscious for many reasons when sexual attention is focused only on herself. This attention can raise guilt about being sexual. For a woman with a negative body image, it may be hard to realize that her partner is focusing so completely on her body. Some women have negative attitudes about the bodily secretions, odors, sensations, and physical reactions that occur while they are highly aroused. These sensate focus exercises often illuminate unresolved concerns and feelings for both partners. If you have a negative reaction pay attention to it. Chances are that your sexuality has been influenced in the past by these reactions. If you honestly appraise your thoughts and feelings, you may discover how they have created problems. Eventually, you may be ready to let go of the problems and move on. Keep in mind that if you can't move beyond them you may need the help of someone trained in this area.

For survivors of sexual abuse, the focus on touch may trigger traumatic memories. Talking through these issues with a therapist in an open and honest discussion can diminish negative feelings. See the section in chapter 4 as well as the 7th treatment module in chapter 9 to learn about how abuse survivors can reclaim their sexuality.

✒ Case 7.9—Nelda and Joey

Nelda and Joey knew that they were nervous about sex, but as they engaged in genital pleasuring they were stunned to realize that neither felt comfortable with oral sex because of the bodily secretions and odors that are a part of oral sex. In the past they had included oral sex occasionally in lovemaking, but neither had felt comfortable either giving or receiving. When giving oral sex, Nelda felt squeamish about seeing, smelling, or tasting Joey's ejaculate. She also worried that he would feel the same about her vaginal secretions.

Over a period of several months they decided to explore this area of making love. First they spent several sessions really looking at the structures of each other's genitals. As they became more familiar with looking, some of the awkwardness disappeared. Then they touched each other without any expectations of sexual arousal. This also lowered their anxiety. As they talked with their therapist they realized they had both made an assumption carried over from childhood: Nelda saw that she associated her genitals with being scolded about being "dirty" if she wet or soiled herself. Now as an adult she began to reconstruct her image of her genitals as clean and beautiful. Joey also made changes in his notions about sex being "dirty" connected to jokes he had heard his friends tell in seventh grade. Nelda and Joey had associated all genital secretions with these negative experiences.

They had both managed to avoid facing these feelings because of the love they felt and their desire to please each other. When they finally understood the issue, they both felt greatly relieved. They decided to slow down and get comfortable with oral sex at a pace that suited both of them. They were soon ready to create new and positive experiences together.

Sensate Focus IV—Non-Demand Exploration of Sensations During Intercourse

Sensate focus IV is a culmination of all your new experience as you build a sexual repertoire. Once you have learned the pleasures of penetration without active thrusting, you can move on to intercourse and practice new experiences, still keeping in mind that this is your opportunity to teach each other and learn what you like and don't like. Give each other a lot of feedback. Use guiding frequently. Play with arousing techniques and experiment with a variety of movements and rhythms— twisting, turning, bending—as you seek out new sensations. While you are having intercourse, try touching each other's genitals in many ways. This is arousing for both partners and an excellent addition to your newfound sexual skills. Some women are able to climax during intercourse if they receive clitoral stimulation along with the natural in-and-out movements of intercourse. As always in this learning experience, orgasm is not the goal, although you may become so aroused you do have an orgasm. There is no set time duration for these exercises. Now is your chance to experience many new and different sensations. Be sure to allow time for pillow talk afterward.

As always, if you feel pain, discomfort, or fear stop and talk about it. You may be able to fix the problem immediately. If not, give yourselves a chance to rest and calm down, and then you may be ready to continue. If you repeatedly find yourself stuck at this point, you may wish to speak to a sex therapist.

Sensate focus IV offers the chance to experience the subtle sensations of penetration and penile containment, and gradually leads to non-demand thrusting. Its

Figure 7.6. Sensate Focus IV: The Quiet Vagina/Non-Demand Thrusting

purpose is to teach the pleasures of sexual connection without driving toward higher excitement or orgasm. It is helpful for all heterosexual couples, but particularly for women with sexual pain or difficulty achieving orgasm. Remember to incorporate earlier sensate focus exercises. These new exercises address one of the most common complaints women have about making love—that their partners don't devote enough attention to the moment but instead rush to orgasm. Such women are often not able to climax during intercourse.

EXERCISE 7.12—THE QUIET VAGINA

This exercise may help women who are fearful of aggression during sex, or who experience pain during penetration or intercourse. The woman is in control of the experience of gradual penetration and then gentle thrusting.

This is an exercise of penile containment that teaches heterosexual couples to relax and enjoy genital sensation while having intercourse. Begin by slowing yourselves down enough to experience quiet connection and intimacy. Bathing, lying together, spoon breathing, and gradual touching can all lead to sexual arousal. When the man is aroused to the point of erection, and you are lubricated, you are ready to begin. If you need to practice safe sex have your partner put on a condom, or do it together as part of making love. The man lies on his back while one of you applies liberal amounts of a water-based lubrication to his penis. Then, you gradually lower yourself onto his erect penis and guide his erect penis into your vagina, thus controlling the depth of penetration to accomodate your needs. Once his penis is in your vagina, allow for some time to become accustomed to the feelings of containment. Using the Kegel exercise, contract and relax your PC muscle. Both you and your partner should feel the resulting sensations. Your partner should simply lie still and provide loving encouragement as you slowly move up and down on his erect penis. The purpose of this movement is for both of you to feel physically and emotionally connected and joined together. Suspend your usual concern for your partner's pleasure and concentrate on yourself. It is important for your partner to hold off his orgasm. If he becomes too excited, he should hold you quietly and rest while he calms down. This has a pleasant and teasing effect for both partners, which often heightens arousal.

Lesbian couples may experience the physical and emotional closeness after orgasm by resting in each other's arms. A woman may want to feel her lover's fingers remaining still within her vagina after orgasm. Use of a dildo might help a partner learn to trust that her partner will move slowly with penetration and she could relax and enjoy the vaginal sensations. Or some partners might be satisfied with no penetration during lovemaking.

EXERCISE 7.13—NON-DEMAND THRUSTING

Non-demand intercourse is an experience of gentle thrusting of the penis with no change in speed or movement. It involves more movement than exercise 7.12. Several positions lend themselves to non-demand thrusting. You can lie together in spoon positions, or you can straddle your partner as he lies on his back. Or try other positions you like. This exercise allows you to get the feeling of your partner's penis moving slowly inside. There is no hurry, nor should you try for orgasm. If the man becomes too aroused to continue, stop and rest, and then resume slow thrusting. Try a variety of movements and positions. This is a time to be selfish and do what you wish. Do a series of slow and fast Kegels to feel the penis. Tease, stop, and rest. The short resting period will allow you to notice sensation more than if you are moving. Then continue.

The exercise is finished when you are tired or you have learned something new about your sensations. Use some time at the end for pillow talk. Afterwards, if either of you wishes to climax, do so in some way other than intercourse.

Possible Reactions to Sensate Focus IV

Many women find these exercises to be gently erotic and intimate. Others experience them as exciting, highly pleasurable, and ultimately orgasmic. When a couple has reached this stage in their sexual growth together, they are usually ready to enjoy intercourse and orgasm in a variety of ways. As you stay in touch with your own real experience and learn to give and receive sensual stimulation, you will deepen both the physical and emotional intimacy in your relationship.

Some women have trouble allowing themselves to be on top, or their partners may not feel comfortable with it. Some women may feel highly aroused yet be unable to reach orgasm and then feel terrible disappointment and frustration. If you or your partner become too focused on orgasm, the exercise may feel rushed and you may feel you have regressed to earlier frustrations. That is a signal to slow down and work through earlier exercises. Some roadblocks at this point, such as persistently painful or difficult penetration, lack of adequate lubrication, or lack of orgasm, require more specific exercises, which are described in chapter 9. However, difficulties at this point also accentuate the importance of sex therapy. Many of these issues can be resolved over time in therapy as the couple gradually feels more comfortable communicating and expanding their sexual repertoire. The therapist serves as a source of encouragement and guidance.

References

Anand, M. 1989. *The Art of Sexual Ecstasy: The Path of Sacred Sexuality for Western Lovers*. New York: Jeremy P. Tarcher/Peregee.

Barbach, L. 1982. *For Each Other: Sharing Sexual Intimacy*. Garden City, NY: Anchor Press/Doubleday.

Bechtel, S. 1993. (Eds.) *The Practical Encyclopedia of Sex and Health*. Men's Health and Prevention Magazines.

Davis, C., J. Blank, H. Lin, and C. Bonillas. 1996. "Characteristics of Vibrator Use Among Women." *The Journal of Sex Research*, 33(4):313–320.

Haas A. and K. Haas. 1990. *Understanding Sexuality, 2nd edition*. New York: Times Mirror/Mosby College Publishing.

Kaplan, H. S. 1974. *The New Sex Therapy*. New York: Brunner/Mazel Publication.

Kaplan, H. S. 1975. *The Illustrated Manual of Sex Therapy*. New York: Quadrangle/New York Times Book Co.

Masters, W. and V. Johnson. 1970. *Human Sexual Inadequacy*. Boston: Little Brown & Co.

Winks, C. and A. Seamans. 1994. *The Good Vibrations Guide to Sex*. San Francisco: The Down There Press.

CHAPTER EIGHT

Overcoming Roadblocks and Resistance

Up to this point, you have been on a journey to discover a deeper understanding of your body, genital anatomy, sexual function, and sexual difficulties. Like any traveler, you no doubt have encountered roadblocks along the way, including external obstructions and internal resistance, which can feel frightening, exhausting, aggravating, or hopeless. Don't despair! Every woman encounters challenges in her life and each woman must find her own way to overcome them. This chapter will provide examples of typical roadblocks and resistance and discuss where they come from and why they exist. The exercises in this chapter are designed to help you build your sexual confidence and overcome your barriers to sexual satisfaction.

Understanding Resistance

Resistance has multiple meanings: in general, it refers to a force that opposes motion; in political terms, it refers to individuals banded together to oppose certain rules or liberate people from oppression; in medicine, it refers to a body's ability to fight off disease. In psychotherapy, resistance refers to a process whereby the conscious, reality-based mind, or *ego*, attempts to block out unconscious wishes or thoughts that are frightening or unacceptable. Our use of the term resistance encompasses all of these definitions and refers to any thought, emotion, or behavior that blocks you from making progress in overcoming your sexual difficulty. Consider these examples:

Jane felt terrified every time she tried to call her gynecologist for an appointment, so she stopped trying.

Barbara told Phil she was too stressed-out from work to do sensate focus exercises.

After learning relaxation techniques, Margie was able to feel relaxed enough to enjoy spoon breathing exercises. However, when it came to sensate focus, she felt that her body was too fat to even consider starting the exercises. After another diet, she reasoned, she might lose enough weight to be attractive enough to feel comfortable being nude in front of her partner.

Vicky appeared to enjoy sensate focus exercises, but after each one she would spring out of bed and refuse to talk about the experience. "It was fine. I just don't have anything else to say about it," she told her partner.

These examples of resistance might sound familiar to you. Look back over your sensate focus exercises and journal entries. Where have you been stuck? What roadblocks have you encountered? Have you put up any specific resistance? Have you found yourself saying any of the following?

- *I'm too busy to do these exercises!*
- *This whole thing is unnecessary; why can't we just get along without sex?*
- *My partner is no help and I can't do this alone.*
- *My problem is too difficult to solve. It's not worth it.*
- *I'm in too much pain to do this. I don't believe any exercises will change the pain.*
- *It will get better on its own.*
- *I'm exhausted every night after dinner—I really can't do it.*
- *No one else cares about me—why should I?*

Many of these statements are rationalizations for not doing the work. We label them "resistance" because most of them have some additional meaning behind them. All excuses are legitimate and have a kernel or more of truth, but if you recognize some of these statements as things you have said or thought, you may have an unconscious reason preventing you from moving forward. If you are too busy, in too much pain, or too tired to do very much, you could use the relaxation exercises as a beginning step. After you feel more relaxed you might be ready to tackle the next step. Resistance basically comes in several forms:

- You are not doing the exercises at all (for various reasons).
- You or your partner is refusing to do one or more of the exercises.
- You can't complete and move beyond a certain exercise (you're stuck).
- You are losing interest in the whole process.
- Fear, anxiety, panic, or pain is preventing you from progressing.

Resistance might be overt, for example, if you are having painful cramps you don't want to do the exercise. Sometimes you can freely recognize and admit that your excuses are forms of resistance, though they have a reasonable explanation: *I am too nervous; I am in too much pain; my partner won't help; this isn't working.* Other reasons do not have clear or reasonable explanations, are acted out rather than verbalized, and suggest an unconscious resistance: *I won't do it; I have no interest; I am confused.* These covert forms of resistance may not be viewed by you or your partner as resistance, but the bottom line is that no progress is being made. For example, if you are afraid of the exercise, you might pick a fight with your partner and then feel so angry you don't want to do the exercise.

A psychoanalytic approach to resistance tries to identify unacceptable unconscious wishes that are preventing progress by causing conflict and anxiety. Consider the following case studies:

❧ Case 8.1—Mary and Ed

Mary had a history of childhood sexual abuse by her father, and as a consequence she had a disorder of sexual desire. As she began sensate focus exercises, she quickly lost interest and felt numb or ticklish when her partner, Ed, touched her. Her loss of interest in the exercises prevented and protected her from having to experience feelings of desire for Ed. These conscious feelings of desire conflicted with her unconscious desires to reject, hate, and fight off her father when he molested her. Resistance occurred because in Mary's unconscious mind, Ed symbolically represented her father. When they talked about Mary's reaction to Ed in therapy they both were able to understand her resistance. This was a major first step for them and it took many months of work for Mary to let go of the past and enjoy her sexuality more easily with Ed.

🙠 Case 8.2—Jennie and Frank

Jennie suffered from a congenitally shortened right leg and was raised by doting parents who attended to her every need. After starting sensate focus, she didn't take any initiative; instead, she expected her partner Frank to plan and carry out all the exercises. Her resistance took the form of dependency on Frank and protected her from taking initiative, because unconsciously she feared that no one would take care of her if she were able to do things for herself. In her unconscious mind, Frank symbolically represented her parents. Jennie loved Frank and liked sex when Frank initiated. As she gained insight into why she was passive, she was able to begin changing her behavior to a more active stance. With the help of the therapist, she agreed to try each week to be responsible for initiating one exercise. After several months, Jennie discovered she liked the sense of competence she felt being an active lover with Frank.

In both examples, a current situation taps into and symbolically raises a previous (but now unconscious) conflict. These conflicts are unconscious because they contain some element that is unacceptable to our reality-based mind, such as hateful, aggressive, inappropriate, or frightening impulses. The goal of psychodynamic therapy is to uncover these conflicts and thus resolve their associated symptoms. Not all sexual dysfunction can be traced to unconscious conflict, however, and not all resistance has underlying unconscious motives. Sometimes *a cigar is just a cigar*—or in resistance terms, sometimes *refusal to do an exercise is just refusal.* However, considering all underlying issues can help in understanding resistance, and usually leads to some valuable discoveries.

Resistance can often be traced to attitudes or actions that prevent you from giving up your sexual problem or linked to feelings that you are helpless to do so. Try asking yourself whether you want to change. If you answer "yes," ask yourself why you want to *maintain* your sexual dysfunction. Although these ideas may seem contradictory (if you see something as a dysfunction, why wouldn't you want to fix it?), remember that many symptoms serve a purpose. They allow a woman to avoid certain challenges or relationships and maintain the status quo. Most women want to fully enjoy their sexuality, but that might mean uncertain and potentially distressing changes in their lives. It might mean they would have to become more socially active or outgoing, more assertive with their partners, or less attentive to the needs of their families. The consequences of change can be painful and may lead to resistance, perhaps tapping into ethical, religious, or cultural values that must be taken into consideration. Of course we do not suggest that you go against your value system. However, if you examine your value system, you may find you have been holding onto a belief that in actuality you no longer agree with. Although people think that their behavior is entirely based on rational decisions, this is not always the case. It is common for a woman in adulthood to unconsciously continue acting on incorrect or misunderstood information she gained in childhood. For instance, if a woman was brought up to believe that premarital sex is bad, she may still unconsciously hold this belief, even though her conscious mind had made a different choice. Thus, although she no longer believes that she must be married to be sexual, a part of her still does hold this belief and when she engages in sexual activity, whether she is married or not, she feels vaguely guilty and bad. Cultural and religious values are strongly embedded in the unconscious. See the section on religion and sex in this chapter. As you progress, take note of how influential these factors are for you. If you are unable to move on after a reasonable amount of time, we strongly urge you to consult with a trained psychotherapist or sex therapist.

Resistance and roadblocks might involve other people. What should you do if your partner refuses to be cooperate, has a sexual dysfunction and won't address it, or scorns your efforts? In those circumstances progress can be difficult. Sometimes the sexual problem is the result of nonsexual conflicts, and sex therapy must wait until you and your partner resolve these issues. Sometimes a partner resists change because of their own physical illness, emotional reasons, or substance abuse. Here again, sex therapy must wait until these other issues are addressed. Sometimes a doctor, therapist, or gynecologist might be dismissive or insensitive to your dilemma, which can cause you to doubt yourself or whether you can work through your problems. If any of these reasons are stopping you, you may have to advocate for yourself. In chapter 10 we discuss how to work with partners and health care professionals. However, when there are legitimate limitations to your progress as a result of your partner, you may need professional counseling to sort these out.

Exercise 8.1—Your Resistance and Roadblocks

Make a list of problems that have come up when trying to work at your sexual problem. These may be similar to your lists from sensate focus in chapter 7.

1. _____
2. _____
3. _____
4. _____
5. _____

Now, list several reasons why you might *not want* to change. This exercise may take some creative thinking, but even tentative or made-up reasons can be revealing.

1. _____
2. _____
3. _____
4. _____
5. _____

Your roadblocks may seem impassable, but we will try to provide you with ways to analyze your resistance and move beyond it. If your resistance focuses on not having enough time or privacy, review chapter 6 for suggestions. If your resistance focuses on excess pain, consult with your physician. If mental anguish (anxiety, depression, insomnia, etc.) is a problem, you may need to consult a psychologist or psychiatrist. If you are faced with a potentially serious gynecological problem, it is important to have it assessed before you continue treatment. Basically, there are many serious areas of resistance having to do with mental or physical ailments that are reversible with the help of a health care professional. Don't delay in dealing with these issues any longer: seek help.

Additional roadblocks you may encounter are negative attitudes towards sex, your own sexual image or identity, or your ability to change. These attitudes are intimately tied to lack of self-knowledge or self-confidence or negative body image.

Sexuality and Religious Beliefs

Many women feel a conflict between their religious beliefs and their sexuality. For some women, it seems impossible to imagine that sex and religion could be reconciled.

Tabitha's mother told her that every time Tabitha had sex, the virgin mother cried.

Sandra's father told her that because she was a woman she tempted men with her sexuality and they fell into sin.

Gwen thought God must despise her for enjoying "animalistic" sex, even though she was married.

Abby believed God was punishing her for having premarital sex by making her infertile now that she wanted a baby with her husband.

Ella believed that a male God could not accept her female sexuality.

These women hold beliefs that are not uncommon, and these beliefs prevent them from integrating sex with their religious beliefs. Their conflicts are not new; throughout history sexuality has been a subject of moral discussion and, often, moral condemnation. A woman's religious views towards sex are often deeply rooted in childhood teachings and carry much influence in her sexuality, even if these views are not currently practiced. On the one hand, a woman might feel that her religious views grant meaning and sanctity to her sexuality. Sexual experiences may represent spiritual experiences that bring her closer to her notion of the divine. A woman may gladly and willingly accept certain limitations on her sexuality in accordance with religious teachings on chastity, modesty, and morality. On the other hand, some women feel a great deal of guilt and frustration when religious views run counter to sexual desires. Our purpose here is not to resolve any moral dilemmas or suggest the rightness or wrongness of any particular beliefs. Rather, we suggest that it is important for each woman to identify ways in which her religious views have an impact on her sexuality in both positive and negative ways. When a sexual disorder is involved, it is especially critical to determine if these views create roadblocks to getting better. In such circumstances, it is important to find ways to adapt exercises or seek religious counseling to reconcile conflicting views.

As with all things, religious beliefs about sex vary widely. Some women believe that sex compromises their religious beliefs and that their expression of faith means avoiding most variations of sexuality. Other women see no conflict between sex and religion and view sex as a positive way to express love as part of a divine plan. In her research on biblical references to sexuality, Debra Haffner (1997) has suggested that the following major ideas can be found in both Jewish and Christian scriptures:

- Sexuality holds a central place in people's lives.

- Sexuality is the source of both great pleasure and satisfaction as well as abuse and pain.

- The body and sexuality are affirmed as good.

- Since sexuality is a powerful force, people must make wise and moral decisions and need support, guidance, and information to make good choices.

- Moral decisions are based on love and respect of each other.

- Equality and mutuality are essential components of adult sexual relationships.

Given Haffner's beliefs that the Bible has such a positive message about sexuality, why do so many women feel shame and guilt about their sexuality that they often attribute to religious sources? Perhaps it is because most religious traditions include teachings that emphasize the wild and uncontrollable side of sexuality that must be restrained. Sex is only seen as a moral act within heterosexual marriages with procreation as its purpose.

In some more ascetic Christian traditions, sexual purity and the denial of all bodily pleasures is considered to be the correct moral choice. From this perspective, the way to salvation is to deny the physical plane through fasting, denial of comfort, and deliberate painful practices to subdue bodily pleasure. Although not all individuals follow these teachings, prevailing theology has historically tended to discourage sexual pleasure, even within marriage. Male sexual desire was projected onto women and women were considered to be less capable of moral thought and more sinful and dangerous because they "tempted" men. Sexual release through masturbation was and is still believed by many to be morally wrong. Hatred of sex and high anxiety and hostility toward sex held sway for many centuries and continues to this day.

Over time, ideas about the place of sex in a spiritual life changed. The Reformation in the Catholic Church in the sixteenth century produced a rapid growth of new ideas including a more liberal view of sexuality. However, sexual practices other than intercourse for purposes of procreation continued to be seen as morally wrong. Many Christian denominations continued to discourage sexual expression. This was true of the Puritans who arrived in New England and set strict guidelines that denied the "pleasures of the flesh" and encouraged a "focus on the spirit." To a certain extent, current antisexual beliefs are the remnants of these ascetic ideas in the United States.

Within the last fifty years there have been some changes in religious acceptance of sexuality among Christian theologians. In his 1962 Encyclical, Pope John XXIII recommended that sexuality could be enjoyed as a personal and intimate experience within marriage, to express love as well as for procreation. Many Christian scholars believe that sexuality is a part of our spiritual development and that sexual expression connects the body, mind, and spirit to the cosmos and the divinity. Sexuality is seen as a vehicle to express intimacy between two people, and the variety of sexual expression in addition to intercourse is a natural, creative way of knowing oneself and one's partner.

Jewish theology does not focus on sexuality as morally wrong, but insists upon strict adherence to laws of chastity and modesty as commanded in the Torah (Five Books of Moses) and expounded upon in the Talmud and other rabbinical literature. According to Orthodox Judaism, sexual enjoyment is considered a vital part of marriage but must be confined to those times of the month when the woman is not menstruating, and only after she has ritually immersed and purified herself in a body of water. Modesty in dress and sexual contact is emphasized. Conservative and Reform branches of Judaism do not emphasize the details of sexual purity and modesty but do adhere to the importance of making sexuality a sanctified act between two people. On the one hand, Judaism does not come down on sex as something dirty or evil; on the other hand, it does have a lot to say about how sex should be practiced.

✎

Exercise 8.2—The Impact of Religious Views on Your Sexuality

Ask yourself the following questions about how your religion influences your sexual practices. If you do not practice a formal religious belief, ask yourself these questions based on the beliefs your parents held or with which you are most familiar. Write down your answers in your journal.

- What are your religion's/denomination's views on sex? How do your own personal views fit with these teachings?

- How have these teachings impacted your personal sexual behaviors?

- Who taught you (or failed to teach you) these religious principles? Were you told not to do certain things directly, or were these instructions implied indirectly?

- Was your father or your mother more influential in your spiritual development as a child? How did this affect your sexual belief system?

- Do you think that the beliefs you accepted as a child accurately represent what you now believe?

- If you believe in God, what gender do you assign to this belief? Can you imagine that God would include both masculine and feminine energy?

- If you view God as purely masculine or purely feminine, what does this mean to you about a woman's sexuality?

As a second step, think about whether any of the information revealed by your responses is relevant to your sexual disorder: Are certain views getting in the way of enjoying sex or of carrying out the exercises in this book? Have you found that your views are actually quite compatible with an enjoyable sexuality? Are there ways in which your religious beliefs could enhance sexuality?

One approach to reconciling religious and sexual views is to develop a spiritual perspective on love and sex that is compatible with both. There are many spiritual views of sex that do not spring out of any particular religious tradition. Snarch (1991) suggests that the experience of desire is the normal consequence of being truly alive, whether one desires bodily or spiritual connection and pleasure. Desire and sexual longing is an integral part of the self which is good. Eros, which means desire and affirmation of life, is a soulful experience that is felt through the body as pleasure. Sexuality grows from deep within as an expression of thoughts and feelings. Spiritual connection occurs as one enters into intimate sex, where both partners allow themselves to be revealed at continually deepening levels. Thomas Moore (1994) calls sex "the soul's limpid mirror" and suggests that "sex has long roots that reach deep into the body's quick and far into the feelings of the heart . . . it is also profoundly involved with the soul." He views sex as having the power to disturb and attract us and shake us from complacency. The dark, disturbing images of sex may be a way to explore the needs of the soul. Finally, he suggests that if people place morality and sex in opposition to each other, they inhibit their growth: "We need a deep-seated, imaginative, constantly deepening moral sensitivity; defensive moralism not only thwarts the souls' thirst for pleasure, it also precludes a truly guiding morality founded in wisdom." A personal morality can be a powerful source of commitment, and loyalty to a sexual partner and belief system does not have to inhibit your sexual longings.

The merger of eros and moral sensitivity can create a life-affirming movement toward depth of soul.

Here are several other suggestions that may help you address religious road-blocks:

- Find a trusted religious or spiritual counselor who knows the teachings of your tradition well. It is common for counselors to have different viewpoints on theological issues, and you may want to speak with more than one counselor if you have questions. Consult with them in order to fully understand your own tradition and place your problem within this context. A therapist might then help you to reconcile conflicting viewpoints from a more objective stance. A therapist will not try to introduce their own beliefs, but will work within your beliefs.

- There is a vast literature on sex, religion, and spirituality. We have listed just a few in the resources section in appendix A. Sometimes readings can help inspire you and provide comfort and guidance in dealing with a sexual problem.

- Think about how exercises can be adapted so as not to conflict with personal moral views. Some women might object to the use of erotic materials or fantasy to enhance sexual desire. Instead, focus on erotic fantasies about your partner. If beliefs about modesty involve limitations on sexual positions, practices, or premarital relations, focus on individual exercises or exercises that maximize what you *can* do. Many religious traditions offer special dispensation when a problem exists that may interfere with procreation. You may want to investigate this with clergy.

Attitudes towards Fear, Anxiety, and Pain

In this workbook, we have focused on the importance of fear and pain reactions in female sexual dysfunction. In chapter 2 we defined fear, anxiety, and pain, and in chapter 6 we provided exercises to lessen its impact.

What happens when relaxation techniques are not enough? On the one hand, it is critical to consult your physician to consider medical treatments and/or medications to help. However, sometimes chronic fear and pain requires less focus on treatment of the pain and more focus on learning methods to cope with it. This change in attitude can have surprising effects on fear and pain. In this section, we will examine ways in which fear and pain reactions are highly influenced by perception and expectation and suggest ways to change these influences.

Although both fear and anxiety can affect sexual experience, there are major differences between these unpleasant feelings. Fear has an identified, external source. There is a possibility, even if it is far-fetched, that what is feared might occur (e.g., you may fear getting pregnant, having your children enter the room while you are making love, or having your partner leave if you don't agree to be sexual).

Anxiety on the other hand, has an unidentified, internal source. It is a vague dread, an unrecognized danger, or a feeling that something awful is looming (e.g., you might feel anxious about "losing control" during sexual activity or orgasm, dread feeling vulnerable when you take off your clothes in front of your partner, or feel anxious that pleasure will lead to "something bad" happening).

Pain is a subjective experience formed by both peripheral and central nervous system stimulation. The experience of pain depends as much on the context in which you perceive it as it does on the size and shape of actual or threatened tissue damage. If a woman views her fear and pain as diffuse, unpredictable, overwhelming, and endless, she will experience it in immense proportions. For example, Mary expected sexual intercourse to cause severe vulvar pain, and so she experienced pain out of proportion to what was warranted; her central nervous system amplified any painful stimulation from peripheral pain receptors. On the other hand, if a woman can predict this same fear and pain, and view it as manageable and temporary, she will experience it differently, perhaps as unpleasant but tolerable. Her central nervous system can override these peripheral signals and lessen the experience of pain. When Mary learned about the causes of her pain during intercourse and understood that it wasn't as serious or long-standing as she thought, the pain was still present, but less intense and much less frightening.

✒ Case 8.3—Sandra

Sandra suffered from chronic leg and back pain due to an injury that occurred many years prior to her entering therapy. More recently she began experiencing superficial and vaginal dyspareunia during intercourse with her husband. She thought it might be heralding menopause. She was referred to psychotherapy because her internist was concerned about her frequent phone calls to him complaining of pain. She often felt overwhelmed by her pain and described it as representing her aging body as it slowly dragged her to an eventual death. There was a physical basis for her pain, but certainly no medical basis to suggest it would kill her. And yet, she perceived it as a harbinger of death.

During treatment Sandra described how she had worked as an army nurse at a military hospital during the Vietnam War, tending to injured soldiers. Her therapist asked her to describe her experiences working with these soldiers. "They never complained," she said, "no matter what their situation. They were so happy to be off the battlefield that their pain seemed inconsequential. They no longer feared death. Their injury and pain meant that they were going to live." Seeing Sandra's emotional reaction to these memories, her therapist pointed out a comparison between the soldier's view of pain and Sandra's own situation. While the soldiers embraced pain as a sign of life, Sandra's own experience of pain was so rolled up with her fears of getting older, having diseases, and dying that it seemed overwhelming and endless. This comparison struck a chord in Sandra, and she began to talk about and define her fears. Her resultant understanding of these influences did not take her pain away, but made it feel more manageable. She felt better able to fine-tune her treatment and was more optimistic about finding ways to alleviate her pain. Medications that never seemed to help before now brought relief, and Sandra consented to having back surgery. She also began treatment for a vulvar condition, which helped reduce painful stimulation.

For Sandra, her dread of fear and pain were greatest when their size and shape had no limits in her mind. Despite her genuine complaint of pain, her medical conditions were neither complicated nor life threatening. Her pain was exacerbated by her mental association with pain and death. She viewed her fear and pain the way a frightened person looks at a large, looming shadow on the wall at night—without realizing that the shadow is caused by a much smaller and well-defined object. In addition, her fear and pain symbolized a scary life change for her—the prospect of getting older and entering menopause. As it turned out, her mother had died during menopause of unrelated problems, but Sandra had always put the two together in her mind. Her memories of Vietnam helped her gain a new perspective by seeing how differently one can view fear and pain.

EXERCISE 8.3—THOUGHT STOPPING FOR FEARFUL, ANXIOUS THOUGHTS

Make use of a technique called *thought stopping* to cope with fear and anxiety. First, pay attention when you're afraid. What are you thinking about? Isolate the fearful or anxious statement and write it down. It might be something like "This is really going to hurt," or "I won't be able to stand it." Negative ideas like these can become a habit of thinking. The next time you find your mind repeating the fearful statement, tell yourself, "Stop!" Say it aloud at least once, so that you can hear yourself say it. Imagine a big red stop sign or other image that means "stop" to you. Flick the fingers of your right hand against your left wrist or wear a thin rubber band and snap it gently on your wrist. Follow this with deliberate thoughts of a different nature. You can imagine a specific scene (such as a relaxing beach), sing the words of a song, count numbers, plan a menu—think of anything else. The mind can only hold one thought in it at a time; as long as you think other distracting thoughts, your fearful thoughts will temporarily abate.

EXERCISE 8.4—SYMBOLS AND METAPHORS

In this exercise, you will devise a ritual to come to terms with your fear or pain. Think of a metaphor or symbol that reduces your fear or pain to an object or situation that you can control. One woman decided she could symbolically put her fears into helium balloons, let go of them, and watch them float away. Another woman imagined her pain as the weeds in her garden and would go out each week and pull them one by one and picture her pain lessening. Some women use exercise to work the fear or pain "sweat" out of their bodies. Religious ritual often makes use of such symbolization. It is a way of taking control over your life and putting all sorts of efforts into getting better.

EXERCISE 8.5—VISUALIZATION

Visualization is a powerful technique you can use to create what you want in your life. The word *visualize* means to imagine a scene in your mind's eye. In this exercise, you will imagine yourself taking part in an experience and achieving a goal you desire. Visualization involves all of your senses; as you visualize scenes, imagine sounds, scents, and physical sensations. Visualization requires sensory detail to create a clear image of what you want. You can use visualization techniques to achieve goals you set for yourself, such as relaxed and enjoyable sexuality. You will need to draw upon an inner well of pleasurable, sensuous experiences to create the right scene. This technique is often used by athletes to improve their performance; they visualize an ideal movement or routine over and over again during practice sessions, and then use these experiences to guide them in actual competition. Your mind has a way of organizing this information and integrating it into the way your body responds physically.

Allow a half hour for practice sessions as you learn to visualize. Later on you will be able to do it quickly and easily. An easy first image is that of being relaxed and peaceful in a beautiful place. Begin by using a relaxation technique to soothe and quiet yourself. In order to make use of your sensory memory you need a method to retrieve it. Usually it helps to imagine a set of stairs, a path or road, or a corridor leading to a place you remember as safe and beautiful. You might choose a path leading to a beach or a meadow, or a door that opens into a secret room. The path acts as a transition from real time into imaginary time and gives you the chance to adjust in your mind to your imaginary place.

Now imagine a door or gateway, or an opening in the natural landscape, through which you can go to be safe and alone. Find a place to lie down and imagine a dream scene opening up before you. Imagine the surroundings with all your senses. Let your mind and body flow with the feelings and sensations of the scene. If you pick a beach, imagine the sun on your body and the breeze blowing gently over you, the sound of the waves and sea birds, the smell of sand and salt air, the brightness of the sand and sky and sparkle of the water. After you have fully visualized the scene, pay attention to the relaxed feelings in your mind and body.

If you aren't able to visualize a scene, you can think about a place that gives you a feeling or an impression in a more abstract way. After you have practiced imagining a peaceful place you are ready to try a more complicated visualization. See the end of this chapter for an example of a visualization script.

As you did before, find a comfortable place to sit or lie down where you can be alone for a half hour without interruptions. Choose a goal; something you want to achieve or feel that is within your reach. Later you can take on more complicated goals. Next, imagine a scene in the present as existing the way you wish it to be. Put yourself in the scene.

Now you can move on and visualize a goal. Start with an idea of what you want and then begin to play a movie of it in your mind. Surround this whole thought with positive energy, perhaps by repeating an affirmation or listening to soothing or inspirational music. Block out negative thoughts or images as you build your scene. Add sounds, scents, and sensations. Imagine yourself as happy, calm, and content in the scene. Thus, if your goal is to be free of the fear and anxiety that is acting as a barrier to your sexuality, visualize lying on a soft bed, feeling as you do when you fall into bed after a stressful day. Feel your muscles relax, your breathing slow, and that contented sense of accomplishment and respite.

Your visualization might then include your lover lying beside you, also feeling relaxed and content, slowly stroking your skin. Let your "camera roll" and add new images. Don't get too complicated and don't add things that make you anxious. It often helps to actually do some relaxation exercises during the visualization. Once you have the ideal scene, visualize it several times each day, as if it already exists. Include affirmations while visualizing, such as "I am enjoying the warmth, sense of safety, and wonderful sexual sensations of being in my lover's arms." An upcoming section will discuss affirmations in more detail.

The very process of visualizing your ideal sexual scene will lead you deeper into understanding of what is limiting you from the satisfaction you seek. Don't be surprised if you find something which stops the visualization process. Tell yourself that a way will occur to you to see what you wish to see. If you are unable to get unstuck, talking with a therapist about the impasse will help you work your way through it.

Sexual Myths

If you examine your attitudes and beliefs about sexuality, you may find that much of what you think is based on cultural myths. These myths try to suggest the "appropriate" or "correct" ways in which women should view sex and dictate how often and in what manner women should have sex. They also emphasize unrealistic goals about "great sex." It is easy to get the impression from romance novels, soap operas, movies, and TV dramas that sex is always an easy and ecstatic experience. The ultimate sexual experience, where everything is possible, is described as the norm. The following common myths represent some of the most troubling, erroneous beliefs about sex, but there may be others. Do any of these myths influence your sexual behavior?

Myth One—If You Love Your Partner, Sex Will Be Wonderful

The truth is that having a good sex life is a learned experience. If you and your partner love each other, that is the foundation for enjoyable sex. But sex is made up of many components, including body image; ability to communicate about sex, romance, and sensuality; and learning techniques to increase desire and passion during lovemaking. Your body is programmed for the basic process of arousal and orgasm, but it requires the other components you and your partner bring to the experience to make it intimate, fulfilling, sacred, and meaningful.

Myth Two—Good Girls Don't Like Sex

Many cultural messages suggest that women are not supposed to show interest in initiating, or enjoying sex. This antisexual message is deeply ingrained in our culture, while at the same time we are bombarded by sexual images in the media. Few women can relate to the ultrasexy, slinky siren in advertising, movies, and music videos, and many have trouble reconciling these images with their own sexuality. The difficulty women have with these mythic images probably stems from the fact that most families have trouble discussing sexual subjects with their children, so TV or uninformed peers become alternate teachers. Some parents try to minimize their children's sexual interest or teach their daughters to ignore their sexual feelings. Some parents are emotionally, physically, or sexually intrusive, and their daughters shut down to avoid the stimulation. Intrusive parents are highly anxious about their children and constantly seek reassurance about the psychological or physical condition of their children by monitoring them. Intrusive parents may also maintain inappropriate boundaries when it comes to talking about their own sexual views, desires, or experiences. When childhood messages continue to influence adult behavior, it can become difficult to enjoy sexual feelings. Some women eventually become conditioned to ignore their bodies when feeling aroused, so they can avoid the guilt, shame, or fear they experience from sexual sensations.

Myth Three—Male and Female Sexuality Is the Same

A lot of people assume that women and men experience sex in the same way. But each woman's sexual response—from desire, to arousal, to orgasm—is unique. Women are not only different from men, but are widely different from each other. For this reason, partners need to teach each other how they experience sexual pleasure. Over time a woman can identify and nurture her own unique sexual feelings.

Myth Four—Sex Should Include Intercourse and Orgasm for Both Partners

This expectation causes trouble when each partner tries to perform for the other. Only 20 to 30 percent of women experience orgasm during intercourse (Kaplan 1983). Simultaneous orgasm is not a common experience. Goal-directed sex is bound to lead to disappointment and frustration. Good sex is enjoyed for what it is, whether one or both partners experience orgasm. Intercourse may or may not be part of the experience. Many people learn this as they age and enjoy their sexuality more as a result.

Myth Five—My Partner Should Know What I Want

You can't expect your partner to read your mind. You wouldn't expect your partner to order for you in a restaurant or choose what clothes you want to wear in the morning—not only do you know your own tastes better, but your desires change hour to hour. Once you learn what you like, you can teach it to your partner and let them know what you want at a particular time. Good lovers continue to communicate their sexual wishes to each other over the years as they share sexual activity.

Myth Six—My Partner's Needs Come First

Women are usually acculturated to be aware of relationships at all times and to take care of others. This carries over to their sexual lives, where many women are so focused on their partners that they do not experience their own sexual feelings. Learning to receive is as important as learning to give. Allow your partner the richly pleasurable experience of being able to give to you.

Myth Seven—Affectionate Touching Always Leads to Sex

Often a sexual encounter begins with affectionate caresses. If a woman doesn't feel like having sexual intercourse, she might feel obliged to stop affectionate touching, worrying that it will lead to sex. It is important to be able to communicate to your partner that you like touching, cuddling, and sensitive touch for its own sake, and not just as a prelude to sex. Let your partner know if you only want sensuous touching and not intercourse. Otherwise, misunderstandings and feelings of rejection can result. You and your partner can learn together to enjoy an array of experiences that don't include genital stimulation.

Myth Eight—Good Sex Is Spontaneous

The myth of spontaneous sex gets us all into trouble. If you think back to the courting days, there was nothing spontaneous about getting ready to see your beloved. You bathed or showered, anticipated the evening, and probably planned every minute. You talked to each other about your likes and dislikes. Most couples need to plan sex into their busy lives, and this type of sex can be just as exciting and enjoyable as spontaneous sex. Sex should not be relegated to the end of a busy day when both partners are tired and want to rest rather than be aroused. Rather, use the planning to add some excitement, anticipation, and intrigue into your sex life.

Myth Nine—An Active Sex Life Is Only Normal for Young, Attractive, Heterosexual Couples—for the Purpose of Procreation

Sex, in one form or another, is a normal part of life. When you go to a public place, look around and realize that every woman you see is probably sexual in some way. She might have an active sex life with a partner, enjoy masturbation alone, or have sexual dreams—and any of these activities might or might not include climax. Good sex does not depend on being beautiful or having a perfect body. Women of all shapes, colors, and sizes enjoy their sexuality. People with an illness or a disability can engage in sexual activity on a regular basis. Couples who have a lesbian or bisexual orientation are just as interested in sex and just as likely to enjoy sex as heterosexual couples. Sex and lovemaking is not solely about reproduction. Most of their lives, people enjoy making love to express affection and enjoy physical pleasure. People who are past the childbearing years or people who do not have children are as involved in sex as those who do. In fact, most older people continue to enjoy sex into their seventies and beyond (Brecher 1984).

Myth Ten—No One Has Sexual Problems Except Me

It is easy to feel alone and different when you are experiencing sexual dysfunction. You may look at family and friends and wonder why you are the only one with a sexual problem. You are far from alone, however. According to research (Masters and Johnson 1970), as many as 50 percent of U.S. adults experience problems with sex at some point in their lives. For many individuals, this problem occurs during times of stress or during a life crisis, but passes when tensions ease. For many others, however, the problem may persist, and they may or may not seek help. Some individuals simply give up sex and lose the opportunity to deal with a problem that can be overcome.

Cognitive Distortions

For centuries, philosophers have known that how you think influences what you feel and how you act. Usually people are so accustomed to their thought patterns that they are unaware of the influence these patterns have over them. The thoughts that run through your head are called *self-talk*. Negative self-talk is often automatic, meaning that you react without questioning the thought. Aaron Beck (1976), David Burns (1980), and Edmund Bourne (1995) have examined these patterns of thought and suggested novel strategies to change them:

- Negative thinking is based on the meaning you make of your life, including your belief systems, cultural background, attitudes, and perceptions. The thoughts you have about a given thing influence your feelings and your behaviors. If you change the thoughts, the feelings and behaviors also change.

- Negative thinking occurs automatically and you are usually unlikely to notice the subtle messages you tell yourself, or how you are affected as a result. By consciously observing your thoughts you can make the connections between how the negative thoughts affect your feelings and behavior. Observation will help you notice what you have not seen before.

- Negative thinking is usually made up of a string of images, phrases, memories, and associations. One or several of these may have no foundation in reality, but can trigger other negative thoughts. Each new image or memory adds a new level of fear or anxiety. When you follow the associations, you will often discover that you have several distortions originating from the first thought.

- Negative thinking can become a habit. Since you learned it, you can unlearn it. Keep in mind that if you have been telling yourself something negative for years, you cannot turn that thought around in a few days. But, if you actively make the effort to notice and then change the thoughts, you can definitely bring about change.

- Negative thinking almost always contains some major distortions of the true situation. But although negative thinking may be irrational, it always seems real. Since the thought is automatic and below your level of awareness, you may accept it without questioning its validity.

- Negative thinking often leads to avoidance of a situation. As a result, two things happen: First, you reinforce the distorted thoughts you have and often feel more anxious. Second, since you avoid the situation, you don't give yourself the chance to check the reality of it and change your perceptions.

Underlying negative thinking are patterns of thought called *cognitive distortions.* The many types of cognitive distortions are listed below. As you read through the list and try the exercises, focus on how your own sexual problem is affected by cognitive distortions. You may discover that at times you engage in several of these patterns, while others are never a problem.

All-or-Nothing Thinking

Perfectionism or all-or-nothing thinking is unrealistic, since nothing in life is all one way or all the other. All-or-nothing thinking forces you to see things as all good or all bad and ignores the fact that there is always a gray zone. Examples:

If I can't have an orgasm tonight, I'll never be able to have one.

If I let her hug me in bed I'll have to have sex with her.

Overgeneralization

This type of thinking occurs when you have one bad experience and assume that this experience will be endlessly repeated in your life. When you hear yourself making absolute statements about the future, you can be sure you are overgeneralizing. Listen to yourself and see if you hear the following words: *you always, you never, I always, I'll never, all, none, everyone else, nobody else.* Example:

He always forgets how I asked him to touch me. He'll never change.

Negative Filtering

This type of thinking occurs when you do the opposite of seeing the world through rose-colored glasses. Instead, you perceive only negative details in a situation and ignore anything positive. Filtering happens sometimes in therapy when you have a setback and forget about all the progress you have made. Examples:

What's the point of trying anymore. I'll never work this through.

So what if we did sensate focus, everything about it felt uncomfortable.

Disqualifying the Positive

This distortion occurs when you not only ignore the positive, but you turn it into a negative. Examples:

He's only willing to work with me on my sexuality because he's a sex addict.

I didn't have vaginal pain last night because my problem has spread elsewhere.

Mind Reading

This type of negative thinking occurs when you believe you know what other people are thinking or feeling without asking them, or you assume that someone should be able to read your mind without your having to say what you are thinking. Nine times out of ten you will be wrong. Examples:

He thinks my body is disgusting.

I shouldn't have to tell him what I like. He should know.

Catastrophizing

This distortion occurs when you expect nothing less than disaster, regardless of the data from your past experience. Examples:

If this doesn't work, my marriage is over.

My vulva really hurts—now I'll have to give up sex entirely!

Minimizing

This mistake in thinking occurs when you refuse to give yourself credit for the positive feedback you are receiving. You deny your own ability this way. Example:

My partner said sex was good just so I won't refuse him the next time he asks.

Emotional Reasoning

This illogical type of thinking occurs when you use your emotions as evidence in evaluating a situation and act accordingly. Of course your feelings are important in evaluating your life situation, but separating thoughts and feelings is very important. Example:

I wouldn't be this frightened unless there was something terrifying ahead.

"Should" Statements

This kind of thinking is based on levels of perfection you expect from yourself or others which are unreasonable and unrealistic. It is a kind of perfectionism with rigid rules of behavior, leading to disappointment in others and self-blame. Examples:

I should be able to ignore this pain during intercourse.

I should be able to enjoy sex.

My partner should be able to give up sex if he loves me.

Personal Labeling

This type of cognitive distortion occurs when you generalize one quality into a negative self-image. Mislabeling often involves language that is emotional, and laden with negative words. Example:

No one will ever want me if I can't have an orgasm. I'm a loser.

Personalization

This mistake in cognition occurs when you believe that everything people say or do is in reaction to you. You assume responsibility for the happiness or pain of everyone around you. Examples:

My partner has trouble getting an erection—it must be because I'm not attractive.

My therapist didn't seem happy today—she must think I'm a hopeless case!

Control Fallacies

You imagine yourself with an external locus of control. This leads to blaming others and feeling victimized and helpless. Examples:

Why does my husband leave that bright light on when we make love—it's his fault that I can't let myself go.

I could probably get interested in sex but I know my partner doesn't really care about me, so why bother?

Fallacy of One Reality

You believe there is only one right way—*your* way. This makes no allowance for multiple realities. Others must be wrong and you will go to great lengths to prove you are right. You must change what others think or do, since your happiness depends on them. Examples:

Why does my partner insist on walking around the house nude? Everybody knows it's wrong to display yourself like that.

Why should I have to wear a flimsy nightgown to have sex? Those ideas are sick.

Fallacy of Fairness

Like the belief in one reality, you assume that you know exactly what is fair and what isn't. If others disagree with you, you are angry and hurt. Examples:

It's not fair that I'm the one who has a problem with orgasm and he has all the fun in bed.

After all I've done for her, it's not fair that she won't help me with my sensate focus exercises.

Fallacy of Change

In this distortion, you put all of your hope for change onto someone else and expect that, with enough pressure, they will change to meet your needs and solve the problem. Examples:

I won't agree to sex if he doesn't show me he loves me.

If he would just be more available at night, I wouldn't have this problem!

Blaming

You blame either yourself or other people for all of your difficulties. Examples:

If it weren't for that insensitive doctor, I would have recovered from vaginismus by now.

It's my fault our marriage is in such trouble. Everything would be fine if I liked sex as much as he does.

Heaven's Reward Fallacy

In this distortion, you feel anger or resentment when all of your efforts and self-sacrifice don't lead to expected returns. Examples:

I've been struggling for two months to get better and nothing is changing. I deserve success after all I've been through.

I always put my partner's needs first. Now he should do what I want without complaining.

Everyone experiences these cognitive distortions at one point or another. They often help people deal with painful realizations by making sense of the situation and giving it some meaning, no matter how unpleasant. Consider the woman who is upset about her vaginismus. She doesn't understand it or know how to resolve it. If she believes her pain is the fault of the doctor because of an insensitive exam (blaming), and she thinks that since this happened once, it will always happen (overgeneralization), she can make some sense of why she has vaginismus and why it won't go away. There are two problems here: her thinking is unrealistic and it is perpetuating the problem. Although she has developed a reason for the problem (it is the doctor's fault), her thoughts prevent her from solving the problem. Over time, mistakes in thinking are woven into your belief system, and consequently affect the way you approach the world. That is why they tend to be repetitive and difficult to change. Change occurs when you acknowledge an unrealistic belief and replace it with more accurate thinking.

The first step to changing cognitive distortions is replacing a negative thought with a more realistic one. Second, replace a negative, or even realistic, thought with a hopeful and positive one. You are more likely to succeed at a given task if you have a positive expectation. Optimism, faith, and self-confidence can make your journey swifter and more successful. To begin, review your journal entries and the notes in this book to see how your attitudes affect your problem. Try to identify whether you are using negative thought patterns. It is not necessary to determine the exact type of cognitive distortion—often several apply. It is more important to identify when you are being guided by mistaken assumptions and then try to counteract them.

EXERCISE 8.6—IDENTIFYING AND COUNTERACTING COGNITIVE DISTORTIONS

In this exercise you will make a list of your own cognitive distortions and try to identify their types. Then, you will devise a more realistic and positive way of thinking about the situation. First, take a moment to look at the following examples:

Jill's Cognitive Distortions

Negative Self-Talk	Cognitive Distortion	Realistic/Positive View
He thinks I take too long to reach orgasm.	*Mind Reading*	*I don't know how he feels—I need to ask him. He might also be concerned.*
We didn't try sensate focus last night! We'll never get started with it!	*Overgeneralization*	*We have the whole week to try. Plus, we did two exercises last week.*
I have to be on the bottom— that's the only position that will work!	*Fallacy of One Reality*	*I've never tried being on top, but many women do—it's worth a try.*
I feel silly when I'm naked—these exercises are humiliating.	*Emotional Reasoning*	*I felt silly last time, but not so much the second time. I also felt excited and interested.*
I should want to have sex whenever my partner wants to.	*"Should" Statements*	*There is no rule here—I can make up my own mind. Plus, it's great that my partner finds me desirable!*

Now that you've gotten the idea of how to do it, try making your own list in your journal or on the chart below.

Negative Self-Talk	Cognitive Distortion	Realistic/Positive View

Affirmations

Affirmations are positive thoughts that you deliberately choose in order to change the automatic negative statements you make about yourself. Using affirmations can help you increase your self-esteem and pride in yourself and your body; alleviate anxiety, helplessness, and feelings of discouragement; lower fear and aversion reactions; and ameliorate pain.

Affirmations can bring about change quickly. You will usually notice a difference in your attitudes within two weeks if you practice daily (Ray 1976; Bloch 1990). Affirmations can help you change your attitude so that you and your partner will progress towards your sexual goals, but should not be used to make you change in some way that does not fit with your value system. Here are several important components to remember when doing affirmations:

- Repetition has a powerful effect. Chances are that if you are having trouble with your sexuality you have repeated hundreds of negative thoughts about yourself for a long time. Affirmations will help you keep track of the changes in your thinking. The consequent changes in your life will in turn reinforce the affirmations.

- Affirmations are most effective if you give them the same emotional charge you give to negative thoughts. When emotion is attached to thought you are more likely to pay attention to the thought.

- Affirmations should be worded so that you make statements about yourself that are actually possible. Look for a happy medium as you design your statements—not impossible to imagine, but advanced from where you are now. You *don't* want to invent something totally unrealistic like "I will have multiple orgasms every time I have sex."

- In order to change you have to be willing. If you can't imagine change, make some affirmations about your willingness to imagine change.

- Affirmations can serve as your personal mantra as you repeat them over and over while breathing deeply. Say them to yourself many times a day. Write them on index cards or Post-its and put them where you can see them. Record them on a tape recorder and listen to the tape before you go to sleep. Keep saying them to yourself daily—*even if you don't believe them*—for at least two weeks. Research shows that individuals with depression start to feel better after two weeks of reciting positive statements (Burns 1980).

EXERCISE 8.7—AFFIRMATIONS

What kind of sexual woman do you want to be? How do you want to feel about sex? You need three main ingredients to make affirmations work for you:

1. The desire to really want something and the clear statement of a wish

2. The belief that you can actually get it

3. The ability to accept into your life the wish you have made

To do this exercise you will need an hour to think and write. Affirmations usually work best if you pick one belief to work on and then design three suggestions that address different components of that main belief. You can choose your affirmations to counteract your cognitive distortions, or you can simply ask yourself what you want. When writing affirmations, use either the present tense ("I am calm and relaxed") or the present progressive tense ("I am becoming more and more calm and relaxed"). Phrase all statements in a positive active manner; instead of saying, "I am not nervous," say, "I am calm and relaxed." Be specific and concrete, and make short declarative statements that condense your idea into the essence of what you want.

For some reason, writing affirmations by hand seems to work much better than using a computer or typing. Starting with a clean piece of paper, fold it in half lengthwise so that you have two columns. On the left side of the paper, write three affirmations that all connect to the main belief. Skip a space and rewrite the same three affirmations. Keep doing this until you have twenty sets of three affirmations.

Next, go back to the beginning and read each one. As you read it, a negative thought, belief, memory, or emotion will automatically pop into your head. Write it down in the right-hand column. Don't try to change it or even think about it now. Go on to the next line, repeating the affirmation. Continue in this manner until you reach the end. As you do this, you'll begin to realize how many thoughts blocked you from your goal as you start to replace old negative beliefs with new positive ones.

The following affirmations are an example of a woman who wanted to be able to relax enough to enjoy sex:

I feel relaxed and open to sexual feelings.

I am safe and secure and enjoy sexual excitement.

I am a sensual, sexual woman, and I deserve pleasure.

If you are having difficulty coming up with affirmations, you might want to adapt your cognitive distortions from exercise 8.3. For example:

Jill's Cognitive Distortion	Suggested Affirmation
I take too long or can't reach orgasm.	*As I enjoy sexual pleasure orgasm will follow.*
We didn't try sensate focus last night! We'll never get started with it!	*Touching is relaxing and gives me pleasure.*
I have to be on the bottom—that's the only position that will work!	*I like the fun of changing sexual positions.*
I feel silly when I'm naked—these exercises are humiliating.	*My naked body is warm and sensuous.*
I should want to have sex whenever my partner wants to.	*I feel good about making my own decisions. OR Giving and receiving sexual pleasure feels good.*

If you really use affirmations, you will notice a change within a week or two in your sense of confidence and hope. The next step is to act on your more realistic, positive, and hopeful affirmations. Some women get stuck here, and spend too much time daydreaming about what is possible without actually doing what is probable and practical. Moving beyond this point requires some assertiveness to ask your partner to help you fulfill your own needs.

Assertiveness Training

Many women are socialized to be agreeable, and consequently they may have difficulty asserting themselves. Being assertive requires belief in the idea that you have a right to ask for what you need. Assertiveness differs from aggression, which has a hostile intent toward the other person.

To be assertive you need to be aware of your feelings first—a task in and of itself. Then you need to be able to ask for what you want or refuse what you don't want. Asking for what you want suggests that you have a right to make requests of your partner. If you are not sure you have the right for a particular request, try saying to yourself, "I deserve _____ ," and see what inner response you get. Becoming assertive is a skill you learn.

You are probably assertive when you order from a menu in a restaurant—you order what you want and do not feel like you are mistreating the waiter with your request. But making your sexual wishes known is much more difficult. No one is really free to say "yes" to sex if they are not equally free to say "no." But since so many women are trained to be aware of the needs of others and to take care of others, they often neglect their own needs and begin to feel resentful. The following exercises start with assertiveness training that doesn't involve your partner, and will move gradually to more difficult, intimate assertiveness training.

Exercise 8.8—Sexual Assertiveness Scale

Some women know what they want sexually but have trouble telling their partners. It might be easy to ask your partner to do the dishes, but not as easy to ask them for a specific sexual touch. Measure your sexual assertiveness with the actions below. If you have made the request of your partner, place a check in the space. Then, whether you've made the request or not, rate your ability to do so on the following scale:

    1 = I could make this request easily.
    2 = I could make the request but with some hesitation.
    3 = I am not sure.
    4 = I probably couldn't or wouldn't make this request.
    5 = I would never request this or am afraid to do so.

After you have scored each one, rank them from the easiest (1) to the most difficult (20). Are there requests you would like to make but can't? You might want to discuss this list with your partner and think of ways to make requests in a comfortable manner.

Sexual Assertiveness Scale

Asking my partner to make love. _____

Telling my partner I don't want to make love. _____

Telling my partner I want to try a new sexual activity. _____

Telling my partner I don't want to try a new activity. _____

Saying I want a specific type of touch. _____

Telling my partner I fantasize. _____

Sharing a fantasy. _____

Telling my partner I masturbate. _____

Showing my partner how I masturbate. _____

Asking my partner to wash before sex. _____

Telling my partner that certain odors turn me off. _____

Telling my partner certain odors turn me on. _____

Asking for oral sex. _____

Asking my partner to include a vibrator in sex. _____

Telling my partner I fake orgasm sometimes. _____

Asking my partner to turn off the TV, or radio, during lovemaking. _____

Telling my partner I'm not ready for penetration.

Telling my partner I want affectionate touch only.   _____
Asking my partner to emotionally connect with me before sex. _____
Asking for continued stimulation if my partner has their   _____
orgasm first.

EXERCISE 8.9—MAKING AND REFUSING REQUESTS
(NONSEXUAL WITHOUT PARTNER)

Many women have trouble asking for what they want. Sometimes this is true even when they are asking themselves. If you want to give yourself something nice, it might be difficult to allow yourself a little pleasure. Problems allowing yourself to have pleasures translates to the sexual arena, where you might believe you don't deserve pleasure and therefore you can't ask for what you want. Another major barrier to asking for what you want is that it might seem risky and affect your relationship in a negative way.

The opposite side of the coin is the difficulty many women have saying "no." Here again, if you say "no," you risk affecting your relationship in a negative way. Also, women are socialized to be helpful and giving. If you say "no," you may feel guilty because you *should* be willing and ready to say "yes" to everything. Some people find it easier to say "no," others find it easier to say "yes," and some people have trouble with both. The following exercises address these issues.

Over a period of one week, ask for three things you want that you would ordinarily not ask for. They can be minor and should not be sexual in nature. You might ask a friend to pick you up after work, or a family member to clean up after dinner. You might let yourself buy a bouquet of flowers, which ordinarily you would think was too expensive. The same week, refuse to do three things that others ask of you, which ordinarily you would agree to do but would rather not. You might refuse an invitation to an event you don't want to attend or refuse to lend out your favorite sweater. You might refuse to go through the pile of paperwork on your desk. Keep track of what it is like to be assertive in this way. If you have trouble asking for things, it may be difficult to convince yourself that you deserve sexual pleasure. Perhaps you have trouble saying "no." This may cause you to feel resentful if you give in.

EXERCISE 8.10—MAKING AND REFUSING REQUESTS
(LOOKING AND TOUCHING, WITH PARTNER)

This exercise is slightly more difficult because you will do this with your intimate partner. Set aside fifteen minutes where you won't be interrupted. You will be practicing assertiveness with looking and touching. You can do this exercise with your clothes on. Sit in front of your partner and greet each other. Now take turns asking to look at each other. For example, you can ask, "May I look at your elbow?" If your partner feels comfortable with your request and says "yes," you may look until you are satisfied. Observe the colors and textures of their body, notice how their skin covers their bones and muscles. When you are done, thank your partner. If your partner feels uncomfortable with your request, they simply need to say "no." Then ask to look at another part of their body. After a few minutes, change roles. When you have finished, talk about the experience. Try to work out ways to make each other more comfortable, and discuss the places on the body you did not want to show the other.

Then sit in front of your partner and take turns asking to touch each other. For example, you can ask, "May I touch your cheek?" If your partner agrees, you can gently explore and when you are finished you can thank them. If your partner says "no," ask if you can touch a less intimate part of their body. The goal of this exercise is to explore slowly—neither of you should rush the other. You both need to be understanding and patient with each other if your partner says "no" to any of your requests. Next, change roles. When you have finished, thank each other and discuss the experience, focusing on how to make the touching as pleasurable and comfortable as possible.

If you become fearful or anxious during this exercise, stop and do some slow, deep-breathing exercises until you feel more relaxed. Then return to the exercise, trying a different part of the body. If you don't know why this made you anxious, talking it over with your partner or a therapist could be very helpful. Keeping track of your reactions in a journal can also be helpful. Go slowly and gradually enlarge the areas of safe touch on your own body or on your partner. This exercise can begin with both partners wearing clothes unless you prefer to be nude. As you continue to increase your ability to feel safe, try being more revealing until ultimately you feel comfortable being nude together and sharing any sensuous touching that you desire.

EXERCISE 8.11—REQUESTING AND REFUSING INTIMATE SEXUAL TOUCH

Allow an hour for this exercise, which will involve being nude with your partner. Before you begin, bathe or shower so that you feel both clean and relaxed. You will be taking turns practicing assertiveness about sexual touch. Start with something that you both agree is easy. Do the exercise as you did the two previous ones, asking and answering, and then talking about the experience.

This is the most difficult of the assertiveness exercises, so be patient with yourselves. Keep in mind that the exercise is about assertiveness, not about testing your sexual boundaries. So say "yes" and "no" to things you could actually do with ease. People always feel hurt when sexual initiations are refused, so be gentle and see what language you find works best for the two of you. Some people find it easier to do this exercise by including guiding to show what they like. If you refuse a request, it is always helpful to offer an alternative so that your partner can learn what you like as well as what you don't like. If you are really shy about asking, tell your partner what you are going to ask for and make sure the partner would agree. Then ask. It might seem mechanical, but actually this type of role-play does help change behavior. If you have trouble refusing, do the same thing. Practice by choosing something you really do like and refuse to do it.

A Visualization Script: White Light

Use the following visualization script as a relaxation method. The first step is to read it into a tape recorder. Then play it back to yourself while you are in a relaxed state. Lie down in a comfortable position and use deep breathing and other relaxation techniques as you quiet your mind:

Find a way to relax your entire body as you sink down ... gradually ... into a state of deep relaxation. ... Breathe in through your nose and out through your mouth ... breathing in the way that is exactly right for you ... slowing your breathing with every breath you take.... Allow yourself to relax and to let go ... let go of tension and take in calm, quiet energy ... feeling universal peace surround you.... You are relaxed and drowsy, very drowsy, and your mind is drifting, floating, easily resting ... quiet.... From the quiet dark emerges a glowing light, a gentle soft white light is shining....

As you breathe in your own natural rhythm, feel yourself surrounded in warm, luminous white light.... The light is shining on you, filling you with peace and quiet ... the light is flowing around you ... radiant ... glowing with energy.... Feel the peaceful sense of glowing health and well-being.... The light is around you, surrounds you.... You are safe, feeling the love of the universe as healing soothing white light swirls around you....

As you rest, calm and relaxed, you feel the stream of white light flowing around you ... and entering into you ... white light ... the light that holds all colors and is no color ... pours through you.... A halo is formed and enters into the top of your head and down your face and neck ... into your throat and chest.... White light is pouring through your arms and hands.... Feel the tingling pleasure in your fingers, warm and safe.... Light is pouring into your body, down into your stomach and abdomen ... streaming through your thighs ... down your legs and into your feet.... Your feet are warm and tingling through your toes ... your body feels the flowing sense of peace and safety as healing white light courses through every cell, healing and warming.... Feel yourself become one with the brilliant and flooding light....

Bathe in this light.... Feel it cascading through you as you breathe in the light ... the light is in you ... you are in the light ... you are of the light. Feel yourself becoming one with the soft sweet light ... as it moves through you ... the brilliant light of the universe pouring through you ... illuminating every part of your body and soul ... soothing and healing ... bathed in an aura of white luminescence.... Feel the peace and health of universal light pour through you ... feel the loving force of light healing you ... know the feeling of peace and rest ... know the healing of body and soul....

Say your affirmations to yourself as you lie quietly filled with the glowing light that heals and warms you.... Rest in the light and say your affirmations.... When you are ready, bring yourself back into the present time and place, holding in your mind the sense of peace.

Roadblocks and Resistance: A Review

Before moving to the next chapter, take some time to review your sexual fears and pains. Look back over your fear and pain lists from chapter 1, and your sexual map from chapter 2. How successful have you been in reducing your sexual fear and pain so far? Have relaxation techniques helped? Sensate focus? Positive statements? Affirmations? Visits to a physician or gynecologist? If these difficulties are persistent there may be several reasons:

- Physical causes are severe and haven't responded to treatment.
- You haven't been able to identify and overcome your resistance.
- You partner is not cooperative.
- You can't get negative thoughts out of your head.
- You are unable to see a future free of fear or pain.

The first three roadblocks have been addressed in previous chapters. Each of these three obstructions are complex and difficult to resolve, and you may need to seek further professional help. Chapter 10 will discuss working with partners in more detail. The last two roadblocks have been addressed in this chapter. Review the different therapeutic techniques you've learned so far:

- Journal writing to identify fears and pains; note feelings and thoughts about yourself and keep track of progress.

- Association webs to find relationships between difficulties.

- Deep-breathing relaxation techniques to lower anxiety and learn to be in the moment.

- Progressive muscle relaxation to gradually relax and experience body sensations.

- Kegel exercises to gain a sense of control over your genitals.

- Sensate focus (with partner) I–IV to learn to give and receive pleasure.

- Cognitive distortion worksheets to change mistaken beliefs.

- Affirmations, imagery, and visualization to gain a positive expectation of your sexual goals.

You may want to repeat one or more of these techniques to get past your roadblocks. Then you will be ready to read chapter 9 and make use of the individualized exercises that suit your needs.

References

Ackerman, D. 1990. *A Natural History of the Senses.* New York: Vintage Books.

Anand, M. 1989. *The Art of Sexual Ecstasy: The Path to Sacred Sexuality for Western Lovers.* New York: Jeremy P. Tarcher/Perigee.

Benson, H. 1975. *The Relaxation Response.* New York: Avon

Benson, H. 1984. *Beyond the Relaxation Response.* New York: Berkeley Books.

Bloch, D. 1990. *Words That Heal: Affirmations and Medications for Daily Living.* New York: Bantam.

Bourne, E. J. 1995. *The Anxiety and Phobia Workbook, 2nd Edition.* Oakland, Calif.: New Harbinger Publications, Inc.

Brecher, E. 1984. *Love, Sex, and Aging.* Boston: Little, Brown & Co.

Burns, D. 1980. *Feeling Good: The New Mood Therapy.* New York: New American Library.

Gawain, S. 1978. *Creative Visualization.* Toronto: Bantam New Age Book.

Haffner, D. W. 1997. "A Sabbatical's Lessons." *SIECUS Developments.* 5(1):2.

Kaplan, H. S. 1983. *The Evaluation of Sexual Disorders.* New York: Brunner/Mazel.

Lowen, A. 1970. *Pleasure.* New York: Penguin Books.

Masters, W. and V. Johnson. 1970. *Human Sexual Inadequacy.* Boston: Little, Brown & Co.

Moore, T. 1994. *Soul Mates: Honoring the Mysteries of Love and Relationship.* New York: Harper Perennial.

Ray, S. 1976. *I Deserve Love.* Berkeley, Calif.: Celestial Arts.

Rico, G. L. 1983. *Writing the Natural Way.* Los Angeles: Jeremy P. Tarcher Inc.

Rosenberg, J. 1973. *Total Orgasm.* New York: Random House.

Rossi, E. L. and D. B. Cheek. 1988. *Mind-Body Therapy: Methods of Ideodynamic Healing in Hypnosis.* New York: W. W. Norton.

Snarch, D. M. 1991. *Constructing the Sexual Crucible: An Integration of Sexual and Marital Therapy.* New York: W. W. Norton.

Zinn, J. K. 1994. *Wherever You Go, There You Are.* New York: Hyperion.

Chapter Nine

Individualizing Your Treatment

In this chapter, we will build upon treatment exercises in chapters 6 through 8, but with a focus on your unique sexual problems. Each treatment module addresses a particular sexual problem by providing suggestions and exercises. These exercises often require some guidance or feedback and are best used with the help of a sex therapist. If you are not working with a therapist, you can request a consultation with a sex therapist to clarify whether you can make changes on your own or whether you need more guidance. In particular, hypoactive desire can be very difficult to treat and the exercises here will only provide a beginning for your work. Likewise, sexual phobias and aversion often require the use of detailed cognitive-behavioral assignments and antianxiety medications and must be conducted with the assistance of a trained psychotherapist and psychiatrist. If your situation is complicated by a medical or psychiatric problem, we urge you to first seek the assistance of a physician you trust and then use the suggestions in this chapter to maximize the ways in which your physician can help. Each module will refer you to the extensive list of helpful readings and resources in the appendix.

These treatment modules require a secure foundation; therefore, we recommend that you master the relaxation techniques taught in chapter 6 and the sensate focus exercises in chapter 7 before you begin. In addition, we suggest that you identify potential resistance to treatment as described in chapter 8. You may become discouraged if you try to solve your problem without enough information, your partner's involvement, or a relaxed and informed environment.

Where do you begin? The module titles are fairly self-explanatory, but table 9.1 can help guide you to a solution for your sexual problem.

Module One—Coping with Medical and Physical Disability

In chapter 4, we discussed the many medical problems that can cause or exacerbate sexual dysfunction. For some women, chronic pain and disability can make sex their last priority; for others, it continues to be an important part of their life. The following suggestions will help you adapt your sexual practices to your unique condition:

- In order to maximize your medical treatment to relieve or minimize symptoms and to achieve adequate pain control you must be your own advocate. Comply with recommended therapies and medications and if you are not satisfied with your treatment talk with your doctor.

Table 9.1. A Guide to the Treatment Modules

Problem/Special Need	Recommended Treatment Module
Complicating medical problem	Module 1
Potential side effects to medication	Module 2
Hypoactive Sexual Desire	Module 3
Sexual Arousal Disorder	Module 3
Orgasmic Disorder	Module 4
Dyspareunia/Vaginismus	Module 5
Vaginal narrowing (strictures/stenosis)	Module 5
Sexual phobia or aversion	Module 6
History of sexual trauma or abuse	Module 7

- Discuss your sexual difficulties with your physician and get recommendations on sexual resources and counseling. Many doctors will not initiate talk about sex. You must be proactive. Most support organizations for chronic illness have published information on sexual function (see the appendix).

- Identify problematic medications and investigate alternative agents or strategies.

- Know your sexual limitations and strengths and focus on sexual activities within these boundaries. You may have to give up unrealistic expectations that you can return to your former state of health, but sex can still be varied, comfortable, and pleasurable.

- Use medications for symptomatic relief before sexual activity. For example, bronchodilators may prevent wheezing during exertion, and analgesics or anti-inflammatory medications may lessen pain.

- Be well rested prior to sexual activity. Do not eat a large meal beforehand.

- If you are worried about whether you have adequate stamina, find an equivalent exercise to practice, such as walking up stairs, to build up endurance and confidence. Consult with your physician to devise an appropriate exercise.

- Take your time during sexual activity and focus on slow and relaxing foreplay.

- Explore sexual positions that decrease exertion or account for equipment such as oxygen tanks or ostomy bags. Suggested positions for intercourse include lying side by side, sitting face to face, or, for heterosexual couples, having the male kneel behind the female as she rests her knees on the ground and her arms on the bed. Several positions are illustrated in figure 9.1.

- Always keep in mind that you are a person—not a disease or disability. Your thoughts and feelings about yourself, your medical problem, and your sexuality are very important.

- Use humor to decrease anxiety over your limitations or self-consciousness. One couple covered the woman's oxygen tank with lingerie, while another couple dealt with their self-consciousness over surgical scars by massaging each other's bodies with opaque body paints.

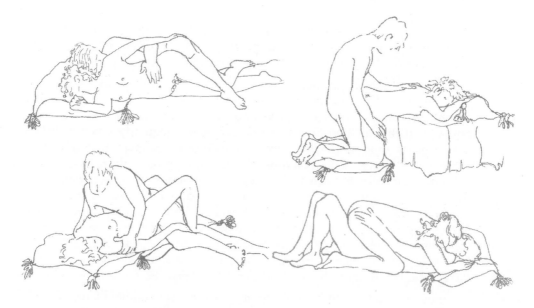

Figure 9.1. Sexual Positions That Minimize Exertion

- Don't avoid or hide from your anxieties, but discuss them openly during relaxed times between sex.

- If you have a gynecologic or urologic disorder, minimize urethral pressure by urinating before sexual activity. Urinate again after sex. Women with interstitial cystitis should be especially careful to follow this recommendation.

- Avoid intercourse during times of increased symptoms or pain.

- Be creative with sexual activities. Minimize activities that cause pain and focus on others that are relaxing and pleasurable. Orgasm can be stimulated in many ways.

The key is to take care of yourself and give yourself time and space to enjoy your sexuality. You may have to develop a new sense of your sexuality with your partner—one less focused on previous sexual patterns and more influenced by your current sexual strengths.

Module Two—Alleviating the Side Effects of Medication

If you suspect that one or more medications are causing sexual dysfunction, you must consult with the prescribing physician. It is never wise to make changes on your own. The following strategies may be helpful and can be reviewed with your prescribing physician:

1. Continue the medication and wait for tolerance of the side effect to develop. Many side effects diminish or go away after several weeks.

2. Reduce the dose of medications with sexual side effects, if possible.

3. Stop the medication and substitute an alternative agent, if available, that has less potential for sexual side effects. For antidepressants, bupropion

(Wellbutrin) and nefazodone (Serzone) have significantly less risk of sexual problems. For antipsychotics, more potent agents risperidol (Risperdal) and haloperidol (Haldol) may cause less dysfunction.

4. For antidepressants, consider the use of medications that work as antidotes to reverse sexual side effects. They can be given one hour prior to anticipated sex initially on an as needed basis, and in increasing doses until success is achieved. If this method doesn't work, consider a regularly scheduled daily dose. Several antidotes include: yohimbine (Yocon), amantadine (Symmetrel), cyproheptadine (Periactin) (**Caution:** this medication not only reverses sexual side effects of SSRIs but can also reverse the antidepressant effect), bethanecol (Urocholine), bupropion (Wellbutrin), nefazodone (Serzone), trazodone (Desyrel), buspirone (Buspar), methylphenidate (Ritalin), and bromocriptine—for antipsychotics (Parlodel). Combinations of antidotes may work as well; for example, Yocon and Ritalin, or Yocon and Periactin. Ask your psychiatrist to review the psychiatric literature for a possible solution. Please note that these antidotes do not always work, and can cause side effects themselves.

5. Attempt to simplify the overall regimen; sometimes combinations of medications cause more sexual side effects than each medication.

6. For certain medications, a "drug holiday" in which the medication is temporarily stopped (such as on weekends) can result in improved sexual function. This has been done successfully for short-acting antidepressants such as Paxil or Zoloft. However, there is the risk of recurrent symptoms during this holiday.

If none of these strategies work, you have to consider the trade-off between the benefits of the medication and the resultant sexual side effects. For some individuals, going off of the medication is just too risky and there may not be adequate alternatives. This is a frustrating situation, and people often stop their medications or abandon sex altogether. In most cases, however, the above strategies will yield some benefit.

Module Three—Increasing Sexual Desire and Arousal

Sexual desire and sexual arousal are complex drives influenced by many different factors. Hopefully you have identified many of these factors in earlier chapters. The relaxation exercises in chapter 6 and the sensate focus exercises in chapter 7 are critical in unblocking the flow of sexual desire and arousal. To further enhance those exercises, this module will help you gauge your levels of desire and arousal and increase your focus on sexual thoughts and images.

Exercise 9.1—Charting Your Sexual Desire

In this exercise, you will chart your current level of sexual interest over several time increments. Many women, especially those with low desire, are surprised to discover that they actually do think about sex on a daily basis. In rating your levels of sexual desire, consider the following questions: How often do you feel a sense of desire within your body? How often do you think about sex or sensual touch, remember recent sexual experiences, or create sensual fantasies? How often do you want to engage in a sexual activity alone? With a partner? We will provide several time charts to record your level of desire, but feel free to make your own charts in your journal. Remember that you are scoring for desire only, which may consist of sexual desires, interests, thoughts, images, or fantasies. You are not scoring for the number of actual sexual experiences you have, nor are you scoring for sexual arousal. Use the following ten-point scale:

    1 = No sexual desires, fantasies, interests, images, or thoughts.
    3 = Mild degree of sexual desires, fantasies, interests, images, or thoughts.
    5 = Moderate degree of sexual desires, fantasies, interests, images, or thoughts.
    7 = High degree of sexual desires, fantasies, interests, images, or thoughts.
   10 = Constant sexual desires, fantasies, interests, images, or thoughts.

This is only a subjective scale since there is no specific standard of sexual desire. The purpose here is for you to take note of your own sexual desire as it fluctuates over time. The *pattern* of desire is as important as the *level* of desire.

Begin by rating your level of sexual desire for two different days, using the charts in figure 9.2. Do not rate two consecutive days. When you chart daily levels of desire, notice slight fluctuations over the course of the day. Passing sensual images, memories of pleasant sexual experiences, body sensations (i.e., tingling in the breasts or genitals), emotional longing for sexual closeness, erotic dreams, and sexual fantasies are all normal kinds of daily sexual thoughts. Keep in mind that desire might be independent of sexual activity; a woman can have sex without feeling much desire for it. Desire occurs foremost in the mind. Does the time of day influence your desire? How long do you think about sex during a given day?

The following explains Susan's "Daily Levels of Sexual Desire" chart:

7 A.M.   She feels sleepy, but aroused to be next to her partner in bed. Level three desire.

8–9 A.M.   Focuses on work. Level one desire.

11 A.M.   Thinks about making love with her partner last night. Level three desire.

12 Noon Receives phone call from partner; anticipates making love that night. Level four desire

1–4 P.M.   Focuses on work. Level one to two desire.

5 P.M.   Thinks about spending the evening with her partner. Level three desire.

6 P.M.   Feels tired after work. Level one desire.

6:30 P.M. Gets ready to go out. Dresses first in silk underwear. Level four desire.

7–8 P.M.   Has dinner with her partner. Level two to five desire.

9 P.M.   Dances with partner. Level eight desire.

10 P.M.   Makes love. Reaches level ten desire.

11 P.M.   Settles down to sleep. Level zero desire.

Once you've charted your daily levels of desire, chart your levels of desire over the course of a week using the chart in figure 9.3. For each day, you can either put in an average number for that day or draw in brackets showing the range for that day. Or, you may simply reflect back on the week and draw a line to represent your subjective sense for your desire over the course of the week. Susan's daily chart shows that she is more desirous when she is relaxing. Desire is not noticeable when her attention is focused on her work. Her desire goes up when she looks forward to being with her partner or remembers previous sexual experiences.

Susan's Daily Levels of Sexual Desire

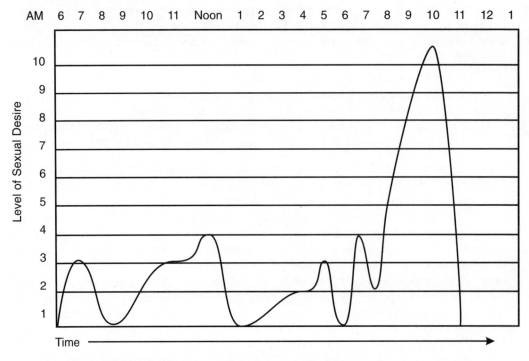

Your Daily Levels of Sexual Desire—1

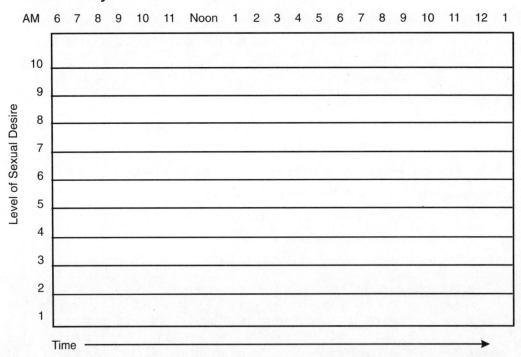

Figure 9.2. Daily Levels of Sexual Desire

Your Daily Levels of Sexual Desire—2

Figure 9.2. Daily Levels of Sexual Desire—*Continued*

The following explains Susan's "Weekly Levels of Sexual Desire" chart:

Monday	Desire at three; remembers weekend of making love.
Tuesday	Busy with deadlines at work, sisters birthday party, desire at zero.
Wednesday	Busy with deadlines at work, rushed with errands after work, goes to the gym, and gets home at 9 P.M., tired. No desire all day. Level zero.
Thursday	Work more relaxed, time to think about her partner, fantasize, plan for evening. Desire between four and ten.
Friday	Beginning of romantic weekend away. Busy during day; desire at zero. But as evening arrives and it's time to leave for trip, desire up to five. Too tired to make love at night, but sleeping together brings desire up to seven.
Saturday	Starts out making love, breakfast in bed, all day relaxing and having fun together. Make love again at night. Desire between three and ten all day.
Sunday	Feeling good but tired. Desire at three for trip home, briefly up to six, and then down to two in the evening as starting to think about work on Monday.

Finally, chart your levels of desire over the course of one month, with day one representing the first day of your period. You can either put in an average score each day or periodically add to the line showing the rise and fall of desire over the course

Susan's Weekly Levels of Sexual Desire

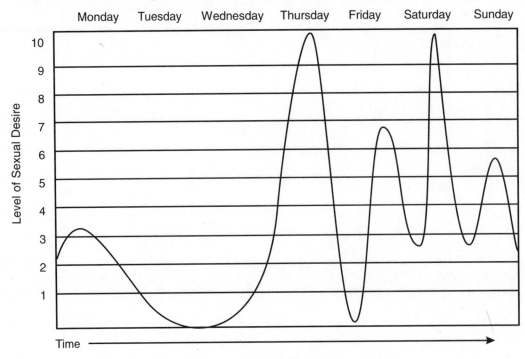

Your Weekly Levels of Sexual Desire

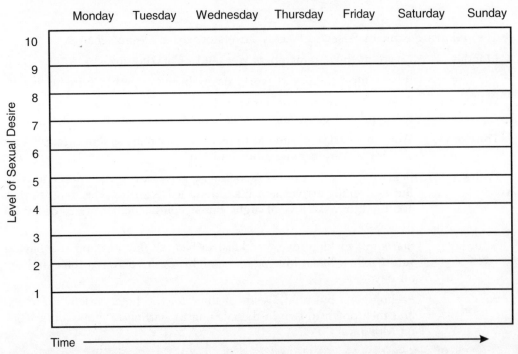

Figure 9.3. Weekly Levels of Desire

of the month. Susan's chart shows that she has two peaks of desire, one during the time of ovulation and the other before she gets her monthly period:

The following list shows fluctuations from one menstruation period to the next. It is illustrated in "Susan's Monthly Levels of Desire" chart in figure 9.4.

Days 1–4	Cramps, bloated, uninterested in sex, breasts are sore. Desire at one to two.
Day 6	Desire between two and ten throughout the day; weekend together with boyfriend.
Day 7	Had a fight, lost desire, mad all day. Level zero
Day 8	Made up with partner, made love. Desire six to nine.
Day 10	Working, busy. Desire zero to three.
Day 11	Special night with boyfriend. Desire nine.
Days 12–13	Desire high all day both days. Made love each day. Ovulating. Always feel sexy at this time of the month.
Days 14–18	Desire at two to four. Out of town on business. Tired and busy.
Days 19–21	Desire two to three. Family visits.
Days 22–23	Desire three to nine. With boyfriend, enjoying each other.
Days 24–26	Desire zero. Angry at boyfriend.
Days 27–28	Desire eight to ten. Made up with boyfriend. Always feel sexy before period starts.
Day 28	Got period, cramps. Desire at one.
Days 29–31	Desire low during period, about one to three.

What have you learned from these charts? Is your average level of desire where you imagined it to be? Are there fluctuations in your level of desire, or is it relatively constant? Are there changes? If so, did these changes surprise you? Is there a pattern to the change? Can you list any factors such as time of day, time of month, proximity to menstruation, or regular daily, weekly, or monthly events that influenced this fluctuation? List them below:

1. _____

2. _____

3. _____

4. _____

5. _____

EXERCISE 9.2—CHARTING YOUR SEXUAL AROUSAL

Now think about your level of arousal during recent sexual experiences. Did your genitals lubricate and become swollen? Were you able to focus on sexual stimulation? Were you aware of any fluctuation of excitement? In figure 9.5, draw your own

Susan's Monthly Levels of Sexual Desire

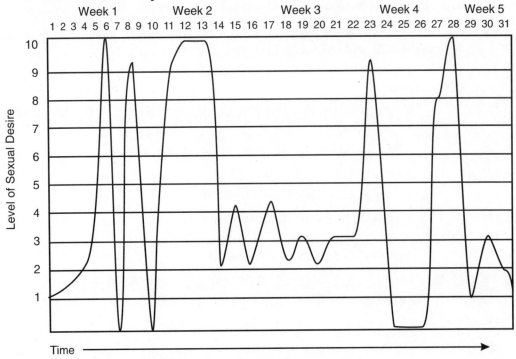

Your Monthly Levels of Sexual Desire

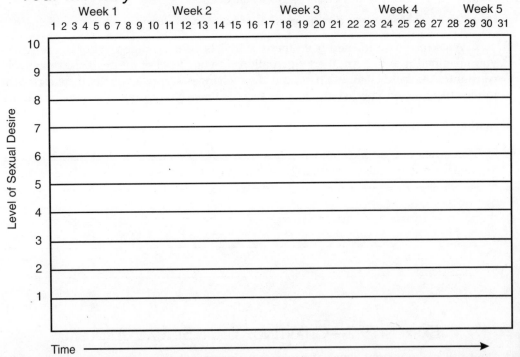

Figure 9.4. Monthly Levels of Desire

sexual response during a recent sexual experience. Note the two thresholds on the chart—one for beginning arousal and one for orgasm. The arousal threshold is reached when any signs of physical arousal begin. It may be helpful to review the section in chapter 1 on the excitement stage as well as the graph of the sexual response cycle in figure 1.6. Except for these two thresholds, the sexual arousal scale we gave you is subjective. You may want to complete this exercise soon after your next sexual experience, when your response is fresh in your mind. You may or may not wish to include length of time, but if you are having trouble getting aroused and notice only two or three minutes of touching, this will be an important piece of information.

❧ Case 9.1—Susan and Stan

Susan filled out her chart of the sexual response cycle after a romantic night out with her partner, Stan. They danced and drank wine, and she enjoyed herself and felt close to Stan. They agreed to have sex when they got home.

Susan enjoyed the process of undressing each other and showering together, and her arousal level rose to three. At the bottom of the chart she later filled out (see figure 9.5), Susan noted that this was about ten minutes long. The phone rang and although they didn't answer, Susan was afraid the call might be important and as her attention was focused on those thoughts her arousal dropped to two (one minute). When Stan began to kiss her neck and ears and fondle her breasts her arousal rose to five (she estimated this took three minutes). She wanted to give him pleasure and while she touched and kissed him her own arousal dropped slightly (three minutes). They decided to have oral sex and as she received Stan's touches and kisses on her genitals her arousal level rose to eight (five minutes). When she pleasured him, her arousal level dropped to six (five minutes). He began touching and deep kissing her again and she decided she wanted intercourse so she straddled him while he entered her and stroked her clitoris (five minutes) until she reached a climax—level ten. Then they rolled over and continued intercourse in the missionary position. Her arousal level dropped to eight and seven and after Stan had his orgasm it continued to drop as she drifted down to no arousal (five minutes).

❧

EXERCISE 9.3—TURN-ONS AND TURN-OFFS

Everyone has unique likes and dislikes that influence how they feel about wanting to engage in a sexual encounter. These can include physical or personality characteristics in a partner, certain settings and ambiance, specific sexual acts, and a variety of sights, scents, sounds, and sensations. You can learn a lot about the factors that shape your desire and arousal curves by looking at these turn-ons and turn-offs. Then, you can make changes to enhance the experience.

Susan's partner, Stan, liked to put a red lightbulb in their lamp during lovemaking to make the room seem "sexy and forbidden." She found herself distracted during sex, however, and eventually realized that the red light was too bright. Susan asked Stan to change the bulb to a softer pink light, which she found very sexy.

Make two lists below of your sexual turn-ons and turn-offs for desire and arousal. What things increase your level of desire prior to sex? What things increase your arousal during sex? Let's look at Susan's sample lists:

Susan's Chart—Sexual Arousal During Sex

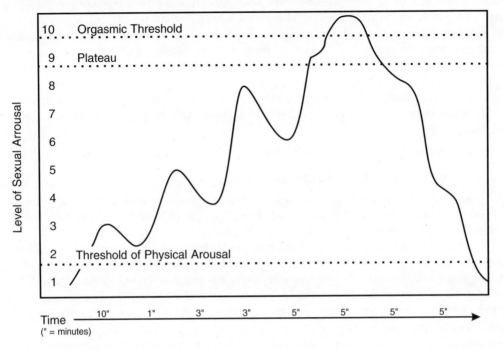

Your Chart—Sexual Arousal During Sex

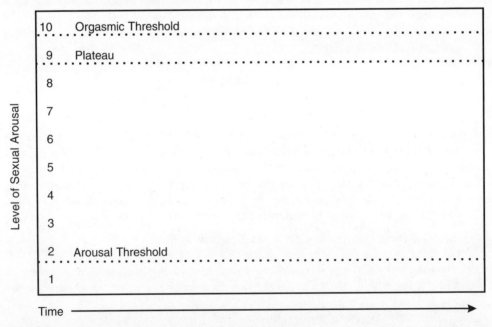

Figure 9.5. Levels of Sexual Arousal During Sex

Things That Increase and Decrease Sexual Desire

Susan's Turn-Ons (before sex)

1. *Slow dancing in a nightclub.*
2. *The scents of wine and of cologne.*
3. *A man with a full mustache.*

Susan's Turn-Offs (before sex)

1. *Having a date order my meal for me.*
2. *A musty or unclean apartment.*
3. *TV shows or movies with violent sex.*

Now make your own list of turn-ons and turn-offs.

Your Sexual Desire Turn-Ons (before sex)

1. _____
2. _____
3. _____
4. _____
5. _____

Your Sexual Desire Turn-Offs (before sex)

1. _____
2. _____
3. _____
4. _____
5. _____

Things That Increase and Decrease Sexual Arousal

Again, let's look at Susan's list as an example. Here she is focusing on turn-ons and turn-offs of sexual arousal or excitement *during* sex.

Susan's Sexual Arousal Turn-Ons (during sex)

1. *Gentle kisses on my breast.*
2. *A scratchy, unshaven face.*
3. *Sex where I'm on top of my partner.*

Susan's Sexual Arousal Turn-Offs (during sex)

1. *Musty pillows or bed linens.*
2. *Loud rock music.*

3. *Oral sex without showering first.*

Now make your own list of turn-ons and turn-offs.

Your Sexual Arousal Turn-Ons (during sex)

1. _____
2. _____
3. _____
4. _____
5. _____

Your Sexual Arousal Turn-Offs (during sex)

1. _____
2. _____
3. _____
4. _____
5. _____

It is important to acknowledge these turn-ons and turn-offs so that you can make changes to increase your interest in being sexual. The main challenge may be asserting your likes and dislikes with a partner. If this is a problem, refer back to the assertiveness section in chapter 8.

Here are several other suggestions to increase sexual desire and arousal:

- Practice giving yourself small physical pleasures each day. Walk on the beach, smell a flower, catch a snowflake on your tongue, listen to music, taste something delicious. List these in your journal and describe the experiences.

- Practice focusing attention on your inner self by using breathing, relaxation, and meditation exercises described in chapter 6.

- Take five minutes and continually focus on the stream of your bodily sensations. It sometimes helps to say out loud what you are feeling to keep from becoming distracted.

By increasing your sensory awareness of pleasures around you and giving in to sensuous desires, you will find that sexual desire and arousal becomes less blocked and flows more freely.

Module Four—Increasing Your Orgasmic Potential

Inhibited orgasm is one of the most common sexual disorders in women. In this module, we will focus on several graduated steps to help you achieve orgasm by yourself and with a partner. The process of achieving an orgasm appears to occur in the last few seconds before orgasm and depends upon a woman's ability to "let go" and surrender to the intense sensations. Orgasm is a reflex response that occurs as a result of three necessary processes. First, a woman needs to have positive expectations, images, and feelings about the sexual experience as it occurs. Second, she needs to focus on the physical stimulation she receives. Third, the stimulation must meet her own unique needs for arousal. Anything that interferes with these factors can inhibit orgasm. For instance, a woman needs to learn what is physically arousing and let her partner know what she likes; otherwise, she will not receive adequate stimulation and orgasm will not occur. Some women lose their positive train of thought during sex or worry that their partners will be turned off by seeing them highly aroused. This interruption in sexual concentration will also inhibit the orgasmic reflex.

Most women *learn* to have an orgasm by practicing how to touch themselves. The first step in learning to have an orgasm requires a sense of privacy and the removal of time constraints or the pressure to perform. This goal is accomplished by focusing on solitary masturbation. Masturbation can provide a sense of competence along with pleasure, as a woman learns to know her body well. By practicing alone in a relaxed setting, she can take her time to learn what type of touch is most stimulating. Then, she can transfer this sense of relaxation and the knowledge of her body to experiences with her partner. Studies by Fisher (1973), Heiman and LoPiccolo (1976), and Barbach (1980) show that women who know how their bodies respond to touch and are assertive with their partners are more consistently orgasmic than women who do not.

Very few men have trouble coming to orgasm. This is probably the case because a man is acutely aware of his penis and touches or fondles his genitals frequently. A man can't avoid touching his penis often (i.e., when he goes to the bathroom; when he experiences spontaneous erections and has to adjust the position of his penis in his pants; and when he masturbates). Most boys begin to masturbate on a frequent basis once they enter puberty. Before long, they know exactly what type of stimulation is most arousing because their goal is almost always orgasm. Girls, however, do not always have the same degree of knowledge and comfort with their genitals. They usually don't masturbate with the same frequency or intensity as boys, perhaps because they may have been taught not to touch themselves "down there." Girls often get the message that their genitals are mysterious and special, but also "dirty," or fragile and that they must guard against touch. Consequently many girls are well into late adolescence before they try to masturbate, and many girls and women feel so uncomfortable touching themselves they don't learn to masturbate to orgasm. As you examine your own attitudes about your sexuality you may discover factors that prevent you from reaching orgasm.

There are a variety of false ideas and frightening notions about masturbation that influence many women. For instance: (1) masturbation is second best, a substitute for being with a partner or enjoying intercourse, (2) it is abnormal and unnatural, (3) it is immature and adults shouldn't masturbate, or (4) it is harmful. Actually, masturbation is a natural function and people in every culture masturbate throughout their lifetimes. It is natural for children to masturbate out of curiosity and for pleasure until someone scolds them. There is no evidence that masturbation is harmful to physical or mental health, and it is the surest way to reach orgasm.

Masturbation means touching yourself for sexual pleasure. Women often touch all parts of their bodies for pleasure, but the genitals are the main focus of masturbation. The advantage to masturbation is that it doesn't require a partner, is relaxing and pleasurable, and (when done alone) has no risk of pregnancy or disease. It is common for married and committed couples to choose solitary masturbation at times, for a variety of reasons. Masturbation can also be an important part of sexual relationships, and for many couples it is as intimate and pleasurable as intercourse. Since most women do not consistently achieve orgasm during intercourse, genital touching is a necessary part of making love. Women may vary when in their cycle and how often they choose to masturbate. Since every woman is unique, each will find a way that suits her best. Some women fantasize during masturbation, while others don't. A woman can masturbate by squeezing her legs together, rubbing her genitals against a bed or pillow, running a stream of water over her clitoris in the bathtub, using a dildo or vibrator, or using her hands and fingers.

The way to learn how to achieve orgasm is to reach this point through masturbation. Every women has the capacity for orgasm, assuming that she has not had a medical problem or procedure that has removed or compromised important genital nerves or structures. Through gradual exploration, a woman can learn about her own responses, and as she feels ready, she can move on to genital touch and then sexually arousing touch. In the vast majority of cases, a woman can learn to have an orgasm alone within a few weeks of experimentation. Having an orgasm with a partner is more complicated, because you have to deal with the distraction from your own sensations while you are paying attention to your partner. You also have to cope with the anxiety of allowing yourself to let go in the presence of another person.

LoPiccolo and Lobitz (1972) have developed a series of exercises that have become the bedrock of treatment for women who want to learn how to achieve orgasm. Heiman and Lopiccolo (1976) have expanded upon these exercises in their excellent book called *Becoming Orgasmic*. In addition to the use of workbooks and individual sex therapy, studies by Barbach (1980), Mills and Kilman (1982), and Heiman and Grafton-Becker (1989) suggest that the treatment of choice for anorgasmic women is to participate in a short-term group with other women (usually lasting eight to ten sessions). This group therapy consists of talks and discussions on sexual function and provides both instruction and support for women to practice attaining orgasm in the privacy of their homes. It does not involve sexual contact among group members. Lonnie Barbach's book *For Yourself* (1973) is an excellent guide to group therapy; it shows how the group process can help a woman in her struggle to achieve orgasm and details common homework assignments.

You have already been taking the overall approach to learning how to achieve orgasm through the many exercises already learned in this workbook. The next step is to complete the following, orgasm-specific exercises.

EXERCISE 9.4—WHAT IS ORGASM?

Begin by writing in your journal about orgasm. Have you experienced it before? If so, what was it like? If not, what do you imagine it to be like? Do you have any fantasies about what orgasm is like? There are many ways to describe orgasm, usually with a focus on the intensely pleasurable sensations in the clitoris accompanied by rhythmic contractions of vaginal muscles. There may be a pleasurable sense of surging, flowing, or contracting throughout the entire pelvis. One's mind is entirely focused on the rush of these pleasurable waves or pulses during orgasm. Orgasm is different from every other pleasurable or sensual experience—there is no mistaking it (Kaplan 1987).

EXERCISE 9.5—PRELIMINARY RELAXATION

Before the initial masturbation exercise, go back to chapter 6 and review the relaxation exercises. What worked best for you? Take some time to practice these techniques. Add the Kegel exercises to your practice sessions. Give yourself some private time and space to relax and focus on your sexuality. While you are relaxed, spend some time touching and exploring your body and then your genitals in a comfortable and sensuous way. When you have done this exercise comfortably several times, you are ready to move on to exercise 9.6.

🙠

EXERCISE 9.6—HOW DO I FEEL ABOUT MASTURBATION?

Ask yourself the following questions about masturbation and write about your attitudes, ideas, and feelings in your journal:

- Beliefs about masturbation vary depending on what you were told as a young person. Some people in every culture masturbate throughout their lifetimes. What did you learn about masturbation as a child? What were your own experiences?

- Do you think that anybody knows that you masturbate? Have you and your partner talked about it?

- Could you tell your partner that you masturbate? Could you show your partner how you touch yourself and what pleases you? If not, why not?

- What would your partner think of you if you talked about how you masturbate? What is the worst thing you can imagine? What is the best thing you can imagine?

- Some people fantasize while masturbating. Do you? Does your fantasy have a story line? a series of images? a combination of the two? Do you imagine erotic experiences you have had? erotic movies or videos you have seen? erotic literature or pictures?

- When you masturbate and get sexually aroused, your body feels different than usual. When you are alone you can take the time to notice what you feel. What feels different?

- Make two lists about masturbation: "Reasons I want to masturbate" and "Reasons I don't want to masturbate."

Some women enjoy masturbation by focusing entirely on their sensations, but if you find yourself getting distracted, fantasy may help.

🙠

EXERCISE 9.7—FANTASY

Look back at your list of turn-ons. What stands out? Can you put several turn-ons together into a fantasy? Some women have a story line and others have a fleeting image, more like a snapshot or series of images. Try to imagine a sensuous or sexual scene that is enjoyable to think about. You may want to write it down in your journal. What emotions come to mind as you try to do this? Excitement? Naughtiness? Guilt? Fear? Some women are reluctant to fantasize because they feel guilty if they imagine being with another partner or doing things they consider wrong or "dirty." Actually, it is normal to fantasize, and you can imagine things you would never want to do in your real life. Fantasies are similar to dreams or thoughts passing through your mind and are harmless. Imagining a sexual scene that arouses you can be very helpful in reaching orgasm. If you feel guilty or uncomfortable about a particular fantasy, you can deliberately stop it and replace it with something you like better or with something that is more within your value system. If you are a woman with an abuse history, you may be plagued with unpleasant and frightening fantasies. If this happens, you may find help by reading module 7 and by talking to your therapist.

If you are having difficulty devising your own fantasy, there are plenty of resources, ranging from erotic stories and pictures to sensuous videos. Many women feel uncomfortable buying such materials in public or are opposed to the idea of pornography. In the appendix we have listed a variety of mail-order catalogs and Web sites that feature erotic materials, some of which are geared towards women. We encourage the use of erotic material only if you feel comfortable with it, but we stress the idea that you need positive sexual images and ideas to become aroused.

Once you have a series of fantasies, see if you can get lost in them. Can you focus on them and forget about things around you? Can you block out other distractions and put yourself into your fantasies? At the very least, can you write it down and concentrate on it while you read it back to yourself? Once you have accomplished this, you're ready for the next exercise.

EXERCISE 9.8—PUTTING TOGETHER FANTASY AND MASTURBATION

Begin this exercise by finding some private time in which to relax in your special space. You will need to either be naked or wearing clothing or lingerie that allows you to stimulate your genitals. Begin to lose yourself in your fantasy, imaging that you are there, experiencing a relaxing but sensual or sexual moment. Massage your body lightly, moving your hands over your breasts, inner thighs, and other arousing areas. As you deepen your focus on your fantasy, explore your clitoris with your fingers. Use a water-based lubricant to enhance the sensation. What kind of touch feels most pleasurable to you? What kind of touch is most delightful? Do you prefer direct or indirect clitoral stimulation? Do you like hard or soft pressure? Do you prefer fast or slow stimulation? Use fingers from both hands on your clitoris or let the other hand drift over your vaginal or anal region. Some women enjoy lightly inserting a finger into their vagina or anus. Other women find that they can increase pleasurable sensations by moaning, rubbing, or pulling on their breasts and nipples, or thrusting their pelvis back and forth. As you build towards orgasm, let the sensations pulse through your body. Close your eyes and stay within your fantasy, and/or focused on the sensations you are feeling in your genitals. As you reach higher levels of arousal, experiment to see what heightens your arousal. You may reach orgasm. ·

There is no rush here, no time limit, and no required "time to orgasm." When a woman is learning to masturbate, she may take as long as thirty to sixty minutes to reach orgasm. You will probably find that you don't even reach orgasm when you first begin to masturbate. That's fine—it will arrive eventually. If you are having difficulty concentrating on your fantasy, try reading or viewing erotic material while you stimulate yourself. Sometimes it is easier to get lost in a sensuous video. If you find that your own fingers or hand is not providing sufficient stimulation to reach orgasm, go to exercise 9.9. If you have been able to consistently reach orgasm in this exercise, move on to exercise 9.10.

EXERCISE 9.9—USING A VIBRATOR

If you are having trouble reaching orgasm by masturbating with your fingers or hand, the use of an electric vibrator will make a nice difference. Vibrators come in all shapes and sizes and either plug into the wall socket or use batteries. Some are shaped to look like penises or dildos, while others are designed to massage the entire body and genital area. We recommend that you use an electric vibrator with variable speeds. These provide enough stimulation to produce orgasm, whereas most battery-operated vibrators may not provide the necessary intensity. There are many places to purchase vibrators, especially since they are sold in most drugstores for body massage. We have listed a number of mail-order catalogs in the appendix, many of which sell a variety of vibrators.

Repeat the exercise from 9.8, but use the vibrator instead of your hand or fingers. Focus on your fantasy or on erotic materials and experiment with pelvic thrusting or massaging your breasts or nipples to increase stimulation. Again, there is no time limit. When first learning to have an orgasm, some women need thirty to sixty minutes of stimulation. As long as you are not causing yourself any pain, continue using the vibrator until you are able to reach orgasm. Do not worry about becoming dependent on it. The success of orgasm will build confidence and will help you learn the most stimulating techniques for yourself. Over time, you will be able to achieve orgasm without it.

Help in Triggering Orgasm

When you reach the plateau stage and have trouble letting go to orgasm, there are several strategies that may help trigger an orgasm:

- Do several fast or slow Kegels in a row. The tensing and releasing of the PC muscle sometimes will allow the orgasm to follow.

- Contracting and relaxing other groups of muscles can also release orgasm. Push your feet against the foot of the bed or against a wall so that you contract your leg muscles, or tighten and release your buttocks and thigh muscles several times.

- Stretching the muscles in your neck by tilting your head back, lifting your head, or hanging your head over the edge of the bed while lying on your back can trigger orgasm. You can increase the sensation by contracting your neck muscles.

- It is common to want the sense of fullness in your vagina at the plateau stage. Accommodate yourself with your own or your partner's finger, or a penis or dildo.

- Change your breathing to release orgasm. Hold your breath and feel the pressure internally on your diaphragm, as if you were trying to blow up a balloon. Then breathe out all at once.

- Role-play that you are having an orgasm. Move your body, thrust your pelvis up and down, squirm, sigh and moan. Thrash around. Sometimes these actions will loosen you up enough to climax.

- Orgasm is the natural reflex action of your body when sexual sensation is intense enough and lasts long enough.

EXERCISE 9.10—ORGASM WITH YOUR PARTNER

Now that you are able to reach an orgasm on your own through masturbation, you can use several exercises to help you reach orgasm with your partner. If you are uncomfortable telling your partner how to stimulate you to orgasm, you can demonstrate or guide their hand to show your partner how and where you like to be touched. Some couples like to show each other how they masturbate to orgasm. As they watch each other, they learn by example. If the idea of sharing masturbation makes you feel self-conscious, you can do it in a set of graduated experiences. You could start with your partner turned away from you but nearby. If this is too close, have your partner stay nearby in the room or just outside the door, perhaps focusing on the TV or reading a book. This might sound a little impersonal, but the goal is to gradually become comfortable with masturbating to orgasm in the presence of your partner. Then you could lie back to back or in a spoon position. Next, your partner could hold you while you touch yourself. And finally, you would show your partner exactly what you do to excite yourself. Your partner could do the same set of exercises so that you slowly become more able to enjoy sexual touching together. If you feel comfortable with oral sex, that can be another way to have your partner stimulate you to orgasm. It is a wonderful experience when you first climax with your partner. Most partners are thrilled by being able to provide such pleasure, and the experience will bring new confidence and joy to your relationship. Be sure to write about both of your reactions in your journal.

As we mentioned earlier, only about 25 to 30 percent of women experience orgasm during intercourse, and this is probably related to the fact that vaginal penetration does not often provide sufficient clitoral stimulation (Kaplan 1974; Heiman and LoPiccolo 1976). If you cannot reach orgasm this way, you should feel no pressure to change. However, if you wish to reach orgasm through intercourse, there is a procedure called the "bridge maneuver" (Kaplan 1987) that can help. Using the Sensate Focus four exercises for nondemanding intercourse, find a position during intercourse that allows for you to thrust onto your partner's penis, while at the same time allowing either you or your partner to stimulate your clitoris, either with a hand or a vibrator. While you are having intercourse, slow down to the point where you are thrusting or moving just enough to maintain your partner's erection. Then, stimulate your clitoris in the way that is most arousing to you. As you approach orgasm, begin thrusting so that your partner's penis moves in and out of your vagina while you continue to stimulate yourself. Use fantasy and body movements in the same manner as in earlier exercises. For some women the thrusting may produce an orgasm without continual clitoral stimulation, but most women need to continue the stimulation to achieve orgasm. This is called the "bridge maneuver" because it provides a bridge between clitoral stimulation and the stimulation of intercourse (Kaplan 1987).

Module Five—Vaginismus and Dyspareunia: Working with Dilators

This treatment module presents a simple method to relax the vaginal muscles to allow for penetration. As you become consciously aware of relaxing and contracting the vaginal muscles around an object, you will gain a sense of control over vaginal penetration. If you have vaginismus, these exercises will help you to eliminate the reflexive spasm that occurs at penetration. If you have dyspareunia, these exercises can give you a sense of control over genital stimulation and penetration so you can focus on reducing pain and increasing comfort and pleasure. For women with vaginal narrowing or shortening (i.e., scars, strictures, stenosis) from surgery or radiation treatment, these exercises will loosen vaginal tissue, ease penetration, and prevent further constriction of the vaginal canal. Many women who suffer from vaginismus find that the services of a sex therapist provide vital and necessary support and quick success. Other types of genital pain are also reduced in sex therapy.

It is important to approach these exercises with a relaxed frame of mind. Use the relaxation exercises from chapter 6 to set the tone for exercises with the dilators. Give yourself private time, and allow yourself as much time as you need to feel comfortable. If you are still feeling apprehensive, look at the exercise where you thought of reasons not to change (see exercise 8.1). Refocus on relaxation techniques that lessen anxiety. If you are feeling too anxious to proceed on your own, you may feel reassured if you work with a sex therapist.

To do the dilation exercises, you will need a set of vaginal dilators and a water-based lubricant. Some women may feel comfortable using their own finger as a dilator. This can work well, but be sure to use a smoothly manicured finger and plenty of lubrication to avoid discomfort. The advantage to using your finger is that you have maximum control over vaginal penetration. The disadvantage is that you are limited to one size and will have to use a larger object eventually. Some women use a tampon cover to begin and others obtain smooth syringe covers from a doctor's office. You can also buy graduated sizes of dildos from mail-order catalogs (listed in the appendix) or find other plastic or rubber cylinders to use. Select items with smooth, rounded edges and blunt ends, that are reusable and easy to clean. Keep them in a private location. You will start with a small size no larger in diameter than your little finger and progress to larger sizes until you are ready to attempt intercourse (or in some cases, a speculum exam). The largest size dildo you use should approximate the size of your partner's erect penis so that the exercises will best simulate eventual intercourse. **Please note:** We do not recommend using any of the following items for dilation exercises: medicine bottles or tubes, metal objects, writing instruments, tools, or anything else that is made of or contains a potentially irritating or reactive material, or that has the potential to splinter, break, or scratch vaginal tissue.

Your doctor or nurse practitioner can prescribe a set of specially designed dilators that come in graduated sizes. They are moderately expensive. These dilators are made of a pliable plastic material with a rim on the bottom, which allows you to hold them as they enter the vagina. In the appendix two manufacturers of vaginal dilators are listed. You can obtain information from the manufacturers to bring to your health care provider or therapist and ask them to order a set for you. It may even be covered by your health insurance. In the long run, these dilators are the best investment to treat your difficulty. They are comfortable, perfectly safe, made of inert materials, reusable, and versatile.

Water-soluble lubricants (e.g., KY Jelly, or Astroglide) should be applied liberally to dilators and reapplied as necessary during the exercises. Do not use creams, lotions, liquid soaps, douches, or petroleum-based products, since they can be irritating to the vagina. If you find the recommended lubricants irritating, consult with your gynecologist for alternate products. If a medical problem causes pain upon insertion, ask your doctor for an anesthetic ointment to use before you begin. Otherwise, there is no need for anesthetic agents and the normal discomfort associated with vaginismus quickly disappears as the exercises progress.

EXERCISE 9.11—PREPARING TO USE DILATORS

Select a relaxation technique from chapter 6 that works well for you. Find a quiet, comfortable, and private place in the house where you can be alone and set aside thirty minutes for this exercise. Make sure that you have a lubricant and the smallest dilator you have. Wear soft and comfortable clothes that allow you access to your vulva or try the exercise in the nude. Some women like to place one small towel beneath their buttocks to catch excess lubricant and keep another one nearby on which to place the dilator and clean it. You might want to avoid this exercise during menstruation since your vulvar and vaginal tissues are more sensitive at that time. Use your relaxation exercise to become fully relaxed. Once you are feeling ready, lightly place your finger or the dilator on your vulva and feel a sense of calm and hopefulness. Imagine the dilator as a part of your body, over which you have full control. It will remain still when you want it still and move slowly and gently when you wish to move it. Lightly rub the dilator over your vulva and let it run into the cleft of your vaginal opening. You should repeat this exercise before each dilator is used to make sure that you feel relaxed and ready to begin. If you have doubts or reservations, feel tense, or are preoccupied, refocus on the relaxation exercise until you feel ready. As you progress, this initial relaxation will require less time.

EXERCISE 9.12—USING DILATORS

Once you achieve a deep sense of relaxation, you are ready to begin using the dilators. This exercise is basically the same for each size and you should repeat it many times until you can comfortably insert the largest dilator. Before you begin, have the well-lubricated dilator next to you. Start by practicing a few Kegel exercises, feeling your PC muscle contracting and relaxing. This muscle will surround the dilator and allow it to gently enter your vagina. Tighten and relax your PC muscle—tighten and relax—tighten and relax. When you are completely relaxed, gently begin inserting the smallest dilator into your vagina. Take your time, breathe slowly and deeply, and slowly advance the dilator. The PC muscle surrounds the first third of your vagina, so you will feel resistance only in this area and may feel the dilator move easily as it passes beyond the PC muscle. Once you have inserted it, leave it in for at least five minutes and focus on relaxing. After five minutes, try a few Kegel exercises to see if you can push the dilator out and then gently push it in again. Remember that when you relax the PC muscle, the dilator will move easily. By feeling your own PC muscle contracting and relaxing in this manner, you will begin to have a sense of control. If you are successful, do the exercise one more time and then move on to the next size. If you have trouble, be sure you are relaxed by breathing deeply. Do Kegels and try again. If you still have trouble a sex therapist can help.

Once you can comfortably insert a dilator, try the next larger size. Repeat the above exercises over a period of time as you gradually progress to the dilator that approximates the size of your partner's penis. Once you have mastered this size, you are ready for the next exercise. If you are using dilators to stretch constricted vaginal tissue to prevent further narrowing or shortening, ask your physician which size dilator you should expect to be able to use. Also ask for ongoing guidelines on how the treatment is progressing and how long you should continue with these exercises.

EXERCISE 9.13—INVOLVING YOUR PARTNER
WITH DILATOR EXERCISES

Once you have mastered putting in the dilators on your own, you are ready to involve your partner. In this exercise, your partner will join you as you practice relaxing and inserting the dilators. This exercise should help you share a sense of control over vaginal penetration as you both practice inserting the dilators.

Start off the exercise with ten to fifteen minutes of relaxed sensate focus. Then, while your partner lies next to you, insert each dilator. Your partner may want to watch how you do this. Next, place your partner's hand on yours as you insert the dilator. Then guide their hand as they insert the dilator (following the guiding exercises in chapter 7). You might also try having your partner slowly insert their lubricated finger as you practice Kegel exercises so that they can feel you control your PC muscle. This experience can be extremely intimate and rewarding for both of you and will hopefully fill you both with confidence. Once you both feel comfortable inserting each of the dilators, you are ready to move on.

Exercise 9.14—Progressing to Controlled, Nondemanding Intercourse

Review the section in chapter 7 on Sensate Focus 4, in particular exercise 7.12 entitled "The Quiet Vagina." You will use a slightly modified form of this exercise to move from insertion of dilators to insertion of your partner's penis. Begin the exercise with some brief sensate focus. Then, as your partner lies on his back, stroke his penis until he is erect. When you both feel ready, straddle his hips with your legs, so that you are sitting above him on your knees, and slowly guide his penis into your vagina. Use plenty of lubrication. It is important for you to guide him into you just as you practiced with the dilators. Contract and relax three times and then gradually allow his penis to enter your vagina. If you feel resistance, stop briefly and focus on relaxation. If you loose focus or become anxious, you might want to then try a dilator before resuming with his penis.

Once he has entered your vagina, he should stay still and not thrust, allowing you to experience the sensation of vaginal penetration. Try squeezing your PC muscle around his penis, feeling the difference between contraction and relaxation of your vaginal muscles. Remain together for several minutes, allowing yourself to move up and down on his penis slowly to provide enough stimulation to maintain his erection. The goal here is not to reach orgasm, but to experience comfortable, nondemanding intercourse. Only after you have practiced this exercise several times successfully should you progress to regular sexual intercourse.

Experiment with other positions, but remember to use your hand to guide your partner's penis into your vagina. This control is crucial to the exercise. Some couples use a side-by-side position and face each other or lie with the woman on her back with their genitals touching and her legs over the man's pelvis. The woman can then take her partner's penis into her vagina in a manner similar to using a dilator. It is important to find a comfortable position in which you feel a sense of control over the insertion of his penis. Your partner might be tempted to start thrusting either because of his excitement or because of his need to maintain an erection. In that case, take a break and stroke his penis with your hands to help him maintain his erection. Use plenty of lubrication. Some couples follow this exercise with oral or manual stimulation and include orgasm.

Some men begin to have erection problems (impotence) following their partner's problem with vaginismus. This may be due to his own sense of rejection, his worry that he can't penetrate his partner, or his lack of adequate stimulation and arousal during sex. If your partner is experiencing difficulties maintaining his erection, allow plenty of time for the sensate focus three exercises that involve genital stimulation and arousal. This is an ideal time to learn a wider repertoire for use during love-making. Use your imagination as you stimulate his penis in a variety of ways before you guide him into your vagina, or have your partner lie on his side and masturbate to stimulate his erection for several minutes before attempting penetration. Some men use a tension ring at the base of the penis to maintain an adequate erection for the exercise. When your partner sees that you are not in pain and are ready for penetration, his own difficulties may improve dramatically. A lesbian couple could make use of many of these ideas to assist in insertion of a finger, dildo, or other object if one partner suffered from vaginal pain. For persistent problems, you may both need to talk with a therapist.

Module Six—Using Desensitization and Medication for Sexual Phobias and Aversion

Treatment for sexual phobias and aversion has already been outlined in chapters 6 and 7: if you can successfully accomplish the relaxation and sensate focus exercises, you have made a good beginning to resolving an aversion or phobia. However, most women with these problems will require assistance from a therapist, often including the use of antianxiety and antidepressant medication. In this module, we will simply outline how this treatment works with a sex therapist, since you will need a professional to prescribe appropriate medications and exercises.

The process of systematic desensitization involves gradual exposure to fearful situations of increasing magnitude while you are deeply relaxed. This technique works extremely well with a variety of phobias, such as fear of heights, fear of flying, fear of public speaking, etc. The first step is to develop a hierarchy, or rank a list of your fears, from the least to the most feared stimulus. Here is part of a sample fear hierarchy for a woman with a phobia of male genitals:

Least Feared ──────────────────────────▶ **Most Feared**

| *Talking about male genitals* | *Seeing pictures of male genitals* | *Seeing her partner's genitals* | *Fondling her partner's genitals* | *Sexual intercourse* |

Your own list will be much longer and more detailed, often with twenty graduated steps. The purpose is to start with a situation that you can tolerate and move slowly closer to the most phobic situation on the list. As you experience each step in your hierarchy, you can utilize relaxation techniques to eliminate anxiety and retrain your mind and body to feel relaxed and comfortable in the situation. You should not move on until you have mastered each step.

For some women, the relaxation techniques may also require the use of medication. There are several strategies that may work. For phobic reactions to specific, predictable situations, you can take a short-acting antianxiety medication (lasting several hours) prior to the situation. See the case of Jane for an example.

✒ Case 9.2—Jane

*Jane had a panic attack every time she went out with her friends to meet men. Her physician gave her a prescription for alprazolam (Xanax) to take thirty minutes before going out. She also joined a ten week group to learn relaxation techniques. The deep-breathing techniques and medication decreased her anticipatory anxiety and prevented her from having a panic attack. (**Note:** She had to avoid drinking any alcohol while on Xanax.)*

For phobic reactions to specific but somewhat unpredictable situations, or phobic reactions accompanied by excessive anticipatory anxiety, a woman can take an anti-depressant medication on a regular basis in combination with a short-acting antianxiety medication on a regular or as-needed basis. Remember that antidepressant medications are also used to treat panic disorder.

❦ Case 9.3—Dana and Jonathan

Dana began dating Jonathan but was gripped with anxiety for several days leading up to each date. She often had panic attacks during the date and had to excuse herself to go to the bathroom and throw up. Dana worked with a therapist who instructed her to practice relaxation techniques on a daily basis and before each date. Dana also started a daily dose of sertraline (Zoloft). After about two weeks the medication kicked in, her panic attacks began to lessen in intensity, and they eventually disappeared after four weeks of treatment. However, she was still anxious prior to and during dates, so her physician added a twice-daily dose of clonazepam (Klonopin). The Klonopin worked immediately to decrease her anxiety. As her anxiety diminished, she learned more about how to face her fear through therapy. With the combination of medications, Dana was able to go on dates and be physically intimate with Jonathan without significant anxiety and panic attacks. She still used deep-breathing relaxation to control intermittent episodes of anxiety.

For unpredictable panic attacks, as occurs with panic disorder, the mainstay of treatment is the use of a daily antidepressant medication.

❦ Case 9.4—Liz

Liz needed an antidepressant medication and also an antianxiety medication to alleviate her debilitating panic attacks, but she had heard that she would lose her sexual interest and excitement as a side effect of these medications. Her doctor recommended that she take Paxil (antidepressant) and Klonopin (antianxiety) in combination. As her condition stabilized, she was able to take a "drug holiday" over the weekend. As her doctor instructed, she continued the Klonopin but stopped the Paxil for the weekend, resuming it again on Monday. Her interest and sexual arousal remained intact.

We listed many antianxiety medications (such as the benzodiazepines) and antidepressant medications in chapter 4. Before starting any medication, ask your doctor what to expect of the medication and how long it will take to work. Also ask about limitations on the use of alcohol, the risks if you were to become pregnant, potential interactions between medications, and potential side effects—especially those that impact sexual function. Some women and physicians put all of their faith in medications and ignore all of the important behavioral and psychological aspects to treating sexual problems. We suggest that the best treatment takes all factors into consideration and combine medications with relaxation techniques and supportive counseling.

Module Seven—Sex Therapy for Survivors of Abuse

Often couples do not realize that previous experiences of sexual or physical abuse or trauma are causing negative effects on their present sexuality. A trauma or abuse survivor with sexual dysfunction may have difficulty establishing her sexuality; she may feel extremely inhibited or exhibit hyperactive sexuality driven by an unconscious need to replay the abuse or a conscious need to please her partner without regard to her own feelings. With therapy, however, women are now able to acknowledge their experiences and transform their lives from that of a powerless victim to that of a capable and confident survivor. In the past ten years, psychotherapists have begun to focus on how to help abused women come to terms with their sexuality. Still, many therapists are not aware that sex therapy can be used as an adjunct to individual treatment. Many certified sex therapists are well trained in working with survivors of abuse and offer specialized information to deal with current sexual concerns. According to experts, therapy for survivors of abuse follows three stages of recovery—from *stabilization*, through *remembering and grieving*, and finally to *integration*. During the first two stages of therapy, a woman might ask her therapist to help her use simple body exercises to learn to feel comfortable (in a nonsexual way) with herself. It is probably unrealistic for abuse survivors to expect to be able to integrate their sexuality without professional help.

Stage One—Stabilization

Initial therapy for survivors of abuse has modest sexual goals. The first step is to provide a woman with a sense of power and control through understanding what has happened to her and how she can recover. The following steps can be useful:

- Establish a sense of safety by creating safe places in your house. Choose a comfortable spot, but usually not a bed. Add locks to doors, pull curtains, or take whatever steps you wish to make a safe and cozy place for yourself. Once there, use relaxation techniques to settle in, and then visualize a safe place in your mind, such as a beautiful beach, a secluded meadow, or anywhere else that is relaxing and peaceful to you. Having this space and time to feel relaxed and safe can help you feel more in control of your life and allow your mind to rest and rejuvenate, taking a break from the emotionally turbulent time when you address your past issues. Also, having a safe place helps you calm down if you are triggered with a memory of abuse. You can go to your safe place in your mind while you calm down.

- Learn to be good to yourself. Give yourself top priority. Do things every day that make you feel pleasure. Write some positive affirmations about yourself.

- Learn deep breathing and progressive relaxation exercises and practice them on a daily basis. Use exercise and meditation to reduce stress.

- Give yourself permission to abstain from sex until you feel ready to resume in a new and positive way.

- Establish boundaries with your partner regarding what is sexually acceptable and what is not. Ask yourself with whom, when, where, and how you will feel good about a sexual experience. Make a safe sexual plan for yourself. If you don't feel good about something, don't do it.

- As you discover areas of sexual comfort, include them in your repertoire. If you know you enjoy sex during the daytime, switch your sexual encounters to daytime hours. If cuddling for a while gets you in the mood, always begin with cuddling.

- Recognize the difference between affectionate and sexual touch. Talk with your partner about boundaries for each type of touch; together, you can reach the understanding that asking for affection is not necessarily asking for sex.

- You can gain your partner's cooperation in your plans for sexual progress by including them right from the start. Establish a safe physical or sensuous connection that doesn't include sex. Enjoy holding hands, hugging, holding each other, and touching each other's hands, faces, or feet. Try asking for permission to touch each other, first agreeing on your approach for this and then deciding on some ways to decline that aren't hurtful.

- Educate yourself. There are many excellent books and videos available which talk about the effects of abuse or trauma and provide suggestions on how to resume normal relationships. We have listed several references and resources for this in the appendix.

- Give yourself permission to move forward when you have established safe boundaries. Challenge yourself with small steps along the way to keep moving toward your goal.

- Review chapter 8 for specific techniques to challenge negative thoughts about sex (e.g., affirmations, thought stopping, etc.)

- Work with your therapist to desensitize yourself to negative sexual images.

- Reduce hyperarousal and other post-traumatic symptoms through the use of medications, relaxation techniques, meditation, and exercise.

- Use distraction techniques to stop thoughts that focus on the past. Try a variety of distractions to learn what works best for you.

- Remember that your partner was not the person who hurt you as a child. The more you can talk together the more your relationship will improve.

Stage Two—Remembering, Grieving, and Staying Grounded

Anxiety, hyperarousal, flashbacks, and symptoms of dissociation sometimes occur during the stage of therapy when you are uncovering traumatic experiences. Dissociation refers to a sense of numbing or reduced awareness to the surrounding environment. As you talk about these memories, your mind and body may react in defensive ways to cope with reemerging feelings from the trauma. Teach yourself and your partner how to comfort you and reconnect or ground you if you have are intensely anxious, or are experiencing a flashback or dissociative episode. The following steps are helpful:

- Learn to stay in the present. If you feel yourself regressing to the past, identify your partner as someone distinct from the person who abused you. Compare the space you are in, the time of day, the furnishings—whatever you can think of that reminds you that you are in the present. Your partner can ask you simple questions such as your name, the time and location, and recent events. Slow repetition of these questions and answers in quiet and calm voices can keep you in the present. Ask your partner to help you use deep breathing techniques, which can reduce intense anxiety and physiologic arousal. For example: *Take a slow deep breath . . . good . . . now look at me . . . tell me your name . . . where are we now? . . . good . . . take another slow deep breath and relax ... great ... stay together with me ... I'm here with you now ... tell me where we are ... good ... (etc.)*

- Identify triggers of flashbacks or other dissociative symptoms so that you can avoid them in the future or desensitize yourself to them. Practice relaxation techniques to use when you are triggered.

- Learn to be aware of the stream of bodily sensations you experience from moment to moment. Practice "staying present" in the moment when you are alone, and then practice staying present in the presence of your partner. Finally, practice staying present when your partner is touching you.

- Gradually explore small increments of physical, but not sexual, pleasure—first alone and then with your partner (e.g., enjoyable sights, tastes, etc.).

- Practice assertiveness exercises from chapter 8.

- Learn to recognize your emotions and distinguish them from each other. Practice talking about your feelings. Start with your therapist or someone you trust. Ask that person to listen but not comment on what you say.

- Learn what is average or common in relationships and sexuality so that you have a variety of choices of how to live your sexual life. Many of the suggested reading under general sexuality in the appendix can help.

Stage Three—Integration

During the integration stage of therapy, a woman often chooses to reclaim her sexuality, and may decide to enter sex therapy if she hasn't yet done so. The role of the sex therapist is to offer a safe and trusting therapeutic relationship to enable the survivor of sexual abuse or trauma to identify her sexual concerns and regain control of her sexuality. The therapist offers information on healthy sexual function and helps the woman grant herself permission to go at her own rate of progress as she becomes a sexual person. The therapist usually works with both the survivor and her partner on shared sexual issues, providing hope and reassurance as the couple deepens their intimate connection. Both sexual and nonsexual issues are addressed.

Many survivors of sexual abuse have not gone through the normal stages of sexual development. They have been bombarded with inappropriate sexuality before they were old enough to manage the powerful feelings that accompany sexuality. Sex therapy can provide a safe environment in which a woman can go through the stages of development that she missed. Here are several suggestions on following a graduated approach to sexuality.

- Practice staying "in" your body and notice the small sensations of touch. Explore your body, by first looking at yourself and then participating in gentle, nonsexual exploratory touch. Touch yourself in a tender and nonsexual way, beginning on the back of your hands and arms. Touch yourself all over and take your time as you notice your sensations and emotions. If you get nervous, stop and breathe deeply until you feel relaxed, then resume your exploration. After you have explored your reactions to touch, talk to your partner and show them what you've learned. Review exercises in chapter 6.

- Share a time of bodily exploration with your partner, providing safe boundaries. First try looking and then touching each other. Have a clear understanding that this will not become a prelude to sexual behavior. Start by touching the hands, head, feet, arms and back only. Gradually learn to stay present and safe with your partner. Refrain from touching the chest, abdomen, or genitals.

- Process your feelings about these exercises with one another. Talk to your partner outside of the bedroom, perhaps during a walk together. Set a timer and talk for no more than twenty minutes. Listen to each other. Use "I" statements: *I like it when you kiss my hair. I like to feel close before we have sex.*

- Avoid goal-oriented sexuality leading to arousal or orgasm. Explore sexual sensations only when ready, allowing excitement to build of its own accord.

- Create new meanings for sex. Discuss what sex used to be and what you want sex to become. Use affirmations to strengthen your new meanings.

- During affectionate or sexual activity, do your best to remain present with your partner. Always feel free to stop if you feel afraid, in pain, or numb. Then take several deep breaths to relax and calm yourself. Tell your partner what is going on. If you find yourself drifting away from the present, your partner can call you back. Discuss and then practice how to do this and how to stop sexual activity if you are in distress. Choose a word both of you recognize to mean stop. This word should be a different word than "no," because often the words "no" and "yes" were involved in abusive situations.

- If you stop a sexual activity, move to a different and safer activity to break the chain of negative associations. A safer activity might be something from a previous exercise or experience that you know you'll feel comfortable with. Once you talk about what happened, you may be ready to begin again.

Dealing with Unwanted Sexual Fantasies

According to Wendy Maltz (1992), survivors of sexual abuse or trauma often experience unwanted sexual memories or fantasies that spoil their sexual experiences. In this case, the term "fantasy" does not have its usual positive or pleasurable connotations. Working to overcome these fantasies should be done in stages with a trusted therapist. First, the woman must learn how to imagine a safe place where she can go in her mind if she gets frightened. Then, she will be better prepared to face the details of the unwanted fantasy by exposing it. Writing out the fantasy helps get it into the light of day where it has less power to frighten her. Maltz recommends underlining the parts that are arousing and noting at which point in the sexual response cycle they occur. The next step is to discover what function the unwanted fantasy plays in the woman's inner life. To do this, a survivor tries to discover the meaning of the fantasy, often by uncovering unresolved conflict within it. She can also use dialogue to confront the characters in the fantasy and to see how each one represents a part of herself. The final step is to reshape the unwanted fantasy or alternative fantasies into arousing but safe and acceptable images. Some women use images from books or movies to create new and satisfying fantasies.

After reading the modules which pertain to your individual problem, you may have questions about how your partner fits into the picture. The next chapter will address how to work with partners. It will also address how to work with doctors, gynecologists, therapists, and sex therapists.

References

Barbach, L. 1976. *For Yourself: The Fulfillment of Female Sexuality*. New York: Anchor Books.

Barbach, L. 1980. *Women Discover Orgasm: A Therapist's Guide to a New Treatment Approach*. New York: The Free Press.

Barbach, L. 1982. *For Each Other: Sharing Sexual Intimacy*. New York: Anchor Press.

Fisher, S. 1973. *The Female Orgasm*. New York: Basic Books.

Heiman, L. and J. LoPiccolo. 1976. *Becoming Orgasmic: A Sexual and Personal Growth Program for Women* (Revised edition). New York: Prentice Hall.

Heiman J. and Grafton-Becker. 1989. "Orgasmic Disorders in Women." *Principles and Practice of Sex Therapy Update for the 1990s*, edited by S. Leiblum and R. Rosen. New York: Guilford Press.

Herman, J. L. 1992. *Trauma and Recovery*. New York: Basic Books.

Kaplan, H. S. 1974. *The New Sex Therapy*. New York: Brunner/Mazel.

Kaplan, H. S. 1987. *The Illustrated Manual of Sex Therapy*. New York: Brunner/Mazel.

Kunzman, K. 1990. *The Healing Way: Adult Recovery from Childhood Sexual Abuse*. San Francisco: Harper and Row.

LoPiccolo, J., and C. Lobitz. 1972. "The Role of Masturbation in the Treatment of Sexual Dysfunction." *Archives of Sexual Behavior*. (2):163–171.

Maltz, W. 1992. *The Sexual Healing Journey: A Guide for Survivors of Sexual Abuse*. New York: W. W. Norton.

Mills, K. H. and P. R. Kilmann. 1982. "Group Treatment of Sexual Dysfunctions: A Methodological Review of the Outcome Literature." *Journal of Sex and Marital Therapy* 8(4):259–296.

Napier, N. J. 1993. *Getting Through the Day: Strategies for Adults Hurt as Children*. New York: W. W. Norton.

Westerlund, E. 1992. *Women's Sexuality after Childhood Incest*. New York: W. W. Norton.

Whitfield, C. L. 1993. *Boundaries and Relationships: Knowing, Protecting, and Enjoying the Self*. Deerfield Beach, Fla.: Health Communications, Inc.

Chapter Ten

Working with Partners, Physicians, and Therapists

The experience of sexual fear and pain is intensely personal and is usually kept secret from others. Sometimes even a partner or personal physician is not aware of a woman's pain. At some point, however, every affected woman must reach out for help, and this process can be difficult. When a woman has trouble with her sexuality, she hopes that the problem will resolve itself in time. This natural and healthy attitude often proves correct. A good percentage of sexual dysfunction is time limited and can be resolved. When it persists, however, a woman must either seek help or learn to live with the problem.

A woman often feels ashamed of her sexual problem and worries how her partner will respond. Sometimes a partner is not willing to hear about a problem, or help resolve it, because they may also have to change. A woman with sexual fear or pain may worry whether her partner will understand her or will respond in a sympathetic way. In the case of phobias or aversion, acknowledging a problem and reaching out is especially difficult. In this chapter we will discuss how you can talk with your partner about your sexual concerns, and how you both can work towards a solution. We will also include suggestions for women who do not have partners.

We will discuss the different types of professional help available, describing the roles of different specialists and providing tips on how to locate them and involve them in the recovery process. Your relationship with your physician, gynecologist, psychotherapist, or sex therapist is important; this chapter will address how to create a comfortable and trusting collaboration. We will discuss what to expect from a gynecologic exam and how these exams can help you better understand certain sexual problems.

Working with Partners

Few sexual problems exist in isolation. Usually sexual problems will have an impact on a relationship. A woman with a sexual problem may have difficulty within a sexual relationship or forming a sexual relationship. Either way, all treatment must at some point involve a partner, which can raise anxiety for both of you. When either partner has a sexual problem, the other must cope with sexual concerns as well as possible strong feelings of anger, resentment, guilt, anxiety, disappointment, or rejection. A woman's partner may also have sexual problems or develop one in response to her difficulties. Couples therapists always think of the problem as a couples issue. Conjoint sex therapy was developed to involve both partners and address the problem as a common challenge. It is never "one person's fault." Although this book is called *A Woman's Guide to Overcoming Sexual Fear and Pain*, it is in essence also a partner's guide and a couple's guide. In this section, we will discuss different aspects and types of relationships relevant to sexual dysfunction and include suggestions and exercises for your partner.

Common Reactions

When a couple experiences a problem with their sexual relationship, there are several common reactions. Some couples will assume that the sexual problem exists in isolation. They will chalk it up to stress or exhaustion, and look no further. Their lack of worry may be realistic, and the problem may resolve itself. On the other hand, this reaction may represent some denial on their part if the problem is recurrent and disruptive. Other couples become mutually upset and worried about the problem, and their emotions either lead to finding a solution or to a more extensive relationship conflict. If the problem turns out to be minor and short-lived, things may return to normal rather quickly, at least until another problem occurs. For example, after the birth of a baby sexuality may change, but in a short while the couple usually resumes their natural sexual rhythm. If the problem is more complex and long-standing, however, it can seriously impair the entire relationship. For instance, if a woman has vaginismus she may be unable to consummate her marriage. Some couples have very different reactions; one partner may appear outwardly unconcerned and the other partner may be quite distressed. These reactions might balance each other out or lead to more serious conflict. Couples with good communication skills will talk about the problem, try to work out solutions together, and seek help if they are not successful in a reasonable amount of time. Your reaction and your partner's may fit one of these models or be entirely different. The nature of the dynamic relationship between you and your partner will have both positive and negative consequences. The goal is to emphasize the positive and communicate about how to lessen the impact of the negative.

～

EXERCISE 10.1—REACTING TO SEXUAL PROBLEMS

Write about how you and your partner have reacted to your sexual problem in your journal. Does your partner acknowledge a problem? Do they see it the same way you do? understand how you feel? Are you both equally concerned or is there a difference in your reactions? How have your reactions influenced the problem? After completing this exercise, ask your partner to read the following section.

A Message for Partners: How Can You Help?

You are probably aware that your partner is experiencing a sexual problem, and you may also be having strong feelings. There are many different types of sexual problems, but all of them are characterized by an interruption at some point in the normal process or cycle of sexual function. Your role in this problem may or may not be clear to you. You might not see the problem as a big deal, or you may feel distressed, confused, or angry about it. Everyone reacts to sexual problems in different ways, but if the problem is not addressed, reactions can lead to considerable conflict.

Regardless of whether you consider yourself part of the problem, you have to become part of the solution. Your attitudes, feelings, and ideas are half of the equation and of equal importance. That is why sex therapy almost always involves both partners.

To become part of the solution you need a clear understanding of your partner's sexual concerns, and you need time to talk it over in a supportive manner. It helps to monitor your own emotional reactions and have an outlet to express them. Ask yourself the following important questions. Then read them aloud to you partner and discuss your answers. Or, if you feel more comfortable doing so, write down your answers and present them to your partner.

1. What is your understanding of your partner's problem? Does it have a name?

2. Why do you think she is having this problem?

3. How has her problem affected you? It is quite normal to feel upset, nervous, guilty, angry, frustrated, or rejected. Do you have any of these emotions? How have you dealt with them?

4. Do you have any difficulty with your sexual function? Have you experienced a decrease in your level of sexual desire or arousal? Difficulty achieving and maintaining erections or ejaculating too quickly? Or difficulty becoming aroused or lubricated? Difficulty reaching orgasm?

5. If you have a sexual problem, did it predate your partner's problem or start afterward? What do you think is the relationship between your problems and those of your partner?

6. Are you willing to help your partner overcome her problem? How do you think you can be helpful? If you are not willing, why not?

7. What have you tried in the past that has had positive effects on her condition? Negative effects?

What have the answers revealed to you? Do you share the same understanding of the problem? Does your partner seem satisfied or supported by your reaction? Sometimes discussing basic questions like these can bring you and your partner closer together, allowing you to see each other's points of view and clear up any misunderstandings.

✐ *Case 10.1—Arnold and Tracy*

Arnold and Tracy had been dating for about three months when they decided to have sex. Up to this point they had enjoyed a lot of physical affection, but had not talked much about their sexual likes or dislikes. When they attempted intercourse, Arnold wasn't able to penetrate Tracy, and with each unsuccessful attempt both of them grew more nervous and confused. They ended the evening with Tracy in tears and Arnold feeling angry and rejected. Tracy didn't understand why this happened: she'd had one previous sexual partner, and although intercourse had been painful, Tracy said it was still possible. Arnold still cared for Tracy and wanted to help her, but every time they tried talking about sex, Tracy became angry and tearful. Arnold finally coaxed her into trying again, but when they attempted intercourse he had trouble maintaining an erection. Reflecting back on the evening, he realized that he had little interest in having sex, because he figured that Tracy was "closing her vagina" because she didn't really want him.

Tracy explained the problem to her physician, who referred her to a sex therapist. Arnold was hesitant to go to a therapist with Tracy, because he felt uncomfortable with the idea that something might be wrong with her. On the other hand, he was surprised that she even wanted him involved, since he perceived her sexual problem as a rejection. The therapist taught them about vaginismus and asked them to talk to each other about their feelings. Arnold spoke about feeling angry, frightened, and rejected. He wanted to help her, but didn't know what to do. Tracy described feeling confused about her vaginismus, because she really wanted to have intercourse with Arnold. This session removed a lot of pressure, and Arnold happily agreed to work with Tracy to overcome her vaginismus. After several months of working with the therapist, Tracy's problem was resolved. Because their sexual problem had been so painful and difficult for them, it had almost ended the relationship before they really had a chance to know each other. After the conjoint therapy, Arnold felt that he was more intimate with Tracy than with any previous partner because he understood her sexuality so well. They continued to have a satisfying sex life after therapy and were married a year later.

We hope that you will commit yourself to helping your partner overcome her problem. There are certainly enough wonderful reasons to do so:

- You will be able to have a satisfying physical and sexual relationship.

- You will remove a major source of personal stress and interpersonal conflict.

- You will have a happier, more intimate relationship.

- You will improve communication and build trust with your partner.

These incentives are not just possible, but *probable* outcomes of working together. Even before you reach your goal, the experience itself of working together will bring many of these benefits to you and your partner. When you learn to overcome a sexual problem as a couple, you will also enhance all other areas of your relationship. In turn, your collaboration can have an enormously positive effect on your current or future family, because they will reap the benefits of your honest and intimate relationship. To understand this better, read the genogram in figure 10.1 to see how family conflict can travel through the generations. What you do now could reverberate for years and generations to come.

We recommend that partners read this entire book and we have provided the following guidelines and suggestions on how to consider yourself as equally involved in the growth of your shared sexuality.

- Be supportive and willing to help. Spend time listening to your partner tell you about her problem without suggesting a solution. If you feel a need to devise a plan—hold back for now, and when you do get involved, use this book as a guide, or use it in conjunction with a sex therapist.

- Keep in touch with your own emotional reactions. Find an outlet to express them—in a personal journal, with your own therapist, or with your partner. Do not discuss it with friends or family unless you and your partner both feel comfortable involving another person. Your sexual problem is a private matter.

- Consider a consultation or trial of couples or sex therapy. Make a joint decision to work together.

- When dealing with a sexual problem, emotions can run high for couples, and arguments may result. You may have a lot of heated or uncomfortable discussions in bed together after an unsuccessful or painful sexual experience. Do not let these situations get you so angry, fearful, or despairing that you give up. Take a time-out from the situation and come back to it later when you are more relaxed. If you remain hopeful it is easier to say to each other, "This too shall pass."

- It is important for your partner to have time and space to work on her problem. She needs private time to get in touch with herself and work through the many exercises in this book. The process of change must flow from her and requires her to take the initiative. Try to assume household or child-care responsibilities several times a week to open up time for her.

- You may both benefit if you take a break from your usual sexual activity for a short while to allow your partner to work on her sexual concerns. Talk it over and make a mutual decision.

- Read the introduction, chapters 1 and 3, and relevant sections from chapters 4 and 5. Ask your partner to discuss what she learned about herself from her sexual history and sexual map in chapter 2. It is important for you to have a full understanding of her difficulty.

- Read through the questions in chapter 2 and think about your own sexual history. Answer those that apply to your gender. How do your own experiences seem relevant to your partner's problem?

- Remember that your partner's journal is private. Do not ask to read it. If she wants to share anything from it, let her take the initiative to do so. Keep your own journal to sort out your thoughts and feelings.

- Take time to do things that give you pleasure. Attend to your own needs. Perhaps you can make a trade-off: your partner can have a free afternoon to read and write in her journal, while you have a free afternoon to be alone, exercise, go to lunch or a movie with friends, or go somewhere else you enjoy.

- Read chapter 6 and practice the deep breathing and muscle relaxation exercises. Use these exercises to settle on your own method of relaxation.

- When your partner is ready for sensate focus exercises in chapter 7, read the chapter and begin working together on the exercises. Be sure to read about pillow talk.

- Read chapter 8 and have a talk about possible roadblocks. Think about your own possible resistance to treatment and how it affects both you and your partner.

- Always practice safe sex together if you have any concerns about sexually transmitted diseases (see chapter 4).

- Spend lots of pleasurable nonsexual time together.

The Choice of Partners

Mastering sexual anxiety is a major task for sexual development. Women with sexual problems often wonder why their difficulties began after they entered a committed relationship, when they felt so sexually free with more casual relationships. Most sexologists agree if anxiety is low and a person is not threatened, sexuality is able to flow easily. In a new or casual relationship, there is usually less to lose and the woman feels safe. Once a commitment is made, the partner becomes loved and valued more highly and anxiety rises. The longer you are together the more importance each person has for the other and the more vulnerable you both feel. The paradox is that the higher value you place on your relationship, the less you are willing to risk losing it. Fear that the partner will leave or be hurtful may cause women to pull back from intimate connections. Sex is more likely to feel risky or awkward at this point. It is important to know that everyone has sexual anxiety to some degree, since you are by necessity vulnerable with your sexual partners.

Then why don't women choose a partner with whom sex is always easy and fun or highly exciting? What causes a woman to commit herself to a specific long-term partner? What factors lead to her infatuation and love for this partner? Although love may seem mysterious and elusive, it is never a random process. Your choice of partners is actually based on a drive to continue your personal growth.

To illustrate this concept, consider that a woman may consciously choose a partner by her preferences for certain physical features, personality characteristics, or common experiences, interests, or cultural, religious, and educational backgrounds. She usually chooses someone who is at about the same degree of maturity as she is. Generally, her partner also has those qualities that are not well developed in herself. For instance, if she is shy, she may choose an extroverted person who makes her feel less timid. Although she is almost never aware of this when she makes her choice, her partner embodies both the positive and negative elements from her original family, elements that hold significant emotional, unresolved issues. She makes this choice because there is a sense of familiarity that replicates her early environment—even the unpleasant aspects of it. Her partner chooses her in the same way. People return to these issues continually in order to gain a sense of control and mastery over them.

How does this process occur in a relationship? Peak infatuation and romance between partners usually lasts for two years at the most during which time partners idealize each other and project their wishes onto their partner. This period is followed by a woman's gradual recognition that her partner will not resolve all of her life issues. Her partner also experiences a similar sense of disappointment. This sets the stage for the couple to reenact their family dramas as they try to rework the unresolved issues they brought to their partnership. It is often during this first major disappointment that each partner learns to cope with the realities of the relationship and to let go of unrealistic fantasies. Over time and with much effort through the challenges of conflict, the couple deepens their understanding for each other and gains a sense of shared control over their personal issues and choices.

Masters and Johnson (1970) suggest that as many as 50 percent of couples have trouble with their sexuality at some time. There is a temptation for the couple to assume that only one person has the sexual problem, but this is never the case. The problem is maintained over time because both people perpetuate it, even though this may not seem apparent to them. In some cases, the problem is associated with one partner and the other partner is therefore caught up in it. For example, if a woman has a history of being sexually abused, her partner has to live with the fact that the abuse always affects their sexual relationship. However, the woman's partner has chosen her for their own reasons and need for mastery. The partner may need to learn patience or how to deal with rejection. The way in which partners relate to each other consists of both positive and negative factors that influence their sexual relationship. For instance, a woman may feel pressured to have an orgasm during intercourse so that her partner's self-esteem will not be damaged and this may lead to orgasm difficulty. Frequently, the sexual problem is connected to fears that the closeness of sex will lead to painful feelings. Because the fear is usually diffuse, many women have trouble identifying just what they are afraid of in their sexual relationships. For instance, a couple may feel bewildered about why they never find time for sex, but despite stated intentions, they still never find time.

Loss of sexual interest is a common problem, especially when couples do not express their anger and instead let resentments build. Many people use their defenses as well as their social skills to ignore and avoid conflict. But internal conflict will raise anxiety regardless of whether it is directly addressed with the partner. Often, the unresolved internal conflicts of both partners are expressed in their sexual relationship and remain unspoken and misunderstood by both people. A successful couple can communicate openly and honestly and work things out; an unsuccessful couple becomes mired in vicious fighting and feuds, smoldering anger and resentment, or silence.

Conflict and Sexual Dysfunction

How does a couple deal with conflict on a daily basis? There are several ways, which we'll demonstrate with the case of Eileen and Jack.

- **They acknowledge the conflict and discuss it openly and honestly.** *Jack yelled at Eileen for refusing to have sex. Later, he apologized for yelling, they sat down and hugged, and Eileen explained that she didn't feel like having sex because she was angry at him for making weekend plans without her input. Jack appreciated Eileen being up-front about her anger, but asked her in the future to tell him right away instead of taking it out on him in bed. He agreed to be more sensitive to her right to say "no" to sex and to talk to her about her refusal instead of yelling.*

- **They avoid conflict and use psychological defense mechanisms to repress feelings about it.** *Jack yelled at Eileen for refusing to have sex. Although Eileen was upset that Jack made weekend plans without consulting her and was demanding of sex, she was not really aware of these sources of her feelings and couldn't talk to him. She felt so awful that she got a terrible headache and went to sleep early.*

- **They acknowledge conflict privately but use social skills to minimize or ignore it in front of each other.** *Jack yelled at Eileen for refusing to have sex. Eileen was furious at Jack for making weekend plans without her and for demanding sex. Although she couldn't get it out of her mind, she kept it to herself, not wanting to start another fight. Later she agreed to have sex but was obviously detached from their encounter. When Jack asked her if there was a problem, she forced a smiled and said "no." Although she said nothing, a quiet resentment began to build inside.*

- **They fight about sex directly or displace anger about sex onto anger about other relational conflicts.** *Jack yelled at Eileen for refusing to have sex. Eileen was furious at Jack for making weekend plans without her and shouted back. He blamed her for deliberately making him miserable and that she always thought up excuses when he wanted sex and, what's more, she never showed him any affection. Eileen accused Jack of choosing his friends before her, for grabbing her instead of asking for affection, and bullying her when she had a terrible headache.* (or) *Jack yelled at Eileen for refusing to have sex. Eileen was furious at Jack for making weekend plans without her. But she felt guilty about not having sex so she changed the subject and agreed that she couldn't have sex because she felt sick. She was too tired and, besides, he had promised to include her in his plans and it was the third time he had not followed through. She and Jack then had a long fight about responsibility, but sex was not mentioned.*

All couples have conflicts; it is impossible for two people to agree about everything. When unresolved conflict remains unspoken and misunderstood, however, sexual relations always suffer. Few people grow up with models of how to deal with conflict. [See resources at end of chapter: Hendrix, H. (1988, 1992) and Snarch, D. (1995).] In the examples, Eileen's unacknowledged and unresolved anger towards Jack led to her avoidance of sex.

Where do these conflicts come from? Why do they affect sexual relations? Many psychologists believe that the roots of interpersonal and sexual conflicts can be traced to unresolved issues from early family life. Conflict, confusion, and isolation from a partner can occur when the current relationship embodies unresolved conflictual situations from the past. A critical juncture occurs as people mature in late adolescence and begin to establish their own identity and form intimate relationships with others. In order to do so, they must become more independent from their parents and family and yet maintain supportive emotional connections. Stable and confident sexual relationships with partners rely on this balance between independence and intimacy. This balance is achieved through disputes, negotiation, and eventual compromise. If a couple shares mutual love, respect, and common goals, conflict and friction will enable the relationship to grow.

Sexual relations can represent a microcosm of this overall tension between partners. Sex requires both the pursuit of pleasure in order to lose oneself in sexual sensations, as well as the willingness to trust a partner and give pleasure to them. The ability to tolerate sexual intimacy requires a woman to maintain a sense of self in the presence of her partner. This can create internal conflict for women who are accustomed to attending to the needs of others. Getting too close to a partner may lead to fears of being abandoned or being engulfed in the needs of the other person. This means that both people must be able to soothe themselves when their partner is unable to provide this crucial service. There are many times when a partner is unavailable when you are angry or distant and you each must be able to take care of yourselves. Everyone faces anxiety about how to balance giving and receiving in a sexual encounter. Each partner in a couple grows at a different pace and this can either enhance a couple's working together or drive a wedge between them. Couples can learn intimacy as they discover that they can maintain their individuality and togetherness at the same time.

Sexual Power Struggles

Sometimes couples find themselves in an unspoken power struggle that plays itself out in the bedroom. One partner appears to have more power, which may be due to an array of actual or perceived attributes: they may be older, stronger, better educated, better looking, or a better wage earner. One may be seen as more outgoing, socially adept, calmer, more organized, or more successful. Whatever the characteristics involved, there is a tendency to rebalance the power in one way or another. If one partner uses this power to make all the decisions or tell the other what to do, the other partner may rebalance the situation by losing interest in sex, thus, creating their own base of power in the bedroom. This struggle for power and control is similar to the struggle for mastery that we discussed before: it is an unconscious drive that causes us to act in repetitive and conflictual ways in relationships. Since this is an unconscious process, you won't necessarily recognize it. But if you find repeating patterns in your fights, it may be about power. A couple's therapist is trained to recognize this and can help if you keep getting stuck in these power struggles.

❤ Case 10.2—Alice and Ron

Power was a problem for Alice and Ron. At the beginning of therapy Ron did all the talking, made all the family decisions, and followed up to see if Alice had carried out his plans. He couldn't understand why Alice was not interested in sex, since she had clearly loved sex when they met. When the therapist helped Ron and Alice look at their process, they could see that Ron was active in his requests for sex, and Alice was both direct and indirect in refusing or avoiding sex. Once Alice began having the power of making more decisions and felt a sense of her equality in their daily life, she warmed up to sex again. She surprised Ron by arranging a romantic weekend getaway in the country.

It is a paradox that people choose as a lifetime partner the very person most likely to make them face their core emotional issue. This occurs for several reasons. Your choice of a certain person may be associated with why you have a problem (e.g., *a woman who always ends up with a partner who is emotionally distant*), and eventually the nature of the relationship influences both of your reactions to the problem, (e.g., *a woman's introverted husband was not upset by her lack of orgasm but tended to blame himself*). You may also be stuck because you are unable to find a compatible partner (e.g., *a woman who is phobic of sex, but only finds herself attracted to insensitive, aggressive men who won't tolerate her difficulty*).

EXERCISE 10.2—CHOOSING PARTNERS

Answer the following questions in your journal:

- If you have a current partner, how did you choose them? What features attracted you?

- On a deeper level, do they have certain characteristics that you don't? Do you think that this influenced your choice?

- Do these characteristics influence your sexual problem? How?

- How does the way in which you and your partner interact affect your problem?

- If you don't have a partner, what characteristics are you looking for? hoping for?

- How do you think those factors will influence your problem?

If you are confused by this exercise and are not able to come up with a link between your partner and your sexual problems, don't worry. As you continue through this chapter, ideas may emerge.

Sexuality in Relationships

When a couple experiences a problem with their sexual relationship, there is a temptation to assume that the sexual problem exists in isolation. This is almost never the case. Many couples have trouble with their sexuality at some time. If there is a sexual problem, the dynamic relationship between the partners has both positive and negative aspects which can either help the couple resolve their problem or make it difficult to do so.

The choice of a long-term partner is actually based on an internal need to continue personal growth. A woman chooses someone who is at about the same level of developmental growth as she is, and has those qualities which are not well developed in herself. Her partner embodies both the positive and negative elements of the woman's parents and siblings—elements which emotionally unresolved issues. Her partner does the same.

After the illusion of romance dissipates, the woman often projects her parents and her own negative characteristics onto her partner and dislikes what she sees. As she realizes that her partner is not her savior after all, she retreats into hurt and anger. Her partner does the same. Then both must master their own personal issues through the natural conflicts which arise in their lives together. In fact, it is through conflict that the person and the relationship grow in breadth and depth. The task of learning to know and love the real person begins at this first major disappointment.

Couples use their internal defenses and social skills to ignore and avoid conflict, but internal conflict will raise anxiety regardless of whether it is directly addressed with a partner. Not infrequently, the unresolved internal conflicts of both partners are expressed in their sexual relationship and remain unspoken and misunderstood by both. According to Scharff (1982), sexual dysfunctions are basically unresolved issues stemming from the family of origin that are given expression in bodily processes.

Everyone has sexual anxiety to some degree, since they are literally naked and vulnerable with their sexual partners. As you learn to master sexual anxiety, you grow into a more developed adult continuing through your life to the next level of mastery. As one partner faces a challenge and changes, the other partner is made anxious by the change in equilibrium and will also feel the push toward growth. Snarch (1991) suggests that the degree to which a person knows themself is the degree to which they can allow intimacy without fear of engulfment or abandonment by their partner. Intimacy occurs when people manage to maintain individuality and togetherness at the same time.

The ability to tolerate sexual intimacy requires maturity and a degree of differentiation from the partner. Bowen (1971, 1975, 1976) developed a theory of differentiation to explain how an individual gains self-mastery in a committed relationship. When partners can maintain their own identities in the presence of the other they are differentiated. Growth occurs as each of the partners disclose more intimate aspects of their core selves over time and are seen by the other for who they really are. When Shakespeare wrote, "To thine own self be true," he was talking about being differentiated from others.

Anxiety, either the fear of abandonment or engulfment, is both a precuser and necessary factor to sexual growth. Mastering sexual anxiety is the major task of sexual development. People having sexual difficulties after they enter a committed relationship often wonder why they felt so free sexually with other, more casual relationships. Most sexologists agree that sexuality can flow when the person is not threatened about their core self; with a new, casual, or uncommitted relationship there is less to lose and the core self is not threatened. But once you make a commitment, the other person is loved, valued highly, and becomes "family," which raises the unfinished agendas from your family of origin. Sex is more likely to feel "dangerous" at this point. In order to understand what goes on below the surface in sexual and emotional relationships you need to understand the past.

Everyone is born into families with characteristics that are both positive and negative, a light and a dark side. The light part of the self is the known part, accepted by yourself and others as your strength. You disown your darker characteristics, which remain out of your awareness. A child is hurt by the darker parts of their parents, but also incorporates those parts into a separate part of the self. When you commit to another person, you believe they will heal all the wounds left from the dark side of your childhood. But instead, you project the dark unowned part of yourself and your parents onto your partner and dislike it heartily. Your partner does the same. Then your life task begins—to work through the disowned dark parts of yourself and see your partner for themselves, rather than as your projections.

⚉ Case Study 10.3—Mary and John

The following example will examine how the past affected the present lives of a couple. After eleven years of marriage, Mary and John were in trouble. In the past, Mary had always agreed to be sexual because she liked to feel close to John, but had never had an orgasm. Her stronger need was to make sure John was satisfied. But Mary had been increasingly angry at John and had withdrawn her affection and sexual availability. John felt sexually rejected by Mary and began an affair. After several months of indecision and guilt, he ended the affair and told Mary the truth.

In John and Mary's family, each generation had extramarital affairs that affected the lives of all the family members and was then reenacted in the next generation. The genogram in figure 10.1 shows the details of John and Mary's families in more detail. John and Mary watched as the therapist added information to their genogram as they talked. He asked about the length of their marriage, their ages, and the ages and gender of their children. He asked them to describe why they were first attracted to each other. They explained that they met and felt entirely comfortable almost immediately. Mary saw in John a warm man who liked to touch her and wanted her to enjoy herself. John saw a friendly, empathic woman who would love and understand him for himself. They fit together "like magic" and decided to marry after a year.

After the initial period of illusion and idealization, where each found the other delightful in every way, reality began to set in. Settling into a home and having two children kept both of them busy, but sex became less frequent and more problematic as time went on. Even though she loved John, Mary felt anxious about initiating or letting go during sex. John couldn't enjoy himself unless she did let go, and after many miserable late night discussions about their poor sexual relationship, he gradually withdrew. Mary was hurt by his withdrawal but afraid of the anger that might emerge if they talked openly about the problem. The more distant John became, the less Mary could respond sexually. In despair, John began an affair with a co-worker.

The affair caused great turmoil for both John and Mary. They loved each other and didn't want to divorce, for their own sake, but especially for the sake of their children. It is no accident that John's affair began when his son was eight-years old—that was his age when his mother, Emma, had her first affair. Mary's father, Anthony, also had an affair when her mother was thirty-seven years old—Mary's exact age when John began his affair. Over and over these connections, seemingly coincidental, are seen when therapists look at the genograms of couples. Often people make impulsive and major decisions around the time of a major loss within their family. They may also reenact unfinished conflict from previous generations.

The therapist asked about the relationships among the parents and siblings in John and Mary's families of origin, and the emotional connections each had to one another. He asked about how the parents related to each other and to their children. John talked about his family. His father had been emotionally and physically absent from his family. His mother was an emotional woman who depended on her husband to supply her with approval and love. As she realized his unavailability, she became angry and carried on a long-term affair. She also turned to her sons for the attention she wanted and was demanding, critical, and angry as she diverted her negative feelings from her husband to her children. John realized that he had known about his mother's affair and been angry at her all his life. As a child, John felt cut off from his father and overwhelmed by his mother's negative feelings. He also absorbed the notion that if you were not happy with your partner you found affection elsewhere.

John was known for his bright intelligence, good looks, confident manner, commitment to his work, and exhuberant sense of play. He was expressive of his passionate feelings, and he was able to express anger easily, although he hid his vulnerable self. John's dark, unacknowledged side included a distrust of women, a sense of powerlessness in relationships, and a fear that he was not lovable. He learned to use his sexuality to get his emotional needs met, as well as to express the anger inside. He wanted a partner who would love him and respond to him sexually so he could feel good about his ability to please her. This distrust of women was coupled with his need for a woman's love and a long-held resentment and hostility, with a belief that in a power game of love he would never win. He felt powerful when his partner wanted him and surrendered to him sexually, but his sense of competence hung on this thin thread. When Mary rejected him he was desperate to regain his sense of masculinity through sex and began an affair.

Mary's father was a successful doctor but when he was with the family he was preoccupied, distant, and unavailable. On several occasions he became involved with other women. Her mother had given up her own dreams for a career and told her children of her resentment and sacrifice as she raised the family by herself. Although she was no longer a practicing Catholic, she passed along the antisexual messages and the anxiety she felt about sex to her daughters. Mary's family message was that men are not involved in family life and women don't like sex.

Mary knew very little about how men thought, felt, or behaved because her father was never home. She was anxious about sexuality and her body, and fearful of expressing anger. She protected herself with a shield of outer friendliness and warmth, but she kept her feelings to herself. She had a bright personality. Like both parents, she was smart, involved with friends, and had a rewarding career. Mary's dark side, put out of awareness, included her anger at not getting enough love or attention from either parent, and her own way of staying safe by being distant, which she hid behind a friendly facade like her mother. Mary denied problems and refused to acknowledge anger or talk about it. She longed for a man who would express his love and affection and who would be at her side as they raised a family together.

When she married, Mary hoped that John's interest in sex would warm her to orgasm. Although she entered into sexual relations easily she could not let go to orgasm. She dreamed of finding a partner who would love her as her parents had not and heal the wounds of childhood. She knew little about her own sexuality and usually agreed to sex because it was harder to say "no."

However, she was not able to acknowledge anger since she had been taught anger was sinful. Unexpressed anger had continued to build over the years, making it harder to feel vulnerable or open to John.

John and Mary looked next at the relationships of their grandparents and realized that both sides of their families had members who had issues about sex. Mary's grandmother passed on messages, from her strict religious training, which included obedience and traditional family values. She also passed on the antisexual messages of the Church, including considerable shame and embarrassment about women's bodies and sexuality in general. Mary's father had an affair when her mother was thirty-seven years old. John's grandfather, Daniel, kept a mistress, like many men in his social circle. His grandfather, James, often had affairs as he traveled on business.

Therapy for Mary and John involved a gradual growth for each of them as they understood the legacies and loyalties they brought from their families of origin and enacted in their marriage. As they began to illuminate their hidden selves, their original love and respect for each other reemerged. They left therapy after two years of hard work, with a deepened intimacy and vastly improved sexual relationship. They had become more autonomous, self-aware, and realistic about each other—more capable of sustaining a truly intimate relationship.

A Family Genogram

Perhaps the best way to illustrate the influence of family dynamics on later emotional and sexual relationships is to construct a family history chart or *génogram*. To understand the complex web of relationships by starting with the grandparents of Mary and John and working through the generations. Each generation is represented visually by being on a different horizontal axis on the page. The youngest generation is at the bottom, and the oldest generation is at the top of the genogram. The symbols at the bottom are used to represent family relationships.

EXERCISE 10.2—CREATING YOUR OWN GENOGRAM

You can create your own genogram by using the symbols provided and the sample genogram of John and Mary. Start near the bottom of the page and mark your children using squares or circles to indicate gender. Include ages, names, and any major life events, illnesses, miscarriages, or abortions. Next, put you and your partner on the chart and draw lines to delineate your families of origin. Include your siblings and their birth order, names and dates of birth, marriages, major illnesses, accidents, or death. Next, show your parents and stepparents, if you have them. Continue up the page and show your parents' siblings and their parents, with any pertinent information. Now draw lines, as shown on the sample chart, to indicate comfortable, distant, critical, or abusive relationships. As you work, look for patterns. Ask your other relatives for information. You should discover many details which will help you understand how your family life has affected your current relationship.

Review the style and symbols in the genogram in figure 10.1. Then make a genogram for your family and one for your partner's family if possible (or have your partner make one). Include information such as name, current age, occupation, medical or psychiatric problems (including substance abuse), major personality characteristics, and cause and age of death if relevant. Ask family members for their memories and dates of significant life events, both positive and negative. Often people make impulsive and major decisions around the time of a major loss within their family. For instance, in the genogram in figure 10.1 it is no coincidence that Mary was 37 when John had an affair; her mother was 37 when her father had an affair. John's mother had an affair when he was eight, the age of his son when he began his affair.

In your genogram, look for details and coincidences, lapses in detail, or things which appear unexplained. Ask several different family members about the same events, since there is always more than one way to think about what happened. This will give you a broader view of your family. Often the *black sheep* of the family will have a valuable contribution based on a more distant perspective of the family. Look for missing links in terms of time, geographical distance, relationships, lost information. These gaps often signal the presence of family secrets. When something is secret or unresolved it is often passed on to the next generation. Many family secrets are about sexual problems, and many sexual dysfunctions appear in several generations.

Sexual Styles

All couples have different sexual styles or ways in which they individually like to approach sex. Some couples like to play out complimentary roles: one likes to play

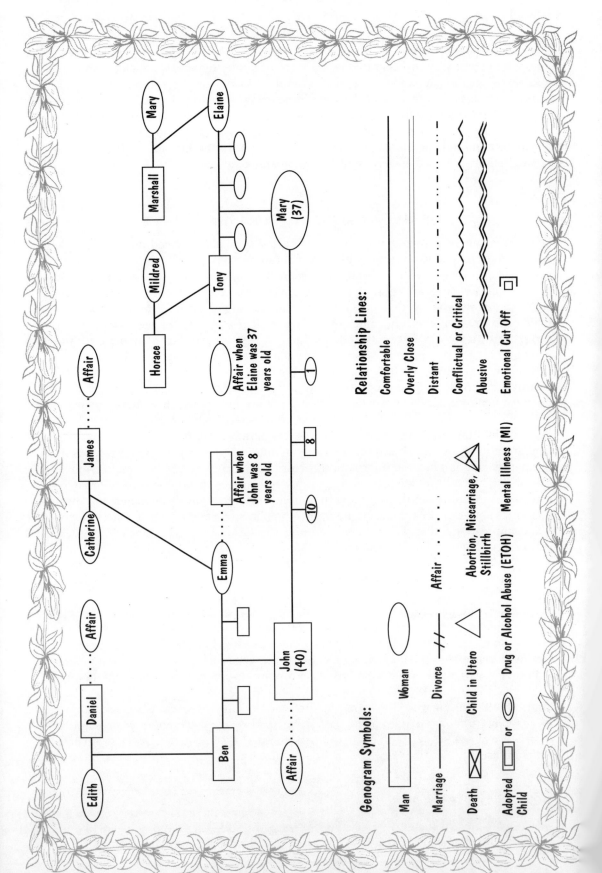

the teacher and the other likes to play the student. Or, both are sensualists and prefer long lovemaking sessions with a wide variety of touching. Sometimes a couple's different styles are not compatible. For instance, both may prefer to be followers rather than leaders during sex. Or, one partner may like drama while the other wants to drift into a trance. It is important, then, for a couple to try out new ideas and find a match between their styles. If you feel awkward about how to begin, there are many good resources listed in the appendix under the subheading Enhancing Sensuality and Sexual Technique.

EXERCISE 10.3—WHAT IS YOUR SEXUAL STYLE?

The following list includes a variety of sexual activities. You and your partner should rate each item from 1 to 5 on your interest or willingness to do it.

    1 = "I won't do this."
    5 = "I would very much like to do this."

Your Style

Activity	Rating
Try a new sexual position such as _____	_____
Be sexual in a different location such as _____	_____
Wear erotic lingerie or clothing	_____
Use a sexual lubricant	_____
Give a sensuous massage	_____
Read erotic literature to each other	_____
Play with sex toys (vibrators, dildos, etc.)	_____
Tell each other a fantasy	_____
Act out a safe fantasy	_____
Watch an erotic movie together	_____
Role-play different people	_____
Play strip poker together	_____
Undress each other	_____
Have a "quickie"	_____
Plan a sexual encounter at a different time of day or night	_____
Write a sexy love letter to each other	_____
Talk on the phone in a sexy way	_____
Give oral sex	_____
Receive oral sex	_____
Try anal sex	_____
Look for the G-spot	_____

Dress up as one another   _____

Include food in sex play (whipped cream, chocolate, etc.)   _____

Surprise each other with something sexual   _____

Take a bath or shower together   _____

Do something together nude (sunbathe, paint a room in your home, etc.)   _____

Try ten different ways to kiss each other   _____

Other: _____

Other: _____

Other: _____

Your Partner's Style

Activity	Rating
Try a new sexual position such as	_____
Be sexual in a different location such as	_____
Wear erotic lingerie or clothing	_____
Use a sexual lubricant	_____
Give a sensuous massage	_____
Read erotic literature to each other	_____
Play with sex toys (vibrators, dildos, etc.)	_____
Tell each other a fantasy	_____
Act out a safe fantasy	_____
Watch an erotic movie together	_____
Role-play different people	_____
Play strip poker together	_____
Undress each other	_____
Have a "quickie"	_____
Plan a sexual encounter at a different time of day or night	_____
Write a sexy love letter to each other	_____
Talk on the phone in a sexy way	_____
Give oral sex	_____
Receive oral sex	_____
Try anal sex	_____
Look for the G-spot	_____
Dress up as one another	_____
Include food in sex play (whipped cream, chocolate, etc.)	_____

Surprise each other with something sexual   _____

Take a bath or shower together   _____

Do something together nude (sunbathe, paint a room in your home, etc.)   _____

Try ten different ways to kiss each other   _____

Other: _____

Other: _____

Other: _____

Lesbian Partners

If you are a lesbian you know that lesbians face the same sexual challenges and problems that heterosexual women do. You may have been exposed to the same negative messages and myths about appropriate female roles and sexual behaviors. Like other women, you have to learn about your sexuality and learn how to communicate openly with your partner. However, lesbians often have to work through an extra layer of fear and anxiety as they acknowledge their sexual orientation. Internalized homophobia can lead to guilt and self-hatred and the acceptance of limiting stereotypes. Lesbians often have to battle internal and external cultural messages that lesbianism is bad, wrong, immoral, disgusting, or dirty. In the past, there have been few resources and even fewer role models for lesbian sexuality. Today, many younger lesbian women are finding a forum to acknowledge and enjoy their sexuality with more ease.

One of the major issues that bring lesbian couples to therapy is loss of sexual desire coupled with a lack of genital sexuality in an otherwise romantic, affectionate, and intellectually satisfying relationship. After the initial stage of sexual infatuation is over, usually lasting in any couple for two years at the most, genital sexuality may dwindle or disappear. When this occurs, each woman may worry that that she is not loved or not sexy enough, or that the relationship is not viable without genital sex. One reason for these concerns is that sex is seen as a major defining factor in a couple's relationship, which distinguishes it from other lesbian friendships. Low desire can also result when the intense closeness and intimacy shared by two women leads to a sense of fusion and fear of being submerged by each other. Heterosexual couples also experience a descrepancy in sexual desire if they fear engulfment or fusion. Avoiding genital sex may provide enough distance for the couple to remain closely connected. Sexual guilt and consequent repression of sexual desire may be the way a woman deals with her internal sexual conflicts at the expense of active sexuality.

Many studies of sexuality suggest that lesbian couples have the least genital activities of all types of couples (Bell and Weinberg 1978). Masters and Johnson (1979) proposed that this was due to the fact that lesbian sexual activity was more suited to female sexual responses, involving more body touching and intimacy. Some feminists believe that the concept of low desire may not apply to women, since it is based upon a male model of sexuality. Some groups of lesbians are exploring a wider repertoire of sex and believe that female sexuality has been contained and limited by male sexuality.

Accordingly, sex therapy for lesbian couples may require a different model from therapy for heterosexual couples. What may be needed is a wider vision of female sexuality that accounts for the possibility that physical pleasure may not be the major factor for women's sexual experience. Woman may enjoy physical pleasure, but the emotional passion may be equally important to their sexual pleasure. Nichols (1988) suggests four important issues to be explored by a lesbian couple with low desire:

1. Is the problem located in the conflictual relationship or in one or both women's individual problems?

2. Do both partners lack desire, or is the problem due to a discrepancy in levels of desire?

3. Is the loss of desire the result of another sexual problem, such as aversion to oral sex? Fear or aversion to oral sex is a common problem which couples bring to a therapist.

4. Is the problem due to a need for a wider repertoire of sex techniques to alleviate sexual boredom?

Loulan (1984) believes that lesbian couples can change their personal definition of sex to suit female sexuality and this might include sexual experiences that would appear quite different from sex with a male partner. For instance, heterosexual couples often engage in sex that is driven by the male's request for sex and wish for orgasm. A lesbian couple will have different sexual desires, preferences, and rhythms. They may need to talk about their differences and explore their unique way of relating sexually. Two women might engage in sex without requiring obligatory orgasm to signal the end of sex. Sexuality could be enjoyed for the sensuous experience itself, since female sexuality is oriented to the whole body and not only to the genitals.

Loulan recommends that women make use of will, rather than depending on a sense of desire to engage in sexual behavior. Willingness is the active decision to be sexual, regardless of whether you feel desire. It is a willingness to allow yourself to enter into a physical connection and pleasure, and stop when you feel you have had enough. Loulan believes that you do not need to continue through to orgasm unless it suits your wishes.

Finding a Lesbian-Affirming Therapist

Though this society is making efforts to allow for diversity, homophobia is still common. Not surprisingly, you want to experience therapy as a safe haven that helps you affirm your life choices. You probably want a therapist who acknowledges that some of your needs are different because of your sexual orientation. A lesbian-affirming therapist may be gay or straight, but their therapeutic philosophy reinforces a lesbian sexual orientation as positive.

Some lesbian women choose a gay-identified therapist because then they don't feel they have to "explain" everything in therapy. They may feel an enhanced sense of safety to explore issues at their own pace. On the other hand, heterosexual therapists can be empathic about a lesbian's experiences and also offer a chance for her to know herself and make her own choice. A good therapist is able to help a woman regardless of her sexual orientation. You need to decide whether having a gay or lesbian therapist will provide an extra perception of safety, understanding, and comfort. Regardless of the type of therapist, it is important for you to discuss any issues in therapy you may have regarding your sexual orientation and decide whether you feel that the therapist understands and affirms your choices.

If you are looking for a lesbian or gay-affirmative therapist, there are a number of resources. We have provided a list of resources in the appendix under Lesbian Issues.

Sex and the Single Woman

At this time there are over fifty million people over the age of eighteen in the United States who are living alone and single, by choice, through divorce, or through the death of a spouse (Hass and Haas 1990). Some people who are single are celibate and intend to remain alone. Others may be looking for a partner and are celibate because they lack a suitable partner. Some single women date several partners but aren't in a monogamous relationship.

As women progress into their 30s and beyond, the ratio of single women to men grows, since men tend to marry younger women and tend to die younger than women. Contrary to the stereotype of "old maids," many single women are happy about their single status. Some are waiting to marry until they finish training in advanced degrees and others are deeply involved in career advancement. Most single women engage in a sexual life in one way or another.

Single women vary widely in their attitudes about being sexual with a partner. A small percentage expect to be married before they engage in sexual activity. A large percentage are sexually active. A midsized percentage of single women think that sex is a natural outgrowth of friendship, provided both people agree.

There are a number of problems a single woman faces regarding her sexuality. Women who wish to marry must decide how they will behave sexually as they look for a mate. Women who have divorced or are widowed usually need time to readjust to the single life before they are ready to date and be sexual again. All women who are not in monogamous relationships should be aware and concerned about using safe sex practices to avoid STDs and pregnancy.

Single women face specific sexual issues in their social lives. Many women may not be sure where to meet interesting partners or how to connect with them once they do meet. Once you meet someone you like, many decisions are required: how soon to be sexual, how to talk about sex, and how to negotiate practicing safe sex are a few examples. Think about your values ahead of time and then you can explain your sexual decisions to a new acquaintance more easily. Be as honest with yourself as you can and don't run the risk of being unprepared for sex just because you didn't want to imagine yourself beforehand as a sexually active woman. It's better to admit to yourself that you *might* want to be sexual and plan ahead to use safe sex practices. Remember you are not obligated to agree to any sexual behavior just because your date asks.

When you are talking to someone new, a few important communication techniques will help you be clear regarding your intentions:

- Use "I" statements when you are explaining your feelings. This is more clear and less blaming of others. *"I would like to talk about how we can both feel comfortable about using safe sex. I would be too worried to enjoy myself otherwise."*

- Ask for their opinions and feelings also. *"How do you feel about waiting until we know one another better?"*

- Choose a time long before you have your clothes off and are both turned on. *"I'd like to talk about the possibility of us having sex before the time comes."*

- Telegraph ahead with a transition statement. *"This is hard for me to say, but I want to talk about sex."*

When a marriage or long relationship ends, there is always a grieving period as you readjust to life as a single person. Women who have been widowed, divorced, or have just ended a monogamous relationship face sexual issues as they work through their sadness and grief or disappointment and anger. Sexual relationships are risky at this time because you may feel insecure about yourself and feel tempted to ignore the need for safe sex. Some women resume sex with their old partner temporarily when either or both of you feel lonely. Widows usually go through a similar adjustment period before they are ready to start a new relationship. If the marriage has lasted a long time, some widows decide not to begin a new sexual relationship. Many widows, however, are ready to engage in sexual activity after they go through a time of mourning.

For most women, the reentry into the dating world is a difficult and painful process. The longer the marriage, the less a woman knows what to expect as a single woman. Women often feel rejected, unattractive, or afraid of being hurt again. Some women, however, welcome the chance to try out their new sexual freedom with a variety of sexual partners. This approach to sex usually decreases after an initial period of exploration. Women who still have children living at home also have to decide how they will introduce a new partner into their family. Within a year or so, most people establish a new relationship which includes satisfying sexuality.

If you are divorced or widowed, or have left a long-standing relationship, the following ideas may be helpful:

1. Discover your sexual self with self pleasuring (masturbation) while you allow yourself time to recover from the loss of your former relationship.

2. Separate you sexual needs from your needs for touch, comfort, affection, and closeness. Take the pressure off fulfilling all your needs through sex by meeting these nonsexual needs with family and friends.

3. Go slowly. Get to know a new partner over time before you become sexual. Enjoy kissing, touching, petting, and sensuality before having intercourse.

4. Discuss issues about safe sex, birth control, sexual activities, monagomy versus multiple partners. Communication is very important.

5. Practice being sexually assertive. Teach your partner what you like, learn what your new partner likes, and try out things new to both of you.

6. If you live with your children, talk with your partner about whether you are ready to acknowledge your new sexual relationship to your family. Trust yourself to make the appropriate decision, considering all of your needs. Remember that it is your right to attend to your needs.

Choosing to live together is becoming increasingly common for couples. If the present trend continues, one out of twenty couples will be living together by the year 2000 (DeMaris and Leslie 1984; Tanfer 1987). Women of all ages may use living together as a transition to marriage. Others see living together as a valid choice if they are not ready for, or don't want a legally binding relationship.

Facing Sexual Dysfunction without a Partner

If you don't have a sexual partner, you may wonder how you can work on your sexual issues. Since sex is so often a part of romantic relationships today, a woman who is dating usually feels the need to include sex as part of the relationship. A woman who has a sexual phobia or sexual aversion may worry that her problem will be immediately apparent to a new partner. Dyspareunia and vaginismus make penetration either painful or impossible. A woman with a desire, arousal, or orgasm problem faces the problem of how to find a partner who is willing to work with her on the problem. She is also faced with deciding how to tell a new lover that she has sexual problems.

This is not an easy dilemma and some women simply forgo sexual relationships. Other women choose partners that, for one reason or another, tolerate their problem. Some women just don't tell their partners early on and only reveal it when it becomes obvious. Hopefully you feel able to be honest about your sexual difficulty and have faith that a partner who truly cares for you will be willing to help. We would like to offer some suggestions:

- Having a sexual problem doesn't mean that you can't have relationships. Don't let it stop you from dating.

- You can work on your problem without having a partner. Women with phobias or aversions can learn relaxation techniques and consider the use of medications. Women with vaginismus and dyspareunia can practice relaxation techniques and work with dilators. Women with desire and arousal disorders can work on relaxation techniques and self-stimulation exercises (with erotic materials, if necessary), and women with orgasm disorders can practice masturbation with or without vibrators. All of these women can start working with a sex therapist on their own.

- When you meet a potential partner, don't rush the relationship. Focus on building trust, friendship, and affection before getting to sex. When you feel ready to have a sexual relationship, you will feel more comfortable discussing your problem.

- If you feel very anxious during the initial few dates, consider setting up a hierarchy of fears and working gradually through them. For instance, one woman went on several first dates to slowly desensitize her fears. She held off on second dates for awhile to keep her level of anxiety in check. Over time, dates became more relaxing, and she progressed to second dates when she and her date enjoyed the first.

- Most sensate focus exercises involve the same touching that occurs with making love. When you are intimate with your partner, lead them through Sensate Focus 1 and 2. You don't have to say, "This is a sensate focus exercise to help my sexual problem." Just present it as a relaxing and sensuous part of sex. Most partners will love the attention. It will give you an opportunity to be sexually assertive.

- Think about how you want to describe your sexual difficulty to your partner and practice it in your head. A conversation about sexuality is less stressful if you talk with your partner while you are away from the bedroom, such as when you are out walking or sitting in the kitchen. Explain that you are working through some personal sexual issues that are not fully resolved. Express your thoughts and feelings and explain how you are coping with your difficulties. Present it honestly and with a calm voice. Listen to what your partner thinks and feels about what you have said. Suggest ways in which they can help you. If you have built a stable relationship up to this point, most partners will want to help. Couples face many challenges together, and your sexual problem might be the first of many life challenges. If your partner is not willing or able to participate in the current problem, it may be indicative of future difficulties together.

- Don't expect a partner to tolerate your problem if you are not willing yourself to take steps to resolve it.

- You can still pleasure your partner without having intercourse. Having a varied sexual style will allow you to have an enjoyable sexual relationship while you work on specific aspects of it. For instance, while one couple worked on overcoming vaginismus, they enjoyed pleasuring each other with mutual masturbation.

- Practice being assertive with your friends about nonsexual issues. Then practice being assertive on your own. This will make it easier to eventually be sexually assertive with a partner. See the requesting/refusing exercises in chapter 8. As you learn to be more aware of your likes and dislikes, you move towards being able to ask someone else to give to you.

As a single woman, you should also keep in mind that periods of celibacy or sexual time-outs can provide the opportunity to tune in to your inner self and explore unresolved issues. Freedom from the commitment of a sexual relationship opens up your time and energy for solitary pursuits. There is no concern for sexual struggles with a partner, hassles from contraceptives, or worries about STDs and unwanted pregnancy. Some women enjoy the opportunity to pursue other interests, develop their independence, or recover from a time of crisis. Sexual abuse survivors often find being single helpful while they work out individual issues and learn to explore other avenues of loving a partner. When couples are troubled with their relationship, brief periods of abstinence can allow time for clear thinking. Long-term abstinence often follows major illness, severe stress, or the death of a spouse. It is not uncommon for women to be unable or unwilling to consider a new sexual relationship after a long marriage ends.

Working with Physicians

The first step in understanding a sexual problem is to address underlying medical issues. We discussed many of these in chapters 1 and 4, and by now you may know whether medical factors are an issue. Try to visit your internist and gynecologist before you see a therapist. Once you have ruled out medical problems or started on a treatment program, you can address psychological concerns with a therapist. If you are too anxious to take this step, you can work through your fear and/or ambivalence with a psychotherapist first. Women with dyspareunia and vaginismus often have reservations about seeing a gynecologist because they fear a painful or unpleasant pelvic examination.

How do you begin working with physicians? Chances are that you already have both an internist and a gynecologist. If not, you can obtain a good referral from a trusted family member or friend or through your health plan. Begin with a visit to your internist for a general overview of your health. As a rule, this physician will not treat sexual dysfunction unless there is an obvious medical cause, but should refer you to a gynecologist or a sex therapist. Fogel and Joseph (1996) write that, "A physician is usually the first, and may be the only, person who has the opportunity to identify a patient's sexual dysfunction. . . . How the physician handles that situation may open doors for the patient or shut those doors for the rest of his or her life." They cite several reasons why doctors sometimes avoid discussing sexual issues with their patients. First, many doctors have little training in sexuality because few medical schools and internship/residency programs include it as part of the curriculum. Without a good understanding of sexuality, many physicians are uneasy about discussing it. As a result, questions about sexual functioning are often left out of physical exams.

Therefore, if you have sexual concerns, you will probably have to initiate the discussion yourself.

Your internist or family practitioner can help address general medical issues, but the next step will be to have a gynecologist take a medical-sexual history and do a pelvic examination. A gynecologist is a licensed medical doctor who has undergone a year of internship training as well as specialty training for three years in the practice of obstetrics and gynecology (they are called OB-GYN specialists). Some gynecologists train for an additional two-year fellowship in a subspecialty such as gynecologic oncology (treatment of female genital cancer) or reproductive endocrinology (treatment of hormonal causes of infertility). Gynecologists handle all problems related to internal and external genital function and structure, including sexual function, reproduction, fertility, contraceptives, family planning and pregnancy, menstruation, menopause, genital pain and bleeding, gynecologic cancers, and sexually transmitted diseases.

All gynecologists encounter women with sexual dysfunction in their practice and are able to identify and treat most underlying physical causes. They do not, however, treat problems of sexual desire, arousal, and orgasm, and do not practice sex therapy. You may want to inquire, however, as to whether the gynecologist has a particular focus to their practice, such as obstetrics, gynecologic surgery, or vulvar disease. This information might help guide you to the most experienced individual for your problem. Many of the resources listed in the appendix can steer you towards appropriate referrals. Large academic research hospitals are always good sources for specialty referrals.

Once you have selected a gynecologist, there are several important steps to prepare for your first appointment. Be prepared to discuss when, where, and how your sexual problem began, and consider beforehand what factors you think perpetuate it. Know your full medical history and bring a list of all the medications you use, including over-the-counter drugs. Be sure to write down a list of questions you want the doctor to answer about your condition. If you are nervous about the appointment, practice some relaxation techniques beforehand (you may even try this while sitting in the waiting room). It is important to let the gynecologist know if you are having trouble with vaginal penetration so that they can tailor the exam to be as slow and comfortable as possible. You should always feel that you have control over an exam; you can ask your doctor to stop or say "no" if you can't go on.

&c& Case 10.3—Sally

Sally had a history of dyspareunia and went to see a recommended gynecologist for an evaluation. She told Dr. Green that she was not able to have intercourse because of her pain and was petrified of having a pelvic exam. Dr. Green listened sympathetically and then asked Sally to position herself on the examination table and relax for ten minutes before beginning. Knowing how painful the exam might be, Dr. Green used a small speculum and lubricated it with an anesthetic jelly. She gave Sally a mirror to watch the exam and asked her to say "okay" or "stop" to let her know if she felt too much pain to continue. Dr. Green was slow and careful in her exam, and this allowed Sally to feel more relaxed. The pain was moderate but tolerable, and Sally left the appointment with a strong sense of trust in Dr. Green.

What Is a Gynecological or Pelvic Exam?

The gynecological or pelvic examination is a physical assessment of the genital and reproductive organs including the vulva, vagina, cervix, uterus, ovaries, and fallopian tubes. A doctor uses a pelvic exam to evaluate if a woman has any diseases or structural problems and to monitor the state of pregnancy at certain points. Doctors usually recommend that women who are sexually active, using birth control, or on hormone replacement therapy should have yearly examinations, including pap smears of the cervix to detect any precancerous cells. Gynecologists usually conduct breast examinations. Pelvic exams should be scheduled to avoid the menstrual period since menstrual flow may affect test results. Breast exams should also be deferred during menstruation since breasts can be enlarged and breast tissue is often more tender, possibly making the exam inaccurate.

Women should not douche for twenty-four hours prior to an exam because douching can mask some disease processes. Recent sexual intercourse will not affect the exam, although some spermicidal products or lubricants may change the vaginal condition and interfere with test results. A patient is encouraged to empty her bladder beforehand, since this makes the exam more comfortable. This also makes it easier for the physician to feel all pelvic structures.

Before the exam, a gynecologist may talk to a woman about her overall health and inquire about any problems. You may feel more relaxed if you ask to meet with your doctor in their office before you go to the examination room. The pelvic exam begins with the woman removing her clothes and covering herself with a sheet or gown. The physician will instruct you to lie on your back on the examining table, bend your legs, and put your feet in footrests or stirrups. An additional sheet is then draped over your pelvis and legs. If you want a better view of the exam, ask the doctor to provide you with a handheld mirror or remove the sheet from your legs. Ask your doctor what to expect before any procedure. If you have never had an internal examination, ask your clinician to show you a speculum and explain how it works. Relaxation techniques will help you feel better and allow the doctor to proceed with ease. You can relax by breathing deeply in through your nose and out through your mouth, imagining the cleansing breath relaxing your abdomen and pelvis.

The first part of an exam is external. Usually the doctor starts with a breast examination, checking for tenderness, lumps, nipple discharge, skin changes, and enlarged lymph nodes in your armpits. Have your doctor explain breast self-examination to you. An abdominal exam is then conducted to check for any pain or masses. Next, the doctor inspects the vulva for irritations, discharges, discolorations, abnormal growths, or painful areas.

The internal exam involves several procedures and usually begins with a speculum exam to look at the vagina and cervix. A *speculum* is a plastic or metal instrument with two curved spoonlike blades that are movable. Speculums come in graduated sizes. First the doctor inserts a finger into the vagina to dilate the opening and relax the muscles. The doctor will press down on the bottom wall of the vagina

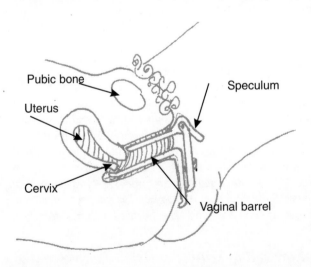

Pubic bone

Uterus

Cervix

Speculum

Vaginal barrel

Figure 10.2.
A Speculum inserted into a vagina

while inserting the speculum into the vagina, advancing it towards the cervix, and then slowly opening the blades until the cervix rests between them. The speculum separates the vaginal walls and holds them open so that the physician can see inside (see figure 10.2).

This procedure may be slightly uncomfortable but is not usually painful. Many doctors warm a metal speculum and insert it very gently and with great sensitivity. If you consciously relax the pelvic muscles, the procedure is easier. If you experience pain or discomfort, tell your physician, and take several deep relaxing breaths while they wait until you are ready to continue. Also, bear down as you relax and push out as if you were relaxing during Kegel exercises. Remember that the vaginal muscles are flexible and elastic enough to accommodate an erect penis or the birth of a baby. A speculum is much smaller. If you take time to breathe in and out through your mouth, these muscles will relax and open. Relaxation can make all the difference. While the speculum is in place the doctor takes a Pap smear using a long cotton swab, brush, or small wooden instrument to collect cells from the cervix. This should not hurt since the nerve endings in the cervix are different than those in the skin. At this point your doctor can inspect placement of an IUD (intrauterine device) or check the fit of your diaphragm. If there is concern about infection, the doctor may take vaginal and cervical cultures using a cotton swab.

After the speculum is removed, a bimanual examination is conducted to assess the shape, firmness, position, and size of the uterus, fallopian tubes, and ovaries. To do this the doctor inserts two gloved, lubricated fingers into the vagina with one hand and presses down on the abdomen with the other hand. By maneuvering their fingers and pressing both hands together the doctor can feel the uterus, fallopian tubes, and ovaries between their fingers. This should not be a painful procedure, but it is important to let the doctor know if you are experiencing any pain or discomfort.

The final part of the exam is a rectovaginal examination, in which the doctor inserts one gloved finger into the vagina and one gloved finger into the anus and feels the surrounding tissue. This examination allows the doctor to feel the space between the vagina and rectum and check for any rectal problems such as hemorrhoids, fissures, bleeding, or abnormal growths. Many women find this part of the exam somewhat embarrassing but no more uncomfortable than the speculum or bimanual exams.

When should a woman have a pelvic examination? Here are several basic indications:

- There is some disagreement as to when a woman should have her first pelvic exam, but it is usually indicated between the ages of sixteen and eighteen or sooner if she becomes sexually active. It is a good idea to have her first pelvic exam before she needs it; that way she can get to know and trust her doctor when she is not worried about any problems.

- If a woman has not begun to menstruate by age sixteen, or if she misses three periods and is too young for menopause.

- After a woman becomes sexually active for the first time.

- If a women has unusual or persistent pelvic or abdominal pain, bleeding, or discharge.

- If a woman has menstrual problems including heavy bleeding, bleeding between periods, severe cramps, or bleeding that lasts longer than ten days.

- If a women wants to discuss options and obtain prescriptions for birth control.

- If a woman experiences itching, redness, sores, unusual odor or discharge, or swelling in the genital area.

- If a woman has pain or muscle spasm at the opening of the vagina during penetration or deep abdominal pain from penile thrusting.

- If a woman is newly pregnant.

- If a woman has sexual relations with a partner who might have a sexually transmitted disease.

- If a woman wants to conceive and first wants to make sure her body is healthy.

- If a woman thinks she might be starting menopause.

- If a woman has been sexually molested, injured, or raped.

- If a woman is experiencing unexplained pelvic pain.

- If a woman's mother took the hormone DES during her pregnancy, yearly checkups are essential for all of her daughters, starting around the age of sixteen. DES daughters are at an increased risk for vaginal cancer.

- A woman should obtain regular checkups including a complete pelvic exam and a Pap smear every year until she has three normal Pap smears in a row, after which she should go for a checkup every one to three years. Yearly visits should continue if a woman has risk factors for sexually transmitted diseases (see chapter 4).

If you are afraid to see a physician because either the exam or the results of the exam seem too hard to manage, work with a therapist who will help you.

Working with Therapists

Why is working with a psychotherapist or sex therapist so important? Many of the exercises in this book are similar to exercises you might do if you were working with a therapist. However, much of the material in this book and many of the exercises may bring up strong feelings that are difficult to identify and overcome alone; If you haven't done so already, you may want to begin working with a therapist. It is always helpful to have a supportive and objective person listen to your thoughts and feelings, help you understand your dilemma, set goals, focus your treatment, and provide feedback as to your progress. Qualified sex therapists can help since they have an understanding of sexual dysfunction and also have experience treating it.

A Guide to Mental Health Professionals and Treatment

What's the difference between mental health professionals? A *psychotherapist* is someone professionally trained and certified to help others deal with psychological difficulties, ranging from mild or moderate adjustment problems to major mental illness. A variety of mental health specialists are trained to practice psychotherapy. *Psychiatrists* are physicians with an M.D. who treat mental illness with prescribed medications and psychotherapy. *Psychologists* are trained extensively in psychotherapy and psychological testing, and have an M.A., a Ph.D., Ed.D., or Psy.D. *Social workers* have expertise and awareness of small and large systems in which the patient participates in the couple, family, and sociocultural setting. Social workers also have training in psychological counseling. Many trained mental health *sex counselors* are also trained in services such as contraception or abortion counseling or rape crisis counseling. *Psychiatric nurses* have received special training in mental illness and are skilled at understanding the physical and emotional symptoms of their patients. Psychiatric nurses provide supportive counseling and some are formally trained in psychotherapy. A *sex therapist* may be any mental health professional who has received specialty training in how to treat individuals or couples with a sexual dysfunction. It is not so much the label but the training, certification, and experience that makes a good therapist.

Although most psychotherapists have some knowledge about sexual dysfunction, they do not have the training or expertise to provide adequate help. You will want to inquire whether a particular therapist has the experience and resources to provide appropriate treatment. Most gynecologists, internists, and family practitioners will know what sexual dysfunction is, but few can provide adequate treatment. Also, they may not be informed enough about treatment options to make an appropriate referral to a sex therapist. These days many nurse practitioners and physician assistants are the first health care workers you will encounter. They are often excellent resources and can make referrals to qualified therapists or counselors if you ask them. We have listed many resources in the appendix for finding referrals on your own.

Sex therapy is similar to many forms of psychotherapy but focuses on your sexual problem, possible causes, and the role it plays within your marriage or relationship. Sex therapists may use one or several approaches to sexual problems. Usually you meet with the therapist weekly to discuss behavioral sexual assignments which you carry out privately at home. Therapy sessions help you identify unresolved issues, couple conflicts, problematic attitudes, and behaviors which interfere with sexual function and treatment. Sex therapy does not recommend any particular philosophy of sexual practice, but works within your own ethical or religious framework to resolve a sexual dysfunction. Thus, the use of varying sexual practices and positions, erotic materials, and sexual aids are adapted to your personal value system. Nothing should be forced upon you. Sex therapists do not need to hear details of your sexual life other than those directly relevant to the problem at hand. Sex therapists do not physically examine patients, do not watch their patients have sex, do not have any physical or sexual contact with their patients, and do not provide surrogate sexual partners.

We have listed a number of national organizations in the appendix to help you find qualified sex therapists. AASECT (American Association of Sex Educators, Counselors and Therapists) acts both as a certifying body and a source of referrals of qualified clinicians. Local Planned Parenthood and other women's centers may be able to help you in your search. Colleges and universities may have programs in human sexuality with faculty members who are trained in sex therapy.

Maximizing the Benefits of Sex Therapy

Before you set up your first appointment, think about what you want to communicate to the therapist. The information you wrote down in chapters 2 and 3 should give you a good base of information. It often helps to write down your symptoms, questions, and concerns. Unless you're single, both partners usually attend the first appointment, since the therapist wants to hear how the problem affects each of you. Start with the important concerns at the beginning of the session, rather than waiting until you are walking out the door. Sex therapists are trained to put you at ease as you discuss difficult or embarrassing issues. Your clinician will want to know when the problem first arose and why you are seeking help now. They will take a sex history similar to the one in chapter 2 in order to identify the type of sexual problem and to illuminate its impact on your life.

After gathering sufficient information from one or more sessions, the clinician will recommend a treatment plan based on the problem, which usually includes a time frame indicating how long treatment might last. No one can categorically state how many sessions you will need, but there are broad guidelines which they use to estimate. Therapists have different theoretical systems and personal styles, yet there is no evidence that any one type is more effective than others. A competent therapist will talk with you about how their treatment will match with your needs. If the match is not right, the therapist can refer you to another clinician. However, remember that all therapy has its ups and downs as people work through difficult issues. Give your treatment a chance to succeed.

If you are dissatisfied with your progress, talk with your therapist before you quit. These impasses often lead to breakthroughs. It is important, however, to trust your inner judgment. Ask yourself whether you have a sense of collaboration with the therapist. Do you feel comfortable enough to ask questions? Do they listen to you? Do they explain any findings from tests and talk about choices of treatment? Can you voice your doubts? If you answered "yes" to these questions, keep working with this therapist. If you could not answer "yes" to some or all of them, think about whether the therapist is just not a good match for you or whether your concerns are actually forms of resistance to making changes in therapy. If you still feel stuck, you and/or you and your therapist together can seek a consultation with another qualified therapist. This may provide the insight you need.

Parting Thoughts

As you reach the end of this book, you have probably been on a long journey exploring many new areas of your sexuality. Ideas you held earlier may have changed and your sense of your own body may be different now that you know yourself better. If you have come through some difficult times in the process, you may have gained confidence in yourself and the process of sexual growth.

If you have had a partner to join you on the way, you may feel closer and understand one another in greater depth. And if you have needed help, you may have found a therapist to guide you on your way.

As you continue your life journey, you will no doubt meet new obstacles and make new progress as you set goals and achieve them. Perhaps you will be able to use some of the techniques you learned in this book. Trust yourself. Your best guide always lies within, and if you follow your inner guide you will always journey well.

References

Bader, E. and P. Pearson. 1988. *In Quest of the Mythical Mate: A Developmental Approach to Diagnosis and Treatment in Couples Therapy.* New York: Brunner/Mazel.

Barbach, L. 1982. *For Each Other: Sharing Sexual Intimacy.* Garden City, NY: Anchor/Doubleday.

Bell, A. and M. Weinberg. 1978. *Homosexualities.* New York: Simon & Schuster.

Bhaerman, S. and D. McMillan. 1986. *Friends & Lovers: How to Meet the People You Want to Meet.* Cincinnati, Ohio: Writer's Digest Books.

Blumstein, P. and P. Schwartz. 1983. *American Couples: Money, Work, and Sex.* New York: William Morrow Co., Inc.

Bowen, M. 1971. "The Use of Family Theory in Clinical Practice." *Changing Families,* edited by J. Haley. New York: Grune and Stratton.

Bowen, M. 1975. "Family Therapy After Twenty Years." *American Handbook of Psychiatry,* Vol. 5, edited by D. Friedman and K. Juzrud. New York: Basic Books.

Bowen, M. 1976. "Theory in the Practice of Psychotherapy." In P. Guerin (Ed.) *Family Therapy.* New York: Gardner Press.

Cargan, L. and M. Melko. 1982. *Singles: Myths and Realities.* Beverly Hills: Sage Publications Inc.

Demaris, A. and G. R. Leslie. 1984. "Cohabitation with the Future Spouse: Its Influence Upon Marital Satisfaction and Communication." *Journal of Marriage and the Family.* 46 (February 1984):77–82.

Douglas, J. D. and F. C. Atwell. 1988. *Love, Intimacy, and Sex.* Newbury Park, Calif.: Sage Publications.

Fogel, D. and J. Joseph. 1996. "Why Physicians Don't Refer." *Contemporary Sexuality,* November, 30 (11):1–2.

Godek, G. P. 1990. *1001 Ways to be Romantic.* Weymouth, Mass.: Casablanca Press.

Godek, G. P. 1992. *1001 Ways to be More Romantic.* Weymouth, Mass.: Casablanca Press.

Hall, M. 1985. *The Lavender Couch: A Consumer's Guide to Psychotherapy for Lesbians and Gay Men.* Boston, Mass.: Alyson Publications, Inc.

Hall, M. 1987. "Sex Therapy for Lesbian Couples: A Four Stage Approach." *Journal of Homosexuality.* 14 (1/2):137–156.

Hass, A. and K. Hass. 1990. *Understanding Sexuality.* St. Louis: Times/Mosby Publication.

Hendrix, H. 1988. *Getting the Love You Want: A Guide for Couples.* New York: Harper Perennial.

Hendrix, H. 1992. *Keeping the Love You Find: A Personal Guide.* New York: Pocket Books.

Hof, L. and E. Berman. 1989. "The Sexual Genogram: Assessing Family-of-Origin Factors in the Treatment of Sexual Dysfunction." *Intimate Environments: Sex, Intimacy, and Gender in Families,* edited by D. Kantor and B. Okun. New York: The Guilford Press.

Kantor, D. and W. Lehr. 1987. *Inside the Family.* San Francisco: Jossey-Bass Publishers.

Kitzinger, S. 1983. *Women's Experience of Sex: The Facts and Feelings of Female Sexuality at Every Stage of Life.* New York: Penguin Books.

Lerner, H. G. 1985. *The Dance of Anger: A Woman's Guide to Changing the Patterns of Intimate Relationships.* New York: Harper & Row/Perennial Library.

Lerner, H. G. 1989. *The Dance of Intimacy: A Woman's Guide to Courageous Acts of Change in Key Relationships.* New York: Harper & Row/Perennial Library.

Loulan, J. 1984. *Lesbian Sex.* San Francisco: Aunt Lute/Spinster Ink.

Loulan, J. 1987. *Lesbian Passion: Loving Ourselves and Each Other.* San Francisco: Aunt Lute/Spinster Ink.

Martin, D. and P. Lyon. 1972. *Lesbian Woman.* New York: Bantam.

Masters, W. and V. Johnson. 1970. *Human Sexual Inadequacy.* Boston: Little, Brown and Co.

McGoldrick, M. and R. Gerson. 1985. *Genograms in Family Assessment.* New York: W. W. Norton.

Moore, T. 1994. *Soul Mates: Honoring the Mysteries of Love and Relationship.* New York: Harper & Row/Harper Perennial.

Mosher, D. 1980. "Three Dimensions of Depth of Involvement in Human Sexual Response." *Journal of Sex Research,* 16(1):1–42.

Nichols, M. 1989. "Sex Therapy with Lesbians, Gay Men and Bisexuals." *Principles and Practice of Sex Therapy: Update for the 1990s,* edited by S. Lieblum and R. Rosen. New York: The Guilford Press.

Peterson, J. R., A. Kretchmer, B. Nellis, J. Lever, and R. Hertz. 1983. "The *Playboy* Reader's Sex Survey: Part I and Part II." *Playboy* January:108, and March:90.

Scharff, D. E. 1982. *The Sexual Relationship: An Object Relations View of Sex and the Family.* Boston: Routledge & Kegan Paul.

Scharff, D. E. 1982. *The Sexual Relationship: An Object Relations View of Sex and the Family.* London: Routledge.

Silverstein, C. 1991. *Gays, Lesbians, and Their Therapists: Studies in Psychotherapy.* New York: W. W. Norton.

Snarch, D. 1991. *Constructing the Sexual Crucible: An Integration of Sexual and Marital Therapy.* New York: W. W. Norton.

Snarch, D. 1997. *Passionate Marriage: Sex, Love, and Intimacy in Emotionally Committed Relationships.* New York: W. W. Norton.

Stewart, F., F. Guest, G. Stewart, and R. Hatcher. 1987. *Understanding Your Body: Every Woman's Guide to Gynecology and Health.* New York: Bantam.

Tanfer, K. 1987. "Patterns of Premarital Cohabitation Among Never-Married Women in the United States." *Journal of Marriage and the Family.* 49 (August):483–497.

Tannen, D. 1990. *You Just Don't Understand: Women and Men in Conversation.* New York: Ballentine Books.

Wincze, J. and M. Carey. 1991. *Sexual Dysfunction: A Guide for Assessment and Treatment.* New York: The Guilford Press.

Readings, Resources, and Referrals

This final section is divided as follows: 1. Readings and Resources—This is a "how to find" section with lists of books, pamphlets, videos, mail-order catalogs, and websites for you to find more information and materials relating to topics on sexuality, and 2. Referrals—a list of organizations that can provide names of local sex therapists for referrals. The lists here are extensive but not complete and we welcome your feedback on any particular item as well as information on additional resources.

Readings and Resources

Aging and Sexuality

Books

Butler, Lewis. 1975. *Sex After Sixty*. New York: Harper & Row.

Doress, P. and D. Siegal, Eds. 1987. *Ourselves Growing Older*. New York: Simon & Schuster. (This book is a feminist interpretation of the issues of aging and women.)

Dosh, R. M. et al. 1997. *The Taking Charge of Menopause Workbook*. Oakland, Calif.: New Harbinger Publications.

Love, L. 1997. *Dr. Susan Love's Hormone Book*. New York: Random House.

Lyons, M. 1997. *Elder Voices: Insights and Reflections*. Cambridge, Mass.: Eldercorps.

Solnick, R., Ed. 1978. *Sexuality and Aging*. Calif.: University of Southern California Press. (A thoughtful collection of articles about sex and aging, including information regarding nursing homes and health care.)

Starr, B. and M. Weiner. 1981. *The Starr-Weiner Report on Sex and Sexuality in the Mature Years*. New York: Stein and Day.

Newsletters

Sex over Forty Newsletter. (A newsletter written by two sex therapists with articles on sexual topics for couples in the second half of life. For more information write to: Sex Over Forty (or S/40) P.O. Box 1600, Chapel Hill, NC 27515.)

Video

Hartman, W. E. and M. A. Fithian. 1978. *Sex at Seventy*. Available from Focus International—Your Sexual Health Education Store, 14 Oregon Drive, Huntington Station, NY 11746. Call (800) 843-0305. Access on the internet at http.//www.sex-help.com/.

Body Image

Books

Cash, T. F. 1997. *The Body Image Workbook.* Oakland, Calif.: New Harbinger Publications.
Hutchinson, M.G. 1985. *Transforming Body Image: Learning to Love the Body You Have.* Freedom, Calif.: The Crossing Press.
Stoppard, M. 1994. *A Woman's Body: A Manual for Life.* New York: Dorling Kindersley.

Dyspareunia

Foundations

The Vulvar Pain Foundation
P.O. Box Drawer 177, Graham, North Carolina 27253
Executive Director: Joanne Yount
Phone: (910) 226-0704 Fax: (910) 226-8518

According to its literature, "The Vulvar Pain Foundation was established in 1992 to help women who suffer with vulvar pain and health care professionals who treat them. The Foundation focuses primarily on pain of noninfectious origin."

The Vulvar Pain Foundation provides educational and other resources on vulvar pain and assists in setting up local support groups. It publishes a quarterly newsletter and coordinates an international network of several thousand women with vulvar pain. The foundation maintains strict confidentiality for anyone who contacts it.

Enhancing Sensuality and Sexual Technique

(See also erotic materials, relationships, and lesbian issues.)

Audiotapes

Love, Pat. *Hot Monogomy.*
There is also an accompanying workbook. You can order a tape from the Sounds True Catalog, 735 Walnut Street, Boulder, Colorado, 80302. Phone: (800) 333-9185.

Books

Anand, M. 1989. *The Art of Sexual Ecstasy: The Path of Sacred Sexuality for Western Lovers.* New York: Jeremy P. Tarcher.
This book has a focus on the spiritual connection to a partner during sex.
Barbach, L. 1982. *For Each Other: Sharing Sexual Intimacy.* Garden City, NY: Doubleday/Anchor Press.
This popular book provides many examples, exercises, and ideas about sex for couples.
Comfort, A. 1974. *The Joy of Sex: A Gourmet Guide to Lovemaking.* New York: Simon & Schuster.
Comfort, A. 1991. *The New Joy of Sex: Gourmet Guide to Lovemaking for the Nineties.* New York: Simon & Schuster.
Godek, G. P. 1991. *1001 Ways to be Romantic.* Boston: Casablanca Press.
Godek, G. P. 1992. *1001 Ways to be More Romantic.* Boston: Casablanca Press.
Hooper, A. 1995. *Ultimate Sexual Touch: A Lover's Guide to Sensual Massage.* New York: Dorling Kindersley Publishing Inc.
Hooper, A. 1996. *Sexual Intimacy.* New York: Doring Kindersley Publishing Inc.
This book deals with relationship issues that occur during sexual interactions.
McCarthy, B. and E. McCarthy. 1989. *Female Sexual Awareness.* New York: Carroll & Graf Publishing Co. Inc.

Videos

Relearning Touch, a video for couples to enhance communication and intimacy, available from Independent Video Services. For an informational brochure call (800) 678-3455, or write to 401 East 10th Street, Suite 160. Eugene OR 97401-3356.

The Secrets of Sacred Sex. To order from Tantra Bazaar write to P.O. Box 10268, Albuquerque, NM 87184. This is one of several videos which provides an overview of Tantric sex. Its inclusion of racial diversity makes it especially valuable.

Vintage Love by Pat Love is a series of tapes which offers a rich array of suggestions how to increase desire in a committed relationship. Write to the Austin Family Institute, 2404 Rio Grande, Austin, TX 78705.

Erotic and Sexual Materials

Contraceptives/Lubricants

Astroglide Personal Lubricant: This water-based lubricant is available in most drug stores. For more information, a list of local vendors, and a free sample, call BioFilm at (800) 848-5900.

Reality—The Female Condom: available from The Female Health Company. Reality is a condom intended to be worn by women during sex to aid in preventing conception and STDs. To receive information and two free samples call (800) 274-6601.

The Rubber Tree: a nonprofit outlet store sponsored by the Seattle chapter of Zero Population Growth (ZPG), that sells nonprescription contraceptives (condoms, spermicidal foams, jellies, and creams) lubricants, rubber gloves, etc. To obtain a catalog call (888) 792-TREE (8733) or write to ZPG-Seattle, 4426 Burke Avenue North, Seattle, WA 98103. You can also access The Rubber Tree on the Web at htttp://www.rubbertree.org/.

Mail-Order Catalogs

Eve's Garden: For a catalog send $2 to Suite 420, 119 West 57th Street, New York, NY 10019.

Good Vibrations Catalog: Contains a wide variety of sex toys and safe sex aids including dildos, vibrators, condoms, lubricants, and dental dams. The Sexuality Library Catalog contains books and videos. To order either catalog call (800) 289-8423 or write to 938 Howard Street, Suite 101 San Francisco, Calif. 94103.

Tantra Bazaar: A catalog of videos with a focus on sex education and secred sexuality. Write to P.O. Box 10268 Albuquerque, NM 87184.

Xandria Collection: A catalog of adult toys and novelties published by the Lawrence Research Group. Catalogs are $4 and can be obtained by calling (800) 242-2823 or writing to P.O. Box 319005, San Francisco, Calif. 94131.

General References on Female Sexuality

Books

Boston Women's Health Book Collective. 1979. *Our Bodies Ourselves.* New York: Simon & Schuster/A Touchstone Book.

Haas A. and K. Haas. 1990. *Understanding Sexuality.* St. Louis, Mo.: Times/Mirror College Publishing.

Kitzinger, S. 1983. *Women's Experience of Sex: The Facts and Feelings of Female Sexuality at Every Stage of Life.* New York: Penguin Books.

Masters, W. M., V. E. Johnson, and R. C. Kolodny. 1994. *Heterosexuality.* New York: Harper-Collins Publishers.

Olds, S. 1985. *The Eternal Garden: Seasons of Our Sexuality.* New York: New York Times Books.

Organizations

CSIE: Council for Sex Information and Education National clearinghouse for information on sexuality.

2272 Colorado Boulevard Number 1228, Los Angeles, Calif. 90041

SIECUS: Sexuality Information and Education Council of the United States

A national organization of sex educators and health care workers that promotes education, research, and dissemination of information about sexuality and sexual health care. SIECUS has numerous position papers on aspects of sexuality and serves as a clearinghouse for publications on all areas of sexuality including sexual dysfunction, sexual identity, and sexual orientation. Contact SIECUS Publication Dept. 130 West 42nd Street, Suite 350, New York, NY, 10036-7802. Phone: (212) 819-9770. E-mail address: siecus@siecus.org.

Websites

Society for Human Sexuality at University of Washington: Short topic papers on every conceivable subject in sexuality. Tap into their search engine at:

http://weber.u.washington.edu/~sfpse/ftpsite.html

Focus International—Your Sexual Health Education Store (videos)

http://www.sex-help.com/

Mental Health Net

http://www.cmhc.com/sxlist.htm

Genital Anatomy and Sexual Function

Books

Carlson, K. S. Eisenstat, and T. Ziporyn. 1996. *The Harvard Guide to Womens' Health*. Cambridge, Mass.: Harvard University Press.

Federation of Feminist Women's Health Centers and S. Gaye. 1981. *A New View of a Woman's Body*. New York: Simon & Schuster.

Stewart, F., F. Guest, G. Stewart, and R. Hatcher. 1987. *Understanding Your Body*. New York: Bantam Books.

Stoppard, M., Ed. 1994. *Woman's Body: A Manual for Life*. London: Dorling/Kindersley.

Genograms

Books

Hof, L. and E. Berman. 1989. "The Sexual Genogram: Assessing Family-of-Origin Factors in the Treatment of Sexual Dysfunction." *Intimate Environments: Sex, Intimacy, and Gender in Families*, edited by D. Kantor and B. Okun. New York: The Guilford Press.

McGoldrick, M. and R. Gerson. 1985. *Genograms in Family Assessment*. New York: W. W. Norton.

Infertility

Books

Clubb, E. and J. Knight. 1996. *Fertility*. Devon, England: David and Charles Book.

Franklin, R. R. and D. K. Brockman. 1990. *In Pursuit of Fertility*. New York: Henry Holt.

Salzer, L. 1991. *Surviving Infertility: A Compassionate Guide Through the Emotional Crisis of Infertility*. New York: Harper Perennial.

Weschler, T. 1995. *Taking Charge of Your Fertility*. New York: Harper Collins.

Zolbrod, A. P. 1990. *Getting Around the Boulder in the Road: Using Imagery to Cope with Fertility Problems*.

To order a copy write to: A. Zolbrod, 12 Rumford Road, Lexington, MA 02143.

Organizations
American Fertility Society: Provides lists of specialists across the country. Write to 2140 Eleventh Avenue South, Suite 200. Birmingham, AL 35205-2800.
RESOLVE: Every state has a chapter of this national group which supplies information, support groups, and referral resources for couples with infertility problems.
Serono Laboratories Inc. 100 Longwater Circle, Norwell, MA 02061. Infertility booklets are free. Phone: (617) 982-9000.

Journal Writing
Books
Goldberg, N. 1986. *Writing Down the Bones; Freeing the Writer Within*. Boston, Mass.: Shambhala.
Rainer, T. 1978. *The New Diary: How to Use a Journal for Self-Guidance and Expanded Creativity*. Los Angeles: Jeremy P. Tarcher.
Rico, G. L. 1983. *Writing the Natural Way: Using Right-Brain Techniques to Release Your Expressive Powers*. Los Angeles: Jeremy P. Tarcher.

Lesbian Issues
Books
Berzon, B. 1988. *Permanent Partners: Building Gay and Lesbian Relationships that Last*. New York: E. P. Dutton.
Cabaj, R. P. and T. Stein, Eds. 1996. *Textbook of Homosexuality and Mental Health*. Washington, D.C.: American Psychiatric Press.
Califia, P. 1988. *Sapphistry: The Book of Lesbian Sexuality*. Tallassee, Fla.: Naiad.
Faderman, L. 1981. *Surpassing the Love of Men: Romantic Friendship and Love Between Women from the Renaisance to the Present*. New York: William Morrow/Quill.
This book considers womens sexuality in the past as known through literature and letters. It suggests that female sexuality has a broader scope than just genital pleasure.
Gay Yellow Pages: The National Edition. Box 292, Village Station, NYC, NY 10014. Published annually.
Hall, M. 1985. *The Lavender Couch*. Boston: Alyson Publications Inc.
This book offers suggestions for lesbians in choosing a therapist.
Loulan, J. 1984. *Lesbian Sex*. San Francisco: Aunt Lute/Spinsters Ink.
Loulan, J. 1987. *Lesbian Passion, Loving Ourselves and Each Other*. San Francisco: Aunt Lute/Spinsters Ink.
Martin, D. and P. Lyon. 1972. *Lesbian Woman*. New York: Bantam.
Sisley E. and C. Cohen, (Eds.) 1978. *The Joy of Lesbian Sex*. New York: Simon and Schuster.
Winks, C. and A. Seamans. 1994. *The Good Vibrations Guide to Sex*. San Francisco: The Down There Press.

Organizations
Parents and Friends of Lesbians and Gays (PFLAG): A national organization providing support and information and working to change discrimination against homosexuals. For more information write to PFLAG, P.O. Box 27605, Washington, D.C. 20038.

Videos
The Sexuality Library. Erotic videos are available from Open Enterprises, 938 Howard Street, San Francisco, Calif. 94103-4163.

Men's Issues

Books

Fanning, P. and M. McKay. 1993. *Being a Man: A Guide to the New Masculinity*. Oakland, Calif.: New Harbinger Publications.

    A workbook for men interested in going beyond male stereotypes and learning to be more in touch with a fulfilling masculinity. Includes sections on sexual relationships.

Zilbergeld, B. 1992. *The New Male Sexuality*. New York: A Bantam Book.

    This is an outstanding book for men with sexual questions or sexual problems. Women with male partners will benefit from reading this relaxed and informative book about male sexuality.

Medical Disorders

Books (Cancer)

Schover, L. and M. Randers-Pehrson. *Sexuality and Cancer: For the Woman Who Has Cancer and Her Partner*. American Cancer Society. To obtain a copy call (800) 227-2345. There is also a version for men with cancer.

Love, S. 1995. *Dr. Susan Love's Breast Book, 2nd edition*. Mass.: Addison-Wesley Publishers. This is a comprehensive book on breast cancer and related issues.

Ostomies (booklets)

    The following booklets on sexuality for individuals with ostomies can be obtained from the United Ostomy Association, Inc., 36 Executive Park, Suite 120, Irvine, Calif. 92714. (714) 660-8624:

    Sex, Courtship, and the Single Ostomate
    Sex and the Female Ostomate

Pulmonary Disease (booklet)

    Being Close is an informational guide on sexuality for individuals with lung disease, published by the National Jewish Center for Immunoloic and Respiratory Medicine. For a copy write to the center at 1400 Jackson Street, Denver, CO 80206, or call (800) 222-LUNG.

Pregnancy

Books

Bing, E. and L. Coleman, L. 1977. *Making Love During Pregnancy*. New York: Noonday Press.

Dunnewold, A. and D. Sanford. 1994. *The Postpartum Survival Guide*. Oakland, Calif.: New Harbinger Publications. Addresses issues after birth of a child, including sections for single, older, and adoptive mothers.

Stoppard, M. 1993. *Conception, Pregnancy, and Birth*. London: Dorling/Kindersley.

Relationships

Books

Hendrix, H. 1988. *Getting the Love You Want: A Guide for Couples*. New York: Harper Perennial.

Hendrix, H. 1992. *Keeping the Love You Find: A Personal Guide*. New York: Pocket Books.

Lerner, H. G. 1985. *The Dance of Anger: A Woman's Guide to Changing the Patterns of Intimate Relationships*. New York: Harper & Row.

Lerner, H. G. 1989. *The Dance of Intimacy: A Woman's Guide to Courageous Acts of Change in Key Relationships*. New York: Harper & Row.

Schnarch, D. 1997. *Passionate Marriage: Sex, Love, and Intimacy in Emotionally Committed Relationships*. New York: W. W. Norton.

This book encourages emotional growth within the context of facing sexual issues.

Tannen, D. 1990. *You Just Don't Understand: Women and Men in Conversation*. New York: Ballentine Books.

Womack, W. M. and F. F. Stauss. 1991. *The Marriage Bed: Renewing Love, Friendship, Trust, and Romance*. Oakland, Calif.: New Harbinger Publications.

A step-by-step guide for couples to increase sexual excitement within their relationship.

Videos

Couple Skills. A series of tapes with topics including conflict resolution, expressing feelings, listening, and coping with anger. Available from New Harbinger Publications: (800) 748-6273.

Religion, Spirituality, and Sexuality

Books

Anderson, S. R. and P. Hopkins. 1991. *The Feminine Face of God: The Unfolding of the Sacred in Women*. New York: Bantam.

Bird, J. and L. Bird. 1970. *The Freedom of Sexual Love*. Garden City, NY: Doubleday & Co.
A book of Catholic doctrine which has been declaired "free of doctrinal or moral error" and deals with concerns about sexuality.

Feldman, D. 1975. *Marital Relations, Birth Control, and Abortion in Jewish Law*. New York: Schlocken Books.

Kosnik, A., W. Carrol, A. Cunningham, R. Modras, and J. Schulte. 1977. *Human Sexuality: New Directions in American Catholic Thought*. New York: Paulist Press.

Lamm, M. 1980. *The Jewish Way in Love and Marriage*. New York: Jonathan David Publishers, Inc.

Moore, T. 1994. *Soul Mates: Honoring the Mysteries of Love and Relationship*. New York: Harper Perennial.

Steinmetz, U. G. 1972. *The Sexual Christian*. St. Meinrad, Ind.: Abbey Press.

Welwood, J. 1992. "Intimate Relationship as a Practice and a Path." *Ordinary Magic: Everyday Life as Spiritual Path*, edited by J. Welwood. Boston: Shambala.

Sex and Disability

Coalitions and Newsletters

Coalition on Sexuality and Disability (CSD)
122 East 23rd Street, New York, NY 10010. Founded in 1978, the CSD promotes sexual health care services for individuals with disabilities. It also promotes research, education, and advocacy in the area of sexuality and disability. A quarterly newsletter is available.

Sexual Abuse

Books

Adams, C. and J. Fay. 1989. *Free of the Shadows: Recovering from Sexual Violence*. Oakland Calif.: New Harbinger Publications.
A guide for women affected by sexual violence as they progress through the recovery process. Includes sections for family members, friends, and therapists.

Barnes, P. P. 1991. *The Woman Inside: From Incest Victim to Survivor*. Racine, Wisc.: Mother Courage Press.

Davis, L. 1991. *Allies in Healing: When the Person You Love Was Sexually Abused as a Child*. New York: Harper Perenial.

Herman, J. L. 1992. *Trauma and Recovery: The Aftermath of Violence from Domestic Abuse to Politcal Terror*. New York: Basic Books.

Kunzman, K. 1990. *The Healing Way: Adult Recovery from Childhood Sexual Abuse*. Available from Hazelden Educational Materials, phone (800) 328-9000.

Maltz, W. 1992. *The Sexual Healing Journey: A Guide for Survivors of Sexual Abuse*. New York: W. W. Norton.

Westerlund, E. 1992. *Womens' Sexuality After Childhood Incest*. New York: W. W. Norton.

Organizations

SIA (Survivors of Incest Anonymous) provides an index of confidential support groups across the country. P.O. Box 21817 Baltimore, MD 21222-6817.

Videos

Partners in Healing, by W. Maltz, is a video for women who suffered from sexual abuse. It is available from Independent Video Services. For an informational brochure call (800) 678-3455, or write to 401 East 10th Street, Suite 160, Eugene, OR 97401-3356.

Sexual Dysfunction

Books (general topics)

Kaplan, H. S. 1974. *The New Sex Therapy*. New York: Brunner/Mazel.

Kaplan, H. S. 1979. *Disorders of Sexual Desire*. New York: Simon & Schuster.

Kaplan, H. S. 1983. *The Evaluation of Sexual Disorders: Psychological and Medical Aspects*. New York: Brunner/Mazel.

Kaplan, H. S. 1987. *The Illustrated Manual of Sex Therapy*. New York: Brunner/Mazel.

Kaplan, H. S. 1987. *Sexual Aversion, Sexual Phobias, and Panic Disorder*. New York: Brunner/Mazel.

Rosen, R. C. and S. R. Lieblum. 1988. *Principles and Practice of Sex Therapy: Update for the 1990s*. New York: The Guilford Press.

Snarch, D. 1991. *Constructing the Sexual Crucible: An Integration of Sexual and Marital Therapy*. New York: W. W. Norton.

Wincze, J. and M. Carey. 1991. *Sexual Dysfunction: A Guide for Assessment and Treatment*. New York: The Guilford Press.

Books (orgasm disorder)

Barbach, L. 1975. *For Yourself: The Fulfillment of Female Sexuality. A Guide to Orgasmic Response*. New York: Doubleday & Co., Inc.

Fisher, S. 1973. *The Female Orgasm*. New York: Basic Books.

Heiman, J., J. LoPiccolo, and L. LoPiccolo. 1988. *Becoming Orgasmic: A Sexual and Personal Growth Program for Women*. New York: Prentice Hall Press.
This is an excellent, comprehensive book on overcoming orgasmic dysfunction.

Videotapes

Focus International, 14 Oregon Drive, Huntington Station, NY 11746. (800) 843-0305. Send for a catalog of excellent videos for all topics about sexuality. Some of them include:

Hartman, W. E. and M. A. Fithian. 1975. *Nondemand Pleasuring*.

LoPiccolo, J. and M. Shoen. 1984. *Treating Vaginismus*.

LoPiccolo, J. and W. C. Lobit. *Becoming Orgasmic: A Sexual and Personal Growth Program for Women*.

Sexually Transmitted Diseases (STDs)/Safe Sex

Audiotapes

Barbach, L. and B. Zilbergeld. 1989. *How to Talk with a Partner about Smart Sex.* This audiotape can be ordered from the Fay Institute, P.O. Box 5 CDN, Montreal, Canada, H3S 2S4.

Books

McIvenna, T. (Ed.), and Institute for Advanced Study of Human Sexuality. 1992. *The Complete Guide to Safer Sex.* Fort Lee, NJ: Barricade Books, Inc.

Whipple, B. and G. Ogden. 1989. *Safe Encounters: How Women Can Say Yes to Pleasure and No to Unsafe Sex.* New York: Pocket Books.

Information Hotlines

AIDS Treatment Informational Service, sponsored by the Centers for Disease Control (CDC): (Open 9 A.M.–7 P.M. EST, Monday—Friday): (800) 448-0440.

CDC National HIV and AIDS Hotline (Open twenty-four hours): (800) 342-2437. Spanish language line (Open 8 A.M.–2 A.M. EST): (800) 344-7432. TDD-TTY (Open 10 A.M.–10 P.M. EST, Monday—Friday): (800) 234-7889.

CDC National STD Hotline (Open 8 A.M.–11 P.M. EST): (800) 227-8922.

National Herpes Hotline (Open 9 A.M.–7 P.M. EST, Monday—Friday): (919) 361-8488.

Journals

Bulletin of Experimental Treatments for AIDS (BETA): This is a quarterly publication of the San Francisco AIDS Foundation that provides the latest information on HIV and AIDS. To order write to P.O. Box 426182, San Francisco, Calif. 94142-6182, or call: (800) 959-1059. You can send E-mail to beta@the city.sfsu.edu or access them via the Web at http://www.sfaf.org/beta.html.

Organizations

Health Awareness Resource Center: A fee-based holistic health information and support service which offers a library, classes, and packets. 18 Old Padonia Road, Cockeysville, MD. 21030. Phone: (410) 664-8980.

HELP (Herpetics Engaged in Living Productively). There are chapters in many cities.

Planned Parenthood: National organization with local chapters. Information on contraception, abortion, STDs, and safe sex.

Single Parents

Organizations

Parents Without Partners (PWP) is a national organization and has local chapters in most cities.

Stress, Fear, and Pain

The resources in this section focus on the mind-body connection and provide strategies for using relaxation techniques and meditation to deal with stress, fear, and pain. All of these techniques are helpful for women learning about their sexuality and dealing with sexual problems.

(See also the section on visualization/affirmations.)

Audio Tapes

Numerous audio tapes with relaxation scripts are available from New Harbinger Publications. You can obtain a catalog by calling (800) 748-6273.

Books

Benson, H. 1975. *The Relaxation Response.* New York: Avon.

Benson, H. 1984. *Beyond the Relaxation Response.* New York: Berkley Books.

Borysenko, J. 1987. *Minding the Body, Mending the Mind*. New York: Bantam.

Bourne, E. J. 1995. *The Anxiety and Phobia Workbook, 2nd edition*. Oakland, Calif.: New Harbinger Publications.

Catalano, E. M. and K. N. Hardin. 1996. *The Chronic Pain Control Workbook, 2nd edition*. Oakland, Calif.: New Harbinger Publications.

Csikszentmihalyi, M. 1990. *Flow: The Psychologiy of Optimal Experience*. New York: Harper Perennial.

Davis, M., M. McKay, and E. T. Eshelman. 1995. *The Relaxation and Stress Reduction Workbook*. Oakland, Calif.: New Harbinger Publications.

McKay, M., M. Davis, and P. Fanning. 1997. *Thoughts and Feelings: The Art of Cognitive Stress Intervention, 2nd edition*. Oakland, Calif.: New Harbinger Publications.

Zinn, J. K. 1994. *Wherever You Go, There You Are*. New York: Hyperion.

Substance Abuse—Recovery

Books

Weinberg, J. R. 1977. *Sex and Recovery*. Published by Recovery Press, 4821 Drake Road, Minneapolis, Minn. 55422.

Rosellini, G. and M. Worden. 1989. *Barriers to Intimacy: For People Torn by Addiction*. Published by Hazelden Educational Materials: (800) 328-9000.

Vaginal Dilators

Catalogs

F. E. Young & Co.
1350 Old Skokie Road, Highland Park, IL 60035
Call for a full catalog: (847) 831-4080.

Milex Vaginal-Hymenal Dilators
Milex Products, Inc., Chicago, IL 60631
Call for a full catalog: (800) 621-1278/or (773) 631-6484.

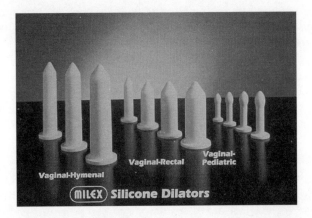

Visualization/Affirmations

Books

Fanning, P. 1994. *Visualization for Change*. Oakland, Calif.: New Harbinger Publications. Teaches the step-by-step use of mental imagery for self-improvement, therapy, and healing.
    Audiotapes are also available through New Harbinger at (800) 748-6273.

Gawain, S. 1978. *Creative Visualization*. Toronto: Bantam New Age Book.

Ray, S. 1976. *I Deserve Love*. Berkeley, Calif.: Celestial Arts. This book shows you step-by-step how to create and use affirmations.

Womens' Development and Sexuality
Books
Gilligan, C. 1982. *In a Different Voice: Psychological Theory and Women's Development.* Cambridge, Mass.: Harvard University Press.
Miller, J. B. 1976. *Toward a New Psychology of Women.* Boston: Beacon Press.
Shinoda, J. B. 1984. *Goddesses in Everywoman: A New Psychology of Women.* New York: Harper Colophon Books.

Referrals

To locate a sex counselor or therapist in your area, the first source of referral is often your physician, health plan, or local yellow pages. Be sure to ask about specific qualifications or certification in sex therapy. You can also check with nearby colleges and universities, which often have psychological health services that may have a list of clinicians who see private patients. Otherwise, any of the organizations listed below can help by providing either directories or specific names for a referral.

Psychiatrists
American Psychiatric Association
1700 13th Street NW, Washington, D.C. 20036

Psychologists
American Psychological Association
1200 17th Street NW, Washington, D.C. 20036

National Register of Health Service Providers in Psychology
P.O. Box 91000, Washington, D.C. 20090-3100

American Board of Family Psychology
6501 Sanger, Suite 15, P.O. Box 7977, Waco, Texas 76714

Clinical Social Workers
National Association of Social Workers
7891 Eastern Avenue, Silver Spring, MD 20901

Marriage and Family Therapists
American Association of Marriage and Family Therapy
1717 K Street NW, Room 407, Washington D.C. 20006

Sex Therapists and Counselors
American Association of Sex Educators Counselors and Therapists (AASECT)
Executive Director: Howard J. Ruppel, Jr., Ph.D.
P.O. Box 238, Mount Vernon, Iowa 52314-0238.

AASECT is an organization of professionals concerned with sex education, counseling, and therapy. It publishes a monthly newsletter and a quarterly journal. To obtain information on aspects of sexuality or sexual dysfunction, or to obtain a list of sex therapists in your area, send a letter with your request and a self-addressed stamped envelope to the address listed above.

Index

A

abdominal breathing, 138-139
abuse. *See* sexual abuse
Ackerman, Diane, 135
adhesions, pelvic, 73-74
affirmations, 194-195; recommended
    readings, 270-271
ageism, 126
aging: enhancing sexual function and,
    132-133; finding positive models of,
    128; menopause and, 128-130;
    questionnaire on sexuality and,
    130-131; recommended resources on,
    261-262; self-image and, 127; sexual
    functioning and, 126-127, 128; sexuality
    time line and, 131-132
Agronin, Marc, 11
AIDS (Acquired Immune Deficiency
    Syndrome), 110-111
alcohol abuse, 106
all-or-nothing thinking, 189
American Association of Sex Educators,
    Counselors and Therapists (AASECT),
    257, 271
American Cancer Society (ACS), 95
Anand, Margo, 156
anatomy: of fear, 27-28; of female genitals,
    15-17; of male genitals, 18-19; of pain,
    29-30
anorgasmia, 76
antidepressant medications, 65, 103, 105,
    204, 225
antipsychotic medications, 106
antisexual messages, 186
anus, 15

anxiety: fear response and, 28-29; learning
    process and, 7-8; medications for
    treating, 103, 105-106; personal
    attitudes toward, 182-185; sexual
    phobias and, 63-65
arousal. *See* sexual arousal
assertiveness, 195-198; making and
    refusing requests, 197-198; sexual
    assertiveness scale, 196-197
association web exercise, 10-11
asthma, 101
atrophic dystrophy, 73
attention, exercise for focusing, 140-141
attitudes: sexuality questionnaire items on,
    53-55; towards fear, anxiety, and pain,
    182-185
audiotapes, recommended, 262, 269
aversion. *See* sexual aversion

B

bacterial STDs, 109-110
bacterial vaginosis, 110
Barbach, Lonnie, 76, 128, 216
Bartholin's glands, 15, 73
Beck, Aaron, 188
Becoming Orgasmic (Heiman and
    Lopiccolo), 216
Benson, Herbert, 136
benzodiazepines, 65, 105
bimanual examination, 255
bipolar disorder, medications for treating,
    103
blaming, 192
blended orgasm, 24
body image: aging and, 127; cancer
    surgery and, 96-97, 98; exploration

exercise on, 18; recommended readings, 262; sexuality questionnaire items on, 53-55

books, recommended, 261-271

boredom, and learning process, 7-8

Bourne, Edmund, 188

breast cancer, 95; and body image, 96-97

breathing exercises, 138-141; abdominal breathing, 138-139; genital focused breathing, 140; pelvic breathing, 139; spoon breathing (with partner), 140, 141; synchronous breathing, 139

"bridge maneuver," 220

Burns, David, 188

C

cancer: case example, 98; recommended readings, 266; sexual dysfunction and, 95-98; treatments for, 96-98

catalogs, recommended, 263, 270

catastrophizing, 190

celibacy, 249, 252

cervical cancer, 97

cervix, 16

change of life, 128

charting: sexual arousal, 208-211, 212; sexual desire, 204-208

chlamydia trachomatis, 109

Christianity, 180

chronic obstructive pulmonary disease (COPD), 101

climacteric, 128

clinical social workers, 256-257, 271

clitoral glans, 15

clitoral hood, 15

clitoral orgasm, 24

clitoris, 15

Coalition on Sexuality and Disability (CSD), 267

cognitive distortions, 188-193; affirmations and, 194-195; identifying and counteracting, 193; sexual trauma and, 92-93; types of, 189-192

cognitive-behavioral therapy, 65

colon cancer, 95

conditioned response, 28

condoms, female, 263

condylomata acuminata, 112

conflicts, 237-238

conjoint therapy, 6

contraceptives, 263

control fallacies, 191

corpus cavernosa, 19

corpus spongiosum, 19

crabs, 110

Csikszentmihalyi, Mihaly, 7

cultural myths about sexuality, 185-188

D

depression: hypoactive sexual desire and, 62; medications for treating, 103

desensitization, systematic, 224

desire. *See* sexual desire

diabetes mellitus (DM), 99

Diagnostic and Statistical Manual for Mental Disorders (DSM-IV), 6

diagnostic decision tree, 59, 78-85

diagnostic flowchart exercise, 78-85

diary exercise, 8-9

dilators. *See* vaginal dilators

disabilities: recommended resource on, 267; sexual dysfunction and, 93-102; treating sexual dysfunction caused by, 201-203

diseases. *See* illnesses; sexually transmitted diseases

disgust, and sexual aversion, 64

disqualifying the positive, 190

dissociation, 227-228

dorsal horn, 29

drug abuse, 106

dysfunction. *See* sexual dysfunction

dyspareunia, 30, 71-76; case examples, 75-76; major causes of, 74; treatments for, 220-224; vaginal and pelvic disorders and, 73-75; vaginismus and, 72; vulva disorders and, 72-73; Vulvar Pain Foundation and, 262

E

ejaculation, 19

elderly. *See* aging

emotional reasoning, 190

emphysema, 101-102

endometrial tissue, 17

endometriosis, 99-100

epididymus, 19

episiotomy, 123

erectile dysfunction, 19, 223-224

eros, 181

erotic and sexual materials, 263

estrogen, 21; and menopause, 128-129

estrogen replacement therapy, 129

excitement stage of sexual response cycle: physical changes during, 22-23; psychological changes during, 26

exploration exercises: on body image, 18; on fear, 30-31, 32-33; on female genital anatomy, 17-18; on genital exploration and arousal, 162-169; on non-demand exploration during intercourse, 171-173; on pain, 31-33

F

fallacy of change, 192
fallacy of fairness, 191
fallacy of one reality, 191
fallopian tubes, 16
family history, 240-243, 244
fantasies. *See* sexual fantasies
fear: anatomy of, 27-28; exploration
    exercises on, 30-31, 32-33; medications
    for treating, 65; personal attitudes
    toward, 182-185; recommended
    resources on, 269-270; sexual phobias
    and, 63-66; sexual response cycle and,
    28-29
female genital anatomy: exploration
    exercises on, 17-18; external, 15;
    internal, 16-17; male genital anatomy
    compared to, 14; recommended
    readings, 264
fibrosis, 97
fight-or-flight response, 28
flashbacks, 93, 227
flow, 7
focal vulvitis, 72
focusing attention exercise, 140-141
For Yourself (Barbach), 216
foreplay, importance of, 148
foreskin, 19
foundations, 262
free association, 10-11
frigidity. *See* sexual arousal disorder
fungal STDs, 109-110

G

gender identity disorders, 78
generalized sexual dysfunction, 66
genital focused breathing, 140
genital herpes, 111-112
genital warts, 112
genitals: comparison of male and female,
    14; exercises for exploring and
    arousing, 162-169; exercises for
    increasing pleasure, 169-170; female
    anatomy, 15-17; male anatomy, 18-19;
    stimulating to orgasm, 169-170; visual
    examination of, 163-164
genograms, 243, 244; recommended
    readings, 264
glans, 18
gonorrhea, 109
Goodwin, Aurelie Jones, 11
grieving, 227
G-spot (Gräfenberg Spot), 16; orgasm
    from stimulation of, 24
guiding exercise, 167-169
gynecological cancers, 95, 96, 97

gynecological examination, 253-256
gynecologists, 253-255

H

Haffner, Debra, 179
heart attacks, 100-101
heaven's reward fallacy, 192
hepatitis, 112
herpes virus, 111-112
history: family, 240-243, 244; of sexual
    functioning, 47-53
HIV (Human Immunodeficiency Virus),
    110-111
homophobia, 247, 248
homosexuals. *See* lesbian couples
hormonal factors: menopause and,
    128-129; sexual desire and, 62, 129
hormone replacement therapy, 129-130
human papilloma virus (HPV), 73, 112
hymen, 15
hyperarousal, 227
hypoactive sexual desire (HSD), 62-63;
    case example, 63; treatments for, 204-214
hypopigmented skin, 73
hysterectomy, 97

I

idiopathic pain, 72
illnesses: physical, 93-102; psychiatric,
    102-107; sexually transmitted, 107-116;
    treating sexual dysfunction caused by,
    201-203
impotence, 19
infertility, 124-125; case example, 125;
    recommended resources on, 264-265
information hotlines, 269
initiating sex, 152-154
inner lips, 15
insulin-dependent diabetes mellitus
    (IDDM), 99
integration stage of therapy, 228-229
intercourse. *See* sexual intercourse
interstitial cystitis (IC), 100

J

Johnson, Virginia, 6, 19
journal writing, 8-9; on feelings about
    masturbation, 217; on orgasmic
    experience, 216; recommended
    readings, 265; on sensate focus
    exercises, 162
Judaism, 180

K

Kaplan, Helen Singer, 6, 20, 21, 76

Kegel, Arnold, 143
Kegel exercises, 16, 143-144; after
    childbearing, 124

L

labeling, 191
labia majora, 15
labia minora, 15
laparoscopy, 99
learning process, 6-8
lesbian couples: "quiet vagina" exercise
    and, 172; recommended resources on,
    265; sexual problems of, 247-248
leukoplakia, 73
lichen sclerosis, 73
limbic system, 21
LoPiccolo, Joseph, 6
lubricants, 263
lumpectomy, 97
lung cancer, 95

M

mail-order catalogs, 263, 270
male genital anatomy, 18-19
Maltz, Wendy, 229
mania, medications for treating, 103
marriage and family therapists, 271
mastectomy, 97
Masters, William, 6, 19
masturbation: exploring your feelings
    about, 217; fantasy combined with, 218;
    reaching orgasm through, 215-216; with
    a vibrator, 218-219
meatus, 18
medical problems: recommended readings,
    266; sexuality questionnaire items on,
    45-47; treating sexual dysfunction
    caused by, 201-203
medications: alleviating side effects of,
    203-204; psychiatric illness and, 65,
    102-107; sexual dysfunction caused by,
    102-107
menopause, 128-130; premature, 97
men's issues, recommended readings, 266
mind reading, 190
minimizing, 190
molluscum contagiosum, 113
mons pubis, 15
mood disorders, 62
Moore, Thomas, 181
morality, 181-182
multiple orgasms, 24
multiple sclerosis (MS), 100
myocardial infarction, 100-101
myotonia, 22
myths about sexuality, 185-188

N

negative filtering, 189-190
negative thinking patterns, 188-193; and
    affirmations, 194-195
nervous system, 28
neuroleptic medications, 106
newsletters, 261, 267
nociceptors, 29
non-demand exploration, 171-173
non-demand thrusting exercise, 172-173
noninsulin-dependent diabetes mellitus
    (NIDDM), 99
nonoxynol-9, 115
nonsexual touching exercises, 155-162;
    assertiveness and, 197-198; case
    examples, 158, 161; facing resistance to,
    161-162; instructions for the giver,
    156-157; instructions for the receiver,
    157-158; journal writing on, 162;
    responses to, 159-161; talking about the
    experience of, 158-159. *See also* sensate
    focus exercises; touching

O

oral sex: pregnancy and, 121; sensate
    focus example, 170-171
organizational resources, 262, 264, 265,
    268, 269; therapist referrals, 271
orgasm: cultural myths about, 187;
    diagnostic flowchart exercise on, 82-83;
    disorders associated with, 76-78;
    exercises for reaching, 216-219; genital
    stimulation to, 169-170; masturbation
    and, 215-216, 218; methods for
    triggering, 219; physical changes
    during, 23-24; psychological changes
    during, 27; reaching with your partner,
    219-220; sexual fantasies and, 217-218;
    types of, 24; vibrators and, 169-170,
    218-219
orgasmic disorder, 76-78; case example,
    77-78; treatments for, 214-220
ostomies, 98; recommended readings, 266
outer lips, 15
ovaries, 16
overgeneralization, 189
oxytocin, 21

P

pain: anatomy of, 29-30; exploration
    exercises on, 31-33; personal attitudes
    toward, 182-185; physical disability
    and, 94; recommended resources on,
    269-270; sexual response cycle and, 30.
    See also sexual pain disorders

panic attacks, 28; medications for treating, 65, 225; sexual phobias and, 64-65

Pap smear, 255, 256

paraphilias, 78

parasitic STDs, 109-110

parasympathetic nervous system, 28

parents, single, 269

Parents and Friends of Lesbians and Gays (PFLAG), 265

Parents Without Partners (PWP), 269

partners: choice of, 235-237, 239-241; conflicts with, 237-238; family-of-origin issues and, 240-243, 244; lesbian, 247-248; power struggles with, 238-239; reaching orgasm with, 219-220; sexual problems and, 231-239; sexual styles of, 243, 245-247; using vaginal dilators with, 222-223. *See also* relationship issues

PC muscle. *See* pubococcygeus (PC) muscle

pelvic breathing, 139

pelvic disorders, 73-75

pelvic examination, 253-256

pelvic inflammatory disease (PID), 74

penis, 18

perineal sponge, 15

periodicals, recommended, 261, 269

personal labeling, 191

personality disorders (PDs), 107

personalization distortion, 191

phobias, 28; medications for treating, 65. *See also* sexual phobias

physical illnesses, 93-102; cancer, 95-98; diabetes mellitus, 99; endometriosis, 99-100; interstitial cystisis, 100; multiple sclerosis, 100; myocardial infarction, 100-101; pulmonary disease, 101-102; treating sexual dysfunction caused by, 201-203

physicians, working with, 252-256

Planned Parenthood, 257

plateau stage of sexual response cycle: physical changes during, 23; psychological changes during, 26

positions. *See* sexual positions

positive affirmations, 194-195

post-traumatic stress disorder (PTSD), 91-92

power struggles, 238-239

pregnancy: positions for intercourse during, 122; recommended readings, 266; sex during and after, 120-124

premature menopause, 97

primary dyspareunia, 71-72

primary symptoms, 59

primary syphilis, 110

primary vaginismus, 68

private space, 136-137

progressive muscle relaxation, 141-143

prostaglandin, 99

prostate gland, 19

psychiatric illnesses, 102-107; anxiety, 103, 105-106; depression, mania, and bipolar disorder, 103; medications for, 104-105; personality disorders, 107; psychotic disorders, 106; substance abuse, 106

psychiatric nurses, 257

psychiatrists, 256, 271

psychodynamic therapy, 177

psychological changes: affirmations for creating, 194-195; in sexual response cycle, 25-27

psychological problems: hypoactive sexual desire and, 62; resistance to change and, 176-177; sexuality questionnaire items on, 45-47; vaginismus and, 70-71

psychologists, 256, 271

psychotherapists, 256, 257. *See also* therapists

psychotherapy. *See* therapy

psychotic disorders, 106

psychotropic medications, 102-107

pubic lice, 110

pubic mound, 15

pubococcygeus (PC) muscle, 16; dilator exercises and, 221-223; identifying, 143; Kegel exercises for, 143-144; vaginismus and, 69

pulmonary diseases, 101-102; recommended reading, 266

Puritans, 180

Q

questionnaires: sexual functioning, 37-57; sexuality and aging, 130-131

"quiet vagina" exercise, 172, 223

R

radiation therapy, 97

radiation vaginitis, 74

Rako, Susan, 129

readings, recommended, 261-271

rectovaginal examination, 255

referrals, therapist, 271

relationship issues: choice of partners, 235-237, 239-241; conflicts and sexual dysfunction, 237-238; family histories, 240-243, 244; lesbian couples and, 247-248; power struggles, 238-239; recommended resources on, 266-267; sexual myths and, 186-188; sexual problems and, 231-239; sexual styles and, 243, 245-247; sexual trauma and,

91; sexuality questionnaire items on, 42-44. *See also* partners

relaxation response, 136, 144

relaxation techniques: breathing exercises, 138-141; creating a place of your own, 136-137; finding time for yourself, 137-138; progressive muscle relaxation, 141-143; suggested routine for, 144-145; visualization, 198-199. *See also* sensate focus exercises

religious beliefs: exercise for examining, 181-182; recommended readings, 267; sexuality and, 179-182

repetition of affirmations, 194

resistance to change: affirmations and, 194-195; assertiveness training and, 195-198; and attitudes towards fear, anxiety, and pain, 182-185; case examples, 176-177, 183; cognitive distortions and, 188-193; listing your reasons for, 178-179; religious beliefs and, 179-182; understanding, 175-179; visualization and, 198-199

resolution stage of sexual response cycle: physical changes during, 24-25; psychological changes during, 27

resources, recommended, 261-271

S

safe sexual practices, 113-116; eroticizing, 116

scabies, 110

scars, vaginal, 73-74

schizophrenia, 106

scrotum, 18

secondary dyspareunia, 72

secondary symptoms, 59

secondary syphilis, 110

secondary vaginismus, 68

selective serotonin reuptake inhibitors (SSRIs), 103

self-image: aging and, 127; sexuality questionnaire items on, 53-55. *See also* body image

self-talk, 188

semen, 19

seminal vesicles, 19

sensate focus checklist, 150-151

sensate focus exercises, 147-173; case examples, 148-149, 154-155, 158, 161, 163-164, 165, 168-169, 170-171; charting your progress with, 149-151; genital exploration and arousal, 162-169; initiating sex and, 152-154; non-demand exploration during intercourse, 171-173; nonsexual touching, 155-162; overview of,

147-148; responses to, 159-161, 170, 173. *See also* relaxation techniques

sensuality, enhancing, 262

sex counselors, 257, 271

sex flush, 22

sex therapists, 257-258, 271. *See also* therapists

sex therapy, 257; maximizing the benefits of, 257-258. *See also* therapy

sexological exam exercise, 164-166

sexual abuse: recommended resources on, 267-268; sexual dysfunction and, 89-93; therapy for survivors of, 225-229

sexual arousal: charting, 208-211, 212; diagnostic flowchart exercise on, 81; disorder associated with, 66-68; genital stimulation and, 169-170; listing turn-ons and turn-offs for, 213; methods for increasing, 204-214; sensate focus exercises for, 167-169

sexual arousal disorder, 66-68; case example, 67-68; treatments for, 204-214

sexual assertiveness scale, 196-197

sexual aversion, 63-66; case example, 65-66; medications for treating, 65; treatments for, 224-225

sexual desire, 21-22; charting, 204-208; diagnostic flowchart exercise on, 79-80; hypoactive, 62-63; lesbian couples and, 248; listing turn-ons and turn-offs for, 213; methods for increasing, 204-214; religious views on, 181

sexual dysfunction: common elements of, 59-61; conflict and, 237-238; definition of, 2; diagnostic flowchart for, 78-85; hypoactive sexual desire and, 62-63; medications and, 102-107; orgasmic disorder and, 76-78; partners and, 231-239; physical illness or disability and, 93-102; physicians and, 252-256; post-traumatic stress disorder and, 91-92; power struggles and, 238-239; prevalence of, 188; recommended resources on, 268; resistance to change and, 175-179; sexual arousal disorder and, 66-68; sexual pain disorders and, 68-76; and sexual phobias and aversion, 63-66; and sexual trauma and abuse, 89-93; sexuality questionnaire on, 37-57; sexually transmitted diseases and, 107-116; single women and, 250-252. *See also* treatments for sexual disorders

sexual fantasies: as aid to reaching orgasm, 217-218; dealing with unwanted, 229; masturbation combined with, 218 sexual functioning: aging and, 126-133; identifying strengths in, 85-86; infertility and, 124-125; menopause and, 128-130; personal sexual history and, 47-53; pregnancy and, 119-124; recommended readings, 263-264; sexuality questionnaire items on, 37-39, 47-53

sexual intercourse: cultural myth about, 187; female orgasm and, 24, 76, 220; non-demand exploration of sensations during, 171-173; progressing from dilators to, 223-224; reaching orgasm in, 219-220; safe vs. unsafe practice of, 113-116

sexual map, 57-58

sexual myths, 185-188

sexual pain disorders, 68-76; diagnostic flowchart exercise on, 81-82; dyspareunia, 71-76; vaginismus, 68-71. *See also* pain

sexual phobias, 63-66; case examples, 65-66, 224, 225; treatments for, 224-225

sexual positions: for intercourse during pregnancy, 122; for minimizing exertion, 203

sexual response cycle, 19-33; diagram of, 20; fear and, 27-29; pain and, 29-30; psychological changes during, 25-27; sexual desire and, 21-22; sexuality questionnaire items on, 39-42; stages in, 19-20, 22-25

sexual strengths, 57, 85-86

sexual styles, 243, 245-247

sexual trauma, 89-93; cognitive aftereffects of, 92-93; PTSD symptoms and, 91-92; relationship issues and, 91; therapy for survivors of, 225-229

sexuality: assertiveness and, 195-198; attitudes and beliefs about, 182-185; choice of partners and, 235-237, 239-241; cognitive distortions on, 188-193; cultural myths about, 185-188; family-of-origin issues and, 240-243, 244; general references and resources on, 263-264; lesbian partners and, 247-248; positive affirmations on, 193-195; religious beliefs and, 179-182; resources for enhancing, 262-263; single women and, 249-252

sexuality and aging questionnaire, 130-131

Sexuality Information and Education Council of the United States (SIECUS), 264

sexuality questionnaire, 37-57; attitudes and self-image, 53-55; history of sexual function, 47-53; medical and psychiatric factors, 45-47; overview of sexual function and dysfunction, 37-39; potential stressors, 55-56; relationship issues, 42-44; sexual response cycle, 39-42; summary questions, 56-57

sexuality time line exercise, 131-132

sexually transmitted diseases (STDs), 107-116; bacterial, parasitic, and fungal, 109-110; infertility and, 124-125; recommended resources on, 269; safe vs. unsafe sexual practices and, 113-116; signs of, 108-109; testing for, 113; transmission of, 108; viral, 110-113

"should" statements, 190-191

side effects of medication: alleviating, 203-204; sexual dysfunction caused by, 102-107

Silverstein, Judith, 70

single parents, 269

single women: sexual dysfunction and, 250-252; sexuality issues for, 249-250

Snarch, David, 6, 21, 23

social workers, 256-257, 271

Solomons, Clive, 73

speculum, 254-255

spermicidal agents, 115

spirituality: recommended readings, 267; sexuality and, 179-182

spontaneity myth, 187

spoon breathing (with partner), 140, 141

stabilization stage of therapy, 226-227

STDs. *See* sexually transmitted diseases

stress: recommended resources on, 269-270; sexual problems and, 55

stressors, 55-56

strictures, 73, 220

substance abuse, 106; recommended resources on, 270

surgery, cancer, 96-97, 98

Survivors of Incest Anonymous (SIA), 268

symbols and metaphors exercise, 184

sympathetic nervous system, 28

symptoms, primary vs. secondary, 59

synchronous breathing, 139

syphilis, 110

systematic desensitization, 224

T

tertiary syphilis, 110

testosterone, 19; and sexual desire, 62, 129

thalamus, 2

therapists: lesbian-affirming, 248; referrals to, 271; working with, 256-258

therapy: for lesbian couples, 247-248; maximizing the benefits of, 257-258; for phobias, 65; for survivors of sexual trauma or abuse, 225-229. *See also* treatments for sexual disorders

thinking: affirmations and, 194-195; negative patterns of, 188-193

thought-stopping technique, 184

time, personal, 137-138

touching: assertiveness and, 197-198; cultural myths on, 187; for genital exploration and arousal, 164-169; guiding exercise for, 167-169; for increasing genital pleasure, 169-170; nonsexual, 155-162. *See also* sensate focus exercises

trance, 25

tranquilizers, 65, 105

trauma. *See* sexual trauma

travel log exercise, 8-9

treatments for sexual disorders, 135-173; breathing exercises, 138-141; creating a space for yourself, 136-137; finding time for yourself, 137-138; hypoactive sexual desire, 204-214; Kegel exercises, 143-144; medical problems and, 201-203; orgasmic disorder, 214-220; progressive muscle relaxation, 141-143; relaxation response and, 136, 144-145; sensate focus exercises, 147-173; sexual arousal disorder, 204-214; sexual phobias and aversion, 224-225; side effects to medication and, 203-204; survivors of sexual trauma and abuse, 225-229; vaginismus and dyspareunia, 220-224. *See also* resistance to change

trichomoniasis, 109-110

turn-ons and turn-offs, 211, 213-214

U

urethral opening, 18
urethral orifice, 15
urethral sponge, 16
urethritis, 73
uterine orgasm, 24
uterus, 16

V

vagina, 15; gynecological examination of, 254-255; pain disorders associated with, 73-75

vaginal dilators, 221-223; involving your partner with, 222-223; ordering from mail-order catalogs, 270; preparing to use, 221-222; progressing to intercourse from, 223-224; using, 222

vaginal narrowing: causes of, 73-74; treatments for, 220-224

vaginal opening, 15; pain in area of, 72

vaginismus, 68-71; case example, 71; dyspareunia and, 72; factors associated with, 70; treatments for, 220-224

vas deferens, 19

vasocongestion, 22, 66

vasopressin, 21

vestibular adenitis, 72

vestibular glands, 15, 73

vestibule, 72

vibrators, 169-170, 218-219

videotapes, recommended, 261, 263, 265, 268

viral STDs, 110-113

visual genital examination, 163-164

visualization: recommended readings, 270-271; as relaxation technique, 198-199; self-improvement exercise using, 184-185

vulva, 15; disorders associated with, 72-73

vulvar dystrophy, 73

Vulvar Pain Foundation, 262

vulvar vestibulitis, 72-73

vulvitis, 72

vulvodynia, 72

W

Web sites, 264
widows, 250
willingness, 22
womens' development, recommended readings, 271

XYZ

More New Harbinger Titles

THE POWER OF TWO
Details the communication and conflict resolution skills that happy couples use to deal with differences—strategies for making decisions together, recovering after upsets, and converting difficulties into opportunities for growth.
   Item PWR Paperback $13.95

COUPLE SKILLS
Unlike other relationship books, *Couple Skills* focuses on action and change—and it lets you choose just the skills that are relevant to your needs.
   Item SKIL Paperback $13.95

THE DAILY RELAXER
Presents the most effective and popular techniques for learning how to relax—simple, tension-relieving exercises that you can learn in five minutes and practice with positive results right away.
   Item DALY Paperback, $12.95

THE ANXIETY & PHOBIA WORKBOOK
This comprehensive guide is the book therapist most often recommend to clients struggling with anxiety disorders.
   Item PHO2 Paperback $17.95

PMS: Women Tell Women How to Control Premenstrual Syndrome
Draws on the experiences of more than 1,000 women to show how to break the vicious PMS cycle of anger, guilt, denial, and depression.
   Item PRE $13.95

NATURAL WOMEN'S HEALTH
New Zealand naturopath and acupuncturist Lynda Wharton brings together the best of traditional and alternative approaches to living well and staying well.
   Item HLTH $13.95

Call **toll-free 1-800-748-6273** to order. Have your Visa or Mastercard number ready. Or send a check for the titles you want to New Harbinger Publications, 5674 Shattuck Avenue, Oakland, CA 94609. Include $3.80 for the first book and 75¢ for each additional book to cover shipping and handling. (California residents please include appropriate sales tax.) Allow four to six weeks for delivery.

Prices subject to change without notice.

Some Other New Harbinger Self-Help Titles

Dr. Carl Robinson's Basic Baby Care, $10.95
Better Boundries: Owning and Treasuring Your Life, $13.95
Goodbye Good Girl, $12.95
Being, Belonging, Doing, $10.95
Thoughts & Feelings, Second Edition, $18.95
Depression: How It Happens, How It's Healed, $14.95
Trust After Trauma, $13.95
The Chemotherapy & Radiation Survival Guide, Second Edition, $13.95
Heart Therapy, $13.95
Surviving Childhood Cancer, $12.95
The Headache & Neck Pain Workbook, $14.95
Perimenopause, $13.95
The Self-Forgiveness Handbook, $12.95
A Woman's Guide to Overcoming Sexual Fear and Pain, $14.95
Mind Over Malignancy, $12.95
Treating Panic Disorder and Agoraphobia, $44.95
Scarred Soul, $13.95
The Angry Heart, $13.95
Don't Take It Personally, $12.95
Becoming a Wise Parent For Your Grown Child, $12.95
Clear Your Past, Change Your Future, $12.95
Preparing for Surgery, $17.95
Coming Out Everyday, $13.95
Ten Things Every Parent Needs to Know, $12.95
The Power of Two, $12.95
It's Not OK Anymore, $13.95
The Daily Relaxer, $12.95
The Body Image Workbook, $17.95
Living with ADD, $17.95
Taking the Anxiety Out of Taking Tests, $12.95
The Taking Charge of Menopause Workbook, $17.95
Living with Angina, $12.95
Five Weeks to Healing Stress: The Wellness Option, $17.95
Choosing to Live: How to Defeat Suicide Through Cognitive Therapy, $12.95
Why Children Misbehave and What to Do About It, $14.95
When Anger Hurts Your Kids, $12.95
The Addiction Workbook, $17.95
The Mother's Survival Guide to Recovery, $12.95
The Chronic Pain Control Workbook, Second Edition, $17.95
Fibromyalgia & Chronic Myofascial Pain Syndrome, $19.95
Flying Without Fear, $12.95
Kid Cooperation: How to Stop Yelling, Nagging & Pleading and Get Kids to Cooperate, $12.95
The Stop Smoking Workbook: Your Guide to Healthy Quitting, $17.95
Conquering Carpal Tunnel Syndrome and Other Repetitive Strain Injuries, $17.95
Wellness at Work: Building Resilience for Job Stress, $17.95
An End to Panic: Breakthrough Techniques for Overcoming Panic Disorder, Second Edition, $17.95
Living Without Procrastination: How to Stop Postponing Your Life, $12.95
Goodbye Mother, Hello Woman: Reweaving the Daughter Mother Relationship, $14.95
Letting Go of Anger: The 10 Most Common Anger Styles and What to Do About Them, $12.95
Messages: The Communication Skills Workbook, Second Edition, $13.95
Coping With Chronic Fatigue Syndrome: Nine Things You Can Do, $12.95
The Anxiety & Phobia Workbook, Second Edition, $17.95
The Relaxation & Stress Reduction Workbook, Fourth Edition, $17.95
Living Without Depression & Manic Depression: A Workbook for Maintaining Mood Stability, $17.95
Coping With Schizophrenia: A Guide For Families, $13.95
Visualization for Change, Second Edition, $13.95
Postpartum Survival Guide, $13.95
Angry All the Time: An Emergency Guide to Anger Control, $12.95
Couple Skills: Making Your Relationship Work, $13.95
Self-Esteem, Second Edition, $13.95
I Can't Get Over It, A Handbook for Trauma Survivors, Second Edition, $15.95
Dying of Embarrassment: Help for Social Anxiety and Social Phobia, $12.95
The Depression Workbook: Living With Depression and Manic Depression, $17.95
Men & Grief: A Guide for Men Surviving the Death of a Loved One, $13.95
When the Bough Breaks: A Helping Guide for Parents of Sexually Abused Children, $11.95
When Once Is Not Enough: Help for Obsessive Compulsives, $13.95
The Three Minute Meditator, Third Edition, $12.95
Beyond Grief: A Guide for Recovering from the Death of a Loved One, $13.95
Hypnosis for Change: A Manual of Proven Techniques, Third Edition, $13.95
When Anger Hurts, $13.95

Call **toll free, 1-800-748-6273,** to order. Have your Visa or Mastercard number ready. Or send a check for the titles you want to New Harbinger Publications, Inc., 5674 Shattuck Ave., Oakland, CA 94609. Include $3.80 for the first book and 75¢ for each additional book, to cover shipping and handling. (California residents please include appropriate sales tax.) Allow two to five weeks for delivery.

Prices subject to change without notice.